Praise for
Redeeming Our Sacred Story

"*Redeeming our Sacred Story* is destined to become a classic in the field of Christian-Jewish dialogue. Carefully researched and gracefully written, it proves that profundity and clarity can go together. I believe that Jews now have a responsibility to deal with our own 'troubling texts' and their implications. Mary Boys has given us a model of sensitivity and wisdom, grounded in a particular religious tradition, but showing that stories that may have previously been interpreted in toxic ways can now be vehicles for compassion, justice, and redemption."

—Dr. Debbie Weissman
President, International Council of Christians and Jews

"*Redeeming Our Sacred Story* does what its title promises. It highlights the New Testament's seeds of anti-Semitism, recounts ways in which those seeds germinated into Christians' biases and persecutions against the Jewish people, and shows how to free the Gospel to become truly 'Good News.' This clear, engaging book by Mary Boys challenges Christians to approach the New Testament and the Christian tradition with a new, sacred respect for Jews and the Jewish tradition."

—Robert A. Krieg, University of Notre Dame

"Every Christian should read this book. It combines the best of contemporary biblical scholarship with the author's personal and deep experience in dialogue with Jews to provide a fresh look at the use and misuse not only of the passion narratives over the centuries but of the central doctrines of the Christian faith. In the light of these studies, the book reinterprets our traditional version of the death of Jesus in a way that will spiritually move Christian readers to new understandings of their faith on the deepest levels."

—Dr. Eugene J. Fisher, *Distinguished Professor of Catholic-Jewish Studies, Saint Leo University*

"In this unflinching analysis, Mary C. Boys provides a comprehensive and accessible overview of New Testament scholarship, medieval and Holocaust history, and liturgy and homiletics in order to explain how and why 'the Jews' were blamed for killing Jesus. But this book is more than a dispassionate work of objective scholarship: Boys speaks as a person of faith who feels ethically and theologically compelled to reach for deeper levels of understanding of this story in the post-Holocaust world of Jewish-Christian reconciliation."

—Katharina von Kellenbach
Professor of Religious Studies, Saint Mary's College of Maryland

Redeeming Our Sacred Story

Studies in Judaism and Christianity

Exploration of Issues in the Contemporary Dialogue Between Christians and Jews

EDITORS
Kevin A. Lynch, CSP
Michael McGarry, CSP
Mark-David Janus, CSP
Yehezkel Landau
Dr. Peter Pettit
Dr. Elena Procario-Foley
Dr. Ann Riggs

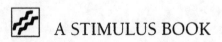 A STIMULUS BOOK

Redeeming Our Sacred Story

THE DEATH OF JESUS AND RELATIONS
BETWEEN JEWS AND CHRISTIANS

Mary C. Boys

A STIMULUS BOOK

PAULIST PRESS ◆ NEW YORK ◆ MAHWAH, NJ

The excerpt from *Le Roman de l'Estoire dou Graal* by Robert de Boron in Chapter 4 is cited in Maureen Boulton, "Anti-Jewish Attitudes in French Literature," in *Jews and Christians in Twelfth-Century Europe,* ed. Michael A. Signer and John Van Engen. Copyright © 2001 by University of Notre Dame Press, Notre Dame, IN 46556.

Cover image by ivgroznii/Shutterstock.com
Cover and text design by Sharyn Banks

Library of Congress Cataloging-in-Publication Data

Boys, Mary C.
Redeeming our sacred story : the death of Jesus & relations between Jews and Christians / Mary C. Boys.
    pages cm
Includes bibliographical references and index.
ISBN 978-0-8091-4817-2 (alk. paper) — ISBN 978-1-58768-281-0
1. Christianity and other religions—Judaism. 2. Judaism—Relations—Christianity. 3. Jesus Christ—Crucifixion. I. Title.
    BM535.B654 2013
    261.2`6—dc23
                                                            2013011454

ISBN: 978-0-8091-4817-2 (paperback)
ISBN: 978-1-58768-281-0 (e-book)

Published by Paulist Press
997 Macarthur Boulevard
Mahwah, New Jersey 07430

www.paulistpress.com

Printed and bound in the
United States of America

Contents

To
Joan Dunham, *in memoriam,*
and
Barbara King Lord

Acknowledgments

The solitary art of writing is at heart a communal practice. Writing a book such as this depends not only on the work of numerous scholars, but also on the support of institutions and colleagues.

I am grateful to the Henry Luce Foundation for naming me a Henry Luce III Fellow in Theology in 2005. In particular, I thank President Michael Gilligan and Program Director for Theology Lynn Szwaja for their hospitality and interest in my project.

My colleague at Union Theological Seminary, Hal Taussig, provided encouragement when I was ready to jettison the project, and gave feedback on an early draft. Others of my Union colleagues from whom I sought advice were generous in providing it. I thank Euan Cameron, Brigitte Kahl, and John McGuckin. Thanks, too, to Barbara Lundblad for the pleasure of working together on our course, "Teaching and Preaching the Cross"—and to our wonderful students. I am also thankful for the commitment of Union's president, Serene Jones, and former academic dean, Daisy Machado, to the continuing development of the faculty.

I had the privilege of leading the 2011 Summer Seminar for Seminary and Religious Studies Faculty at the United States Holocaust Memorial Museum with Victoria Barnett, Staff Director for Church Relations. I thank Vicki for her leadership and scholarship. The commitment of the seminar participants and the resources of the museum and its staff contributed significantly to this project.

Over the years, I have tried out ideas for this book in lectures at Boston College, Creighton University, Fairfield University, Flagler College, Florida Atlantic University, The Jewish Theological Seminary of America, Iona College, Manhattan College, Sacred Heart University, Saint Joseph's University, St. John's College (in Sydney, Australia), and the University of Richmond. Workshops for rabbis at the Oraita Institute for Continuing Rabbinic Education and for teachers for Facing History and Ourselves, the Museum of Jewish Heritage, and the Hartford Catholic Biblical School have sharpened my awareness of the complexity of teaching about Christianity in relation to antisemitism. Lectures and workshops sponsored by Bat Kol for the Archdioceses of St. Boniface and Winnipeg, the Ukrainian Catholic Archeparchy of Winnipeg, and the Diocese of Saskatoon have added new dimensions to my understanding of liturgical and pedagogical issues with regard to the death of Jesus.

I am grateful to Amy-Jill Levine, who provided meticulous response to a draft; Robert Krieg, who offered insight and encouragement; Adam Gregerman and Kevin Spicer, who responded with alacrity and expertise to my requests for advice; Brenda Gaydosh, for sending material from her dissertation on Bernhard Lichtenberg; Karyn Carlo, who commented on an early draft; Mary Garvin, who died before this book appeared; Miriam Malone and Kathleen A. Ross; and Nancy de Flon, my editor at Paulist Press. My thanks, too, to Carol Ingall and Sara Lee for rich conversations over many years that have taught me so much about Jewish life.

Meeting twice a year, the Christian Scholars Group on Christian-Jewish Relations has been a vital part of my continuing education. I thank the members for their collegiality, scholarship, and friendship. Katharina von Kellenbach and Björn Krondorfer were especially helpful in suggesting resources to me, and Michael McGarry in leading me to Paulist Press. Similarly, participants in the international "Christ and the Jewish People Project" have been great partners in learning. I thank Philip Cunningham and John Pawlikowski, longtime colleagues in matters Catholic-Jewish, for our many joint ventures and their good company.

I thank those members of my community, the Sisters of the Holy Names of Jesus and Mary, who read all or parts of the manuscript and provided sage counsel: Mary Garvin, Miriam Malone, and Kathleen A. Ross. My gratitude extends as well to the leadership of our U.S.-Ontario Province and to friends across the congregation for their continuing support.

I dedicate this book to two beloved women. Joan Dunham (1927–2008) was indefatigable in her efforts to bring Jews and Catholics together. Until her death, she co-chaired the Albany, New

York, Jewish–Roman Catholic Dialogue and a similar group in the Diocese of Venice, Florida, during her sojourns as a "snowbird." Joan was great company: She was compassionate, smart, serious, and zany. She has been a presence throughout my writing, her memory a blessing.

In the many years we have been friends, Barbara King Lord has been like a sister to me, and I treasure our relationship. Her hospitality on numerous weekends and summer days provided a beautiful place to write, a professional editor's counsel, and a friend's encouragement. I am deeply grateful for the interest she has taken in this project, for her journalist's expertise—and, above all, for her friendship.

Easter 2012

Introduction

Rabbi and medieval scholar Michael Signer frequently drew upon the image of the mirror to speak about dialogue between Jews and Christians. He quoted the twelfth-century poet and theologian Alan of Lille: "All creatures of the world, like a book or a picture, are a mirror for us."[1] Jews and Christians, Signer believed, mirror each other: "When we are at our best with respect to our two traditions, we can see 'through the glass darkly' the outlines of the other's tradition. As we recognize those outlines, we come to see parts of ourselves that we might otherwise overlook."[2]

In this book I focus on a dimension of Christian life that we have long overlooked: the crucifixion of Jesus of Nazareth as mirrored in Jewish experience. My interest lies first in what we see in this mirror, when we were clearly not "at our best." Indeed, what we see is disconcerting. Edward Flannery, the late priest and historian, prefaces his book *The Anguish of the Jews* with a personal experience that gave impetus to his work:

> One evening several years ago, I walked north on Park Avenue in New York City in the company of a young Jewish couple. Behind us shone the huge illuminated cross the Grand Central Building displays each year at Christmas time. Glancing over her shoulder, the young lady—ordinarily well disposed toward Christians—declared: "That cross makes me shudder. It is like an evil presence."
>
> This disturbing comment evoked many questions in me, not least of which was: How did the cross, the supreme symbol of universal love, become a sign of fear, of evil for this young Jewess?[3]

1

In the nearly fifty years since Flannery's encounter—and thanks in part to his pioneering book—some Christians have taken a long look in the tarnished mirror of our tradition's history with Jews.[4] Revealed in that mirror is a shadow side of Christianity. Christians have reiterated for nearly two millennia that the Jews were responsible for the death of Jesus Christ, thereby unjustly maligning Judaism and inflicting bitter suffering on Jews. In some periods, the violence inherent in the rhetoric of odious contrast was used to justify bloodshed.

The accusation that Jews are implicated in the death of Jesus suffuses the New Testament, most explicitly the Gospel of John, but also the other three canonical Gospels, the Acts of the Apostles, and Paul's First Letter to the Thessalonians. Moreover, these texts are proclaimed in Christian worship. As Scripture, they are sacred and normative writings; they cannot merely be set aside.

Furthermore, the fundamental plot line of these texts is widely known, even among those largely unschooled in the Christian tradition. While its underlying argument is the more abstract claim that Jews "rejected" Jesus, this allegation comes alive through a drama of good versus evil, of innocent suffering and ultimate vindication. The characters are memorable, especially the villainous ones (for example, Judas, Caiaphas, the chief priests and elders of the people, "the Jews"), especially as enacted in passion plays and tableaux. Scenes from the various passion narratives have dominated Christian art and have been a staple of sacred music. One need never have picked up a New Testament to know the basic contours of the story of the crucifixion of Jesus and the events leading to it.

Yet, while familiar with the plot, relatively few Christians are cognizant of its consequences for Jews. In part, this stems from the demographic reality that most Christians in the world do not encounter Jews in their daily lives. As a result, the church's relationship with Judaism seems tangential to their practice of Christianity. In some respects, this is understandable, particularly in communities overwhelmed by poverty and violence; their degree of dislocation is already so severe that further immersion in the shadow side of the tradition could be paralyzing. Yet it is also likely that Christians in such communities, typically lacking the resources and opportunities for knowledge of the history, will therefore continue in the inadequate view of Judaism that has been part of the tradition. Still others prefer to look away from our tradition's shadow side, lest it give credence to contemporary secular critics who revile theism, claiming that "religion poisons everything."[5]

But whether or not Christians encounter Jews in their daily lives, we are obliged to honor the commandment, "You shall not bear false witness against your neighbor" (Exodus 20:16; Deuteronomy 5:20). To put it plainly: Christians have used texts to bear false witness against Jews, albeit often because they assumed that the texts were factual. In this graced moment, however, we have both the resources to read ancient texts in new ways and the ethical obligation to do so. This is not a matter of rewriting but of rereading and reinterpreting them.

It is crucial that we Christians scrutinize our sacred texts, asking how we might be faithful to them in light of history. We will live our discipleship if we draw on the death of Jesus in ways that animate the lifelong process of conversion to the God who is merciful and just. Facing what is revealed in history's tarnished mirror involves dying to the old self disfigured by antagonism to Jews and transfigured by living in just relationship with them.

By redeeming our sacred story from its sacrilegious uses, we will bear witness to the power of religion to engage in the work of reconciliation. In so doing, Christian religious belief will neither be an opiate (contra Marx) nor a poison (contra Hitchens), but a healing balm for a world roiled by intolerance and violence. Honest and unsparing confrontation with our tradition's sinful past enables a different future—the future Jesus envisioned in his teaching about the reign of God.

OVERVIEW

Three major sections constitute this book. In the first, "A Trembling Telling," I describe how the New Testament accounts have caused Christians to "tremble, tremble, tremble," in the words of the African American spiritual. Yet these accounts have not always been told in life-giving ways. The second section, "A Troubling Telling— and Its Tragic Consequences," reviews the texts that assign responsibility for the death of Jesus to Jews (whether groups of Jews or the Jews as a people). These are "troubling texts," not simply in themselves but because of their effects on Jews over the course of history. In our time, however, these texts may and must be reinterpreted, thus the third section on "A Transformed Telling."

Stories of Jesus' death lie at the core of Christian identity. They offer an encounter with his experience of the human condition: betrayals by those closest to him, his own fear of death, uncertainty about God's will, and the endurance of terrible suffering and an ignominious death. These stories cause us to "tremble, tremble, tremble," as the great spiritual "Were You There?" expresses it. Moreover, the death and resurrection of Jesus lie at the center of Christian liturgical life, spirituality, creeds, and doctrines. It has evoked centuries of reflection, given rise to meaningful rituals, inspired art and music, been the subject of theological exploration, motivated persons to sacrifice themselves for a cause greater than they, and sustained persons through times of suffering. The stories of Jesus' death lie at the heart of what is sacred in Christianity.

Yet these "tellings" have also glorified suffering, condoned passivity in the face of violence, and constricted the meaning of salvation by associating it only with Jesus' death—as if his life and ministry held little meaning. These "troubling tellings" are the subject of considerable reappraisal today, as I document in the first chapter. Yet insufficient attention has been paid to an even more troubling telling: misinterpretations of the passion narratives that have rationalized hostility to and violence against Jews as "Christ killers." This sacrilegious telling cries out for redemption—an unfinished task for Christians.

Redeeming Christianity's sacred story requires respect, even awe, for its power, as I suggest in the second chapter. It also demands painstaking analysis of how it has functioned over the centuries. This critical assessment, which constitutes Part II, begins by examining New Testament texts about the death of Jesus that provided raw materials for hostility toward Jews (chapter 3). It then follows the way in which Christians have interpreted those narratives in apocryphal texts, commentaries, sermons, formal teaching, and popular culture (chapters 3 through 5). Chapter 6 probes the element of continuity between Christian teaching and preaching and the Holocaust.

But respect and critique must be complemented by reconstruction. This reconstructive task is multifaceted. It involves drawing on contemporary modes of biblical scholarship that shed new light on the historical circumstances of the death of Jesus (chapter 7), and on complicated matters of religious identity in the early centuries of the Common Era (chapter 8). It also entails formulating principles for interpreting New Testament texts in our time (chapter 9) and exploring ways in which new understandings of the passion and death of Jesus might become transformative for the lives of Christians today (chapter 10).

A few notes to situate this book and to aid in reading. First and foremost, I call attention to the many perspectives from which the death of Jesus has been, and continues to be, approached within Christianity, whether in technical theological treatises on topics such as redemption, salvation, and atonement or in the more pastoral approaches of the church's everyday life. The literature is massive, and I have only touched upon some of it. In the course of my research, I encountered numerous insightful works that consider various aspects of the crucifixion; wherever appropriate, I make reference to them. This book, however, carves out a distinctive path. It initially follows connections between alleged Jewish culpability for Jesus' death and the consequences suffered by Jews. It then pursues interpretations more faithful to the historical context of first-century Judea and to the intellectual and moral insights of our own time. Thus I am boring down on just one element of a much larger and immensely complicated set of theological questions and issues.

Second, this is a work of synthesis, drawing on a considerable array of biblical, theological, and historical resources. Necessarily, much has been left out in working on such a broad canvas; the notes offer nuance and suggest sources for further exploration. Perhaps the most glaring omission is the lack of sustained attention to the Christian belief in the resurrection of Jesus from the dead. Typically in Christian theological literature, one would speak of the "passion, death, and resurrection" of Jesus; our belief is that his death was not the final word and, therefore, that his death and resurrection need to be mentioned in tandem. Precisely because of the focus on the Christian-Jewish dimensions of the passion and death, I have largely bracketed the resurrection. I note, however, that in our time a Jewish

5

and a Christian scholar have collaborated to publish *Resurrection: The Power of God for Christians and Jews.*[6]

Third, many Christians across the ecumenical spectrum have heard in various contexts that our sins are responsible for the death of Jesus. A classic formulation in my own Catholic tradition states:

> The reasons why the Saviour suffered are also to be explained, that thus the greatness and intensity of the divine love towards us may the more fully appear. Should anyone inquire why the Son of God underwent His most bitter Passion, he will find that besides the guilt inherited from our first parents the principal causes were the vices and crimes which have been perpetrated from the beginning of the world to the present day and those which will be committed to the end of time. In His Passion and death the Son of God, our Saviour, intended to atone for and blot out the sins of all ages, to offer for them to his Father a full and abundant satisfaction.
>
> Besides, to increase the dignity of this mystery, Christ not only suffered for sinners, but even for those who were the very authors and ministers of all the torments He endured....In this guilt are involved all those who fall frequently into sin; for, as our sins consigned Christ the Lord to the death of the cross, most certainly those who wallow in sin and iniquity crucify to themselves again the Son of God, as far as in them lies, and make a mockery of Him. This guilt seems more enormous in us than in the Jews, since according to the testimony of the same Apostle: If they had known it, they would never have crucified the Lord of glory; while we, on the contrary, professing to know Him, yet denying Him by our actions, seem in some sort to lay violent hands on him.

This excerpt from the *Roman Catechism* composed in the wake of the Council of Trent (1545–1563) has many variants.[7] The consistent substratum, however, is that human sinfulness, not simply "the Jews," caused Jesus to die. By way of illustration, not long ago I heard a minister say that on Good Friday he invites his congregation

to come forward and pound a nail in a cross as a way of acknowledging their responsibility as sinners. While I have my reservations
about such a practice, I have chosen not to address in depth this linkage between the sins of humankind and Jesus' death. It has coexisted
for many centuries with the accusation of Jewish culpability. The
abstract character of this teaching that "our sins" caused Jesus' death
carries far less force than do the vivid narratives of the Gospels in
which Jews are the primary perpetrators. The twists and turns of the
development of Christian doctrines regarding human sinfulness as
having "consigned Christ the Lord to the death of the cross" would
also have required discussing the intricacies of various atonement
theories, which in turn would dissipate my focus.

Ultimately, I hope that this study might contribute to the revival
of relations between Jews and Christians in which we become true
mirrors of one another, revealing the profundity of our respective traditions and witnessing to the world that reconciliation is possible.

PART I

A TREMBLING
TELLING

CHAPTER 1

The Cornerstone and a Stumbling Block

The chief actual sufferers from Jesus' death by crucifixion have been, paradoxically, not Christians but Jesus' fellow Jews. From an early period—the mid-second century can be documented—the apparent complicity in his death of the priestly leadership of the Jerusalem Temple with the Roman prefect of Palestine was extrapolated by Christians to the whole city, the whole land, and before long the whole people. Jews have suffered untold indignities at the hands of Christians, even to their liquidation, as a result of the way Jesus died.[1]

I f there is one book that many readers across diverse cultures have in common, it may well be *Night* by Elie Wiesel. Already a classic, published in some thirty languages, its inclusion in Oprah Winfrey's Book Club in January of 2006 widened its circulation even further. The backstory of its publication illumines my reasons for this book.

After World War II, Wiesel (b. 1928) did not write about his experience for a decade. In 1954, however, he composed a lengthy manuscript in Yiddish, *Un di Velt Hot Geshvign* (And the World Kept Silent), that was published in Argentina. But this publication attracted little notice.[2] A 1954 interview in Paris with the eminent French writer François Mauriac, however, led to what was eventually published as *La Nuit* (Night).

Wiesel tells about their initial meeting when he was twenty-seven and Mauriac was seventy. In his view Mauriac was "famous, old and rich, covered with honors, comfortably ensconced in his Catholic faith," whereas he was "young, poor, riddled with doubts, a

11

solitary stateless person, unknown and Jewish."[3] Seeking to put his younger interviewer at ease, Mauriac spoke of his admiration for the Jewish people. He continued by speaking at length about Jesus, the Jew from Nazareth. In Wiesel's view, it was an "impassioned, fascinating monologue on a single theme: the son of man and son of God, who, unable to save Israel, ended up saving mankind. Every reference led back to him." Both fascinated and angered, Wiesel spoke:

> "Sir," I said, "you speak of Christ, Christians love to speak of him. The passion of Christ, the agony of Christ, the death of Christ. In your religion, that is all you speak of. Well, I want you to know that ten years ago, not very far from here, I knew Jewish children every one of whom suffered a thousand times more, six million times more, than Christ on the cross. And we don't speak about them. Can you understand that sir? We don't speak about them."[4]

Having responded with uncharacteristic boldness, Wiesel left, taken aback by his audacity before this revered figure. While waiting for the elevator, he felt a hand on his arm. It was Mauriac, asking him to return. So he did: "And suddenly the man I had just offended began to cry...wordlessly, never taking his eyes off me, he wept and wept." Mauriac wanted no apologies; to the contrary, he wanted to know why Wiesel hadn't written:

> I shall never forget that first meeting. Others followed, but that one left its mark on me. It was brought to a close by Mauriac's escorting me to the door, to the elevator. There, after embracing me, he assumed a grave, almost solemn mien. "I think that you are wrong not to speak....Listen to the old man that I am: one must speak out—one must *also* speak out."[5]

Encouraged by Mauriac, Wiesel revised and abbreviated his Yiddish work, and about a year later brought the French version to Mauriac, who helped him find a publisher and contributed the foreword. It is clear that Mauriac was deeply moved by Wiesel and his testimony.[6] He wrote in his foreword:

And I, who believe that God is love, what answer could I give my young questioner, whose dark eyes still held the reflection of that angelic sadness which had appeared one day upon the face of the hanged child? What did I say to him? Did I speak of that other Israeli, his brother, who may have resembled him—*the Crucified, whose cross has conquered the world? Did I affirm that the stumbling block to his faith was the cornerstone of mine, and that the conformity between the Cross and the suffering of men was in my eyes key to that impenetrable mystery whereon the faith of his childhood had perished?* Zion, however, has risen up again from the crematories and the charnel houses. The Jewish nation has been resurrected from among its thousands of dead. It is through them that it lives again. We do not know the worth of one single drop of blood, one single tear. All is grace. If the Eternal is the Eternal, the last word for each one of us belongs to Him. This is what I should have told this Jewish child. But I could only embrace him, weeping.[7]

The two remained friends until Mauriac's death in 1970. Wiesel reports that Mauriac even dedicated a book on Jesus to him: "To Elie Wiesel, who was a crucified Jewish child."[8]

The conversation between Mauriac and Wiesel was both candid and poignant. Yet in their friendship we see profoundly different sensibilities about the cross. And in those differing sensibilities lies what has been the great theological divide between Jews and Christians: the cross as the cornerstone of faith for Christians and as a stumbling block to Jews.[9] As Naomi Seidman notes, "Mauriac, in his Christological reframing of the Jewish Holocaust, never touches on the question of Jewish guilt for Christ's crucifixion; *but what vanishes in his reading of Jewish catastrophe is the other half of that story—the historical animosity of Christian against Jew.*"[10]

In a sense, my book revisits the terms of the Mauriac-Wiesel encounter by entering into the "other half of that story": the catastrophic consequences for Jews of the accusations that they were (and, in some perspectives, continue to be) responsible for Jesus' death. This charge evolved over time, but originated in a number of texts in the New Testament that assign primary responsibility for the death of Jesus to Jews, whether to groups of Jews (for example, the chief priests, elders, and scribes) or to "the Jews" as a people. Early church writers heightened this accusation with significant rhetorical effect, and it became a common staple of church teaching and preaching for nearly two millennia. The charge that Jews were "Christ killers" constitutes the theological core of anti-Judaism. Over the centuries it has at times functioned in various ways, often as the basis for the charge that the Jews were unfaithful to God, but in some periods as a rationalization of persecution and as fuel for pogroms.

Relatively few Christians are aware of the extent to which interpretations of the crucifixion have been a major stumbling block to a just relationship with Jews. Thus, we must learn this history and take responsibility for it. Too much violence, both rhetorical and physical, has been rationalized by vilifying Judaism as a tradition unfaithful to God for rejecting Jesus and putting him to death. This stumbling block, this scandal, requires our repentance.

Yet repenting of the stumbling block need not—indeed, should not—result in diminishing the importance of Jesus as the cornerstone of Christian faith.[11] To the contrary, the stories of the death of Jesus in the four canonical Gospels and in Paul's Letters are essential to Christian identity. Collectively, they give rise to a story as elemental to Christianity as the Exodus is to Judaism. The accounts of the death and resurrection of Jesus lie at the heart of Christian spirituality, liturgy, and theology. They are sacred stories.

Sacred stories used sacrilegiously cry out to be redeemed. Razing the stumbling block will reveal new perspectives on the cornerstone.

RAZING AND REVEALING: THE EXPERIENCE OF CHRISTIAN-JEWISH DIALOGUE

In the more than fifty years since Mauriac and Wiesel met, many Jews and Christians have spoken at length about issues that have divided our traditions. While the conversations have ranged widely, one theological issue has been a constant: how responsibility for the death of Jesus affects relations between Judaism and Christianity.

This is evident in the proceedings of the first major post–World War II Jewish-Christian dialogue, the International Emergency Conference on Anti-Semitism, more often referred to as the Seelisberg Conference (named after the Swiss village where sixty-five Jews and Christians from nineteen nations gathered in the summer of 1947). The participants met to express their profound grief over the Holocaust, their determination to combat antisemitism, and their desire to foster a better relationship between their traditions. The participants acknowledged antisemitism not only as a sin against God and humanity, but also as a danger to modern civilization. They also placed interpretation of the crucifixion at the center of their deliberations.[12]

At the conclusion of the conference, the Christian participants (Protestant, Catholic, and Orthodox) issued a statement to the churches that included a ten-point recommendation. Points seven and eight deal explicitly with how the churches should teach and preach about the death of Jesus, but points six and nine also do so implicitly:

6. Avoid using the word *Jews* in the exclusive sense of the enemies of Jesus and the words *The Enemies of Jesus* to designate the whole Jewish people.
7. Avoid presenting the Passion in such a way as to bring the odium of the killing of Jesus upon all Jews or upon Jews alone. It was only a section of the Jews in Jerusalem who demanded the death of Jesus, and the Christian message has always been that it was the sins of mankind which were exemplified by those Jews and the sins in which all men share that brought Christ to the Cross.
8. Avoid referring to the scriptural curses, or the cry of a raging mob: *His Blood be Upon Us and Our Children* [Matthew 27:25], without remembering that this cry should not count against the infinitely more weighty words of our Lord: *Father Forgive Them, for They Know not What They Do* [Luke 23:34].
9. Avoid promoting the superstitious notion that the Jewish people are reprobate, accursed, reserved for a destiny of suffering.[13]

These points anticipated later statements from various churches, the most famous of which is the Second Vatican Council's 1965 declaration *Nostra Aetate*. This brief document, which consists of five sections in its final form, went through a lengthy and contentious drafting process.[14] The fourth section, the longest, expresses an understanding of the passion and death never previously articulated in the history of the Catholic Church. Without explanation of what had changed from previous teachings, the document asserted that "what happened in His passion cannot be charged against all the Jews, without distinction, then alive, nor against the Jews of today." Yet it did not exculpate Jews entirely: "True, the Jewish authorities and those who followed their lead pressed for the death of Christ."

In recent years, biblical scholarship, which I will draw upon in later chapters, offers a far more nuanced reading of the passion accounts. Nevertheless, despite its lacks, *Nostra Aetate* inaugurated a serious reassessment of Christian teaching in many churches, and subsequent documents from the Catholic Church reflect the fundamental arguments of contemporary scholarship.[15]

Today, statements from various churches, regional associations, consultations, and study groups abound; virtually all are available online. This documentation serves as a textual witness to changed (and changing) attitudes and ideas about Christianity's relationship with Judaism. Although these teachings are widely available, earlier problematic views persist. This is due in large measure to the fact that far too few Christians have (1) been exposed to just how deep and broad has been their tradition's disparagement of Jews as "Christ killers," and (2) been taught to read the New Testament accounts of the death of Jesus with attention to and appreciation for their complexity.

Thus, I believe it is necessary to document the extent of Christian denigration of Jews because of their purported responsibility for the crucifixion *and* to reveal alternate readings of the death and resurrection that make possible a more profound understanding of the Christian story. Ultimately, my intent is constructive, that is, I hope to show ways of passing on this sacred story that do greater justice both to its complex origins and to its meanings in our time. In the course of achieving this end, it is necessary also to look critically at sacrilegious tellings of the passion, which I have termed "troubling tellings."

TAKING ON OTHER TROUBLING TELLINGS

I am, of course, not the only critic of troubling tellings. Elizabeth Dreyer notes that certain ways of speaking about the death of Jesus have contributed to a false asceticism, a neglect of ego-development, and suppression of one's needs and gifts in imitation of Christ. Moreover, misunderstandings of the death of Jesus have led Christians into "masochism, guilt, depression, and paralysis when faced with the crying needs of the world."[16] Particularly in our time, a number of theologians and pastoral counselors argue that the story of the death of Jesus has been told in ways that valorize suffering and self-sacrifice. For example, victims of domestic abuse have been counseled to be forgiving, like Christ, who "when he was abused, he did not return abuse" (1 Peter 2:23a). Advice that condones passivity and forgiveness in the face of violence has had a particularly deleterious effect on women: "For women, a theology of the cross as self-giving love is even more detrimental than that of obedience because it colludes with the cultural 'feminine' calling to self-sacrificing love for the sake of their families. Thus, it renders the exploitation of all women in the name of love and self-sacrifice psychologically acceptable and religiously warranted."[17] Moreover, the passion has been interpreted in ways that suggest that redemption has been completely achieved, and that fixate on the crucifixion while disregarding other Gospel narratives. Similarly, many tellings have constricted the meaning of salvation by associating it only with the death of Jesus, as if his life and teaching about God's reign hold little meaning.[18] These troubling tellings have rightfully evoked criticism, many of which come from women mindful of ways in which interpretations of Christ's sacrificial death have constricted their lives. In Colleen Carpenter Cullinan's words, the wrong story has been told—to the harm of many.[19]

In general, these critics take issue with ways in which metaphors used in the New Testament to reflect on the meaning of the death of Jesus—such as sacrifice, blood of the Lamb, scapegoat, justification, martyr, ransom—have been used in literalistic ways that glorify or condone violence. Atonement theories in particular receive a great deal of criticism; one such theory, "penal substitution," is the subject of much recent discussion. While there are varying articulations of this theory, it might be summarized as Jesus' receiving the penalty due to us because of our sinfulness. That is, in dying Jesus offered himself to God, thus bearing the punishment God would otherwise have inflicted on sinful humankind. Jesus, therefore, has saved us from the punishment we deserve; by his death he reconciles us with God, and so is the source of our "at-one-ment."[20]

The penal substitution theory has played an important role in Christian piety, especially in certain Protestant circles. It also has enjoyed a long life in Catholic spirituality. Some versions are highly problematic in suggesting God's need for vindication through Jesus' torturous death. Consider the following excerpts from widely circulated promotional materials for the Mel Gibson film *The Passion of the Christ.* "For Jesus, dying was His reason for living. He died for you so that you might live forgiven." God has diagnosed the problem of human sinfulness: "If there were another way to God, Jesus' death would have been unnecessary....Our problem is our sin that separates us from God, and Jesus' death is our only cure."[21] Potential movie-goers were instructed: "Your sin and guiltiness had to be punished and paid for. That's how serious God is about your guilt. Jesus was brutally beaten and killed because that is what it took for us to be forgiven of our sins. It was an enormous cost that He was willing to pay for you."[22]

Analysis of the "wrong story" of the crucifixion has given rise to an abundant and important literature that complements the latter part of my book. But to deal with it in the depth it deserves takes me away from my principal focus on Jewish-Christian relations. Accordingly, I feature below several voices of that criticism. In so doing, I situate my own project, suggesting both common lines of inquiry and points of disagreement.

Ironically, among those who criticize the "wrong story," virtually no attention is given to what Seidman calls the "other half of that story—the historical animosity of Christian against Jew" that tellings of the passion have helped to fuel.[23] This inattention suggests the tone deafness many Christians have when it comes to our tradition's relation with Judaism.

STORIES WRONGLY TOLD: VARIOUS VOICES

In a number of cases, poignant first-person accounts testify to the toxic effects of the story wrongly told. Roberta Bondi, a historian of the early church, recounts a vivid dream in which she is sobbing in a green-tiled bathroom: Her husband Richard is about to be knifed to death by a powerful man whom she believes has come to kill her instead. "Don't hurt her," Richard says. "Take me; just don't hurt her; take me."[24] As Bondi reflects on this dream, she sees it as mirroring what she had been taught about the crucifixion in the revivals she participated in as a child at Pond Fork Baptist Church. The message conveyed was that her own sin and worthlessness, which angered God, were the cause of Jesus' murder; that as a woman she was to be selfless, sacrificing herself for her husband and children as Jesus had sacrificed his life; that God had made Jesus come to earth to pay back the debt of sinners like her.

It took three years after that dream for Bondi to come to another understanding of the crucifixion. As she attended church services in Holy Week and participated in her ordinary round of responsibilities as a mother, wife, and professor, she experienced herself "standing in the yellow dust of Golgotha at the very foot of the cross," no longer an anonymous observer but standing "by Jesus as his mother."[25] She assumed another perspective on Good Friday, listening to the proclamation of the passion and Jesus' cry from the cross: "My God, my God, why have you forsaken me?" She heard this cry "from within the truly unendurable pain and yearning love of God, his heavenly mother."

Bondi continues:

> Suddenly, the meaning of Gospel narratives, Jesus' action
> and his teaching, presented itself clearly to me in a way it
> never had before. God had never wanted, and certainly
> never needed, Jesus' death. Jesus himself was no passively
> obedient, selflessly suffering deflector of God's wrath at

human imperfection. Jesus was no subordinate of God, mindlessly doing God's will in submissively loving obedience. It was Jesus who had made the choices leading to the cross.[26]

Bondi wonders how she could have been caught up by the depiction of an "all-powerful, angry parent God whose love somehow demanded the blood-payment of the world."[27] As she came to understand Jesus as one who had "cast his lot" with all whom the world had shamed, Bondi reclaimed an insight from the early church that in the cross lay the possibility of the healing of humankind's wounds, the restoration of vision, and the ability to love.

Other theologians, however, find interpretations of the death of Jesus so harmful that they turn away from its telling. While ultimately I disagree with their solution, their critique raises important questions about our purposes in telling the story of the passion and death of Jesus.

Rita Nakashima Brock and Rebecca Ann Parker offer a poignant critique of ways in which the "wrong story" of the passion has sanctioned violence and fostered acquiescence in the face of terrible suffering. By interpreting the death of Jesus as foreordained by God and requisite for salvation, they argue that the Christian tradition has, in effect, portrayed God as a child abuser, or at least as a bystander to the cruel death of his son. By situating the cross at its heart, Christianity made sacrificial love preeminent. Too many people, particularly women, internalized that message as a call to endure, thereby confusing pain and the "emotional entrapment of abuse with love."[28]

Their poetic style heightens the disclosure of experiences of searing pain. Each has endured considerable suffering in her own life, including sexual abuse, racism, and broken relationships, for which they found conventional theological understandings inadequate. For example, Brock, born in Japan of a Japanese mother (and, as she finds out only after her mother's death, of a Puerto Rican father), writes:

> I realized long after I was a theologian that my interest in religion and my focus on the violence done to Jesus are

grounded in my childhood experiences of racism. I have concluded that the Christian theological tradition has interpreted Jesus' life in ways that reinforced trauma. I was isolated by the traumatic events of my childhood. The tradition has isolated Jesus as a singular savior, alone in his private relationship with God. Jesus is depicted as unique and separate, carrying salvation on his own solitary shoulders. His relationships to others are described paternalistically, as if they needed him but he did not need them. To be saved, I was supposed to have an isolated relationship with him, to need him when he did not need me.[29]

Moreover, as ordained clergy, pastoral involvement with victims of violence intensified their dissatisfaction with how Christianity has proclaimed the death of Jesus. Brock and Parker are, in a word they used some twenty-four times in their book *Proverbs of Ashes*, "haunted" by the harm inflicted by telling the "wrong story."

Brock and Parker follow their critique with stories of their own experience of redemption through the steady witness of those who hear others into speech, the support of mentors and colleagues, the love of those closest to them, the healing power of beauty. "In our efforts to cleave to life," they say, "we have found the presence of God."[30]

They conclude:

Jesus' death was not unique. The torture inflicted on Jesus had been visited on many. It continues in the world, masked by the words "virtuous suffering" and "self-sacrificing love."…We cannot say what would have happened if Jesus had not been murdered, but unjust, violent death is traumatizing. His community retained the scars and limitations of those who survive violence. Christianity bears the marks of unresolved trauma. Jesus' resurrection and the continuation of his movement are not triumphs, but a glimpse of the power of survival, of the embers that survive the deluge. To know that the presence of God endures through violence is to know life holds more than its destruction. The power of life is strong. Salvation is

21

sometimes possible....Discovering that love endures, we come to the moment when we know that our hearts have room for more, that loss and regret have not snapped shut the clasp on our hearts. We unlock latches for repair and hope....Nothing can separate us from the love of God.[31]

Another well known critic of atonement theories is womanist theologian Delores S. Williams.[32] She argues that theologies that speak of Jesus as a substitute for humankind and thus as the "ultimate surrogate figure" present a problem for African American women. African American women have a long history of oppression by serving as surrogates. In the antebellum years, their surrogacy was coerced: as house slaves, acting as mammies; as field slaves, laboring under the command of overseers; and as sex slaves, fulfilling the lust of white men. In the post-bellum period, their surrogacy may have been voluntary, but cultural and economic factors often meant that African American women continued to do back-breaking labor and to serve as domestics. Williams suggests a kinship between the role of mammy and the institution of "Mothers of the Church," who, while having substantial power in the church, must nevertheless exercise their power in such a way that they do not challenge the "power and authority of the patriarchal head of the church, usually a male preacher."[33] Moreover, she traces negative stereotypes of African American women to their surrogacy roles. The mammy tradition has given rise to images of African American women as "perpetual mother figures, religious, fat, asexual, loving children better than themselves, self-sacrificing, giving up self-concern for group advancement." The antebellum notion of the hard-laboring field slave has contributed to the image of African American women as "unfeminine, physically strong, and having the capacity to bear considerably more pain than white women." The sexual slavery to white men has created the image of African American women as Jezebel. Such surrogacy roles rob African American women of "self-consciousness, self-care, and self-esteem."[34]

Thus, Williams proposes to "liberate redemption from the cross and to liberate the cross from the 'sacred aura' put around it." For this task she turns to the Synoptic Gospels, in which Jesus redeems through a "perfect ministerial vision of righting relationships." She writes:

> Thus, to respond meaningfully to black women's historic experience of surrogacy-oppression, the theologian must show that redemption of humans can have nothing to do with any kind of surrogate role Jesus was reputed to have played in a bloody act that supposedly gained victory over sin and/or evil….Perhaps not many people today can believe that evil and sin were overcome by Jesus' death on the cross; that is, that Jesus took human sin upon himself and therefore saved humankind. Rather, it seems more intelligent to understand that redemption had to do with God, through Jesus, giving humankind new vision to see resources for positive, abundant relational life—a vision humankind did not have before.[35]

Sally A. Brown offers insightful analysis of the various ways in which preachers have misconstrued God's redemptive action in the death of Jesus. She identifies four fundamental arenas in which "cross talk" goes awry: (1) it may portray a wrathful God who will be "satisfied" only by the death of his son Jesus; (2) it may speak of sin in narrow and individualistic ways that fail to account for social and systemic sin and evil; (3) it may valorize suffering; and (4) it may depict divine justice as retributive rather than reparative, and the violence of Jesus' death as a necessary response to human sinfulness.[36] To counter this "cross talk gone wrong," she offers a guiding principle for revitalizing preaching and teaching: Examine the potential impact of a particular image or interpretation "on concrete persons, including the most vulnerable persons, who will hear the sermon [or teaching] and have their imagination of redemption affected by that image."[37]

DEADLY DIRECTIONS AND LIBERATING POSSIBILITIES[38]

Bondi, Brock, Parker, and Williams have provided instances of what New Testament scholar Barbara E. Reid calls the "deadly directions" of interpretation. For Brock, Parker, and Williams, the story of the cross no longer holds much redeeming power.[39] Reid, though no less conscious of the way troubling tellings have harmed women, sees more "liberating possibilities" in these stories. What is requisite is great care in how we tell them, as Reid writes:

> It is vitally important how we tell the story of the cross. What we say of Jesus' passion reflects how we understand God's involvement in our suffering. Any way of telling the story that does not take us more deeply into the freeing and empowering love of God and impel us to radiate that to others is not an adequate version of the story. Nor is it an adequate version if it ignores, trivializes, or increases the suffering of real women and men, particularly those who suffer most in our world. It is particularly incumbent on preachers, teachers, and ministers to tell the story well and to help deconstruct and replace versions that are especially abusive toward women.[40]

I could not agree more, though I add to her final sentence, "*and Jews*." It is to those liberating possibilities that I turn in chapter 2. Rightly told, the story of the passion, death, and resurrection of Jesus holds power for living in the freedom to which God calls us. The key is stories "rightly told," and cross talk mindful of the other half of that story, the historical animosity of Christian against Jew.

CHAPTER 2

Power in the Story
Stories Rightly Told

The cross, then, represents not primarily a cry of pain, though that is not silenced, but the exuberance of life as it breaks free from the control and violence it has confronted and moved through.[1]

In the course of working on this book, I have found myself frequently using the phrase, "the story of the death and resurrection of Jesus." In fact, however, there is no one such story. From the beginning this "event" has been told in different ways; even the four canonical Gospels differ in their rendering.[2] Over the centuries Christians have created various "tellings" of the passion and resurrection—in theology and spirituality, music, visual art, drama, poetry, and prose—and drawn upon them for varied ends, not all of them salutary. Subsequent chapters chronicle the disedifying and destructive uses that have had such a toxic effect on Christianity's relationship with Judaism, and offer a transformed interpretation that does greater justice to our bond with Jews.

The sacrilegious uses to which the stories have been put disrupt conventional readings of the death of Jesus. To focus, however, only on the troubling tellings is to lose sight of the enormous power in the story as it is lived out in Christian communities for whom it has been a life-sustaining source of commitment to God's reign. The more we grasp how some renderings have functioned in sacred— even saving—ways, the greater will be our resolve to repent of and transform troubling tellings. Thus, in this chapter I have chosen voices from varied Christian sources that serve as testimonies to salutary ways Christians are telling the story. Just as Barbara Reid has listened in on Latin American women discovering "liberating possibilities" through biblical study, so, too, am I listening in on conversations among biblical scholars, theologians, and pastors seeking to unleash the power of the story in their communities of faith.[3]

Readers might wonder what criteria determine the inclusion of the accounts that follow. Perhaps my most important criterion was an evident connection between the historical and theological context of the death-resurrection of Jesus in relation to the contemporary situation of a community. Karyn Carlo expresses this as linking the cross of Jesus with the crosses of history; she calls for a theology of the cross that speaks to the complexity and ambiguity of life.[4] A second criterion was an indication that the memory of the passion enlivened a community, offering it hope amidst difficulties and sorrows. A third was a theological wisdom evident in a given community's particular narrative, a wisdom that does not assume that suffering is inherently redemptive but that contemplation of the crucified one should result in a commitment to reduce suffering. A fourth criterion is related to the overall arguments of this book: a reading of the passion that does not blame "the Jews" for the death of Jesus; this charge cannot be sustained by historical evidence.

Admittedly, these criteria have a subjective element; readers may decide for themselves if what follows is indeed a manifestation of the "power in the story."

AFRICAN AMERICAN CHRISTIANITY AND THE DEATH AND RESURRECTION OF JESUS

The spirituals provide a point of departure for grasping some of the deep connections many African American Christians find in the death and resurrection of Jesus. The spirituals speak of the death of Jesus with a "deep and personal poignancy."[5] As the slaves sang spirituals, Howard Thurman said, they were placing themselves at the foot of the cross, entering the "fellowship of His suffering."[6]

The spirituals offer us a glimpse into the power of passion stories for an enslaved people. Because slaves knew the meaning of pain and humiliation, they saw themselves with Jesus on the cross. As James Cone writes:

> Through the blood of slavery, they transcended the limitations of space and time. Jesus' time became their time, and they encountered a new historical existence. Through the experience of being slaves, they encountered the theological significance of Jesus' death: through the crucifixion, Jesus makes an unqualified identification with the poor and the helpless and takes their pain upon himself.[7]

This "unqualified identification" is eloquently expressed in one of the most famous spirituals:

> Were you there when they crucified my Lord?
> Were you there when they crucified my Lord?
> Oh, sometimes it causes me to tremble, tremble, tremble.
> Were you there when they crucified my Lord?
>
> Were you there when they nailed him to the tree?
> Were you there when they nailed him to the tree?
> Oh, sometimes it causes me to tremble, tremble, tremble.
> Were you there when they nailed him to the tree?
>
> Were you there when they laid him in the tomb?
> Were you there when they laid him in the tomb?
> Oh, sometimes it causes me to tremble, tremble, tremble.
> Were you there when they laid him in the tomb?
>
> Were you there when God raised him from the tomb?
> Were you there when God raised him from the tomb?
> Oh, sometimes it causes me to tremble, tremble, tremble.
> Were you there when God raised him from the tomb?

Slaves "trembled" because they were contemplating a terrible, violent event. They trembled because the crucifixion of Jesus mirrored the degradation of their historical existence. They trembled because they sensed the scandal of the crucifixion.[8] To the question, "Were you there?" James Noel responds:

When addressed to white America, the answer is: you are already there. Christ is present in the people you work to death, rape, whip, and lynch. The crucifixion is taking place right before your eyes, in your own time, through the system of racial exploitation that you uphold. However, white America was prevented from contemplating Christ's crucifixion with the same seriousness and intensity as African American Christians because it participated in this evil. For the slave, the crucifixion, with all its horror, was a central focus of their theological gaze. Their insight was identical to Martin Luther's, who perceived God doing something entirely new and unheard of in Christ.[9]

Noel is not alone in linking the crucifixion with lynching.[10] Cone, who terms the crucifixion a "first-century lynching," argues that the cross and the lynching tree must be seen together, each interpreting the other.[11] Both were public spectacles. "The crowd's shout, 'Crucify him!' (Mark 15:14) anticipated the white mob's shout, 'Lynch him!'"[12] Holding the cross and lynching tree in tandem is requisite for healing the racial divide in the church and society.

Cone acknowledges the importance of the critique of Delores Williams and others who have questioned maintaining the centrality of the cross in light of its misuse, but he differs with them. He contends we should not turn away from the cross because people have used it to justify evil. To the contrary, "The cross is the most empowering symbol of God's loving solidarity with the 'least of these,' the unwanted in society who suffer daily from great injustice."[13] And the lynching tree is a metaphor for race in the United States, "a symbol of America's crucifixion of black people. It is the window that best reveals the theological meaning of the cross in this land."[14]

Cone takes his title, "Strange Fruit," from a haunting song Billie Holiday recorded in 1939:

> Southern trees bear a strange fruit,
> Blood on the leaves and blood at the root,
> Black body swinging in the Southern breeze,
> Strange fruit hanging from the poplar trees.

> Pastoral scene of the gallant South,
> The bulging eyes and the twisted mouth,
> Scent of magnolia sweet and fresh,
> And the sudden smell of burning flesh!
> Here is a fruit for the crows to pluck,
> For the rain to gather, for the wind to suck,
> For the sun to rot, for a tree to drop,
> Here is a strange and bitter crop.[15]

African Americans embraced the story of the crucified Christ and claimed that it gave them life, just as God had raised Jesus into the life of the early community of his followers. "While the lynching tree symbolized white power and 'black death,' the cross symbolized divine power and 'black life'—God overcoming the power of sin and death."[16]

Similarly, Christopher Pramuk draws upon this song as "reve-latory of what should not be," as disintegrating the "White mythos of America, the myth of innocence, in the 'sudden smell of burning flesh.'"[17] He sees the specter of magnolia trees changed into gallows as analogous to gas chambers in the heart of Christian Europe, cast-ing an "accusatory shadow over White American Christianity and White Catholicism."[18] Christian complicity in racism, symbolized most vividly in the lynching tree, means that for "Whites, the blood-letting of Jesus' cross foreshadows the revelatory power of 'strange fruit' as a divine word of judgment: *You killed him.*"[19] To gaze on the

> senseless suffering of another human being—"Strange fruit hanging from the poplar trees"—without compassion, without mourning, without a word of protest, is to betray not only the God of all life, but to deny one's own human-ity, the imago Dei within. For Whites the Black cloud of witnesses breaks upon a lock-tight, self-referential, and thus thoroughly impoverished (i.e., racist) horizon.[20]

Prominent among this "Black cloud of witnesses" is Martin Luther King, Jr., for whom the cross symbolized the struggle against the injustice of racism. To challenge this injustice was "the cross that we must bear for the freedom of our people."[21] King himself was aware that he bore a weighty cross. Particularly after a mentally ill woman stabbed him at a book signing in Harlem in 1958, King was aware that the many enemies he made in the course of leading non-violent resistance against racial and economic oppression and in his outspoken criticism of the war in Vietnam might cost him his life. While preaching in Albany, Georgia, in 1962, he told the congregants: "It may get me crucified. I may die. But I want it said, even if I die in the struggle, that 'He died to make me free.'"[22] And indeed his advocacy exacted the ultimate cost: his assassination on April 4, 1968.

In response to the assassination, Nicholas Flagello composed the oratorio *The Passion of Martin Luther King*.[23] In a variant of the Bach passion, in which the passion and death of Jesus are told in narrative form and the chorus offers a commentary and meditation, Flagello fashions his narrative from King's own words and uses Latin liturgical texts in place of the German chorales. After the soloist sings "It may get me crucified...," the chorus sings:

> *Pro peccatis suae gentis videt Jesum in tormentis,*
> *Et flagellis subditum:*
> *Videt suum dulcem natum moriendo desolatum,*
> *Dum emisit spiritum.*[24]

For many on the underside of history, the passion of Jesus functions as a symbol of resistance to evil and inspires lamentation that leads to protest. One of the most powerful examples of this is found in the words of Mamie Till Mobley, whose son, Emmett (b. 1941), was brutally beaten and killed by two white men in Mobley, Mississippi, in 1955 for allegedly whistling at a white woman.[25] Mobley demanded that her son's casket be open at his funeral and gave permission for her son's disfigured and bloated body—after his death from gunshot wounds, he had been thrown into the Tallahatchie River—to be photographed so that the world could witness the vicious consequences of racism her son had endured. "Lord," Till Mobley said, "you have your only son to remedy a condition, but who knows, but what the death of my only son might bring an end to lynching."[26] Her courageous decision to allow people to view the broken body of her son did help to end lynching; artists helped to bring Till's death to the attention of the nation.[27] Along with Rosa Parks's refusal to sit in the back of the bus in Montgomery, Alabama, in December 1955, it was a catalyst in the civil rights movement.

Although the cross symbolizes "death and defeat," James Cone says:

> God turned it into a sign of liberation and new life. The cross is the most empowering symbol of God's loving solidarity with the "least of these," the unwanted in society who suffer daily from great injustices. Christians must face the cross as the terrible tragedy it was and discover in it, through faith and repentance, the liberating joy of eternal salvation. But we cannot find liberating joy in the cross by spiritualizing it, by taking away its message of justice in the midst of powerlessness, suffering, and death.[28]

THE WAY OF THE CROSS

Since the late medieval period, many Christians have meditated on the passion of Christ through pilgrimages to shrines or "making the stations of the cross" or processions or tableaux that mark the events that led to his death and resurrection. As devotional expressions that manifest popular religiosity, these encounters are varied, culturally embedded, and beyond the control of religious authorities. Thus, they differ significantly in quality, insight, and emphasis.

The five contemporary examples I have chosen for this section originated in particular communities and circumstances: in an African American theologian's reflections on the Stations of the Cross in tandem with the paintings of a Tanzanian artist; in an exhibit marking the sixtieth anniversary of the atomic bombing of Hiroshima and Nagasaki juxtaposed with Stations of the Cross; in another Stations of the Cross dedicated to all the victims—civilian and military—of the wars in Iraq and Afghanistan; in the "Way of the Cross from Latin America, 1492–1992" by the 1980 Nobel Peace Prize winner Adolfo Pérez Esquivel; and in the reenactment of the passion in a predominantly Mexican neighborhood in Chicago. These five selections illustrate ways that particular Christians draw upon the passion, death, and resurrection of Christ to help makes sense of their own lives—and to protest against violence, racism, torture, poverty, and militarism.

Diana L. Hayes, a theologian, fashions fourteen meditations around the paintings of Stations of the Cross on the walls of St. Joseph Musaka Church in Mwanza, Tanzania, by Charles S. Ndege.[29] Ndege depicts Christ as a black man: "Just as he has been depicted over the centuries attired in the robes of the Jewish poor, Middle Eastern nobility, Renaissance princes, Flemish merchants, and English nobles, he is today rendered in a style and manner representative of the largest and fastest-growing Catholic community in the world, the church of Africa."[30]

At the sixth station, Hayes considers "Veronica Wipes the Face of Jesus." This apocryphal story of a woman brazenly defying soldiers to offer consolation to Jesus, only to have his image left on her cloth, evokes a meditation on the perseverance and fidelity of African American women.[31] As women, they have been blamed across the ages for the "entry of evil into the world." As African American women, they have been plagued at every step by stereotypes: as "overbearing matriarch, emasculating wife and oversexed seductress." Yet in spite of seemingly insurmountable odds, they have refused, as did Veronica, to back down in the face of danger.

> Veronica, unaware, receives a further blessing: the image of Jesus' face on her cloth as a sign of her faithfulness. So many women today remain unknown, faceless and forgotten, despite the courageous and countless acts of mercy they have performed down through the years. The unknown Black slave woman who knew the alphabet and a little bit of reading, knowledge that could have led to her death if discovered, who held classes at night after a hard day in the fields and taught class after class. Many took their new knowledge, forged passes, and fled, but she stayed behind, providing a way to the future. The women who sewed quilts, today seen as valuable pieces of folk art but

then only as scraps sewn together to keep warm....These were women then of strength....[32]

Just as Veronica and her companions "boldly walked up to Jesus, ignoring the soldiers and their weapons," so today "other women walk with their children, of every nation and tongue, with their sons, in jail, in school, or in corporate or political office, with their daughters, college-bound or pregnant at too young an age. They walk because they must, because they love, because they care. They reveal the inner strength of women. They reveal the courage of women. They reveal the faith of women."[33]

A similar reading of the legend of Veronica may be seen in the Stations of the Cross composed by Eastern Oklahoma Pax Christi members for an exhibit they sponsored in 2005 on the occasion of the sixtieth anniversary of the nuclear devastation of the Japanese cities of Hiroshima and Nagasaki.[34] As they paused at the sixth station, they prayed:

> Veronica saw the true face of God incarnate because she saw pain and did what she could to relieve it, wiping the face of Jesus, a condemned prisoner. Women wiping the tears of those who are brokenhearted, tending the wounds of those who are injured and in pain, going into places of danger to love and serve those in great need, responding with mercy, showing true nonviolent love, also will see the face of God. Bless those who show the courage to come forward and be seen. Protect them as they show mercy and compassion for your people.

The national Pax Christi organization also offers a version of the Stations of the Cross on their website.[35] Composed by Rev. Sebastian L. Muccilli, who had served as Catholic chaplain during the Vietnam War and at a veteran's hospital, these meditations aptly express the Pax Christi aversion to violence and militarism.[36] For example, at the eleventh station, "Jesus Is Nailed to the Cross," Muccilli writes:

No matter how much we want to look away from this excruciatingly painful experience you were sentenced to undergo, Jesus, we cannot. Its demonic overtones have riddled history with unnecessary anguish superimposed on the ordinary, everyday trials of persons caught in the crosshairs of enmity and cruelty.

The cross looms starkly over a world plunged in terrorism. It has taken on proportions undreamed of until March of 2003, when the United States preemptively and savagely attacked Iraq with the deceptive claim that Iraq was hiding weapons of mass destruction. Nonviolence is a strategy whose effectiveness dawned on Gandhi's India over 70 years ago. Called the Mahatma (Great-Souled), Gandhi asserted humanity's unity under one God by espousing Christian, Muslim, and Hindu scriptures. Our conflicted, prejudiced world needs to learn a strategy of nonviolence as it stretches to implement social justice as a world-wide reality to save itself from annihilation.

At the sixth station, Muccilli contemplates Veronica's "act of courage and compassion, so graced with tenderness and respect that no one dares interrupt or interfere." He continues:

There are non-combatants in war: nurses, corpsmen, physicians, chaplains, and Red Cross volunteers, who minister with devotion and healing in their eyes and hands. Their mission is to serve and care for those who have been traumatized by a conflict they never imagined could personally touch them with such grave consequences. The angelic presence of care-givers injects hope into the horror of war allowing the wounded to cope with their undeserved fate.[37]

Muccilli's stations are accompanied by war photos, and this visual effect focuses the viewer on the horror of war.

Even more visually startling are the fifteen paintings of Argentinian sculptor, architect and human rights activist Adolfo Pérez Esquivel, the "Way of the Cross from Latin America,

1492–1992."[38] Painted for the 500th anniversary of the colonization of the Americas, Esquivel's water colors depict the events of the passion in the context of suffering Latin Americans. For example, his first station, in which Jesus is condemned to death, portrays Jesus being led from prison through the Plaza de Mayo in Buenos Aires, where the "Mothers of the Disappeared are holding placards saying (in Spanish): "No more repression." "Where is my son?"[39] Here Esquivel refers to the mothers who protested the "disappearance" of their sons and daughters during Argentina's "Dirty War" from 1976 to 1983 in which thousands of person were killed or simply "disappeared" under a military junta.

Esquivel composes the sixth station with Indian women surrounding Jesus, evoking the time before Hernán Cortés's entrance to Mexico in 1519 when there were some twenty-two million Aztecs, but only a million a year later. The commentary accompanying the painting reads in part:

> They have wiped the face of Jesus. His features, now imprinted on the cloth, are their features. Could they be ours too? Once, we were all indigenous peoples. Perhaps today we must rediscover this quality if we are to re-make communities of place and care for the Earth whereon we tread. But we must shape identity *inclusively*—just as Jesus was challenged to be inclusive by the Canaanite woman (Mark 7:24–30).

Esquivel's paintings reveal his vision of the passion of Jesus in his own peoples. So, too, does the *Via Crucis* of the Pilsen neighborhood on Chicago's Lower West Side. Originally settled by Irish and German immigrants in the mid-1880s and named by Czech immigrants of the late nineteenth century after the city of Pizeň, Pilsen has been home to a predominantly Mexican community since the 1960s. According to 2000 figures, the neighborhood is 89 percent Latino/a, with 37 percent of its population lacking citizenship; it has seen a "modest rise" in owner-occupied housing and more households had income above the poverty level (38 percent) than below (27 percent) it.[40] When the *Via Crucis* began in 1977, however, conditions were considerably worse; the neighborhood, with its

REDEEMING OUR SACRED STORY

dilapidated housing, unemployment, and violence, revealed munici-
pal neglect. In particular, apartment house fires on Christmas Day
1976 and New Year's Day 1977, in which seventeen persons died,
seemed to have been key catalysts for parishioners of St. Vitus
Parish to organize the first *Via Crucis*. Some two thousand people
walked with players representing the major figures of Jesus' passion
and death. Their Stations of the Cross expressed both their faith and
their protest against their substandard living conditions. As cultural
anthropologist Karen Mary Davalos observed, "By turning to this
Catholic devotion, they communicated multiple messages to Pilsen
and the city, including a call to cultural heritage and faith, an act of
solidarity, collective remembrance of the people who had died in the
fires, and a moment of consciousness-raising about conditions in
Pilsen."[41]

Originally the various stations were enacted in the seven
Catholic churches along or near the main commercial and residential
thoroughfare, 18th Street (*El Dieciocho*). Since the 1980s, however,
the stations have become prayer in the streets, including 18th Street
and Racine Avenue, notorious for its gang violence. In the words of
one of the coordinators, "The *Via Crucis* is something we live in the
barrio. The Virgin Mary cried for her son and now the mothers cry
for their sons who use drugs and are in gangs. It's real."[42]

The third station, "Jesus Falls for the First Time," is typically
recited in front of a place of employment, and prayers are recited for
workers suffering economic and human injustice. By linking the
pain of Jesus to that of workers, "the reflection calls attention to an
employer or corporation that ignores the plight of workers. It
invokes the sacred to legitimate class struggle. Naming the sources of
oppression, such as absentee landlords and ruthless employers, is an
important step in community empowerment."[43] For example, in
1994 the procession stopped at El Rey Tortillería, remembering
employees working in harmful conditions that became a stimulus to
the owners to create a healthier working environment.

One of the most eloquent interpretations of the Pilsen *Via
Crucis* comes from one of its coordinators, Patricia Luz. In an interview with Davalos, Luz says:

Christ suffered way back two thousand years ago, but he's still suffering now. His people are suffering. We're lamenting and wailing. And also we are a joyful people at the same time....So what we try to do is incorporate some of that. So this is not a story, not a fairy tale. It happened and it's happening now....We must be Christlike. He fought [against] injustices. We should also fight [against] injustices, to make our life and our world a better place to live....And in order to do that we have to bring these things to focus, to mind. And what we did is [connect] where Jesus meets his mother; we picked this spot, the *El Rey Tortillería* or the school and the theme we use there is Mary laments for her son who will be put to death. And here a lot of women lament for their sons who are killed because of the craziness of the gangs. Or they lament that their children are not fed properly. They do not receive the nourishment that they should receive. They do not receive the nourishment of the education [system]. They are discriminated against because they are poor.[44]

Luz captures what unites these five versions of the Stations of the Cross: "It happened then and it's happening now." So the residents of Pilsen reenacted the death of *"Jesus de Nazaret, Rey de los Indios"*—"Jesus of Nazareth, King of the Indigenous."[45] Their authors and artists connect the story of the passion to their own communities, mindful that we "deny his death when we turn our backs to the death on our streets."[46]

Yes, the death of Jesus happened *then*. Thus I situate his death in succeeding chapters in its full context of first-century Judean life in the Roman Empire. And yes, it is happening *now*—thus the importance of the power in the story.

THE CROSS AS A MIRROR OF A PEOPLE'S SUFFERING

In the previous chapter, I drew upon the criticism of Rita Nakashima Brock and Rebecca Ann Parker that Christianity has placed too much emphasis on sacrificial love. Parker specifically has raised question about the way certain liberation theologies speak about the "crucified people of God." Such language, she asserts, idealizes the acceptance of violence: "Perpetrators should not be hidden by language that praises the death of martyrs as nourishment for the world."[47] It may be, however, that Brock and Parker have generalized in ways that do not take account of the way images and languages work for others. Serene Jones offers an important corrective in her observation that as feminist theologians construct Christian doctrine, they need to be mindful of the need for "localized thick descriptions." For example, "[I]mages of the broken body of Jesus on the cross may be violent and abusive to a battered woman in the United States, whereas in Guatemala, they may serve to remind a mother that God grieves the loss of a child to political torture and military repression."[48]

The response to the assassination of Archbishop Oscar Romero in El Salvator on March 24, 1980, seems to belie the Brock-Parker critique. Rather, Romero's life and the response to his martyrdom[49] are testimony to the "power in the story." He was, by all accounts, a dedicated yet theologically conservative priest—"predictable, an orthodox, pious bookworm who was known to criticize the progressive liberation theology clergy [who were] so aligned with the impoverished farmers seeking land reform."[50] Like many conservative priests, he regarded with suspicion theological viewpoints associated with statements of the Latin American Episcopal Conference that had met in Medellín, Colombia, in 1968.[51] But less than three months after being named archbishop of San Salvador, Romero experienced a "profound spiritual awakening" when confronted with the murder of Jesuit priest Rutilio Grande, an elderly man and a young boy by a death squad on March 12, 1977, in the village of El Paisnal.[52] An advocate for the right of *campesinos* (peasants, farmworkers) to organize farm cooperatives, Grande had preached a sermon just a week prior to his death in which the country's "institutionalised disorder before which the very proclamation of the Gospel is subversive." Grande continued: "I fear that if Jesus were to cross the border...they would crucify him again, because they prefer a Christ of mere buriers and undertakers. A Christ dumb, without mouth, who can be carried in procession through the streets. A Christ with his mouth muzzled....That is not the Christ of the Gospel, the young Christ, 33 years old, who died for the most noble of causes."[53]

Romero, while hesitant about Grande's involvement with the campesinos, nevertheless considered him a close friend. "When I looked at Rutilio lying there," Romero said, "I thought: if they killed him for doing what he did, then I, too, have to walk the same path."[54] Jon Sobrino, a Jesuit theologian whom Romero had initially criticized as having Marxist leanings, speaks of Rutilio's death as occasioning a conversion, a moment in which the scales fell from his eye:

> In the presence of Rutilio's dead body, Archbishop Romero had felt what St. Ignatius Loyola felt in his contemplation on sin, when in the eyes of his imagination he stood before Christ crucified. There the question comes thundering in, down to the deepest recesses of one's being: "What will I do for Christ?" I believe that it was Rutilio's death that gave Archbishop Romero the strength for new activity.[55]

While Romero seems always to have been sensitive to the needs of the poor, after Rutilio's death he became far more forthright in challenging the institutions and ruling powers that were the beneficiaries of structural injustice. He demanded that the president investigate Grande's murder, and notified him that representatives of the archdiocese would no longer appear with government leaders on public occasions. He wrote to President Jimmy Carter, requesting the cessation of U.S. military aid, which armed the right-wing groups.[56] He established an archdiocesan commission to establish truth and document abuses of human rights. Yet the violence continued unabated. Death squads targeted church people who advocated for the *campesinos*. Five more priests were killed in his years as archbishop. Many walls in San Salvador bore graffiti that read: "Be a patriot: kill a priest."[57] Many church workers disappeared or were killed; nearly three thousand *campesinos* died each month. With the country on the brink of civil war, Romero used his nationally broadcast Sunday sermons to challenge the violence and to denounce the chasm between rich and poor. In his last Sunday homily, March 23, 1980, he specifically addressed the police and rank-and-file military: "In the name of God, then, and in the name of this suffering people, whose screams and cries mount to heaven, and daily grow louder, I beg you, I entreat you, I order you in the name of God: Stop the repression!"[58]

Romero's advocacy for the poor was costly. He drew the ire of the government, the army, the oligarchy, and even many of his fellow bishops, thus enduring the "long Calvary of hierarchical misunderstanding and rejection."[59] The archdiocesan radio station was jammed and then fire-bombed twice, and the newspaper office also fire-bombed. He received numerous death threats, but refused the offer of secret service protection offered by El Salvador's president: "I hereby inform the president that, rather than my own security, what I should like to have is security and tranquility for 108 families and their 'disappeared.'...A shepherd seeks no security as long as the flock is threatened."[60]

Romero admitted that he feared for his life, yet he proclaimed: "If they kill me, I shall rise again in the Salvadoran people....But if God accepts the sacrifice of my life, may my blood be the seed of freedom and the signal that hope will soon be a reality."[61] On March 24, 1980, Romero was shot through the heart while presiding at Eucharist; his blood spilled over the altar. By some estimates, a crowd of some 250,000 mourners filled the cathedral and cathedral square for his funeral. It was, as Jesuit John Dear says, the "largest demonstration in Salvadoran history, some say in the history of Latin America. The government was so afraid that they threw bombs into the crowd and opened fire, killing some thirty people and injuring hundreds. The funeral Mass was never completed and Romero was hastily buried."[62] His blood mingled with all the blood spilled by the people of El Salvador.[63]

Romero became a "dangerous memory." The military harassed people who possessed even his photo or a book about him. Yet there is little question that Romero remains very much alive in the Salvadoran people, especially the poor. As one woman said, he helped to change "the idea that God did everything and we just had to suffer."[64] He is a "very present memory of what ought to be," inspiring women to assert their rights and consoling the Co-Madres, the "Mothers of the Disappeared," for whom "speaking to Romero and our dead children" helps us to know that "we are not alone."[65] As one person in the slum parish of *Madre de los Pobres* testified, "I may not understand the resurrection of Jesus, but Monsignor Romero has not died, but is resurrected in our people. It is easier to understand the resurrection of Jesus through Romero."[66]

Anna L. Peterson suggests that the passion and death of Jesus offered an explanatory narrative by which many were able to find meaning in the deaths of those who sought a more just society. She cites research showing that those who have a clear political or religious interpretative frame and value system recover more quickly from trauma and have less lasting damage from political repression. By drawing on the passion story, the Salvadorans neither glorified martyrdom, which remains "death before its time and against justice," nor passively accepted suffering.[67] Rather, it motivated many to resist political oppression and to situate their grief and pain in a larger picture of the "slow march toward the reign of God."[68]

Peterson identifies the social functions of the martyrs. They showed that resistance is possible; in the end the oppressors may win, but they can be defied. Their boldness makes others take note of their convictions, and their dedication inspires survivors to continue the struggle: "Martyrdom forges both a community of believers and a tradition of resistance. The deaths create a covenant with survivors who continue working for the same cause."[69] She cites the comment of Daniel Vega: "This dead man can't say anything to me, but he left his example and his ideals. I have to keep resurrecting him in my work." They are sharing with God the responsibility for resurrecting the dead. In the words addressed to the government and military by a Base Ecclesial Community, "The one that you assassinated is alive in the people. S/he is resurrected in every hand that is raised to defend the people from the exploiter's power. S/he lives in the firm, the factory, and in the school."[70]

In El Salvador, stories about Jesus and other martyrs provided a utopian horizon, reasons for hope, and evidence that human history holds room for the unexpected (heroic virtue, self-sacrifice, visions of a new earth) as well as the expected (repression and suffering). Narratives of martyrdom and resurrection not only described the suffering that activists encountered, but also proposed a new and better way to live.[71]

Serene Jones offers the image of the "mirrored cross": In the cross we see our own suffering reflected, although this mirroring is more complex than a simple reflection.[72] It is an image that speaks to the life of Archbishop Romero and so many of the "crucified peoples" of El Salvador.

A FUNERAL IN THE CONTEXT OF A BAPTISM

In Christianity, particularly in the liturgical churches, the sacrament of baptism is linked with the death and resurrection of Jesus. In large part this connection arises from the multivalent symbol of water. Water is a cosmic symbol; life originates in primordial waters. It symbolizes purification, cleanliness, and regeneration as well. Yet water also represents destruction and death. It is, as Alexander Schmemann writes, "the mysterious depth which kills and annihilates, the dark habitation of the demonic powers, the very image of the irrational, uncontrollable, elemental in the world."[73] So water is the principle of life and the principle of death in this "essentially ambiguous intuition" of Christianity.[74]

Paul draws upon this ambiguity in his Letter to the Romans (ca. 57 C.E.) when he speaks of the baptized person being "buried" in the baptismal waters, as Christ died on the cross. But death is not the final word:

> But if we have died with Christ, we believe that we will also live with him. We know that Christ, being raised from the dead, will never die again; death no longer has dominion over him. The death he died, he died to sin, once for all; but the life he lives, he lives to God. So you also must consider yourselves dead to sin and alive to God in Christ Jesus. (Romans 6:8–11)

Because baptism in the early church was typically by immersion and thus the candidate entered the waters naked, baptisteries were constructed as a way of insuring proper decorum. In keeping with Paul's metaphor, they were often designed to look like mausoleums, with the font inside shaped like a sarcophagus. Yet the design of the baptisteries and the mood of the liturgy were festive rather than morbid.[75]

This intimate bond of death and life is evident in a moving account of a funeral in the context of a baptism as recounted by a British parish priest, Rev. Tom Grufferty.[76] He describes the funeral of Anna Stevenson, who had developed liver cancer two months after the birth of her first-born son; she died just four weeks later. Her husband, Edmund, a parishioner, asked that her funeral include the baptism of their son, Edmund, Jr., a request Grufferty accepted after brief reflection.

The baptism of Edmund, Jr., led to a few adaptations to the funeral liturgy. Grufferty received the coffin at the door of the church in the typical manner, but postponed sprinkling it with holy water until after the water had been blessed and the baby baptized in order to stress that baptism is a gateway into eternity; one's baptismal day inaugurates the journey into life eternal. As Anna's coffin was borne into the church, her husband followed immediately behind, with their baby in his arms. Once the procession reached the front of the church, the father, godparents, and grandparents marked Edmund, Jr., with the sign of the cross. Following the readings—including the text from Romans cited above—and a tribute by Edmund to his beloved wife, the priest and Edmund blessed her coffin with the holy water from the font from which their son had just been baptized.

The next part of the liturgy involved lighting a candle for the newly baptized baby; the candle was dipped three times into the waters of the baptismal font, accompanied by a prayer used at the Easter Vigil: "May all who are buried in Christ, in the death of baptism, rise also with him to newness of life."

Embodying the cross, the baptized person becomes a member of the Body of Christ.

A CROSS CARVED IN AN AUSCHWITZ CELL

In August 2004 I went to Auschwitz.[77] At the end of our visit to Auschwitz I, the administrative headquarters and site of the major labor camp, and Auschwitz II (or Auschwitz-Birkenau), the extermination camp where about a million Jews were gassed to death, I purchased some materials in the bookstore. Among my purchases was *Auschwitz: The Residence of Death*, a book with many photos from the archives, accompanied by some textual explanations.[78] I thought the photos would enable me to review and reflect on what we had seen that memorable August day.

Near the end of the book a photo captures an etching I had not seen: a crucifix scratched on the wall of cell #21 in the infamous "Death Block," or Block 11 of Auschwitz I, a place of torture and death primarily for non-Jewish political prisoners.[79] In this central prison of the camp, the Nazis had fashioned "standing cells," where four men were made to stand all night in an area measuring approximately 3 feet by 3 feet, then sent off to labor by day. Block 11 also housed starvation cells and suffocation chambers. Outside, the Nazis fashioned a "Death Wall" in the courtyard between it and Block 10: a black wall placed against a stone fence where prisoners were shot to death. The first experiments with Zyklon B, the gas that came to be used in the various crematoria, were made in Block 11, gas being far cheaper than bullets.

I know nothing further about the prisoner who carved that crucifix into the wall of his cell. I can only imagine his fear and emotional turmoil—and yet also I sense in that etching the depth of his faith. Was he not asking for the courage to endure, even to face an agonizing death, like the Crucified One? Was he not invoking the presence of Christ even in the hell in which the Nazis had imprisoned him? It is this crucifix that enables me to understand in new ways what it might mean that Christ died "for us." Not as substitute for us sinners, not as an appeasement to a vindictive God, not as the restoration of God's honor, but rather as one who endured terrible suffering and a violent death. As Gerard Sloyan writes, Jesus' death has been "strangely consolable" for some: "Both the wretched of the earth and the more comfortable in their time of extremity—war, famine, illness, separation, death—have taken comfort from their faith that deity itself was acquainted with injustice, abandonment by friends, physical pain, and mental anguish. It is not likely that the Christian masses will soon desert a God who has experienced their pain."[80] However painful the "troubling tellings" of Christ's death are, I find myself returning to that crucifix scratched into a cell in Auschwitz.

PART II

A TROUBLING TELLING— AND ITS TRAGIC CONSEQUENCES

CHAPTER 3

Troubling Texts
Raw Materials for Hostility to Jews

The reader does not rewrite the text any more than the Christian
individual erases his or her sinful past or the Church its checkered
history. The oppressiveness in the text remains both as a witness to
that from which we have been saved and as a challenge to action
on behalf of justice. But just as we must not cling to our sins as a
paradigmatic definition of ourselves, just as the Church must not
continue to affirm its mistakes as if they were Tradition, so we
must not propose the oppressive patriarchalism [or the Christ-killer
charge] in the text as the Word of God.[1]

It is difficult to face the reality that the New Testament, so beloved
and vital to Christianity, includes texts that have provided the raw
materials for harsh depictions of Jews as enemies of Christ. Identifying
this raw material constitutes the principal focus of this chapter, and
this, in turn, offers the foundation for the subsequent chapters that
document how these texts functioned in the church vis-à-vis the synagogue.

Raw materials, basic material from which something is made or
manufactured, may be used for salutary or deadly ends. Consider the
diamond, the hardest and toughest natural material. As a prized
gemstone, "diamonds are forever." Industrial grade diamonds make
excellent cutting and grinding tools. But the diamond trade has also
been used to fund and fuel conflict; the so-called "blood" diamond
has been at the basis of so much criminal and insurgent activity that
nations have banded together to regulate trade.

So, too, the texts reviewed here. As elements in a larger narrative that has inspired and sustained the lives of Christians, they are "gospel," good news. Rightly told, they are part of a powerful story. Yet these texts, often wrenched from their historical and literary contexts, have been used as proof texts that became the basis of condemning Jews as unfaithful to God.

I believe that these troubling texts should neither be isolated from the rest of the narratives of which they are a part, nor regarded as historically reliable accounts of the passion and death of Jesus. In the third part of this book (chapters 7–10), I make an extensive case for an alternative interpretation of the passion stories, and suggest ways in which this rereading might be incorporated into Christianity spirituality. This rereading reflects a "growth in insight into the realities and words that are being passed on," in the words of one of the key documents of Vatican II.[2]

But here the task is more limited: to identify the New Testament texts most troubling in the history of the Jewish-Christian encounter. Complicating the task are the varied modes in which the New Testament treats the crucifixion and the extent to which these accounts are deeply embedded in the lives of Christians through liturgical celebration, popular religiosity, and artistic expressions.

The New Testament tells about the death of Jesus in numerous and variant ways. The four canonical Gospels contain the most extended accounts. Each enfolds a "passion narrative," that is, several chapters devoted to the events leading up to the crucifixion.[3] Moreover, details differ in the four passion narratives, as each evangelist shaped his story according to a distinct perspective. Nor do the passion narratives constitute the totality of New Testament tellings. Paul, in particular, had a great deal to say about the meaning of the death of Jesus; disciples of Paul, writing in his name, added to the Pauline point of view. Luke appended a second work to his Gospel; his Acts of the Apostles offers more material on the passion. So, too, do other writings, such as 1 Peter, and the Letter to the Hebrews. And beyond the canonical texts lie apocryphal materials, some of which include passages about events surrounding the death of Jesus. In short, textual material abounds.

Moreover, the accounts of the death of Jesus transcend the pages of the New Testament. Each year in Holy Week, churches enact solemn rituals retelling the story. In some Christian traditions, one of the passion narratives is proclaimed on Passion (Palm) Sunday, and another (usually that of John) on Good Friday. Many participate in devotions such as the Stations of the Cross or services for the "Seven Last Words" of Jesus. Pilgrims retrace Jesus' journey to Golgotha as they walk the *Via Crucis*—the Way of the Cross—in Jerusalem. Passion plays enhance the drama; a film such as *Jesus of Montreal* (1989) contemporizes the passion. Music—from Bach's two monumental works for chorus and orchestra, *St. Matthew's Passion* and *St. John's Passion*, to the simplest of chants and spirituals—evokes deep emotions. Artists over the ages and throughout the world have depicted the death of Jesus in a range of media and with various intentions. For example, Marc Chagall portrayed Christ as a crucified Jew amid a pogrom in his "White Crucifixion." Harlem Renaissance painter William H. Johnson, in his "Jesus and the Three Marys," depicted Jesus as a victim of a lynching in the posture of the Grünewald crucifixion scene in the Isenheim altarpiece of the early sixteenth century.[4] Composer Nicholas Flagello has interpreted the 1968 assassination of Martin Luther King, Jr., in the mode of a Bach passion in his "The Passion of Martin Luther King"; the libretto consists of excerpts from King's speeches and writings juxtaposed with Latin liturgical texts.[5] Thus, for many Christians stories about Jesus' death are familiar and sacred.

Their familiarity and sacredness contribute to the difficulty of acknowledging the toxic potential in the texts and of rethinking how we might interpret them.

RAW MATERIALS IN THE PASSION NARRATIVES, THE ACTS OF THE APOSTLES, AND PAUL

In identifying texts that served as a source for Christian hostility to Jews, the passion narratives of the canonical Gospels are the most important. They constitute the most extended accounts, are regularly proclaimed and ritualized in Christian worship, and capture the imagination as well-told stories.

As stories with character, plot, settings and points of view, the Gospels present Jesus as an itinerant Jewish teacher from Nazareth in Galilee. He teaches through word and deed—through parables, sayings, healing, and meals with people many others deemed sinful or marginal (see Luke 15:2). They show Jesus interacting with the men and women who accompany him as disciples, with specific groups (such as Pharisees, scribes, and Sadducees), and with Jewish crowds. Occasionally they tell of his encounters with Gentiles, such as the Syrophoenician woman who begs him to cast a demon out of her daughter (Mark 7:25–30).[6] In the passion narratives, the conflict is principally between Jesus and other Jews; Jesus is depicted as the innocent victim of those who reject his message. These Jewish figures interact with officials who exercise rule in Judea on behalf of the Roman Empire, but the imperial authorities are portrayed as less obviously hostile to Jesus. In the Synoptic Gospels, the Pharisees, along with scribes and Sadducees, are depicted as Jesus' principal opponents. They take issue with his message about God's reign, challenge his authority, and serve as foils for his teaching. In the Synoptic passion accounts, however, the chief priests and scribes, often in tandem with the "elders" and the "whole council," lead the opposition to Jesus. In the Fourth Gospel, Jesus' adversaries are more typically generalized as "the Jews," although the Pharisees do on occasion play the role of antagonists, such as in the account of the man born blind in John 9.[7] In John's passion narrative, the high priest Caiaphas plays an important role, but it is "the Jews" who stand out for their vociferous insistence that Pilate put Jesus to death.

The texts in the Acts of the Apostles that provide toxic raw materials are lesser known, but because they appear to give the history of the early church, they readily reinforce the accusation that Jews were responsible for the death of Jesus. Paul has one highly problematic text connecting Jews to the crucifixion, though his seeming link of Judaism with legalism has contributed to another layer in its denigration by Christians.

The texts that provide the most dangerous raw materials for condemning Jews can be placed in two principal categories: those that attribute responsibility for the death of Jesus to Jews and those that heighten the traitorous role of Judas.

(text)

ALLEGED JEWISH RESPONSIBILITY FOR
THE DEATH OF JESUS

If one assumes (and I do not) that the New Testament is factual in its explanation of those who sought the death of Jesus, then the conclusion is clear: Jews, whether specific groups or as a whole, were responsible for his crucifixion.

Consider the Markan passion narrative, beginning with the arrest of Jesus (14:43–52) and culminating in the crucifixion (15:33–39). Judas arrives in Gethsemane with a "crowd" from the chief priests, scribes, and elders; they are armed with swords and clubs. Having given them the sign that the one he kissed should be arrested and led away under guard, Judas approaches Jesus, calling him "Rabbi," and kisses him, thereby signaling the crowd to arrest him.[8] A minor scuffle seems to have broken out in which "one of those who stood near"—one of the Twelve?—drew his sword, cutting off the ear of the high priest's slave. But Jesus rebukes them: "Have you come out with swords and clubs to arrest me as though I were a bandit? Day after day I was with you in the temple teaching, and you did not arrest me. But let the scriptures be fulfilled."[9] Mark then reports: "All of them deserted and fled," and adds a brief scene peculiar to his Gospel in which a young man, wearing only a linen cloth, was following Jesus when they—presumably the crowd—caught hold of him. He escaped by leaving the linen cloth and running off naked (14:51–52).

Mark counters the brevity of this scene with a more elaborately constructed account of Jesus before the high priest, with the chief priest, elders, and scribes also in attendance. Before providing details, however, he first notes that Peter had followed Jesus at a distance and was sitting in the high priest's courtyard, warming himself at the fire. Inside, the chief priests and council sought testimony to convict Jesus of a capital crime, but "they found none" (14:55). In contrast, false testimony abounded, but those who testified falsely did not agree with one another (14:59). The climactic moment of this scene arises when the chief priest stands to ask Jesus, "Have you no answer? What is it that they testify against you?" Mark observes that Jesus remained silent and gave no answer.[10] The high priest intensifies his interrogation: "Are you the Messiah, the Son of the

Blessed One?" Now Jesus responds, "I am; and 'you will see the Son of Man seated at the right hand of the Power,' and 'coming with the clouds of heaven.'"[11] At this response the high priest tears his clothes, calls what Jesus has said blasphemy, and calls for the assembly to make a decision: "All of them condemned him as deserving death" (14:64). After this condemnation, Mark says that some began to spit at Jesus, blindfold him, and strike him, saying, "Prophesy!" The guards join in this mockery, beating Jesus.[12]

The scene then shifts below to the courtyard, where a servant of the high priest notices Peter warming himself. She notes that he was with Jesus from Nazareth, but Peter denies knowing or understanding what she is talking about. As Peter walks out into the forecourt, a cock crows. Seeing him again, the servant observes to bystanders that Peter is "one of them" and then the bystanders say to Peter, "Certainly you are one of them; for you are a Galilean" (14:69–70). Cursing, Peter responds with an oath: "I do not know this man you are talking about." At precisely this moment, a cock crows—a second time—and Peter remembers that Jesus had told him he would deny Jesus three times before a cock crowed twice: "And he broke down and wept" (14:72).

The next scene takes place in the morning. After conferring with the elders, scribes and whole council, the chief priests bind Jesus, and hand him over to Pilate. Now another interrogation proceeds, with Pilate initially asking, "Are you the King of the Jews?" Jesus responds, "You say so." The chief priests accuse Jesus "of many things" (15:3), so Pilate asks Jesus how he responds to their charges. "But Jesus made no further reply, so that Pilate was amazed" (15:5).

Mark then tells of a custom connected with the festival in which Pilate released any prisoner for whom they asked, and he reports that a certain Barabbas was imprisoned with "rebels who had committed murder during an insurrection" (15:7). The crowd asks Pilate "to do for them according to his custom," to which Pilate replies, "Do you want for me to release for you the King of the Jews?" Mark adds, "For he realized that it was out of jealousy that the chief priests had handed him over" (15:9-10). The chief priests continue to stir up the crowd, agitating for them to release Barabbas rather than Jesus. Pilate banters with the crowd, asking what they wish him to do with "the man you call the King of the Jews." In response, the crowd shouts, "Crucify him!" Pilate retorts, "Why, what evil has he done?" The crowd's shouting grows louder, "Crucify him!" So Pilate, "wishing to satisfy the crowd, released Barabbas for them; and after flogging Jesus, he handed him over to be crucified" (15:15).

Soldiers then lead Jesus into the courtyard of the prefect's palace, summoning the whole cohort. They clothe Jesus in a purple cloak, twist some thorns into a crown, put it on Jesus' head, and salute him: "Hail, King of the Jews." Their mockery continues. They strike him with a reed, spit on him, and kneel in homage before him. Then they strip him of the purple cloak, dress him in his own clothes, and lead him out to be crucified, compelling a passer-by, Simon of Cyrene, father of Alexander and Rufus, to carry his cross (15:21).

The soldiers bring Jesus to Golgotha, which Mark says means the "place of a skull" (15:22). Although they offer him wine mixed with myrrh, Jesus refuses it. "And they crucified him, and divided his clothes among them, casting lots to decide what each should take" (15:24).[13] It was, Mark says, nine in the morning when they crucified him, and the inscription of the charge against him read, "The King of the Jews." Two bandits were crucified on each side of Jesus, and passers-by mocked him, "shaking their heads and saying, 'Aha! You who would destroy the temple and build it in three days, save yourself and come down from the cross!" (15:29–30). The chief priests and scribes similarly mocked Jesus: "He saved others; he cannot save himself. Let the Messiah, the King of Israel, come down from the cross now, so that we may see and believe." Even those crucified with Jesus taunted him (15:31–32).

Then at noon darkness covered the entire land until three in the afternoon, when Jesus cried loudly, *"Eloi, Eloi, lama sabachthani,"* "My God, my God, why have you forsaken me?"[14] Some of the bystanders misinterpret this as Jesus calling for Elijah. Someone ran to fill a sponge with sour wine; putting it on a stick, he gave it to Jesus to drink, saying, "Wait, let us see whether Elijah will come to take him down" (15:36). "Then Jesus gave a loud cry and breathed his last" (15:37).

Mark then says that the curtain of the temple was torn in two, from top to bottom and that the centurion, who stood facing Jesus and watched him draw his last breath, exclaimed, "Truly this man was God's son!" (15:38–39). He notes also the presence of women who looked on from a distance, including Mary Magdalene; Mary, the mother of James the younger and of Joses; and Salome. "They had followed him and provided for him when he was in Galilee; and there were many other women who had come up with him to Jerusalem" (15:41).

In sum, Mark assigns primary responsibility for Jesus' death to Jewish figures. The chief priests, scribes, and elders come to arrest Jesus, armed with swords and club. After Judas ironically betrays his teacher (rabbi) with a kiss, they seize Jesus and take him to the high priest; the chief priests and the "whole council" seek testimony that would result in Jesus' death—even if the testimony were to be false. The high priest, following their lead, interrogates Jesus, who assents to being "the Christ, the Son of the Blessed." In response, the high priest rips his robes and accuses Jesus of blasphemy. He invites those present to decide Jesus' fate: "They all condemned him as deserving death" (14:64), with some among them striking Jesus, even spitting at and mocking him. The next morning the chief priests, elders, scribes, and "the whole council" confer, binding him and bringing him to the governor of Judea, Pontius Pilate.

So the soldiers (presumably those of Rome) take Jesus inside, dress him in a purple cloak, and crown him with thorns. Like the chief priests, elders, scribes, and whole council, they strike him, spit at, and mock him. Although it is the soldiers who bring Jesus to Golgotha, and who oversee his crucifixion, they are bit players in this drama. The leading roles are played by Jews: chief priests, the high priest, elders, scribes, the council, the crowd. Even the Roman-appointed governor, Pilate, acquiesces to their demands that Jesus be crucified. As Jesus breathed his last, the temple curtain is torn in two. It is the centurion—a Gentile—who exclaims, "Truly this man was the Son of God!" (15:39).

Matthew's passion narrative is essentially a variation on Mark's. He differs in some details, both by way of additions (for example, in the scene of Jesus' arrest [26:50–52], the dream of Pilate's wife [27:19], the earthquake following Jesus' death [27:51]), and by way of omissions (for example, shortening the material about Barabbas). Two major departures from Mark, however, function to accentuate Jewish complicity. A Matthean addition, unique to his Gospel, highlights Pilate's reluctance and the crowd's blood thirst. In Matthew's depiction, Pilate sees that he can do nothing; mindful that a riot was beginning, Pilate takes water and washes his hands before the crowd: "I am innocent of this man's blood; see to it yourselves" (27:24). In contrast, "the people as a whole answered, 'His blood be on us and on our children!'" (27:25). If the two accounts are looked at in parallel, the additions become more obvious (principal additions are in boldface):

Mark 15:7–15	Matthew 27:15, 20–26
[7] Now at the festival he used to release a prisoner for them, anyone for whom they asked.	[15] Now at the festival he used to release a prisoner for them, anyone whom they wanted.
[8] So the crowd came and began to ask Pilate to do for them according to his custom.	[20] Now the chief priests and the elders persuaded the people to ask for Barabbas and to have Jesus killed.
[9] Then he answered them, "Do you want me to release for you the King of the Jews?" [10] For he realized that it was out of jealousy that the chief priests had handed him over.	[21] The governor again said to them, "Which of the two do you want me to release for you?"
	And they said, "Barabbas."
[11] But the chief priests stirred up the crowd to have him release for them Barabbas instead. [12] And Pilate spoke to them again, "Then what do you wish me to do with the man you call the King of the Jews?" [13] They shouted back, "Crucify him."	[22] Pilate said to them, "Then what shall I do with Jesus who is called the Messiah?" They all said, "Let him be crucified!"
[14] Pilate asked them, "Why, what evil has he done?" But they shouted all the more, " Crucify him."	[23] Then he asked, "Why, what evil has he done?" But they shouted all the more, "Let him be crucified!"
[15] So Pilate, wishing to satisfy the crowd, released for them Barabbas;	[24] **So when Pilate saw that he was gaining nothing, but rather that a riot was beginning, he took water and washed his hands before the crowd, saying, "I am innocent of this man's blood; see to it yourselves." [25] And all the people answered, "His blood be on us and on our children!"**
and after flogging Jesus, he handed him over to be crucified.	[26] Then he released for them Barabbas, and having scourged Jesus, delivered him to be crucified.

Matthew also embellishes the story of Judas, as does Luke. Those embellishments will be discussed in detail in a separate section.

Luke orders his account of the arrest of Jesus somewhat differently from Mark and Matthew, and in addition to the chief priests and elders who had come to seize Jesus were "officers of the temple police" (22:52). Again, Luke has Jesus being mocked before he is interrogated (22:63–65), then brought before the council of chief priests and scribes, a scene generally congruent with Mark and Matthew, although there is no verdict given, as in Mark 14:64 and Matthew 26:66. When this assemblage brings Jesus to Pilate (23:1), Luke attributes to them charges solely in his Gospel: "They began to accuse him, saying, "We found this man perverting our nation, forbidding us to pay taxes to the emperor, and saying that he himself is the Messiah, a king" (23:2).[15] Pilate then questions Jesus, as he has in Mark and Matthew: "Are you the king of the Jews?" And he receives the same response: "You say so." He then tells the chief priests and crowds that he finds no basis for an accusation against Jesus, but they insist, in language unique to Luke: "He stirs up the people by teaching throughout all Judea, from Galilee where he began even to this place" (23:5). Hearing the reference to Galilee, Pilate inquires about whether Jesus was a Galilean; as such, Jesus came under the jurisdiction of Herod Antipas. This becomes the basis of a scene found only in Luke, a trial before Herod and then Pilate's declaration that neither he nor Herod found Jesus guilty of the charges brought against him (23:7–16):

> And when he learned that he was under Herod's jurisdiction, he sent him off to Herod, who was himself in Jerusalem at that time. When Herod saw Jesus, he was very glad, for he had wanted to see him for a long time, because he had heard about him and was hoping to see him perform some sign. He questioned him at some length, but Jesus gave him no answer. The chief priests and the scribes stood by, vehemently accusing him. Even Herod with his soldiers treated him with contempt and mocked him; then he put an elegant robe on him, and sent him back to Pilate. That same day Herod and Pilate

became friends with each other; before this they had been enemies. Pilate then called together the chief priests, the leaders, and the people, and said to them, "You brought me this man as one who was perverting the people; and here I have examined him in your presence and have not found this man guilty of any of your charges against him. Neither has Herod, for he sent him back to us."[16]

Thus, Pilate declares, "Indeed, he has done nothing to deserve death. I will therefore have him flogged and release him."

But the crowd will hear nothing of this, shouting for Pilate to release Barabbas, whom Luke briefly identifies as a "man who had been put in prison for an insurrection that had taken place in the city, and for murder." Pilate, "wanting to release Jesus" (23:20), addressed the crowd, although Luke does not report what he said; rather, Luke reports, the crowds keep shouting, "Crucify him, crucify him!" Pilate faces the crowd a third time: "I have found in him no ground for the sentence of death; I will therefore have him flogged and then release him."[17] This is to no avail: "But they kept urgently demanding with loud shouts that he should be crucified; and their voices prevailed" (23:23). So, Luke tells us that "Pilate gave his verdict that their demand should be granted" and "released the man they asked for, the one who had been put in prison for insurrection and murder, and he handed Jesus over as they wished" (23:24–25).

Luke's additional material, such as the trial before Herod, only reinforces the complicity of Jewish figures, such as the chief priests and scribes. His exculpation of Pilate is even stronger than that of Mark and Matthew; three times Pilate declares Jesus innocent of the charges (23:4; 23:14; 23:22). Luke omits the cry of desolation. Rather, Jesus dies, "crying with a loud voice, 'Father, into your hands I commend my spirit.' Having said this, he breathed his last" (23:46).[18] Luke's centurion exclaims, "Certainly, this man was innocent."[19] The evangelist adds, "When all the crowds who had gathered there for the spectacle saw what had taken place, they returned home, beating their breasts" (23:48).

Despite some divergent details, the Synoptic Gospels speak in one voice: Jewish figures—most notably the high priest, the chief priests, scribes, elders, and council—desperately want Jesus' death. They stir up the crowd to such frenzy that Pontius Pilate finally accedes to their demand, "Crucify him! Crucify him!" Over the ages, much tragedy would result from the way their raw material was used.

John's Gospel is stylistically very different from the Synoptic Gospels; his passion narrative is no exception to his characteristic approach. The arrest happens in a garden, a place where Jesus often met with his disciples, so Judas, "who betrayed him," knew of it. He had brought a detachment of soldiers and police from the chief priests and Pharisees; they were armed with lanterns, torches, and weapons.[20] The variant ways the Gospels render the scene of Jesus' arrest illustrate the distinctive flourishes of the Fourth Gospel:

Mark 14:43–51	Matthew 26:47–56	Luke 22:47–53	John 18:2–11
[43] Immediately, while he was still speaking, Judas, one of the twelve, arrived;	[47] While he was still speaking, Judas, one of the twelve, arrived;		[2] Now Judas, who betrayed him, also knew the place, because Jesus often met there with his disciples.
and with him there was a crowd with swords and clubs, from the chief priests, the scribes, and the elders.	with him was a large crowd with swords and clubs, from the chief priests and the elders of the people.	[47] While he was still speaking, suddenly a crowd came, and the one called Judas, one of the twelve, was leading them.	[3] So Judas brought a detachment of soldiers together with police from the chief priests and the Pharisees, and they came there with lanterns and torches and weapons.
[44] Now the betrayer had given them a sign, saying, "The one I will kiss is the man; arrest him and lead him away under guard.	[48] Now the betrayer had given them a sign, saying, "The one I will kiss is the man; arrest him."		[4] Then Jesus, knowing all that was to happen to him, came forward and
[45] So when he came, he went up to him at once and said, "Rabbi!" and kissed him.	[49] At once he came up to Jesus and said, "Greetings, Rabbi!" and kissed him.	He approached Jesus to kiss him; [48] but Jesus said to him, "Judas, is it with a kiss that you are	asked them, 'For whom are you looking?' [5] They answered, 'Jesus of Nazareth.'

Mark 14:43–51	Matthew 26:47–56	Luke 22:47–53	John 18:2–11
	[50] Jesus said to him, "Friend, do what you are here to do."	betraying the Son of Man?"	Jesus replied, 'I am he.' Judas, who betrayed him, was standing with them. [6]When Jesus said to them, 'I am he,' they stepped back and fell to the ground. [7] Again he asked them, 'For whom are you looking?' And they said, 'Jesus of Nazareth.' [8]Jesus answered, 'I told you that I am he. So if you are looking for me, let these men go.' [9]This was to fulfill the word that he had spoken, 'I did not lose a single one of those whom you gave me.'
[46] Then they laid hands on him and arrested him.	Then they came and laid hands on Jesus and arrested him.		
[47] But one of those who stood near drew his sword and struck the slave of the high priest, cutting off his ear.	[51] Suddenly, one of those with Jesus put his hand on his sword, drew it, and struck the slave of the high priest, cutting off his ear.	[49] When those who were around him saw what was coming, they asked, "Lord, should we strike him with the sword?" [50] Then one of them struck the slave of the high priest and cut off his right ear. [51] But Jesus said, "No	[10] Then Simon Peter, who had a sword, drew it, struck the high priest's slave, and cut off his right ear. The slave's name was Malchus.
	[52] Then Jesus said to him, "Put your sword back in its place; for all who		

Mark 14:43–51	Matthew 26:47–56	Luke 22:47–53	John 18:2–11
	take the sword will perish by the sword. 53 Do you think that I cannot appeal to my Father, and he will at once send me more than twelve legions of angels? 54 But how then would the scriptures be fulfilled, which say it must happen in this way?	more of this!" And he touched his ear and healed him.	11 Jesus said to Peter, 'Put your sword back into its sheath. Am I not to drink the cup that the Father has given me?'
48 Then Jesus said to them, "Have you come out with swords and clubs to arrest me as though I were a bandit? 49 Day after day I was with you in the temple teaching, and you did not arrest me. But let the scriptures be fulfilled. 50 All of them deserted him and fled. 51 A certain young man was following him, wearing nothing but a linen cloth and ran off naked.	55 At that hour Jesus said to the crowds, "have you come out with swords and clubs to arrest me as though I were a bandit? Day after day I sat in the temple teaching, and you did not arrest me. 56 But all this has taken place, so that the scriptures of the prophets may be fulfilled." Then all the disciples deserted him and fled.	52 Then Jesus said to the chief priests, the officers of the temple police, and the elders who had come for him, "Have you come out with swords and clubs as if I were a bandit?" 53 When I was with you day after day in the temple, you did not lay hands on me. But this is your hour and the power of darkness!"	

The exchange between Jesus and this group is a classic Johannine rendering. "Then Jesus, knowing all that was to happen to him"—a claim found only in John—steps forward and asks, "Whom are you looking for?" (18:4). When they respond, "Jesus of Nazareth," he in turn answers, "I am he." As is so often the case in this Gospel, Jesus' words must be read on more than one level. In this case, "I am he," evokes the various claims Jesus has used throughout: "I am he [the Christ]," "I am the bread of life," "I am the light of the world," "I am the gate for the sheep," "I am the good shepherd," "I am the way and the truth and the life," "I am the true vine."[21] John's Jesus repeats the "I am he," at which point "they stepped back and fell to the ground." Again, he asks for whom they are looking. "Jesus of Nazareth." Now for a third time, "'I told you that I am he. So if you are looking for me, let these men go.' This was to fulfill the word he had spoken, 'I did not lose a single one of those you gave me.'"[22]

The arresting party consists of "soldiers, their officer, and the Jewish police," who bound Jesus. First, they take him to Annas, former high priest and father-in-law of the high priest that year, Caiaphas, whom John identifies as the "one who had advised the Jews that it was better to have one person die for the people" (18:14).

John skillfully alternates scenes of Peter's denial that he was a disciple (18:15–18 and 25–27) with the interrogation of Jesus by Annas (18:19–24) and then by Pilate (18:28). When Annas interrogates Jesus, he asks no specific questions, unlike the Synoptic accounts. Rather, Jesus speaks: "I have spoken openly to the world; I have always taught in synagogues and in the temple, where all the Jews come together. I have said nothing in secret. Why do you ask me? Ask those who heard what I said to them; they know what I said" (18:20–21). At this a member of the police strikes Jesus in the face, saying, "Is that how you answer the high priest?" Jesus answers in characteristic Johannine fashion: "If I have spoken wrongly, testify to the wrong. But if I have spoken rightly, why do you strike me?" His question is left unanswered; John tells us that Annas then sends Jesus bound to Caiaphas, the current high priest.

Early in the morning they take Jesus from the place Caiaphas had questioned him to Pilate's headquarters. But the party does not enter the headquarters so as to avoid ritual defilement that would interfere with their observance of Passover (18:28c). Thus, Pilate goes out to them, inquiring about their accusation against Jesus. They respond, "If this man were not a criminal, we would not have handed him over to you," but Pilate parries, "Take him yourselves and judge him according to your law." Now the Jews reply, "We are not permitted to put anyone to death" (18:30–31).[23] John adds, "This was to fulfill what Jesus had said when he indicated the kind of death he was to die."

Now Pilate returns inside his headquarters to confront Jesus, asking, "Are you the King of the Jews?" In the Synoptic accounts, Jesus answers, "You have said so." In John, however, Jesus engages in an extended exchange with Pilate (18:35–38):

> "Do you ask this on your own, or did others tell you about me?"
>
> Pilate replied, "I am not a Jew, am I? Your own nation and the chief priests have handed you over to me. What have you done?"
>
> Jesus answered, "My kingdom is not from this world. If my kingdom were from this world, my followers would be fighting to keep me from being handed over to the Jews. But as it is, my kingdom is not from here."
>
> Pilate asked him, "So you are a king?"
>
> Jesus answered, "You say that I am a king. For this I was born, and for this I came into the world, to testify to the truth. Everyone who belongs to the truth listens to my voice."
>
> Pilate asked him, "What is truth?"

As in the Synoptic Gospels, Pilate finds no case against Jesus, so he goes out to report this to the Jews. He raises the custom of releasing someone at Passover, asking them whether they want him to release the King of the Jews. "They shouted in reply, 'Not this man, but Barabbas!'" John adds, "Now Barabbas was a bandit" (18:39–40).

Back inside, Pilate has Jesus flogged, the solders weave a crown of thorns to put on his head, and they dress him in a purple robe. They mock Jesus, saying, "Hail, King of the Jews," striking him on the face.

The governor returns outside and says to the Jews, "Look, I am bringing him out to you to let you know that I find no case against him." Jesus emerges, wearing his crown of thorns and purple robe. "Here is the man," Pilate proclaims. But the chief priests and police shout, "Crucify him! Crucify him!" Pilate repeats his previous instruction in 18:29 that the Jews should take him themselves and crucify him, because he finds no case against him. But the Jews respond, "We have a law, and according to that law he ought to die because he has claimed to be the Son of God" (19:6–7).

"Now when Pilate heard this," John observes, "he was more afraid than ever" (19:8). John continues with the extended encounter between Jesus and Pilate, as Pilate returns inside his head-quarters and asks Jesus, "Where are you from?" Now Jesus gives no answer, as he had to Pilate in Mark (15:5) and Matthew (27:14). Pilate calls attention to his authority: "Do you refuse to speak to me? Do you not know that I have power to release you, and power to crucify you?" But the Johannine Jesus refuses to acknowledge Pilate's authority: "You would have no power over me unless it had been given you from above; therefore, the one who handed me over to you is guilty of a greater sin."

From then on, John says, Pilate tried to release Jesus, only to be thwarted by *the Jews,* who exclaim, "If you release this man, you are no friend of the emperor. Everyone who claims to be a king sets him-self against the emperor" (19:12). Hearing this, Pilate now brings Jesus outside, and he "sat on the judge's bench at a place called The Stone Pavement, or in Hebrew, *Gabbatha*" (19:13). It was about noon on the day of Preparation for the Passover. Pilate says to *the Jews,* "Here is your King!" But they have none of this: "Away with him! Away with him! Crucify him!" Pilate asks them, "Shall I crucify your King?" The chief priests answer, "We have no king but the emperor" (19:15).

Then, as in the Synoptic Gospels, Pilate hands Jesus over to be crucified (19:16). Standing near the cross were his mother and her sister, Mary, the wife of Clopas; Mary of Magdala; and "the disciple whom he loved."[24] Knowing that "all was finished," Jesus "bowed his head and gave up his spirit" (19:30).

Raw material for portraying Jews as unfaithful abounds in the Fourth Gospel. The high priest Caiaphas and his father-in-law, Annas, are malevolent characters who have no compunction about interrogating Jesus and bringing him to Pontius Pilate. Yet John portrays them as punctilious in their observance of ritual law. Once they have brought Jesus to Pilate, accusing him of being a criminal, they largely disappear from the narrative. We hear primarily of the Jews, who, as a nation, along with their chief priests, have handed over Jesus to Pilate. In the artfully constructed scenes where Pilate goes back and forth from inside his headquarters to the courtyard where the Jews are gathered, the emphasis on Jewish responsibility reaches a climax. Pilate says to the crowd that he has no case against Jesus (19:4), but the chief priests and police urge, "Crucify him! Crucify him!" (19:6). When Pilate retorts, "Take him yourselves and crucify him; I find no case against him," the Jews answer that he must die because according to their law Jesus claimed to be the Son of God (19:7). Remarkably, John says that after this exchange, the Roman governor—the most powerful man in Judea— was "more afraid than ever." Again, Pilate attempts to release Jesus, but the Jews object that were he to do so, he would be no friend of the emperor. "Everyone who claims to be a king sets himself against the emperor" (19:12). Finally, Pilate returns outside, this time with Jesus, saying to the Jews, "Here is your King." But the Jews cry out, "Away with him! Away with him! Crucify him!" Pilate seeks their assurance: "Shall I crucify your King?" And the chief priests give their response: "We have no king but the emperor" (19:14–15). At Golgotha the chief priests of the Jews (19:21) object that the inscription on the cross, "Jesus of Nazareth, the King of the Jews," should instead read, "This man said, I am King of the Jews."

Luke's understanding of the passion and death of Jesus is also apparent in his second volume, the Acts of the Apostles. Luke calls his writings a diēgēsis, a narrative; he tells his patron, Theophilus, to whom he dedicates his work, that his aim is to write an "orderly account" (Luke 1:3). Although this seems to suggest that he is writing history, in fact his volumes give precedence to theological interpretation and preaching.

Acts has no passion narrative, but speeches attributed to Peter, John, Stephen, and Paul reveal whom Luke held accountable for the death of Jesus. This is apparent in Peter's speech after the event of Pentecost, which famously begins: "Men of Judea and all who live in Jerusalem, let this be known to you, and listen to what I say. Indeed, these are not drunk, as you suppose, for it is only nine o'clock in the morning" (2:14–15). He goes on to say, "You that are Israelites, listen to what I have to say: Jesus of Nazareth, a man attested to you by God with deeds of power, wonders, and signs that God did through him among you, as you yourselves know—this man, handed over to you according to the definite plan and foreknowledge of God, you crucified and killed by the hands of those outside the law" (2:22–23). Similarly, after curing a man lame from birth who begged by the temple's Beautiful Gate, Peter addresses a crowd "filled with wonder and amazement at what had happened" (3:10): "The God of Abraham, the God of Isaac, and the God of Jacob, the God of our ancestors has glorified his servant Jesus, whom you handed over and rejected in the presence of Pilate, though he had decided to release him. But you rejected the Holy and Righteous One and asked to have a murderer given to you, and you killed the Author of life, whom God raised from the dead. To this we are witnesses" (3:13–15). Addressing the rulers, elders, and scribes assembled in Jerusalem, including Annas, Caiaphas, and other members of the high-priestly family, Peter says, "Let it be known to all of you, and to all the people of Israel, that this man is standing before you in good health by the name of Jesus Christ of Nazareth, whom you crucified, whom God raised from the dead" (4:7).

Throughout Acts, Luke presents the Followers of the Way as constantly harassed by Jewish leaders. The "priests, the captain of the temple, and the Sadducees" arrest Peter and John (4:3), annoyed that they are teaching about Jesus of Nazareth and proclaiming the resurrection from the dead. Joined by members of the high-priestly family, they order them not to speak or teach in the name of Jesus (4:18). After threatening them, they release the pair. But not for long; the high priest, along with the Sadducees, "filled with jealousy," arrested the apostles and put them in prison (5:17–18); an angel, however, opens the prison doors to free them and they continue teaching in the temple. Brought again to the Jewish authorities, Peter and the apostles proclaim, "We must obey God rather than any human authority. The God of our ancestors raised up Jesus, whom you had killed by hanging him on a tree. God exalted him at his right hand as Leader and Savior that he might give repentance to Israel and forgiveness of sins" (5:29–30). Enraged by this speech, they want to kill the apostles. Only the sage advice of the Pharisee Gamaliel saves them: "I tell you, keep away from these men and let them alone; because if this plan or this undertaking is of human origin, it will fail; but if it is of God, you will not be able to overthrow them—in that case you may even be found fighting against God!" (5:38–39).[25]

Luke names Stephen as one who did great "wonders and signs among the people." But certain members of the synagogue of the Freedmen resisted his wisdom and the Spirit. They stir up the people, accusing Stephen of blasphemy and bringing him before the Sanhedrin, where false testimony is given about Stephen. The high priest quizzes him: "Are these things so?" Unlike Jesus, largely silent at his own trials, Stephen speaks at length, testifying to God's work in Israel and accusing the Sanhedrin of infidelity: "You stiff-necked people, uncircumcised in heart and ears, you are forever opposing the Holy Spirit, just as your ancestors used to do. Which of the prophets did your ancestors not persecute? They killed those who foretold the coming of the Righteous One, and now you have become his betrayers and murderers" (7:51–52). Stephen's accusation enrages his hearers, who drag him out of the city and stone him to death. As he is dying, Stephen cries, "'Lord Jesus, receive my spirit.' Then he knelt down and cried out in a loud voice, 'Lord, do not hold this sin against them.' When he had said this, he died" (7:59–60). Luke notes that Saul approved of this killing (8:1); later, Luke says that the chief priests authorized Saul to bind all who invoked the name of Jesus (9:14). After his encounter on the road to Damascus, however, he became increasingly more powerful; his confrontation with Jews in Damascus led them to plot to kill him (9:23).

Much of Acts focuses around the conflict between the miracles and testimony of the followers of Jesus and the rejection of their message by Jews. Herod Agrippa I lays "violent hands" upon some who belonged to the church. He not only had James killed; he saw that this "pleased the Jews." He has Peter arrested, only to have the angel once again free the prisoner (12:7–10). The Jews are jealous of the crowds that Paul and Barnabas draw (13:44) and drive them out of Pisidian Antioch (13:50), and then out of Iconium (14:1). Paul argues with Jews in a synagogue in Thessalonica (17:1); when Paul and Silas go to Beroea, they find Jews who are more receptive—until

Thessalonian Jews arrive to incite the crowds against them (17:13). Paul argues with Jews in the synagogue each Sabbath during his time in Corinth (18:4) and resolves he will preach instead to the Gentiles (18:6). But in Luke's depiction of the Apostle to the Gentiles, most of his conflicts are with Jews and with Roman officials to whom Jews had complained about Paul (see 20:3; 21:27; 23:12; 24:9, 27; 25:2, 7, 9,15, and 24). Despite charges brought against Paul by Jews, Herod Agrippa II declares, "I found he had done nothing deserving of death" (25:25). Yet his persecutors continue (26:7, 9–10, and 21).

In sum, the Acts of the Apostles not only makes the Jews responsible for the death of Jesus, but also presents the community of Jesus' followers as harassed and even persecuted by Jews. Because Acts reads as if it were a historical account, most Christians assume it has accurately reported "what really happened" in the early church. As later chapters will reveal, the history is much more complex.

Unlike the Gospel writers, who constructed a narrative of the death of Jesus, Paul was a writer of letters. His letters are a dense weave of instruction, pastoral counsel, arguments, admonitions, hymn fragments, metaphorical language, Scripture quotations and allusions, prayers, and greetings to fellow workers. Thirteen documents in the New Testament are attributed to Paul, but not all are considered of his own composition. Most scholars conclude that Paul authored 1 Thessalonians, Galatians, Philippians, Philemon, 1 and 2 Corinthians, and Romans; these seven are typically regarded as the "genuine" Pauline letters. Some scholars also consider him to have written Ephesians and Colossians, and fewer still that he wrote 2 Thessalonians, Titus, and 1 and 2 Timothy. Moreover, as was evident in the above section, Paul is a central figure in broad swaths of the Acts of the Apostles. Yet not all of what Luke writes about Paul accords with Paul's own writings.

Moreover, Paul's letters are "occasional documents," directed to particular audiences at a particular time.[26] We have Paul's responses to situations and questions from the various communities to whom he wrote, but we lack reliable knowledge about the specifics of the audiences, situations, and queries. Thus, we must be wary of grand syntheses, of treating Paul as if he were a systematic theologian and not a peripatetic pastor. We can at best discern *elements* of "Paul's theology of the cross," even as we acknowledge that any such synthesis depends in large part on the assumptions we bring to our reading of Paul.

Paul wrote in the 50s of the first century, well before the Gospels and Acts. It may seem odd, then, to place this section on Paul after my synopsis of the evangelists' telling of the story of Jesus' death. If, however, Paul comes first chronologically, his views seem to have exercised a more subtle influence on the religious imagination of Christians. The Gospels have been far more significant in the way most people think about the events of the passion, hence my decision to give precedence to their narratives over Paul's more fragmentary perspectives.

That being said, the death of Jesus is a preeminent theme in Paul—and far more than a theme. Paul's encounter with Jesus as the crucified one "energized his entire apostolic endeavor (of which his letters represent only a small part), through which he sought to order the lives of Christian congregations by pulling everything into the tremendous gravitational field of the cross."[27] It was Paul himself who was first drawn into this gravitational field. He tells the Galatians that "it is no longer I who live, but it is Christ who lives in me. And the life I now live in the flesh I live by faith in the Son of God, who loved me and gave himself for me" (2:20). In that same letter, he exclaims, "May I never boast of anything except the cross of our Lord Jesus Christ, by which the world has been crucified to me, and I to the world" (6:14). To the Corinthians, Paul writes the following: "When I came to you, brothers and sisters, I did not come proclaiming the mystery of God to you in lofty words of wisdom. For I decided to know nothing among you except Jesus Christ, and him crucified" (1 Corinthians 2:1–2). He and those who follow the way of Jesus are "always carrying in the body the death of Jesus, so that the life of Jesus may also be made visible in our bodies. For while we all live, we are always being given up to death for Jesus' sake, so that the life of Jesus may be made visible in our mortal flesh" (2 Corinthians 4:10–11).

Paul's message to the communities to whom he writes is not one of "lofty words or wisdom" (1 Corinthians 2:1). Rather, he proclaims the cross, which is "foolishness to those who are perishing, but to us who are being saved it is the power of God" (1 Corinthians 1:18). The crucified Christ is a "stumbling block to Jews and foolishness to

Gentiles, but to those who are called, both Jews and Greeks, Christ, the power of God and the wisdom of God" (1 Corinthians 1:23–24). Yet this "foolishness" constitutes the moral core of Christian life for Paul. He exhorts the community at Philippi to take on the same mind as had Jesus, who had assumed the form of a "slave...[and who] humbled himself and became obedient to the point of death—even death on a cross (2:7–8). Just as Jesus had died, been buried, and raised, so, too, his followers must let the "old self" be crucified with Jesus. In a famous passage to the community at Rome that has become a key text for Christian liturgical life, Paul wrote:

> Do you not know that all of us who have been baptized into Christ Jesus were baptized into his death? Therefore we have been buried with him by baptism into death, so that, just as Christ was raised from the dead by the glory of the Father, so we too might walk in newness of life. For if we have been united with him in a death like his, we will certainly be united with him in a resurrection like his. We know that our old self was crucified with him so that the body of sin might be destroyed, and we might no longer be enslaved to sin. For whoever has died is freed from sin. But if we have died with Christ, we believe that we will also live with him. (Romans 6:3–8)

Another liturgically significant text is Paul's admonition that when the community gathers to eat the bread and drink the cup, they are proclaiming "the Lord's death." Those who do so in an "unworthy manner will be answerable for the body and blood of the Lord" (1 Corinthians 11:26–27).

In general, Paul shows little interest in the actual events of the passion, death, and resurrection. In the text from the 1 Corinthians regarding the Eucharist, he says, "For I received from the Lord what I also handed on to you, that the Lord Jesus on the night when he was handed on/betrayed took a loaf of bread..." (1 Corinthians 11:23), but Paul provides detail neither about the betrayer(s) nor how the betrayal took place.[28] There is, however, one text in which he does assign specific blame:

> For you, brothers and sisters, became imitators of the churches of God in Christ Jesus that are in Judea, for you suffered the same things from your own compatriots as they did from the Jews, who killed both the Lord Jesus and the prophets, and drove us out; they displease God and oppose everyone by hindering us from speaking to the Gentiles so that they may be saved. Thus they have constantly been filling up the measure of their sins; but God's wrath has overtaken them at last. (1 Thessalonians 2:14–16)

It is a matter of debate whether Paul actually authored this passage or whether it was added by a later editor.[29] Even if Paul were not its author, the accusation remains in the canon of the New Testament as raw material for hostility to Jews.

THE NEW TESTAMENT'S DEPICTION OF JUDAS

Judas Iscariot may well be one of the best known figures of the Bible—if the least loved, since his name is synonymous with betrayal and treachery. Judas has captured the imagination of many, intriguing all manner of commentators and artists (including the band Judas Priest). Recently, Judas has been in the forefront of discussion since the controversial translation of *The Gospel of Judas*, published in 2006 by the National Geographic Society and shortly thereafter the subject of a television special.[30] Indeed his notoriety—and, in some cases, fame—is so widespread that an entire book could be written on the many ways artists, religious leaders, and scholars have interpreted his character.[31] As will become evident in subsequent chapters, the traitorous Judas of the Gospels and the Acts of the Apostles came to exemplify the treachery of Jews.

Yet as familiar a character as Judas is, historically reliable information about him is negligible. He receives no mention from Paul, whose letters precede the Gospels by some two decades. Paul, however, does mention that Jesus was "betrayed": "For I received from the Lord what I also handed on to you, that the Lord Jesus on the night when he was betrayed took a loaf of bread" (1 Corinthians 11:23). When Mark, Matthew, and John identify Judas among the

Twelve, they name Judas Iscariot as the one who betrayed Jesus.[32] Yet the term frequently translated as "betrayed" in all these passages is more ambiguous; the Greek *paradidomai*, some argue, should more correctly be translated as "handed over."[33] Luke, in contrast, terms Judas a "traitor" (Greek, *prodotēs*), a term with the more negative connotation of one who engages in a treacherous act.[34] Luke's overall portrait of Judas, moreover, is harsher than Mark's and Matthew's; so, too, is John's.

Mark, as is typical of his Gospel, has the least embellished depiction of Judas, mentioning him explicitly three times: among the Twelve (3:19); as the one who went to the chief priests in order to betray/hand him over to them (14:10); and as betrayer/deliverer who arrived with the chief priests, scribes, and elders and kissed Jesus to signal that it was he who should be arrested (14:43–44). Mark also includes a scene at the Last Supper in which Jesus speaks about one of the Twelve (without naming him) who will betray/hand over the Son of Man. "It would have been better for that man," says Jesus, "if he had not been born" (14:18–21).

Matthew follows Mark in identifying Judas as the betrayer/ deliverer among the Twelve (10:4), and his scene of the arrest largely follows Mark, with slight variations. So, too, in his account of the Last Supper, although Matthew explicitly names Judas as the betrayer/deliverer, and Judas asks, "Is it I, Master?" (26:25). Yet Matthew departs from Mark in adding a scene whose details have become important aspects of the way Judas has been remembered:

> When Judas, his betrayer, saw that Jesus was condemned, he repented and brought back the thirty pieces of silver to the chief priests and the elders. He said, "I have sinned by betraying innocent blood." But they said, "What is that to us? See to it yourself." Throwing down the pieces of silver in the temple, he departed; and he went and hanged himself. But the chief priests, taking the pieces of silver, said, "It is not lawful to put them into the treasury, since they are blood money." After conferring together, they used them to buy the potter's field as a place to bury foreigners. For this reason that field has been called the Field of Blood to this day. Then was fulfilled what had been spoken

through the prophet Jeremiah, "And they took the thirty pieces of silver, the price of the one on whom a price had been set, on whom some of the people of Israel had set a price, and they gave them for the potter's field, as the Lord commanded me."(Matt 27:3–10)

Matthew's memorable account has given us the details of the thirty pieces of silver and the phrases *innocent blood* and *blood money*.

Luke also has an account of the death of Judas in the Acts of the Apostles (1:15–20), but it differs markedly from Matthew's:

> In those days Peter stood up among the believers (together the crowd numbered about one hundred twenty persons) and said, "Friends, the scripture had to be fulfilled, which the Holy Spirit through David foretold concerning Judas, who became a guide for those who arrested Jesus—for he was numbered among us and was allotted his share in this ministry." (Now this man acquired a field with the reward of his wickedness; and falling headlong, he burst open in the middle and all his bowels gushed out. This became known to all the residents of Jerusalem, so that the field was called in their language Hakeldama, that is, Field of Blood.) "For it is written in the book of Psalms, 'Let his homestead become desolate, and let there be no one to live in it'; and 'let another take his position of overseer.'"

Note the differences: In Matthew the chief priests took the thirty pieces of silver Judas had returned, regarded it as "blood money," and used it to buy a potter's field as a place of burial for foreigners. Matthew reads this as fulfilling Jeremiah.[35] In Luke, it is Judas himself who acquired the field with the thirty pieces of silver, that is, "With the reward of his wickedness." Luke, while not reporting the cause of his fall, vividly describes the death of Judas: "falling headlong, he burst open in the middle and all his bowels gushed out."[36] Luke reads the Field of Blood as evoking the Psalms (69:25 and 109:8b), and justifying the need for someone "to take the place in this ministry and apostleship from which Judas turned aside to go to his own place" (Acts 1:25).

As will become evident, the association of Judas with the grotesque became a staple of Christian preaching and teaching. Before leaving the New Testament, however, two further characteristics Luke and John attributed to Judas require mention. The first is Luke's connection of Judas with Satan: "Then Satan entered into Judas called Iscariot, who was one of the twelve; he went away and conferred with the chief priests and officers of the temple police about how he might betray him to them" (Luke 22:3–4). John has similar texts. In the conclusion to the long discourse on the Bread of Life, Jesus says to Simon Peter and the others: "'Did I not choose you, the twelve, and one of you is a devil?' He spoke of Judas the son of Simon Iscariot, for he, one of the twelve, was to betray him" (6:70–71). And in the account of the Last Supper, John notes that "The devil had already put it into the heart of Judas son of Simon Iscariot to betray him" (13:2).

John adds another detail that has been taken up in Christian memory: Judas as a thief. In recounting the story of Mary of Bethany anointing the feet of Jesus with a "pound of costly perfume," he tells us that Judas asked, "Why was this perfume not sold for three hundred denarii and the money given to the poor?" The narrator assigns a motive to Judas' question: "He said this not because he cared about the poor, but because he was a thief; he kept the common purse and used to steal what was put into it" (12:5–6). John then brings together the satanic element and, at least implicitly, the thievery in his account of the Last Supper:

> After saying this Jesus was troubled in spirit, and declared, "Very truly, I tell you, one of you will betray me." The disciples looked at one another, uncertain of whom he was speaking. One of his disciples—the one whom Jesus loved—was reclining next to him; Simon Peter therefore motioned to him to ask Jesus of whom he was speaking. So while reclining next to Jesus, he asked him, "Lord, who is it?" Jesus answered, "It is the one to whom I give this piece of bread when I have dipped it in the dish." So when he had dipped the piece of bread, he gave it to Judas son

of Simon Iscariot. After he received the piece of bread, Satan entered into him. Jesus said to him, "Do quickly what you are going to do." Now no one at the table knew why he said this to him. Some thought that, because Judas had the common purse, Jesus was telling him, "Buy what we need for the festival"; or, that he should give something to the poor. So, after receiving the piece of bread, he immediately went out. And it was night.

In sum, the depiction of Judas in the New Testament develops considerably beyond Mark's characterization of him as the one who betrayed or handed over Jesus. Matthew's additions that Judas betrayed "innocent blood" and that the thirty pieces of silver constituted "blood money" evoke the accusation unique to his Gospel that the whole crowd cried, "His blood be on us and on our children" (27:25). Both Matthew and Luke describe Judas as dying in a terrible way: by hanging himself (Matthew) or by falling headlong in such a manner that he split open, his bowels gushing out (Luke). Furthermore, Luke and John associate Judas with Satan or the devil, and John portrays him as a thief.

Given the way in which New Testament texts developed the character of Judas, it is difficult to ascertain the precise history, if any, underlying his role in the passion and death of Jesus. Did he merely hand Jesus over, as Klassen has argued, or was he in fact the betrayer? Many scholars regard his portrait in the New Testament as more a literary invention than as a historically reliable report. Kim Paffenroth, for example, maintains that by the end of the first generation of Christian storytellers, Judas was little known; perhaps some knew that he was the disciple who had cooperated with authorities who arrested Jesus. Yet when later generations looked at Judas, they saw "the perfect cipher on which to practice their art, shaping him into the kind of man or monster that their individual stories needed."[37]

The raw materials accusing Jews of responsibility for the death of Jesus and demonizing Judas had tragic consequences, as the next chapters document. Insofar as the raw materials were used in this fashion, they became, in Adrian Thatcher's terminology, "savage" texts, that is, biblical passages used to marginalize or persecute or victimize "any of the people or creatures for whom (according to the Christian Gospel) Christ died."[38] A savage text should not be confused with the Bible itself, not even those parts that depict or authorize violence:

> No, the savage text is not the Bible. It is what Christians have made of the Bible when they have used its pages to endorse cruelty, hatred, murder, oppression, and condemnation....The savage text is what the Bible, or parts of it, becomes when it enables Christians to convert the good news of God's revealed love in Jesus Christ into the bad news that people are the wrong color, or race, or gender, or denomination, or orientation, or religion, or class, or empire, just because they differ from the Christians who are preaching this bad news....The savage text makes hatred holy.

A crucial aspect of redeeming our sacred texts from their sacrilegious uses is a willingness to look straight into the tarnished mirror of our history. To this mirror we now turn.

CHAPTER 4

Christ Killers

A Consistent Refrain

Certainty of God's will leads to intolerance,
to threats of violence, to murder.[1]

In this chapter and the next, I follow over the course of centuries the allegation that Jews were responsible for the death of Jesus. Tracing the journey of this accusation reveals how the raw materials of biblical texts functioned to buttress Christian belief and practice over against Jewish belief and practice. The charge that the Jews killed Jesus became a crucial component of the rhetoric of Christian identity formation. It was a key element in its rivalry with the synagogue in the complex and extended process by which Christianity ultimately separated from Judaism. As a fundamental part of the "us/them" binary, it stood at the center of the assertion that the Way of Christ, the crucified Savior, was the only faithful way to God and that the followers of Christ had become God's people. God now rejected the Jews, the former people of God, because of their infidelity in killing Jesus. In many cases, particularly before the High Middle Ages, the clash remained primarily in the rhetorical realm. Later, however, Jews paid a much steeper price as the violence of the rhetoric too often inspired violent—and vile—deeds.

I shall generally proceed chronologically, not to suggest an evolutionary trajectory, but rather to provide some order. Having shown its origins in the raw material of certain New Testament texts in the previous chapter, my point of departure here is with apocryphal texts and writers of the early church, from the Epistle of Barnabas to the highly nuanced writings of the prolific Augustine of Hippo. Then in a second section my analysis shifts to a more virulent form of anti-Judaism evident in the Crusades, in popular and devotional literature, and finally in the charge of ritual murder.

I am not implying a direct line from the early church to the medieval church. Many of the texts cited from the early period were not known in the medieval realm, and the socio-political situations differed from age to age and region to region. Moreover, the image of the Jews projected by the New Testament texts did not necessarily accord with social realities, thus a distinction between the "real" Jew and the "hermeneutical" Jew, that is, between the actual Jews and the image of the Jews projected and propounded by Christian teachers. Yet despite significantly changed contexts, the linkage with Jews and the death of Jesus was a consistent refrain.

The subsequent chapter continues the narrative first by analysis of the passion play enacted in the Bavarian village of Oberammergau from the seventeenth century through the present, and then explores how the church's traditional anti-Jewish teaching fused with aspects of racial antisemitism. The refrain of Jewish responsibility for the death of Jesus returns again and again.

APOCRYPHAL TEXTS: INNOCENT PILATE, GUILTY JEWS

One of the intriguing elements in New Testament apocryphal literature was the way in which Pontius Pilate, under whose authority as the governor of Judea from 26–36 C.E. Jesus was crucified, came to be exonerated. Instead, texts tended to place full blame on the Jews. For example, in a relatively early apocryphal text, *The Gospel of Peter*, Pilate has little to do with Jesus' death and seems to be sympathetic to his centurion's report that "In truth he was the Son of God." Pilate responds, "I am clean from the blood of the Son of God" (*Gos. Pet.* 11:45–46).[2] In the *Acts of Pilate*, "the Jews" repeatedly return to Pilate, insisting that he put Jesus to death. At one juncture, Pilate summons his messenger to get Jesus, and instructs him, "Let Jesus be brought with gentleness" (I.2).[3] Various disciples of Jesus and those whom Jesus had healed appeared before Pilate, testifying to Jesus' innocence; they convinced Pilate of this. It was only "the Jews" who resisted their testimony. Finally, Pilate gave in when "the Jews" told him that Jesus was the one Herod had sought in Bethlehem. Pilate then said to Jesus, "Your nation has convicted you of claiming to be a king" (IX.5). Another section of the *Acts of Pilate* contains a report by Pilate to Emperor Claudius (although the emperor to whom Pilate would have reported was Tiberius) in which he accuses the chief priests of "bringing forward lie after lie" about Jesus. Pilate, believing them, orders Jesus to be scourged. "And they crucified him." But Jesus rises from the dead, and even though the Jews bribe Pilate's soldiers to say that his body had been stolen, "they were unable to keep silent about what had happened. For they testified that he had arisen, and that they had seen it, and that they had received money from the Jews."[4]

Still another section of the *Acts of Pilate,* known as the *Paradosis* or "Handing Over," exalts Pilate. After his report to the emperor, Pilate is brought to Rome and placed before Caesar, the senate, army, and "all the great ones of the empire." Caesar demands that Pilate account for "his wicked daring [by which] you have destroyed the whole world." Pilate responds, "Almighty Caesar, I am innocent of these things; it is the multitude of the Jews who are guilty instigators....This nation is rebellious and refractory, and does not submit to your power." Caesar, however, rebukes Pilate for not having recognized the signs that "Jesus was the Christ, the king of the Jews."

> And when Caesar said this and named the name of Christ, all the gods fell down, where Caesar sat with the senate, and became as dust. And all the people who stood by Caesar trembled by reason of the naming of the name and the fall of their gods, and gripped by fear they all went away....And Caesar commanded that Pilate should be kept in custody, in order that he might learn the truth about Jesus.[5]

Caesar's interrogation of Pilate continues the next day. The governor confesses, "I did it because of the unlawful insubordination of the lawless and godless Jews." Enraged, Caesar orders a decree against the Jews:

To Licianus, chief governor of the East, greeting! At the present time the Jews who live in Jerusalem and the neighbouring towns have committed a lawless crime in forcing Pilate to crucify Jesus who was acknowledged as God. Because of this crime of theirs the world was darkened and dragged down to ruin. Therefore by this decree proceed there with all speed with a strong body of troops and take them prisoner. Obey, and advance against them, and dispersing them among all the nations enslave them, and expel them from Judea, making the nation so insignificant that it is no longer to be seen anywhere, since they are men full of evil.[6]

Caesar then orders Pilate to be executed. En route to his execution, Pilate "prayed silently" and asks that he not be destroyed with the "wicked Hebrews." His action had been done in ignorance. "Therefore, do not condemn me because of this sin, but pardon me, Lord, and your servant Procla [Pilate's wife], who stands with me in this hour of my death...." Then, remarkably, the narrator wrote:

And behold, when Pilate had finished his prayer, there sounded a voice from heaven: "All generations and families of the Gentiles shall call you blessed, because in your governorship all was fulfilled which the prophets foretold about me. And you yourself shall appear as my witness at my second coming, when I shall judge the twelve tribes of Israel and those who have not confessed my name." And the prefect cut off Pilate's head, and behold, an angel of the Lord received it. And when Procla his wife saw the angel coming and receiving his head, she was filled with joy, and immediately gave up the ghost, and was buried with her husband.[7]

No wonder that the apologist Tertullian (ca. 155–225) noted that he had heard that Pilate "was now in fact a Christian in his own convictions" (*Apology*, 21). As Daniel Schwartz observes, such an apologia was a necessary tool in justifying Christianity: "its spokesmen had to be able to argue that the empire's representative who had actually had the closest contact with Jesus, far from considering him a criminal worthy of condemnation, in fact thought him innocent or even more."[8] Yet the exoneration of Pilate intensified the charge of Jewish culpability and falsified history.

EARLY CHURCH WRITERS ON JEWS
AND THE DEATH OF JESUS

The Epistle of Barnabas (late first or early second century) provides a striking example of oppositional identity formation. Throughout, the anonymous writer, whose precise location remains uncertain, refers to "us" and "them." By "us" Barnabas means those for whom the meanings of types such as the scapegoat and red heifer are "clear"; by "them" he means those to whom the meanings are obscure, "because they did not hear the voice of the Lord" (8.7). In chapters 5–8, Barnabas cites or alludes to a wide variety of Old Testament texts as proof that the new covenant, grounded in Jesus' suffering and death, provides salvation for his followers but destruction for them. Hostility to Judaism pervades the letter.

Already by the mid-second century, the accusation that the Jews had killed Jesus had become a matter of disputation. The apologist Justin Martyr, likely writing from Rome ca. 155–160 C.E., accused the Jew Trypho: "He was pierced by you" (*Dialogue with Trypho*, 32.2).[9] This "dialogue"—Trypho's relatively few lines sound suspiciously like Justin's creation—offers another instance of the formation of Christian identity by way of contrast with Judaism.[10] For Justin, "We have been led to God through this crucified Christ, and we are the true spiritual Israel" (*Dialogue*, 11.5). The Jews, on the other hand, are the "very instigators of that evil opinion they have of the Just One and us" (*Dialogue*, 17.1), unable to correctly interpret their own Scriptures: "For we believe and obey them, whereas you, though you read them, do not grasp their spirit" (*Dialogue*, 29.2). Jews had murdered Jesus, "the Just One and his prophets before him," and now they were rejecting "those who hope in him and in him who sent him, namely almighty God, the Creator of all things" (*Dialogue*, 16.4). By their evil deeds, Jews were beyond redemption: "Indeed, your hand is still raised to do evil, because, although you have slain Christ, you do not repent; on the contrary, you hate and, whenever you have the power, kill us who through him believe in God, the Father of the universe" (*Dialogue,* 133.6).

Justin's *Dialogue with Trypho* established a polemical template that centuries of successive Christian authors drew upon. Justin fashioned a reading of Scripture in which the Jews were blind to the meaning of "their" Scriptures (now "ours"), obdurate (thus necessitating the Law), idolatrous (for which God tolerated sacrifice), and sinful. They deserved to be deprived of homeland and temple, yet even after all that, they continued to reject Christ and observe the Law according to the flesh (especially circumcision). Ironically, by continuing to practice circumcision, they facilitated their own exile, since it was by that mark they could be identified as Jews.

Once Justin had established this interpretive context for reading Scripture, it was possible to read the texts that eventually comprised the Christian canon as testimony to Jewish blindness. Thus, the missions of Jesus and Paul were directed against the Jews. The vicissitudes suffered by Jews, such as the failed revolts against Rome, the devastation of Jerusalem and the temple, could be adduced as proofs that the "Jews, in rejecting Christ, had sealed their rejection of God; God, in turn had conclusively rejected them."[11] As will become evident in many of the texts cited in this chapter, Christians began to use the term *Jew* as a negative code word within their internal debates against doctrinal diversity within and perceived persecution without.[12]

Late in this same second century, the bishop of Sardis (in modern Turkey), Melito (d. ca. 190), preached a powerful sermon known now as "Homily on the Passover." His rhetoric was brilliant, but his heightened language conveyed a shocking depiction of Judaism:

> O wicked Israel, why did you carry out this fresh deed of injustice, bringing new sufferings upon your Lord—your master, your creator, your maker, the one who honored you, who called you Israel? But you were discovered not to be Israel, for you have not seen God or acknowledged the Lord. (#81)[13]

As a consequence, life has become bitter for Jews, as it is written, "'You will eat unleavened bread with bitter herbs.'" In a flourish of repetitions—the rhetorical device of anaphora—Melito continued his skillful oratory:

> Bitter for you the nails which you sharpened. Bitter for you the tongue which you sharpened. Bitter for you the false witnesses which you set up. Bitter for you the bonds which you prepared. Bitter for you the whips which you plaited. Bitter for you Judas whom you rewarded. Bitter for you Herod whom you obeyed. Bitter for you Caiaphas in whom you trusted. Bitter for you the gall which you furnished. Bitter for you the vinegar which you produced. Bitter for you the thorns which you gathered. Bitter for you the hands which you stained with blood. You did your Lord to death in the midst of Jerusalem. (#93)

Reaching a climax, Melito cried, "And who has been killed? Who is the killer?" He answered his own question:

> I am ashamed to say and compelled to speak....Who was it? It is a heavy thing to say, and a most fearful thing to refrain from saying. But listen, as you tremble in the face of him on whose account the earth trembled. He who hung the earth in place is hanged. He who fixed the heavens in place is fixed in place. He who made all things fast is made fast on the tree. The Master is insulted. *God is murdered*. The King of Israel is destroyed by an Israelite hand. (## 94–96, emphasis added)

It is this disturbing claim that made Melito infamous as the "first poet of deicide"—in killing Jesus, Jews have killed God.[14] Melito's sermon draws on similar anti-Jewish traditions in the *Gospel of Peter* that emphasize the centrality of the Jews—"wicked Israel"—in mocking, judging, and crucifying Jesus. Melito has followed his predecessors in assigning responsibility for the death of Jesus to the Jews, but heightened their infamy. He is both an heir and the source of many different threads of anti-Jewish rhetoric.[15]

A less harsh verdict was rendered in a lengthy mid-third century treatise by Origen (ca. 185–254). A refutation of the anti-Christian polemics of pagan philosopher Celsus, it reflected both the typical rhetoric of *Adversus Judaeos* literature and yet a defense of Judaism as superior to Greek myths. The learned Origen, famed for his compilation of the Hexapala (Hebrew and Greek texts of Tanakh/Old Testament in parallel columns), seemed to have interacted with Jewish scholars. His work revealed awareness of rabbinic exegesis and halakhic debates, perhaps a reflection of his years in Caesarea Maritima, where he likely encountered Jewish scholars. His major argument with the Jews was that they read their Scriptures without grasping their import, that is, that they read them literally and were blind to their spiritual meaning.[16] So the Old Testament was a book about Christ and belonged more truly to the church than to the Jews. Such a view echoed that of his contemporaries, as did his accusation that the Jews had committed "a crime of the most unhallowed kind," when they conspired against the Savior of humankind in the "city where they offered up to God a worship containing the symbols of mighty mysteries [Jerusalem]." Accordingly, the city where Jesus suffered and died must "perish utterly," and "the Jewish nation" be overthrown, "and the invitation to happiness offered them by God to pass to others—the Christians" (*Contra Celsus*, IV.22). Yet Origen was not uniformly hostile to Judaism; even as he believed that "after the advent of Jesus the Jews were altogether abandoned....[with] no indication of any Divinity abiding amongst them," he respected the wisdom and insight of Jewish tradition (*Contra Celsus*, Book II.8).[17] Nicholas de Lange observes:

> Yet whenever he opens his mouth to criticize the Jews, he almost stifles himself in his attempt to remain calm and reasonable. He shows no malice, only amazement at the ingratitude of the Jews, who were especially chosen to witness the divine incarnation which was foretold by their own prophets, and yet refused to accept it.[18]

In contrast, John Chrysostom (347–407), the "golden tongued" rhetorician of Antioch (and later the bishop of Constantinople), rendered Jews in an unambiguously negative fashion. His eight

"Homilies against the Judaizers" constitutes the "most vituperative and vindictive attack on the Jews from Christian antiquity."[19] Historians dispute the precise identity of Judaizing Christians. Robert Wilken considers them typically to be gentile Christians "whose acquaintance with Judaism was mediated through Christianity; who, in contrast to the majority of Christians, adopted certain aspects of Jewish law, even though before becoming Christians they had not observed it."[20] John McGuckin offers a more expansive understanding of the term:

> I think the Judaizers were simply the majority of the common people in Alexandria who seem to have gone to the synagogue for their great feasts and then to the church for their great feasts—much to the annoyance of the Christian bishops who started (because of this) arguing for the need for religiously strong boundaries between the communities. In my reading the boundaries did not exist between the Jewish and Church factions...in major cities like Alexandria and Antioch. For me, this also explains why Chrysostom is so virulent against the Jews in Antioch and Constantinople.[21]

Whoever the Judaizers were, Chrysostom inveighed against them in scathing terms:

> Here [in the synagogue] the slayers of Christ gather together, here the cross is driven out, here God is blasphemed, here the Father is ignored, here the Son is outraged, here the grace of the Spirit is rejected. Does not greater harm come from this place since the Jews themselves are demons. (*Discourse,* I.6.3)[22]

Chrysostom preached these homilies in Antioch, a city where Jews had become increasingly prominent since the third century B.C.E. and were relatively numerous.[23] A significant Christian populace had developed; "it was in Antioch that the disciples were first called Christians"(Acts 11:26b). But what the term *Christian* precisely meant in relation to "Judaism" in the late third and early fourth centuries is a matter of debate. This debate, which will be taken up at some length in later chapters, suggests the importance of recognizing the fluidity of religious borderlines. Given this fluidity, the pluralism of Antioch, with its pagans, Jews, and Samaritans, posed a challenge to authorities eager to maintain order. Emperor Constantine had forbidden conversions to Judaism in 315, although in his rule there was no consistent policy regarding Jews. A harsh tone, however, was evident in the legislation, which referred to Judaism as an "abominable" and "dangerous sect."[24] The ascension of Constantine's nephew Julian as emperor in 361 proved particularly threatening to Christian authorities. Julian, known as "the Apostate" because of his rejection of and hostility to Christianity, regarded both Hellenism and Judaism as superior religious systems. He overturned the anti-Jewish laws (for example, Jews forbidden to seek male proselytes or to own Christian slaves), removed tax exemptions for clergy, and forbade Christians to teach rhetoric.[25] Most disquieting was his decision—made while living in Antioch—to rebuild the temple in Jerusalem. Because Christians had interpreted the destruction of Jerusalem and its temple as a sign of divine punishment for Jewish infidelity in crucifying Jesus, Julian's decision appeared as a rebuke to Christianity.[26] Robert Wilken writes that "in the Christian mind, the attempt to rebuild the temple in Jerusalem was a profound attack on the truth of Christianity."[27]After Julian's reign, which ended with his death in June of 363, Antiochene Christians began to manifest increasing hostility toward Jews, even though the temple was never rebuilt.[28]

None in Antioch was more eloquently hostile than John Chrysostom. Some members of his congregation were attracted to Jewish ways of life, although "most members of my flock are free of this disease [of attraction to Judaism]" (*Discourse*, III.1.4). This segment of the congregation apparently observed Jewish fasts and festivals and attended the synagogue as well as the church. Chrysostom's sermons functioned as a sort of Christian "border control," accentuating what he held to be the sharp distinction between Judaism and Christianity:

> The difference between the Jews and us is not a small one,
>   is it? Is the dispute between us over ordinary, everyday

matters, so that you think the two religions are really one and the same? Why are you mixing what cannot be mixed? They crucified the Christ whom you adore as God. Do you see how great the difference is? How is it, then, that you keep running to those who slew Christ when you say that you worship him whom they crucified? (*Discourse,* IV.3.6)

To those who believed that participating in the life of both the church and synagogue were compatible, Chrysostom presented a stark dissimilarity: "Finally, if the ceremonies of the Jews move you to admiration, what do you have in common with us? If the Jewish ceremonies are venerable and great, ours are lies. But if ours are true, as they *are* true, theirs are filled with deceit" (*Discourse,* I.6.5). Hence, in Chrysostom's perspective, it was necessary to draw well-defined contrasts premised on Jewish infidelity, of which the ultimate exemplar was the crucifixion:

You did slay Christ, you did lift violent hands against the Master, you did spill his precious blood. This is why you have no chance for atonement, excuse, or defense. In the old days your reckless deeds were aimed against his servants, against Moses, Isaiah, and Jeremiah. Even if there was ungodliness in your acts then, your boldness had not yet dared the crowning crime. But now you have put all the sins of your fathers into the shade. Your mad rage against Christ, the Anointed One, left no way for anyone to surpass your sin. (*Discourse,* VI.2.10)

Thus, it should be clear why God has turned his back on the Jewish religion: "It is again obvious that he did so because of him whom you crucified and because of your recklessness in committing this outrage....After the cross...you endure a greater vengeance and have none of your former blessings" (*Discourse,* 6.4.7). And the sign of God's rejection was the destruction of Jerusalem: "[God] made Jerusalem what we might call the keystone which held together the structure of worship. When he overthrew the city, he destroyed the rest of the entire structure of that way of life" (*Discourse,* 4.6.9).

Ambrose (ca. 337–397), bishop of Milan, was no rhetorical match for Chrysostom, but his justification of the destruction of synagogues portended a more violent turn. In 388 a Christian mob, incited by their local bishop, had burned a synagogue in Callinicum (in Mesopotamia) in retaliation for a raid on the Christian quarter by the Jewish quarter. When the emperor, Theodosius I (346–395), received word of the incident, he ordered that those taking part in the destruction be punished and that the bishop have the synagogue rebuilt at his own expense.

Lest, however, this burning of a synagogue be regarded as an indication of Christian intolerance, it is important to situate it in the larger context of ancient cities. Mob rule typically prevailed, governmental enforcement was largely ineffective, and society's various factions habitually engaged in violence against other groups.[29]

Nevertheless, this incident is pertinent to our narrative because the bishop, Ambrose, drew upon the "Christ killer" charge in his redress to the emperor. He protested to Theodosius: The people responsible should not be so severely punished for the mere burning of a building, "and much less since it is the burning of a synagogue, a home of unbelief, a house of impiety, a receptacle of folly, which God Himself has condemned." What, Ambrose asked, "could the scheming Jews lose by the fire?" Furthermore, "who is to avenge the Synagogue? Christ, Whom they slew, Whom they denied? Will God the Father avenge those who do not receive the Father, since they have not received the Son?"[30] Eventually, the emperor acceded to Ambrose, who promoted the elimination of Jewish religiosity by violent action.[31]

Augustine of Hippo (354–430), however, presented a more complex case. In his earlier years as a Manichean—a follower of Mani (ca. 210–276), a Persian religious figure who established a Christian religious movement that flourished widely until about the seventh century—Augustine followed their dualistic perspective. God, who alone is good, is opposed by Evil, substance in itself. Good and evil war within humankind; the incorruptible soul, composed of light, reflects the good, whereas the body, composed of earth, reflects the evil.[32] Among the corollaries of this system of thought was that the body—fleshy, material—is evil. In such a system of thought, Judaism, premised on the God of the Old Testament, who had created the material universe and engaged in unseemly acts (as had many Old Testament figures), was a carnal and corrupt religion. So, too, in the Manichean perspective was Catholic Christianity, which had retained the Scripture of the Jews and professed belief in an incarnate Christ.

Gradually, however, Augustine, found the Manichean world-view unsatisfactory. He became a catechumen, was baptized into Catholic Christianity in 387, called into priesthood by the people of Hippo in 391, and ordained as bishop in 396. His "conversion" involved radical change, a transformation that transcended the out-ward move from Manichee to Catholic: "With astounding courage and sheer acuity, he rethought absolutely everything that he had come into this phase of his life with."[33] An innovative and nuanced understanding of Judaism comprised a significant aspect of this rethinking.

Paula Fredriksen analyzes the evolution in Augustine's view of Judaism, arguing that his *Against Faustus* (398–400) reflects his reas-sessment of "received ideas about Christianity's relationship with Judaism, and about Judaism itself, past and present."[34] A Manichee, Faustus had authored *Capitula* in 386; Augustine recapitulated the major arguments of that work in his reply. Faustus hewed to the Manichean line: railing against the bloodthirsty god of the Jews, the morally flawed Old Testament figures, and the carnal practices of blood sacrifices and circumcision. Debate with Faustus allowed Augustine to draw upon the extensive biblical study in which he had engaged in the years since his conversion, including a serious engagement with Paul's writings.

Fredriksen identifies five prominent dimensions of Augustine's new teaching about Judaism in *Against Faustus*. First, Augustine read the Bible not only typologically (in which a present event, situation, thing, or person suggests a likeness to an event, situation, thing, or person in the past) but also literally (that is, that the text itself meant what it said).[35] As a consequence, he recognized that God had cho-sen Israel and bestowed the Law as a good for the people, who had in turn received it. Second, Jewish practices, grounded in the Law, conformed to God's will; this included not only Sabbath, ritual wash-ing, festivals, and the dietary laws, but also two practices consistently disparaged in the *Adversus Judaeos* tradition and among the

Manichees: blood sacrifices and circumcision. Third, Augustine insisted that Jesus, the twelve apostles, the churches of Judea, and Paul were faithful in keeping the commandments. Fourth, although the Jews were blind to the Gospel's truth—blinded by God's secret justice—they served the church as the guardians of the books for the sake of the church, "bearing the Law and the Prophets, and testifying to the doctrine of the church, so that we honor in the sacrament what they disclose in the letter" (*Against Faustus*, 12.23). Fifth, just as God protected Cain, who murdered Abel (Genesis 4:8), so God protects the Jews, who murdered Christ. Their ancestral practices, commanded in the Law, serve as the "mark of Cain"—not a badge of shame but a sign that no ruler should "kill" Jews, that is, force them to cease being Jews.[36]

In Augustine's theological reasoning, the Jews were essential to the church as "wandering book slaves who witness to Christian truth":

> Book custodian (*custos librorum*), librarian (*bibliothecarius, librarius*), guardian of the book cask (*scriniarius, capsarius*). The Law and the prophets universally speak about Christ; the Jews, reading wrongly, unwittingly carry these books that they think are theirs but that actually belong to the church. In this way, the Jews help the church to spread the gospel.[37]

To be sure, Augustine held the Jews responsible for the death of the Son of God. Yet he believed they were ignorant of his true identity because they misread their own Scriptures. Jews preserved faithfully the books of Scripture, but read them "as the face of a blind man appears in a mirror—by others it is seen, but by himself it is not seen" (*City of God*, 18.46). In this same text Augustine cites Psalm 59:11–12: "As for my God, his mercy will go before me; my God has shown me this in the case of my enemies. Do not slay them, lest at some time they forget your Law; scatter them by your might." These verses served as the basis for a decisive admonition. The world must not "slay" them, that is, not end their existence as a distinctive people, lest "they might forget the Law of God and thus fail to give convincing testimony." Yet the psalmist had to add "Scatter them," because if Jews lived "only in their own land and not everywhere, then the Church, which is everywhere, would not have them available among all the nations as witnesses to the prophecies given beforehand about Christ" (*City of God*, 18.46).

Certainly, elements of the *Adversus Judaeos* tradition surfaced throughout the extensive corpus of Augustine's work; in 429 he had written *Adversus Judaeos* as a critique, in part, of Judaizing Christians. Nevertheless, Augustine was distinctive in his recognition of the importance of Judaism as an embodied community whose witness was essential to the flourishing of Christianity. His dictum that Jews not be killed held force for centuries. "Do not slay them" became even more important once Emperor Theodosius I declared Christianity the official religion of the Roman Empire in 380 C.E., enabling the church to exercise its theology in the political and cultural sphere.[38] Jews became subject in many areas to decrees that restricted their rights and effectively reduced them to second-class citizens. Yet, thanks in large measure to Augustine, Christian society *tolerated* the presence of Jews in *their* society—hardly a virtue, yet a far better situation than would later develop.

Such an attitude prevailed for centuries in the Christian West. Alleged Jewish culpability for the crucifixion of Jesus—and thereby the Jews' rejection of the Son of God—resulted in consistent denunciation of Jewish faithlessness and disparagement of Judaism. The hostility to Judaism, however, was largely doctrinal, with legal ramifications: Jews were relegated to a subordinate position in society by exclusion from political office, separation from Christians, prohibition from ownership of Christian slaves, and left out of the feudal network.[39] Although Pope Gregory I (r. 590–604) intervened to prohibit forced baptisms and from Christians taking over synagogues, his decrees nonetheless reflected his contempt for Judaism: "When anyone is brought to the font of baptism, not by the sweetness of preaching but by compulsion, he returns to his former superstition, and dies the worse from having been born again." So preachers should be persuasive that Jews would seek conversion and turn away from their "former vomit."[40]

The rhetoric of the *Adversus Judaeos* literature should not be taken as a mirror of social reality. Despite tensions, there is considerable evidence of continuous interaction between Jews and Christians. As Fredriksen notes, the vitality of this "habitual contact accounts in part for the increasing shrillness of anti-Jewish invective."[41] She concludes:

> The ideology of separation was initially an optative principle, intimately and immediately allied to textual practices, articulated and developed by an intellectual minority...beginning, perhaps in the early second century C.E. It was an ideal vociferously—or, depending on our degree of empathy for figures like Chrysostom, perhaps plaintively—urged in the fourth. It was a policy ineffectually legislated, in pockets of the old Roman world, in the sixth. It was never in this culture, for the entire period from the coming of Christianity to the coming of Islam, a native reality universally lived.[42]

In the medieval world, however, the social reality changed.

THE EMERGENCE OF A VIRULENT ANTI-JUDAISM IN THE MIDDLE AGES

It was not until the eleventh century that virulent anti-Judaism emerged among the populace particularly in northern Europe, where unofficial crusaders fueled enmity and slaughtered Jews.[43]

Pope Urban II called for the liberation of the churches of the East from Islam in 1095 at the Council of Clermont.[44] French Benedictine chronicler Guibert of Nogent (ca. 1055–1124) provided one of the first definitions of a crusade:

> In our time God has initiated a holy manner of warfare so that knights and common people who, after the ancient manner of paganism, were formerly immersed in internecine slaughter, have found a new way of winning salvation. They no longer need, as they formerly did, entirely to abandon the world by entering a monastery or by some other similar commitment. They can obtain God's grace in their own manner and dress, and by their ordinary way of life.[45]

While primarily aimed at protecting the church from the threat posed by Muslim expansion, the Crusades also resulted in dire consequences for Jews. The first widespread massacre of Jews in Europe occurred in 1096 when bands of peasant crusaders swept through towns of the Rhineland—Speyer, Worms, Mainz, Cologne, Trier, Metz, Bamberg, Regensburg—killing God's enemies, the Jews, who were closer at hand than were Muslims.[46] This pogrom "augured heightened tensions ahead."[47] Crusaders, after all, were those who "took the cross" (crucesignati).[48] At least some crusaders were charged to take vengeance because of what the Jews had done in the crucifixion:

> Rouse yourselves, members of Christ's household....Give heed to Christ, who today is banished from that city and is crucified...and forcefully take Christ away from these impious crucifiers....Every time they torment them [the Crusaders' Christian brothers] and kill them they lance Christ's side....If an outsider were to strike any of you down would you not avenge your blood relative? How much more ought you to avenge your God, your father, your brother, whom you see reproached, banished from his estates, crucified; whom you hear calling, desolate and begging for aid.[49]

As a consequence, the cross, the preeminent symbol of Christianity, took on an ominous meaning, particularly for Jews.[50] James Carroll argues that the Crusades represent the church's alienation from its Jewish roots. By its violence against those it perceived as opposed to Christianity, the church failed to engage in the sort of self-criticism characteristic of the prophets of Israel. By its "embrace of the ethos of violence" in a "total war waged under the sign of the cross," the church had betrayed the meaning of the cross.[51] Christopher Tyerman notes that the preaching of the cross during the Crusades conflated "meritorious Christian violence, the legitimacy of revenge and religious vendetta and the suffering of Christ Crucified."[52]

The Crusades heralded not only an intensified invective against Jews, but also a tragic turn to violence against them in the twelfth and thirteenth centuries. In addition to their reputation as Christ killers, Jews were further stereotyped as usurers, bribers and secret killers. "It had become easier to think of Jews as less than fully human and to treat them accordingly"; they were even depicted as imaginary monsters.[53] Thomas Bestul argues that the formation of attitudes that intensified hostility toward Jews in the later Middle Ages was both reflected in and actively supported by the way narratives on the passion treated Jews.[54]

Bestul shows that from about the middle of the twelfth century the role of Jews was magnified in accounts of the passion. In part this arose from a more affective piety that followed upon the theological reinterpretation of the meaning of the incarnation and redemption among eleventh- and twelfth-century theologians. Greater focus on the humanity of Christ in turn led to greater focus on his suffering—and thereby on those regarded as responsible for his crucifixion, the Jews. A literature of spirituality focused on the suffering Christ as his medieval followers sought to imitate him by bearing "Christ's cross...in our heart, by recollection and compassion; in our mouth, through frequent and devout thanksgiving; and in our body, by flagellation and castigation."[55] It is not surprising that these meditations often included negative references to the Jews who had crucified Jesus.

In the late twelfth century a form of meditation developed in which the person meditating entered into the events of Christ's life as if he or she were there, visualizing and involved in the scenes.[56] But the same affective piety that meditated on the suffering Christ in graphic detail depicted Jewish malice in similarly physical terms. For instance, Bonaventure writes in his *Vita Mystica*:

> The third shedding of blood occurred when they plucked
> his cheeks, as the prophet testifies speaking in the person
> of the lovable Lord Jesus: I have given my body to strik-
> ers, and my cheeks to them that plucked them. Some
> interpret this to mean that the wicked Jews tore his face
> with their fingernails; others, that they plucked his beard.
> Neither could have been done without the shedding of
> blood. I see the sacrilegious hands of this most impious
> mob, who are not content with striking, slapping, and
> covering with spittle the adorable face of Jesus all-good,
> but now, in their burning rage, also pluck his cheeks and

93

draw from the most sweet face the blood that reddens our rose. I see in this lamb without blemish a patience worthy of admiration and imitation, as He turns in all meekness his cheeks most pure to the harrowing of impure claws.[57]

In a wider societal context, a variety of factors created turbulence: the weakening of the feudal order, the development of an economy based on markets and exchange, the emergence of an urban merchant class contesting the privileges of the landholding lords, the social dislocations instigated by the Crusades, and terror of the Black Death in the fourteenth century. Perhaps in response to this instability, the church shored up its own borders, delineating and enforcing qualifications for membership. The Fourth Lateran Council of 1215 exemplified this in its pointed refutation of heresy and its legislation directed against Jews: forbidding them to engage in usury, requiring them to wear special clothing so as to be distinguishable from Christians, forbidding them to appear in public during the Passion (Palm) Sunday and the Triduum (Holy Thursday, Good Friday, and Holy Saturday), forbidding converted Jews to return to Jewish practice, and reiterating prohibitions against Jews holding public office.[58] By requiring Jews to dress in a distinctive manner, they became "spectacles of alterity."[59] What had emerged, in the analysis of R. I. Moore, was a "persecuting society," in which certain "others"—Jews and heretics, but also lepers, female prostitutes, and homosexuals—were pushed to society's margins.[60]

Yet even as their villainy was enlarged in the popular imagination, one theme remained a constant: Jews had crucified Jesus Christ, and thereby become despicable and loathsome. As the enemies of Christ and his followers, they were deserving of contempt. A popular devotional poem by Franciscan friar John Pecham (d. 1292), *Philomena*, emphasized Jewish perfidy:

The sixth hour, when he wished to be bound, scourged
    and spit at
And cruelly tortured by the perfidious (*a perfidies*);
to be wickedly treated by the perfidious Jews (*a Iudaeis
    perfidies*)
finally fixed to the cross, to be pierced with nails.[61]

"Perfidious," which in its Latin original means unbelieving but has more negative connotations in English, became part of the prayer for the Jews on Good Friday in the Roman Missal of 1570.[62] Moreover, a number of thirteenth-century ecclesiastical documents linked Judaism with perfidy, even speaking of the *damnata perfidia* of the Jews.[63]

An especially disgusting depiction of Jewish treachery involved a fixation on spittle.[64] In his *Stimulus Amoris*, Ekbert (ca. 1132–1184), Benedictine abbot of Schönau (near Trier, Germany), meditating on the sufferings Jesus experienced, wrote of the impiety of the wicked Jews (*perfidorum Judaeorum*) who befouled Jesus with the "spittle of defiled lips" (*polluti labii*). Bonaventure likely borrowed this phraseology in his *Lignum Vitae*; he wrote that Jesus' face, "which fills the heavens with joy, was defiled by spittle from impure lips." It was, however, the Carthusian monk Ludolphus of Saxony (d. 1377) who worked most extensively with this detail:

> Indeed it was the custom of the Jews, out of contempt, vituperation, and scorn to spit in the face of one they despised. And they spit so horribly and ceaselessly into the faces of men that sometimes they suffocated them. What is more shameful? What more despicable? What more shameful and contemptible than to spit in the face, and especially in that most beautiful face, on which angels long to gaze.[65]

The spittle, however, was not of the ordinary variety: it was their "most foul excretions," which made the "blessed face" of Jesus "as abominable from the spitting and the blows which they gave it as if it were a leper's." In such representations, Jews have become objectified, a poison on Christian society—indeed, a plague on Christianity.

The highly graphic and detailed description of the torture visited upon the suffering Jesus correlated with the revival of Roman juridical practice that had fallen into disuse after the empire's fall. The shifts in narrative art from the latter half of the thirteenth century paralleled the restoration of juridical torture in the civil realm. This was matched in the ecclesiastical world. Various papal documents expressed contempt for the "treason" of heresy. The encyclical *Ad extirpanda* of Innocent IV in 1252 permitted the torture of heretics. Bestul argues that the religious intentions of the passion narratives had thereby become subverted. They promoted "values and beliefs about torture and punishment"; they supported an "outlook that certain ways of behaving" were "expected and legitimate."[66] The passion narratives sanctioned the construction of categories of persons on the margins of society and subject to persecution and violence:

> These victims of violence are not Christ, but they can be seen as forming a context, even a necessary context, against which we are meant to measure the magnitude of Christ's suffering for us. *That is, the suffering of Jews, heretics and lepers provides a reference point in the contemporary material world that helps the Christian to reconstruct imaginatively, as much as it is humanly possible to do so, the immeasurably greater and finally inexpressible pain that Christ had endured in the cause of human salvation.*[67]

Bestul's disturbing conclusion is that during the Middle Ages, the graphic representations of the passion in Latin devotional literature neither desensitized their audiences to violence nor anesthetized them to brutality. Rather, they seemed to "instruct them that this was not an unthinkable way to treat the flesh of a fellow human being."[68] Whether or not one accepts Bestul's correlation between the graphic depictions of the passion in Latin devotional literature and torture of those regarded as enemies of the state or church, it is clear that Jews were depicted as less than human.

A similar tone, if a different image, of anti-Jewish hostility in late twelfth-century France, may be seen in the romances of Chrétien de Troyes (d. 1189/90):

> The wicked Jews,
> Whom we should kill like dogs,
> Brought harm to themselves
> And did us great good when in their malice
> They raised him on the cross:
> They damned themselves and saved us.[69]

Antagonism toward Jews because of their role in the crucifixion was also evident in a poem by another French writer, Robert de Boron. His poem on the legend of Joseph of Arimathea, *Le Roman de l'Estoire dou Graal*, enjoyed further life in various prose versions that circulated widely in the thirteenth and fourteenth centuries. In her analysis of the poem, Maureen Boulton concludes that its cumulative effect was "to focus the guilt of the Crucifixion exclusively on the Jews, even to the point of exonerating Pilate." Jews are "base-born people" (*la gent de pute aire*). When Joseph of Arimathea, the poem's protagonist, seeks to verify Jesus' identity, he asks him if he is:

> The one whom Judas sold for thirty pieces of silver
> To the Jewish scoundrels
> And whom they struck and beat
> And then hung on the cross?[70]

Later in the poem, Jesus himself refers to "wicked misbelieving Jews" (*mauveis Juïs mescreanz*). Pilate reinforces this attitude toward the Jews:

> When they saw that I did not wish to judge him,
> They became angry,
> For they were very powerful people,
> Endowed with wealth and rich;
> And they said that they would kill him
> And would not leave him alone....
> They took him and led him
> And beat him and struck him
> And he was bound to a stake
> And crucified on the cross
> Which you heard before you came here.

As de Boron's poem continues, the emperor's son, Vespasian, who had been struck by leprosy, is healed by the sight of the Grail (the chalice of the Last Supper).[71] In gratitude he asks his father if he might be allowed to avenge Jesus' death by "those thieving, stinking Jews" (*cil larrun puant Juïs*). Vespasian proclaims:

I wish to destroy all these Jews
And don't want there to be one who does not die;
They have indeed revealed everything
For which they ought all to die.

After Vespasian concludes his proclamation, the emperor kills thirty Jews. Vespasian becomes a Christian convert—and "did as he pleased with the Jews."

Across the Channel in the twelfth and thirteenth centuries, negative judgments about Jews connected to their status as "Christ killers" also developed. Margery Kempe (b. ca. 1373), for example, spoke in Mary's name of "cruel Jewys leydyn hys precyows body to the crosse....Alas, ye cruel Jewys, why far ye so wyth my swete sone and dede he yow nevyr non harm? Ye fille myn hert ful of sorwe."[72] As one commentator observed, Kempe was "both a consumer and a producer of religious dogma, and a creator of literature in which anti-Judaism is a structural component and a declaration of Christian orthodoxy."[73] Ironically, Kempe most likely never met a Jew; England had expelled its Jews in 1290, and though Kempe was widely traveled, it seems improbable she would have interacted with Jews. But the raw materials of the New Testament texts and their long usage in the church provided Kempe the resources for her association of cruelty with Jews.

From England emerged the charge that Jews engaged in ritual crucifixion, and that nation "remained its most consistent exponent."[74] The unfolding of this accusation is a fascinating, if unedifying, tale. A concise, if historically unreliable, account is found in a document ca. 1155, the *Anglo-Saxon* Chronicle:

> In his [King Stephen's] time, the Jews of Norwich bought a Christian child before Easter and tortured him with all the torture that our Lord was tortured with; and on Good Friday hanged him on a cross on account of our Lord, and then buried him. They expected it would be concealed, but our Lord made it plain that he was a holy martyr, and the monks took him and buried him with ceremony in the monastery, and through our Lord he works wonderful and varied miracles, and he is called St. William.[75]

The full story of St. William, as the chronicler calls him, is attributed to a Welsh-born monk of Norwich's cathedral priory, Thomas of Monmouth. Between 1149/1150 and 1172/73, Thomas composed seven books of *The Life and Passion of Saint William the Martyr of Norwich.* His tale revolves around the death on Good Friday of 1144 (March 25) of twelve-year-old William, an apprentice to a furrier. William's apprenticeship meant that he had dealings with some of Norwich's Jews:

> For they [the Jews] esteemed him to be especially fit for their work, either because they had learnt that he was guileless and skillful, or, because attracted to him by their avarice, they thought they could bargain with him for a lower price, Or, as I rather believe, because by the ordering of divine providence he had been predestined to martyrdom from the beginning of time, and gradually step by step was drawn on, and chosen to be made a mock of and to be put to death by the Jews, in scorn of the Lord's Passion, as one of little foresight, and so the more fit for them.[76]

The insertion of Thomas' opinion offers a clue to the genre: hagiography rather than history. Its aim was to extol William, and edify others—and to provide a patron saint for Norwich. While much of the *Life* involves attribution of various miracles to William, far more significant is Thomas' depiction of the mode and timing of William's death and the motives of his alleged killers. As he tells it, on the first day of Passover, having sung the appointed hymns in the synagogue, the "chiefs of the Jews" seized William as he was blithely eating his dinner. They inserted a wooden gag in his mouth, drawing it tightly. Then they used a short rope to tie his head at both the forehead and neck and shaved the boy's head:

> Having shaved his head, they stabbed it with countless thorn points, and made the blood come horribly from the wounds they made. [Jesus had worn a crown of thorns before his death.] And so cruel were they and so eager to inflict pain that it was difficult to say whether they were

more cruel or more ingenious in their tortures. For their skill in torturing kept up the strength of their cruelty and ministered arms thereto.

And thus, while these enemies of the Christian name were rioting in the spirit of malignity around the boy, some of those present adjudged him to be fixed to a cross in mockery of the Lord's Passion, as though they would say: "even as we condemned the Christ to a shameful death, so let us also condemn the Christian, so that, uniting the lord and his servant in a like punishment, we may retort upon themselves the pain of that reproach which they impute to us."

Conspiring, therefore, to accomplish the crime of this great and detestable malice, they next laid their blood-stained hands upon the innocent victim, and having lifted him from the ground and fastened him upon the cross, they vied with one another in their efforts to make an end of him.

Like Jesus, William was eventually stabbed with a lance on his left side. Streams of blood were pouring out of his body, so the Jews poured boiling water over him to clean him and staunch his many wounds.

Thus then the glorious boy and martyr of Christ, William, dying the death of time in reproach of the Lord's death, but crowned with the blood of a glorious martyrdom, entered into the kingdom of glory on high to live for ever. Whose soul rejoiceth blissfully in heaven among the bright hosts of the saints, and whose body by the Omnipotence of the divine mercy worketh miracles upon earth.

Thomas claimed that a certain Theobald, who had converted from Judaism when he learned of the glorious miracles of William, explained the reasons for the Jews' crucifixion of the boy:

As proof of the truth and credibility of the matter we now adduce something which we have heard from the lips of Theobald, who was once a Jew, and afterwards a monk. He verily told us that in the ancient writings of his fathers it was written that the Jews, without the shedding of human blood, could neither obtain their freedom, nor could they ever return to their fatherland. Hence it was laid down by them in ancient times that every year they must sacrifice a Christian in some part of the world to the Most High God in scorn and contempt of Christ, that so they might avenge their sufferings on Him; inasmuch as it was because of Christ's death that they had been shut out from their own country, and were in exile as slaves in a foreign land.

Historian Gavin Langmuir speculates that Theobald must have been a real person, although why he might have passed on such a patently false account is unclear. He also notes that Theobald made mention only of blood sacrifice, not of crucifixion.[77] Despite the fact that Theobald's story contradicts "everything we know from massive evidence about classical, medieval, and modern Judaism," once Thomas of Monmouth's *Life* was published, the charge of ritual crucifixion had taken on a life of its own.[78] The story was known in France by 1170; in 1255 Jews were accused, without any evidence, of crucifying eight-year-old Hugh of Lincoln (England), for which King Henry III executed nineteen Jews.

The charge of ritual murder found its way into chronicles and ballads. In the "Prioress's Tale," Chaucer (ca. 1343–1400) tells of a young Christian boy in Asia who sang *Alma Redemptoris* ("Mother of the Redeemer") as he walked through a Jewish area en route to and from school. The Jews set upon him:

Our first foe, the serpent Satan, who has his wasp's nest in the Jewish heart, swelled up and said, "O Hebrew people, alas, is this honorable to you that such a boy shall walk at will in spite of you and sing of such matter as is against the reverence due your faith?"

From this point on the Jews conspired to drive this innocent one out of the world. To this purpose they hired a murderer who took up a secret place in an alley, and as the child went by, this cursed Jew seized and held him tight, and then cut his throat and cast him into a pit. I must say that they threw him into an outhouse, where these Jews purged their bowels.

O cursed race of modern Herods, what good is your evil intent? Murder will be revealed, truly it will not fail, and chiefly where it touches the honor of God. Blood cries out on your cursed deed. O martyr made strong in virginity (the Prioress cried), now may you sing, following always the white celestial Lamb. St. John, the great evangelist, wrote of you in Patmo and said that they, those who never knew women in the flesh, go before the Lamb and sing an ever-newsong.[79]

At the end of the tale, the Prioress evokes Hugh of Lincoln:

O young Hugh of Lincoln, slain also by cursed Jews, as all men know (for it is only a little while ago), pray also for us, sinful unstable people, that God in His mercy may multiply His grace upon us in reverence of His Mother Mary. Amen.

During this period, the church became more preoccupied with rooting out heretics, and as Christians began to learn more about rabbinic Judaism (in part through the infamous disputations), they realized that contemporary Judaism was shaped by the Talmud. This realization led to new charges against Jews. They were no longer merely blind to the Christ whom their Scriptures prophesied, but practitioners of a heretical religion.[80] Moreover, in theological circles, most notably in the work of Thomas Aquinas, the Jews who killed Christ were not so much ignorant as they were guilty of "voluntary ignorance," that is, an express desire to be ignorant. Voluntary ignorance increases the degree of sinfulness:

It must, however, be understood that their ignorance did not excuse them from crime, because it was, as it were, affected ignorance. For they saw manifest signs of His

Godhead; yet they perverted them out of hatred and envy of Christ; neither would they believe His words, whereby He avowed that He was the Son of God. Hence He Himself says of them (John 15:22): "If I had not come, and spoken to them, they would not have sin; but now they have no excuse for their sin." And afterwards He adds (John 15:24): "If I had not done among them the works that no other man hath done, they would not have sin." And so the expression employed by Job (21:14) can be accepted on their behalf: "(Who) said to God: depart from us, we desire not the knowledge of Thy ways."[81]

All this led to the conviction among many that Jews no longer deserved the protection of the church. The legends about Jews as ritual murderers became more widespread, amplified by charges that Jews desecrated the eucharistic bread so as to reenact their original deicide. Preachers spread tales based on such fabrications and vilified Jews in passionate sermons. The raw materials of biblical texts had been used in ways that made Jews less than human.

CHAPTER 5

Christ Killers

A Deadly Accusation

The anti-Jewish libels that translated the Christ-killer myth into a regimen of demonic rituals in which the Jews regularly engaged— a regimen that teaches much more about Christian beliefs and doubts than it does about Jewish behavior—have withstood the passage of time. Reason, science, enlightenment, progress, and all the other bywords of modern civilization that we believe distinguish us from our medieval predecessors have not succeeded in overcoming a way of thinking about Jews that extends back to the first Christian centuries.[1]

As the previous chapter has shown, anti-Jewish teaching varied in tone and effect, yet with the steady drumbeat of Jewish responsibility for the death of Jesus. This chapter reveals the intensification of hostility to Jews that resulted from the bonding of traditional anti-Jewish teachings with racial antisemitism. It proved a lethal linkage.

THE OBERAMMERGAU PASSION PLAY

Passion plays reached their apotheosis in the production of the Bavarian village of Oberammergau in mid-seventeenth century that continues to the present. First performed in 1634, the Oberammergau Passion Play has been staged virtually every decade since 1680. The 2010 production, which ran about five hours and included a three-hour break, was performed 102 times between May 15 and October 3 in a theater seating 4,700 persons. The 2000 production drew an audience of over a half million between late May and early October.[2]

Oberammergau is defined by the play, both religiously and economically. Only natives or villagers who have lived there over twenty years are eligible to play one of the 2,000 roles, 120 of which are speaking roles. Families jealously guard major roles, and the village vociferously debates proposed changes to the script, production, or set design.

Since the mid-1960s, the most controversial dispute has centered on the play's depiction of Judaism. Oberammergau's play took up the legacy of medieval vituperation—Jews as "base-born people," "enemies of the Christian name," "wicked Jews," "cursed race of modern Herods"—and impressed upon its audiences just who killed Jesus and what punishment they deserved. After a performance in 1860, Scottish writer Alexander Craig Sellar revealed how the play electrified him, exciting in him the kind of "outbursts of hatred against the Hebrew race" associated with the Middle Ages:

> With strange emotions you gazed upon the executioners as upon wild beasts when they tore his mantle into shreds, and cast lots for his vesture; and the Jewish race appeared hateful in your eyes, as you watched them gathering round the cross, looking upon the man they had crucified, and railing at him, and taunting him with his powerlessness and his pain. Then for the first time you seemed to understand the significance of those ungovernable explosions that in the history of the middle ages one reads of, when sudden outbursts of hatred against the Hebrew race have taken place, and have been followed by cruelties and barbarities unrivalled in history. Just such a feeling seemed excited in this Ammergau audience by this representation.[3]

Although it is difficult to measure precisely how the play might have inculcated anti-Jewish attitudes, an account from an American photographer and travel writer, E. Burton Holmes, during the 1900 season offers a memorable case in point. Holmes was captivated by the children, whom he watched being coached for their roles in the various tableaux or as part of the "Jewish rabble." While rooming in

the home of the play's director, Ludwig Lang, Holmes overheard
Lang's young son practicing his role. Curious, Lang opened his door
and looked down the corridor:

> There, striding up and down, play-book in hand, was
> Herbert Lang, the young son of the house, in the gabar-
> dine of old Jerusalem. Showing no trace whatever of self-
> consciousness, he was practicing at the top of his full,
> ringing voice, the cries and shouts uttered in union by all
> the Jewish population on the stage. "Hosanna! Hosanna!"
> he would cry in triumph; then in an altered tone, with
> boyish simulation of frenzy and fanatic hate, voice the
> unreasoning judgements of the mob, "*An's Kreuz mit Ihm!*
> *Den Barrabas [gibe uns] los! Den Galiäer an's Kreuz!*" "To
> the cross with him. Release Barrabas! Crucify the
> Galilean!" And then in still another tone, "His blood be
> upon us and upon our children." All this over and over.[4]

It is not surprising, then, that Jewish quarters in Europe were sealed
off after performances of the Oberammergau Passion Play, "lest exit-
ing viewers, bent on avenging Jesus' death, kill any Jew in sight!"[5]

As recently as the 1984 production, Jewish responsibility for
the death of Jesus was accentuated considerably beyond the New
Testament accounts. Compare the scene in Matthew 27 with that of
the Oberammergau script.

Matthew

> The governor again said to them, "Which of the two do
> you want me to release for you?" And they said,
> "Barabbas." Pilate said to them, "Then what should I do
> with Jesus who is called the Messiah?" All of them said,
> "Let him be crucified!" Then he asked, "Why, what evil has
> he done?" But they shouted all the more, "Let him be cru-
> cified!" So when Pilate saw that he could do nothing, but
> rather that a riot was beginning, he took some water and
> washed his hands before the crowd, saying, "I am innocent
> of this man's blood; see to it yourselves." Then the people
> as a whole answered, "His blood be on us and on our chil-

dren!" So he released Barabbas for them; and after flogging Jesus, he handed him over to be crucified. (27:21–26)

Oberammergau

Annas: And may the Galilean die....

Nathaniel: Let us demand his death.

People: Away to Pilate! The Nazarene must die!

Caiaphas: He corrupted the law. He despised Moses and the Prophets. He blasphemed God.

People: To death with the false prophet! The blasphemer must die. Pilate must have him crucified.

Caiaphas: He will pay for his misdeeds on the cross.

People: We shall not rest until the sentence is spoken....We demand the conviction of the Galilean! The Nazarene must die!...

People: Judge him! Sentence him!

Pilate: See what a man!

High Council: To the cross—

Pilate: Cannot even this pitiful sight win some compassion from your hearts?

People: Let him die! To the cross with him!

Pilate: So take him and crucify him, for I find no guilt in him.

Caiaphas: Governor, hear the voice of the people of Jerusalem. They join in our accusations and demand his death.

People: Yes, we demand his death.

Pilate: Lead him down and let Barabbas be brought here from prison.

Annas: Let Barabbas live. Pronounce the death sentence on the Nazarene.

People: To death with the Nazarene.[6]

Later, Pilate asks the people—"in reality a howling mob of Jews"—whether Jesus should be released. Their response was "Crucify him, crucify him."[7]

Given the heightened emphasis on Jewish villainy, it is not surprising that Adolf Hitler praised the play. Hitler first attended Oberammergau's play in 1930, and then came as the Führer on August 13, 1934, for the 300th anniversary.[8] In 1942, Hitler said that it was vital that the play be continued, since it provided "knowledge of the menace of Jewry." Oberammergau outshone all others, in Hitler's judgment:

> Never has the menace of Jewry been so convincingly portrayed as in the presentation of what happened in the times of the Romans. There one sees in Pontius Pilate a Roman racially and intellectually so superior that he stands out like a firm, clean rock in the middle of the whole muck and mire of Jewry.[9]

Many members of Oberammergau's cast were members of the Nazi party, with a higher proportion of belonging among those who played the major roles. Moreover, Nazi officials welcomed both the foreign capital the play engendered and its possibilities to advance Nazi ideology.[10] The program for the 1934 production recorded gratitude that the "German people and its tribes" had been spared not only the wretchedness of the plague but of "Bolshevism, this pestilence of abandonment of the race created by God." It continued: "Is there any time more favorable than these days of the suppression of the antichristian powers in our fatherland to remember the price the Son of God Himself paid for His people, the people who adhere to Him and to His banner"—a question repeated in the program of the first postwar production in 1950.[11]

While Oberammergau's Passion Play provided a dramatic enactment of the longstanding Christian accusation that the Jews were responsible for the death of Jesus, the development of race "science" intensified negative consequences for Jews. Racial antisemitism, developed in more secular circles, became all the more treacherous when promulgated to populations already disposed by religious teachings to think of Jews as perfidious.[12]

RACISM AND THE "JEWISH QUESTION"

Over the course of the Enlightenment, Jews were granted rights that enabled them to leave ghettos and Jewish districts and to participate more fully into political and cultural life.[13] This was an uneven process, differing from region to region and from ruler to ruler; often rights were later rescinded, only to be restored by another ruler. As Jews became more prominent, however, many believed that their presence in society was a problem. This became known as the "Jewish question": What is the place of Jews in the body politic? Is it possible that a group with such a distinctive identity could be integrated into the developing nation states? The Jewish question, J. Kameron Carter argues, "lies at the core of modernity's problems with race, religion and the rise of the modern state."[14]

Carter attributes a decisive formulation of the Jewish question to Immanuel Kant. In his 1775–1777 essay "Of the Different Human Races," Kant had delineated a hierarchy of races: white, Negro, Hun (Mongol and Kalmuck), and Hindu. Whites, however, stood apart, a "race" that wasn't really a race insofar as it had achieved "developmental progress" toward perfection. The other races, however, were, as Cameron says, "held hostage to their own particularity....Indeed, they suffer under the entropy of their own particularity: they can't get over themselves. Thus, the racialization process has occurred for the darker races in such a way that their racial existence is an impediment to their human existence, where 'human' here stands for the universal."[15] In a private note, Kant wrote that "All the races will be stamped out…, they will undergo an inner rotting or decay leading to their utter eradication (Americans and Negroes can't rule themselves. They serve therefore only as slaves), but never that of whites."[16] And of the whites, the German nation, *das Volk*, was the embodiment of the ideal, because the cosmopolitan Germans rose above the differences that led, for example, to the constant feuding of the French and English. Such wars diminished the progress of the species.

Having accounted for the races outside Europe, in *Anthropology from a Pragmatic Point of View* (1798) Kant then wrestled with what to do with "contagion" within: the Jews, aliens within the body politic of Prussia and within Europe's white nations. They were

Orientals in the midst of the Occident, "Palestinians living among us."[17] In Carter's analysis, Kant has made the *Judentum* (that is, all things Jewish, including the Jewish people and Judaism) a symbol for all nonwhite flesh; thus, the race question became a moment within the Jewish question. What had been Kant's fourfold schema of races "reduces to a binary opposition between white and nonwhite flesh qua white and Jewish flesh, between occidental whiteness and oriental (Palestinian) Jewishness."[18] And unlike the Negro, the Mongol, or the Hindu, Kant viewed the Jew as a contagion *within* Europe.

In Kant's perspective, ancient superstitions held Jews bound. Materialism and empiricism enslaved them. Jesus, representative of the overthrow of Judaism, affirmed what humankind could become. Jesus Christ ceased being a Jew, at least at the level of ethics and morality. Thus, Kant reimagined Christianity as "racially" severed from and ethnographically triumphant over its oriental Jewish roots.[19] Were Jews to accept the religion of Jesus, however, then one would witness the "euthanasia" of Judaism.[20]

The movement from Kant's "euthanasia of Judaism" to the Nazi's "Final Solution" encompassed many developments; only the broad contours can be given here. Some argued vehemently that Jews were impediments to national identity and cohesion. In 1843, Bruno Bauer published *Die Judenfrage* (The Jewish Question), arguing that Jews should abandon Judaism entirely. In 1881, Karl Eugen Dühring, mindful that a number of Jews had entered more fully into society through baptism and assimilation, proclaimed that "Jews are to be defined solely on the basis of race, and not on the basis of religion."[21] Just two years later Theodor Fritsch published "The Racists' Decalogue" in his *Anti-Semitic Catechism*. Among his commandments given to the German people was this: "Thou shalt keep thy blood pure. Consider it a crime to soil the noble Aryan breed of thy people by mingling it with the Jewish breed. For thou must know that Jewish blood is everlasting, putting the Jewish stamp on body and soul unto the farthest generations."[22]

Meanwhile, the medieval accusations of blood libel reappeared in Hungary (1882), Germany (1891), and Bohemia (1899). Moreover, the late nineteenth and early twentieth centuries witnessed the formation of various antisemitic organizations, publications of race theory and Teutonic supremacy, including Houston Stewart Chamberlain's *The Foundations of the Nineteenth Century* (1899) and the *Protocols of the Elders of Zion (1905)*, a spurious account of a Jewish conspiracy to destroy Christianity and control the world.[23] The Dreyfus Affair in France in the 1890s unleashed a frenzy of antisemitic activity. While ultimately Alfred Dreyfus, a Jewish army captain accused of selling secrets to the Germans, was exonerated in 1906—nine years after his first trial, humiliation, and imprisonment—the scandal revealed serious antisemitism among the army and in sectors of the French Catholic Church.

One political ramification of the Dreyfus Affair was the enactment of a law in 1905 that separated church and state in France. In contrast, during the period of the Dreyfus Affair, a French royalist movement developed, Action Française, that opposed "internal foreigners": Jews, Protestants, Freemasons, and foreigners. Headed by Charles Maurras, an agnostic who nevertheless championed the Catholic Church as the state religion that provided a cohesive French identity, the movement was politically influential; beginning in 1908, it published a daily paper, *Action Française*.[24]

Philosopher Jacques Maritain was one of the few prominent Catholics to take issue with antisemitism in France. Despite his early attraction to the reactionary Maurras, by the late 1920s Maritain had turned in a quite different direction. He spoke of the "vocation of the Jewish people" and of the "race" of Jesus as the "trunk to which we have been grafted." He urged Catholic writers to guard against "all hatred and contempt against the Jewish race and the religion of Israel" and to differentiate themselves from the political antisemitism in the secular press.[25]

Maritain, however, had little company. As detailed below, the Vatican issued a number of statements condemning racism, and antisemitism as a form of racism, in the early decades of the twentieth century, but its statements were typically ambiguous and ineffective. As Martin Rhonheimer argues, these statements were never intended to help Jews. Given the church's dominant view of Jews in the Nazi period, "it would have been astonishing if the Church had mounted the barricades in their defense."[26]

TWO TYPES OF ANTISEMITISM:
A PROBLEMATIC DISTINCTION

A controversy in the late 1920s between certain Vatican offices and a group advocating better relations with Jews offers a case study of the varying attitudes toward Judaism in official church circles. Under Pope Pius XI, the Vatican's first official condemnation of anti-semitism was issued on March 25, 1928. In a profound and tragic irony, however, this condemnation was formulated as part of a *Monitum* (warning) from the Holy Office suppressing *Amici Israel*, a Catholic association founded in 1926 with the goal of promoting reconciliation between Jews and Catholics. Primary source materials from 1922–1939, recently released from the Vatican archives, provide the details of the disedifying process by which this warning and its accompanying condemnation transpired.[27]

While the mission of *Amici Israel* originally included praying for the conversion of Jews, the group also sought to enhance understanding of Judaism, to avoid negative references to Jews in preaching and liturgy (for example, speaking of Jews as the "people who killed God"), and to counter untrue allegations against Jews, such as ritual murder. The group's founding was inspired by a convert from Judaism, Sophie Franziska van Leer (1892–1953). By 1928 it included 19 cardinals, 278 bishops and archbishops, and about 3,000 priests among its members.

In early January of 1928, *Amici Israel* appealed to Pope Pius XI for reform of the Good Friday prayer for the Jews. Specifically, their letter called for removal of the terms *perfidis* (perfidious) and *perfidiam* because they connoted something hateful. They also recommended that the practice first specified in the 1570 Roman Missal of not genuflecting during the prayer for the Jews on Good Friday be abolished.[28] They offered a sample prayer as an alternative to that in current use. According to Hubert Wolf's analysis of the archival material, the pope forwarded their request to the Congregation of Rites. In turn, this office sent it to a liturgical expert, Benedictine abbot Ildefons Schuster, who indicated his approval of the arguments of *Amici Israel* as "fully justified by the classical tradition of the Roman liturgy."[29] Then the liturgical committee of the Congregation on Rites examined the issue, concluding that the Good Friday prayer should be revised in accordance with the recommendation from *Amici Israel.*

Despite the approval of liturgical experts at the highest level of the Catholic Church, any reform of a prayer that dealt with matters of faith also required the approval of the Congregation for the Doctrine of the Faith. Its expert, papal court theologian and Dominican priest Marco Sales, came to a different conclusion about the request of *Amici Israel.* Drawing upon biblical texts such as Acts 7:51 ("You stiff-necked people") and Matthew 27:25 ("His blood be upon us and our children"), Sales concluded that the Bible bore witness to Jewish faithlessness. Only the Jews, Sales said, had a "pact with God and a covenant with him, and only the Jews constantly violated this pact, and only they would continue constantly to violate it. It should come as no surprise, then, that they are called perfidy, and that we use the expression *perfidia Judaica* to distinguish them from the pagan."[30] Nothing should be changed, he recommended.

As the secretary of the Holy Office (that is, its head), Cardinal Rafael Merry del Val, one of the opponents of the so-called "modernists," concurred with Sales.[31] Moreover, in identifying a list of "erroneous or offensive-sounding statements" that had appeared from advocates for reform of the Good Friday liturgy, an expert commissioned by Merry del Val asked, "How it was possible that the Jews, who had made common cause with those who nailed Jesus to the cross, thereby killing the son of God, could even have belonged to the Kingdom of the Eternal Father in the first place?"[32] As Sales had, Merry del Val found ample evidence in the biblical texts. The Good Friday prayers, he maintained, were about "stiff-necked Jewish people burdened with the curse that they as a people with their principles undertook the responsibility for having spilled the blood of the holiest of the holy."[33] Cardinal Merry del Val wrote that the Good Friday liturgy had been "inspired and sanctified" over the centuries. It aptly expressed the "abhorrence for the rebellion and treachery of the chosen, disloyal, and deicidal people."[34] He warned against the possibility that *Amici Israel* could fall into the "trap devised by the self-same Jews who everywhere insinuate themselves into modern society and attempt by all means to dispel the memory of their history, and to exploit the good faith of Christians."[35]

Wolf documents how the pope worked with Merry del Val in editing the statement from the Holy Office, "taking pain with the wording so as to avoid even the slightest appearance of anti-Semitism in the dissolution of *Amici Israel* and everything connected with it."[36] The condemnation applied to antisemitism only in a racial (rather than religious) sense—an implicit differentiation that would become explicit in later documents.

While the statement from the Holy Office praised the organization's desire for the conversion of Jews (although the association's founders had in fact begun to rethink the desirability of fostering such conversions), it censured it for "a manner of acting and thinking that is contrary to the sense and spirit of the Church, to the thought of the Holy Fathers and the liturgy."[37] In the course of suppressing the association for its "erroneous initiatives," the statement read:

> The Catholic Church has always been accustomed to pray for the Jewish people, the recipients of divine promises up to the coming of Jesus Christ, *in spite of this people's blindness. More than that, it has done so on account of that very blindness.* Ruled by the same charity, the Apostolic See has protected this people against unjust vexations, and just as it reproves all hatred between peoples, so it *condemns hatred against the people formerly chosen by God, the hatred that is commonly designated today under the name of "anti-Semitism."*[38]

As Anna Łysiak observed, the decree, although condemning hatred of Jews, nonetheless retained the idea of a sinful Jewish people whose rejection of Jesus led to their suffering.[39] Nevertheless, this first repudiation of antisemitism by the official magisterium indicated at least an awareness of the dangers of racial antisemitism.[40]

The decision of the Congregation for the Doctrine of the Faith did not go unnoticed among Jews. An article in the *Jewish World* on April 16, 1928, recorded strong objections. In response and at the behest of the pope, Jesuit priest Enrico Rosa, publisher of the journal *Civiltà Cattolica*, contributed an article to a May 1928 edition of that journal.[41] He distinguished between two types of antisemitism.

On the one hand, there was an "un-Christian type" of antisemitism—a racial antisemitism that "fed on party politics or passions...or material interests." This, of course, must be condemned. On the other hand, the church must be wary of "danger emanating from the Jews"; they had become "presumptuous and powerful" and were engaged in revolutionary activity throughout Europe. Moreover, Jews were "forging plans for world hegemony."[42]

Before examining another appearance of this alleged distinction between two types of antisemitism, it is important to situate the case in its wider ecclesiastical context. Wolf argues that the antisemitism evident in the Curia (for example, Marco Sales and Merry del Val) and in the work of Enrico Rosa are a "facet of the manner in which...an influential group with the [Catholic] Church positioned itself vis-à-vis modernism....What we are really dealing with here is the intransigent, radical-ultramontane, antimodernist Catholicism that took control of the Church in the nineteenth century and was swept away only by Vatican II."[43] The controversy in the late 1920s over the reform of the Good Friday liturgy revealed a variety of positions, even within the various Vatican offices. Although the Catholic magisterium condemned racial antisemitism before the Nazis came to power, the refusal to reform the Good Friday liturgy and dissolution of *Amici Israel* are marks of "moral impoverishment"—an all too convenient condemnation of hatred of Jews by those outside the church while turning a blind eye to antisemitism within.[44]

The distinction between two types of antisemitism became even more prominent in subsequent years. Gustav Gundlach, a Jesuit, published an encyclopedia article in which he differentiated between two types of antisemitism. Gundlach opposed a racial antisemitism in which Judaism was condemned "simply because of its racial and national foreignness." It was un-Christian because it opposed a group "solely because of the difference in their nationality, rather than because of their actions."[45] On the other hand, he considered that a "politico-governmental" antisemitism was "permissible" when it "combats, by moral and legal means, a truly harmful influence of the Jewish segment of the population in the areas of economy, politics, theater, cinema, the press, science, and art [liberal-libertine tendencies]." Even as Gundlach asserted that the church has "always protected Jews against anti-Semitic practices proceeding from false jealousy, false Christian zeal, or from economic necessity," he claimed that it had "inspired and supported measures opposing the unjust and harmful influence of economic and intellectual Judaism."[46]

The distinction was developed at greater length in a draft encyclical (circular letter) for Pope Pius XI in 1938 by Gundlach and fellow Jesuits Gustav Desbuquois and John LaFarge. Although never published, for reasons about which one can only speculate, the logic of the draft provides a glimpse of the kind of thinking in the highest levels of the church in the late 1930s.[47] On the one hand, the authors decry the "struggle for racial purity [that] ends by being uniquely the struggle against the Jews." As a consequence, millions of people have been denied their rights as citizens; by denying human rights to Jews, "many thousands of helpless persons" have been left without resources. "Wandering from frontier to frontier, they are a burden to humanity and to themselves."[48] Nevertheless, while "unjust and piti-less," it does lead to awareness of the "authentic basis of the social separation of the Jews from the rest of humanity. This basis is directly religious in character." Thus, the authors conclude, "the so-called Jewish question is not one of race, or nation, or territorial national-ity, or citizenship in the state. It is a question of religion and, since the coming of Christ, a question of Christianity."[49] From the Jewish people, the only people in history to have a call from God, came Jesus Christ, the fulfillment of Israel's prophecies and types. Yet:

> The Savior, whom God had sent to His chosen people after they had prayed and longed for Him for thousands of years, was rejected by that people, violently repudiated, and condemned as a criminal by the highest tribunals of the Jewish nation, in collusion with the pagan authorities who held the Jewish people bondage. Ultimately, the Savior was put to death.[50]

Although the redemption gained by the suffering and death of Jesus was for all of humanity, the consequences for Jews were dire:

> Blinded by a vision of material domination and gain, the Israelites lost what they themselves had sought....[T]his

unhappy people, destroyers of their own nation, whose misguided leaders had called down upon their own heads a Divine malediction, doomed, as it were to perpetually wander over the face of the earth, were nonetheless never allowed to perish, but have been preserved through the ages into our own time.[51]

Yet Jewish rejection of Jesus allowed the Gentiles to enjoy the fruit of the promises rejected by the Jews. Israel may have incurred God's wrath, but thereby it "hasted the evangelization and…conversion of the Gentiles." Thanks to God's mercy, Israel may eventually share in redemption, but this possibility exists in the realm of the supernatural. In the realities of historical time, however, "we find a historic enmity of the Jewish people to Christianity, creating a perpetual tension between Jew and Gentile which the passage of time has never diminished, even though from time to time its manifestations have been mitigated."[52]

With the world on the brink of World War II, traditional tropes of theological antisemitism, most notably that of condemnation of the Jews for their alleged responsibility for the death of Christ, were reiterated. The crucifixion served as a symbolic event: the "crucifying Jew" as personifying evil, the crucified Jesus as embodying good.[53] The church that had "gone on red alert" in reaction to modernity and modernism "always saw a plot, concocted above all by Jews, to undermine the Christian order of international society."[54] As a consequence, most Catholics were ill prepared to resist antisemitism in any guise.

One group of theologians and politicians, however, mounted a protest, urging that the church speak out against the heresy of racism as an "archenemy of the gospel and the Church."[55] They took issue with the "permissible" or moderate antisemitism that Gundlach and others had identified and advocated protest against ostracizing Jews. Johannes Oesterreicher, a priest and Jewish convert, was the editor of the Viennese journal in which the protest had appeared. While in exile in Paris in 1940, he published *Racisme—antisémitisme, antichristianisme* (Racism: Antisemitism, Anti-Christianity).[56] Oesterreicher considered the fundamental error of racism to be considering humans *only* as members of race, thereby denying individuality and personhood. He believed that people succumbed to the error of racism because of the sin of blasphemy:

> "The 'Aryan' man feels himself called to be the creator and master of the world, which he imagines exists for his own glory....The racist folly is a rebellion against God, who on Sinai...gave his commandments to the people of Israel and to all of humanity....[Thus] the myth of superiority of the 'Aryan' race...in the end is a protest against the election of Israel." Such rebellion led to hatred of Christ. All persecution of Jews "touches" Christ.[57]

Similarly, Jacques Maritain often spoke of antisemitism as ultimately a hatred of Christ, "Christophobia." He viewed the antisemitism of the Nazis as a desire to "exterminate the race of Christ from history"; thus, the Nazis sought the destruction of "the Jews for the Messiah who has come from them."[58]

PROTESTANT AND CATHOLIC CHURCHES DURING THE THIRD REICH

The churches were certainly not immune from the forces of nationalism, anti-liberalism, anti-communism, or the racist antisemitism that the Nazis exploited. In some cases, outright complicity was evident, such as the German Christian Movement (*Deutsche Christen*), which tried to Nazify Christianity. This movement had some 600,000 members; eventually it encompassed between one quarter and one third of German Protestants.[59] Other Protestants, organized under the umbrella of the Confessing Church (*Bekennende Kirche*), objected to the dominance of Nazi ideology in the church.[60] In its 1934 Barmen Declaration, the Confessing Church accused the German Christian Movement of teaching false doctrines, such as the state taking over the "church's vocation" and that the church is an "organ of the state." Although a protest against "alien principles" being taken into the church, the Barmen Declaration did not contain an objection to antisemitism.[61] One of the major points of contention between the German Christians and the Confessing Church was that the former declared that baptized Jews were to be excluded from the churches.[62] Heinz Erich Eisenhuth explained the rationale for this: "[Martin] Luther saw the Jews above all as murderers of Christ. We see in them destroyers of God's creation, whose defense is the duty of all Germans and also of the German Protestant Church."[63]

The German Christian Movement disseminated its ideology in part through the Institute for the Study and Eradication of Jewish Influence on German Church Life (*Institut zur Erforschung und Beseitigung des jüdischen Einflusses auf das deutsche kirchliche Leben*), with its headquarters in Eisenach. It drew its members from Germany, Austria, Czechoslovakia, Romania, and Scandinavia, including professors of theology, pastors, bishops, and laity.[64] It published a hymnal that removed all references to Jewish terms (for example, amen, alleluia, Jerusalem, Zion) and a catechism that taught that Jesus was not Jewish. Sensitive to the Nazi charge that Christians worshipped the God of the Jews and thus could not be loyal National Socialists, the Institute's founding director and its pre-eminent ideologue, Walter Grundmann, told a 1941 conference: "Our Volk, which stands above all else in a struggle against the satanic powers of world Judaism for the order and life of this world, dismisses Jesus, because it cannot struggle against the Jews and open its heart to the king of the Jews." [65] Thus, Grundmann and colleagues developed elaborate, if entirely specious, theories purporting to demonstrate that Jesus was a Galilean of Aryan stock.

In 1940, the Institute published a revised version of the New Testament, *Die Botschaft Gottes* (The Message of God). Its chief characteristic was "dejudaization": removal of any neutral or positive references to Judaism, a harmonization of the Synoptic Gospels in order to avoid what its authors regarded as Matthew's pro-Jewish perspective, and omission of apocalyptic passages as well as those claiming fulfillment of Old Testament prophecies. The Sabbath becomes a holiday (*Feiertag*) and Pesach becomes Easter (*Osterfest*).[66]

The Institute emphasized Jewish responsibility for the death of Jesus. Grundmann wrote that Jews stood under divine judgment, "marked by the curse of God" because they did not recognize Jesus as God's son and instead crucified him. Thus, the Nazis were justified in protecting the German nation from the "demoralizing and destructive" influence of the Jews.[67] Adolf Schlatter, whom Grundmann considered his mentor, wrote that the Jews forced Pilate to crucify Jesus; it was the "climax" of Jewish guilt and the "act of the nation."[68] A considerable portion of the Institute's dejudaized New Testament was devoted to accounts of the passion. Its 1941 catechism, *Deutsche mit Gott: Ein deutsches Glaubensbuch* (Germans with God: A German Catechism), explained that Jesus was the "savior of the Germans":

> Jesus of Nazareth in the Galilee proves in his message and behavior a spirit that is in opposition to Judaism in every way. The struggle between him and the Jew became so bitter that it led to his deadly crucifixion. Thus Jesus cannot have been a Jew. Until this day the Jews persecute Jesus and all who follow him with unreconcilable hatred. By contrast, Aryans in particular found in Jesus Christ the answer to their ultimate and deepest questions. So he became savior of the Germans.[69]

Although the Institute's members blamed the degenerate Jews for the death of Jesus, their portraits of the Aryan Jesus tended not to focus on the anguish of the crucifixion but on the heroism of the "manly warrior whose life was the focus, not his death."[70] Catholic priest and scholar Philip Haeuser (1876–1960) propounded a similar depiction to a group of Nazi party members in December 1930. For Haeuser, Jesus was a warrior, a soldier who had engaged in battle against the Pharisees: "Only because of this will to do battle, because of his courage to do battle, was he fated to be whipped and crucified."[71] God sent this militant Jesus to establish a church purified of Jewish tradition. Haeuser, who had written his doctoral dissertation on the *Epistle of Barnabas* and translated Justin Martyr's *Dialogue with Trypho*—two staples of the *Adversus Judaeos* literature, albeit radically different in tone—was a prominent antisemite whose views were widely circulated through public appearances and publications. Christ, he wrote, campaigned against Jewish leaders, "against the scribe, the Jewish preachers, the representatives of Jewish law, and the inhabitants of Jerusalem." Jews had "condemned their Messiah to death in their blindness, stubbornness, and depravity....The Jewish people ceased once and for all to be an instrument of divine grace and mercy."[72]

Haeuser saw Hitler as a modern savior. In a 1936 address, he proclaimed that "Christ emphasizes the great law of life…he leads the struggle against inaction, against the synagogue—Hitler does the same thing today." Christ was unable to finish his task because he was crucified. "Hitler will see his task through."[73]

Given Haeuser's rightwing views, adulation of Hitler and anti-semitism, it is not surprising that his negative depiction of Jews included holding them responsible for the death of Jesus and thus rejected by God. Haeuser never retracted his views. In contrast, Romano Guardini (1885–1968), a priest and scholar who taught at the University of Berlin until the Nazis forced him to retire, wrote a book in 1937 with the goal of turning people away from devotion of Hitler and back to worship of Jesus. Still in print (and with an introduction to the 1997 edition by then Cardinal Josef Ratzinger), *The Lord* became well known. No friend of Nazi ideology, Guardini nevertheless harshly portrayed the Jews in *The Lord*.[74] By crucifying Jesus, the Jews precipitated humankind's second Fall as Adam's sin had the first. They had rejected the Lord because they had been preoccupied with the details of the Mosaic Law; their hearts had become hardened and their sacrifices at the temple were mere ritualism rather than true worship. Jesus preached the message of grace. "But the Jewish people did not believe. They did not change their hearts, so the kingdom did not come as it was to have come."

> The Jewish people, the Pharisees and Scribes and high priests, how "grown up" they are! The whole heritage of sin with its harshness and distortion looms at us. How old they are! Their memory reaches back more than one and a half millennia, back to Abraham—a historical consciousness not many nations can boast. Their wisdom is both a divine gift and fruit of long human experience; knowledge, cleverness, correctness. They examine, weigh, differentiate, doubt; and when the Promised One comes and prophecy is fulfilled, their long history about to be crowned, they cling to the past with its human traditions, entrench themselves behind the Law and the temple, are sly, hard, blind—and their great hour passes them by. God's messiah must perish at the hands of those who "pro-

tect" his law. From his blood springs young Christianity, and Judaism remains prisoner of its hope in the coming of One who has already come.[75]

The Lord became a bestseller. It was even passed around in bomb shelters as a way of maintaining people's hope that Jesus Christ was the savior, not the self-proclaimed Führer Hitler. Yet its negative representation of Judaism reinforced the longstanding view of Jews as Christ-killers and Judaism as a desiccated religion that had given way to Christianity. Guardini later expressed regret for what he had written about Jewish responsibility for the death of Jesus and urged Germans to assume moral responsibility for the Holocaust.[76] Yet the fact that a scholar and priest of such learning and integrity, as well as a critic of Nazi ideology, could portray Judaism as rejecting Jesus' message of grace shows how deeply embedded that charge had become in Christianity.

In reviewing the work of theologians supportive of the Third Reich, both Protestant and Catholic, it is evident that alleged Jewish responsibility for the death of Jesus was but one element in vilification of Judaism that permeated society. Judaism was degenerate and Jews were foreigners. They constituted a separate race inferior to Aryans that nonetheless sought world domination. Jews were avaricious and polluted German society. They were inhuman and thus expendable.

Yet without dismissing the influence of these views or underestimating the force of Nazi propaganda and the ruthlessness with which they enforced their regime, it seems undeniable that the teachings of Christianity about Judaism played their own nefarious role. And at the heart of Christian teaching about Judaism was the accusation that Jews had killed Jesus and thus rejected God. To claim, as Catholic theologian Bernhard Bartmann did, that by killing Jesus the Jews had rejected God was to provide a religious buttress for Nazi race hatred. "Jerusalem had not wanted salvation, and it was no longer able to receive it. Israel now lacked God's grace, for God no longer gave it to Israel."[77]

Even when leading church officials challenged the ideology and actions of the Third Reich, they seldom challenged the regime's anti-semitism. This is particularly clear in the case of the bishop of

Münster, Count Clemens August von Galen (1878–1946), who was beatified in 2005 by Pope Benedict XVI. Once heralded as among the few "churchmen who defied Hitler," von Galen preached three sermons in the summer of 1941 that earned him the sobriquet "Lion of Münster."[78] Analysis of the sermons reveals his audacity—and his apathy regarding the persecution of Jews.

The first, preached in St. Lambert Church in Münster on July 13, 1941, was an impassioned denunciation of the Gestapo's unlawful assault on the church: confiscation of property and expulsion of "blameless and highly respected German men and women." Because the actions of the Gestapo had no redress before an administrative tribunal, "None of us is safe." Von Galen addressed his congregation as "a bishop, a promulgator and defender of the legal and moral order willed by God" who believed himself called upon "courageously to assert the authority of the law and to denounce the condemnation of innocent men, who are without any defence, as an injustice crying out to heaven."[79]

Not only was the church subject to persecution by the Gestapo; the city of Münster came under heavy bombardment from the Royal Air Force. So in the second sermon, preached a week later at the *Liebfrauenkirche* (Church of Our Lady), von Galen exhorted the people, "Become hard! Remain firm!" He continued his condemnation of Nazi violations of the rights of the church, accusing the regime of a "deep seated hatred of Christianity, which they are determined to destroy."[80]

In the third sermon, preached at St. Lambert's on August 3, 1941, von Galen again protested the Gestapo, accusing them of conducting a "campaign of annihilation" against Catholic religious orders. It is on this occasion that he famously denounced Hitler's so-called "euthanasia" program. The Nazis had murdered persons who were mentally ill because they judged them "unproductive." Von Galen thundered from the pulpit: "Have you, have I, the right to live only so long as we are productive, so long as we are recognised as productive?" Once it is admitted that society has the right to kill "unproductive" people, he argued, "then the way is open for the murder of all unproductive men and women." He reported that he had protested to local authorities because the German penal code forbade such murders. Even more, God had commanded: "Thou shalt not kill."[81]

This third sermon included another distinctive theme, based upon the Lukan text of Jesus weeping over Jerusalem (19:41–44). Jesus was weeping for his "fellow-countrymen," von Galen claimed, because they had refused to "recognize the only thing [Jesus the Son of God] that could avert the judgment foreseen by his omniscience and deter in advance by divine justice." Later, he accused "Jerusalem and its inhabitants" of setting their "will against God's will. Foolishly and criminally, they defy the will of God! And so Jesus weeps over the heinous sin and the inevitable punishment. God is not mocked!" Yet it may be that Israel was not the only one who "rejected God's truth, [who] threw off God's law and so condemned itself to ruin." Might not Jesus also be weeping over Germany because of the violence done to the mentally ill, the persecution of the church, and the widespread failure to obey God's commandments? In a final word, he excoriated the Nazis and urged his congregants to separate themselves from their godless ways.

Without question, von Galen defied the Nazis, both in his preaching and in various letters of outrage written to officials of the Third Reich. Psychiatrist Robert Jay Lifton observed that von Galen's third sermon of 1941 "probably had a greater impact than any other one statement in consolidating anti-'euthanasia' sentiment."[82]

And yet *his sermons had not a word in defense of Jews*. In fact, his only references to Jews in the sermons disparaged them as having "set their will against God's will," having rejected "God's truth," and thereby "condemned" themselves to "ruin." In a 1940 sermon, he spoke of "degenerate Jews as a threat to children."[83] When Münster's Jews were deported in December 1941, he made no protest.

Like so many church leaders of his time, the Catholic bishop of Münster had little regard for the situation of Jews. He was "heroic," Kevin Spicer writes, "only when National Socialism targeted the Catholic Church," but was also "disfigured by his tolerance of anti-semitism and his bewildering if not shameless indifference to the persecution and murder of European Jews."[84] Von Galen "did not protest the April 1933 boycotts, the September 1935 Nuremberg Laws, the pogrom of 1938 [Kristallnacht], or the countless other discriminations and acts of violence perpetrated against men and

women who had lived in his diocese for years."[85] Beth Grieche-
Polelle writes of von Galen:

> Until his death in 1946, the bishop refused to recognize
> that referring to Jews as "degenerate," "rejected," and
> "lost," combined with an ardent opposition to Jewish
> anarchy and liberalism, only aided the Nazi regime.
> Agreeing with the state that the true enemy was a "Judeo-
> Bolshevik conspiracy" and attempting to rally Catholics to
> the regime's fight against that enemy did not work to
> mobilize the Catholic population to defend a persecuted
> minority. The imagery of the Jews employed by von Galen
> leaves one with the feeling that the Jews were responsible
> for their own damnation. His continuing fear of "godless
> Communism," the subtle suggestion that the Jews were
> behind the forces of Communism, and his ultranational-
> ism "made him and the whole German episcopacy useful
> in propping up the Third Reich."[86]

For several decades after World War II, "good Germans" were
not regarded as responsible for the catastrophe of the Holocaust;
rather, the "evil Hitler" and his minions were assigned the guilt.
Historiography with regard to the role of the churches in the Shoah
has undergone significant change. Two generations of historical
scholars have analyzed considerable evidence exposing the falsity of
the postwar myth that German churches church leaders had been
"brave and long-suffering moral opponents and also victims of the
Nazi state."[87]

Nevertheless, we must acknowledge the heroism of those who
resisted Hitler by undermining the Nazi regime, rescuing Jews, or
countering the unspeakable barbarism in the heart of European civilization. Among such valiant persons were Christians, but overall
too many Christians were perpetrators and bystanders rather than
"righteous Gentiles." In some instances, church leaders and groups
spoke out in condemnation, but there was no long-term, comprehensive, and coordinated program of opposition:

Perhaps at the heart of those failures was the fact that the
Churches, especially in Nazi Germany, sought to act, as
institutions tend to do, in their own best interests—
narrowly defined, short-sighted interests. There was little
desire on the part of the churches for self-sacrifice or heroism, and much emphasis on "pragmatic" and "strategic"
measures that would supposedly protect these institutions' autonomy in the Third Reich. Public institutional
circumspection carried to the point of near numbness; an
acute lack of insight: these are the aspects of the churches'
behavior during the Nazi era that are so damning in retro-
spect....Ultimately, the churches' lapses during the Nazi
era were lapses of vision and determination. Protestant
and Catholic religious leaders, loyal to creeds professing
that love can withstand and conquer evil, were unable or
unwilling to defy one of the great evils of human history.
And so the Holocaust will continue to haunt the Christian
Churches for a very, very long time.[88]

Christian teaching was not limited to the ecclesial realm. It is
clear that the Nazis drew significantly on the Christ-killer myth in
the curriculum of German schools. Most notable is the 1938 work of
Ernst Hiemer, *Der Giftpilz* (The Poison Mushroom), a collection of
seventeen short stories for young readers and a key text making the
ideology of the Third Reich widely accessible. Among its chapters is
"What Christ Said about the Jews." A peasant mother, returning from
working in the fields, stops with her three children near a roadside
shrine of Christ:

Children, look here! *The Man who hangs on the Cross was
one of the greatest enemies of the Jews of all time. He knew
the Jews in all their corruption and meanness.* Once he drove
the Jews out with a whip, because they were carrying on
their money dealings in the Church. He called the Jews
killers of men from the beginning. By that he meant that
the Jews in all times have been murderers. He said further to the Jews: Your father is the Devil! Do you know,
children, what that means? It means the Jews descend

from the Devil. And because they descend from the Devil, they live like devils. So they commit one crime after another. *Because this man knew the Jews, because He proclaimed the truth to the world, He had to die. Hence, the Jews murdered him. They drove nails through his hands and feet and let him slowly bleed. In such a horrible way the Jews took their revenge. And in a similar way they have killed many others who had the courage to tell the truth about the Jews. Always remember these things, children. When you see the Cross, think of the terrible murder by the Jews on Golgotha. Remember that the Jews are children of the Devil and human murderers.*[89]

Gregory Paul Wegner observes that "No other society has ever devoted such a focused effort at integrating anti-Semitic thinking into curriculum intended for young children." He continues:

> The language of religion expressed by various Nazi curriculum writers became another effective way in which Jews could be categorized as the negative other. The image became all the more potent through the exploitation of Golgotha. The charge of deicide against the Jews, one which survives to this day in anti-Semitic circles, carried a powerful emotional appeal for Nazi propagandists both inside and outside schools.[90]

By identifying the Nazi appeal to religious language, Wegner implicitly raises the question of how aware Nazi leaders were of Christian teaching about Jews and Judaism. Richard Steigmann-Gall argues that while the Nazi worldview assigned ontological priority to race, it was often framed within the language of Christianity.[91] For example, Dietrich Eckart, an important mentor of Hitler in Munich, said, "Wonders never cease; from the deluge is born a new world, while the Pharisees whine about their miserable pennies! The liberation of humanity from the curse of gold stands before us! But for that our collapse, but for that our Golgotha!"[92] In a poem titled "The Riddle," Eckart wrote:

The New Testament broke away from the Old
as you once released yourself from the world
and as you are freed from your past delusions
so did Jesus Christ reject his Jewishness.[93]

Joseph Goebbels, one of Hitler's closest collaborators and the Reich Minister of Propaganda from 1933 to 1945, also drew upon Christian religious terminology: "Money is the power of evil and the Jew its servant. Aryan, Semite, positive, negative, constructive, destructive. The Jew has his fateful mission to once more dominate the sick Aryan race. Our salvation or our ruin is dependent on us." Hitler was "an instrument of divine will shaped by history....Nothing exists outside of God."[94] Goebbels's use of racial and religious tropes in describing Jews is most evident in his 1933 novel, *Michael*. His protagonist, Michael Vormann, muses:

Christ is the genius of love, as such the most diametrical opposite of Judaism, which is the incarnation of hate. The Jew is a non-race among the races of the earth....Christ is the first great enemy of the Jews....That is why Judaism had to get rid of him. For he was shaking the very foundations of its future international power. The Jew is the lie personified. When he crucified Christ, he crucified everlasting truth for the first time in history.[95]

References to Jesus expelling the money-changers from the temple were prominent among Nazi leaders, including Goebbels: "He drives the Jewish money-changers out of the temple. A declaration of war against money. If a man said that today, he would wind up in prison or a madhouse."[96] Similarly, Julius Streicher, publisher of the notoriously antisemitic newspaper *Die Stürmer* and of the children's book referred to above, claimed in 1924: "[We] relentlessly fight the shady mixing of religion and Jewish party politics, and fight to keep the religion pure, as did the Lord when he threw the hagglers and usurers out of the Temple."[97] Adolf Hitler, too, drew upon this passage:

[The Jew's] life is only of this world, and his spirit is inwardly as alien to true Christianity as his nature two thousand years previous was to the great founder of the new doctrine. Of course, the latter made no secret of his attitude toward the Jewish people, and when necessary he even took to the whip to drive from the temple of the Lord this adversary of all humanity, who then as always saw in religion nothing but an instrument for his business existence.[98]

Another influential Nazi party official, Walter Buch, spoke of the Jew as "not a human being: he is a manifestation of decay." Thus, any mixing of Jews and Germans violated the "divine world order." The liberalism unleashed in the late eighteenth century had allowed the Jew to contaminate society: "The heresies and enticements of the French Revolution allowed the pious German to totally forget that the guest in his house comes from the *Volk* who nailed the Savior to the cross."[99]

When Hitler met with Bishop Wilhelm Berning, representative of the German Catholic Bishops' Conference on April 26, 1933, he admitted, "I have been attacked because of my handling of the Jewish question." He rationalized, however:

The Catholic Church considered the Jews pestilent for fifteen hundred years, put them in ghettos, etc., because it recognized the Jews for what they were. In the epoch of liberalism the danger was no longer recognized. I am moving back toward the time in which a fifteen-hundred-year-long tradition was implemented. I do not set race over religion, but I recognize the representatives of this race as pestilent for the state and for the Church, and perhaps I am thereby doing Christianity a great service by pushing them out of schools and public functions.[100]

Not only did Hitler use the church's long history of anti-Judaism to justify the ideology of the Third Reich; he seemed also to suggest implicitly that he was Christ-like, since Christ "must be regarded as a popular leader who took up his position against

Jewry." Like Hitler, Jesus had "set Himself against Jewish capitalism." For that the Jews "liquidated him."[101] Hitler intended to reverse that ending.

AN ACCUSATION RESCINDED?

The longevity and tragic consequences of the "Christ killer" charge provide the critical backdrop for the dramatic declaration by an ecumenical council, the highest level of authority in the Roman Catholic Church, on October 28, 1965, that "...neither all Jews indiscriminately at that time, nor Jews today, can be charged with the crimes committed during his passion." This excerpt from section four of the Second Vatican Council's Declaration on the Church's Relation with Non-Christian Religions—*Nostra Aetate* in its Latin title—seemingly overturned nearly two millennia of preaching and teaching in its claim that responsibility for the death of Jesus ought not to be ascribed to Jews as a people.[102] Yet this same section is filled with ambiguities, such as the phrase that introduces the sentence from which the above excerpt was taken: "True, the Jewish authorities and those who followed their lead pressed for the death of Christ."[103]

During the Council itself, political intrigue and entrenched theological positions complicated the possibility of a more frank recognition of the church's anti-Jewish teachings. In light of formidable barriers—the paucity of conciliar participants who possessed accurate knowledge of Judaism (and other religions of the world), the depth and breadth of anti-Jewish teachings in Christianity, the resistance from a block of traditionalists who contested any significant changes in church teaching, and the opposition of Eastern bishops, especially those from Arab lands—it is a wonder that even a weakened document finally emerged from the fourth and final session of the Council. Scurrilous antisemitic tracts were distributed by anonymous or pseudonymous parties at all the sessions, although, according to one of the commission members involved in the drafting of *Nostra Aetate*, their "arguments were so vile, their allusions so repulsive, their origin apparently so uncertain and even suspect" that this literature exercised no influence on the conciliar participants.[104]

The various drafts, five in all (although the first never made it to the floor of the Council), were hotly contested. In the summer preceding the promulgation of the final text on October 28, 1965, some most involved in its drafting feared it would never see the light of day. Without recognition of the contentious history of *Nostra Aetate*, the reader will detect only a "portentous blandness."[105] Too little of this contentious history is known. Even more significantly, too few know of the long history of anti-Jewish teaching that the declaration began to reverse. As a consequence, the vast majority of those who learn of this declaration have little idea of its significance as the most radical change in the ordinary magisterium of the church emerging from Vatican II.[106]

Nevertheless, *Nostra Aetate* made a tremendous difference in formal relations between the Catholic Church and the Jewish People. As the foundational text of dialogue—its Ur-text, as it were—*Nostra Aetate* prompted initiatives that would have left previous generations of both Jews and Catholics incredulous: diplomatic relations between the Holy See and the State of Israel, visits by two popes to Auschwitz and Yad Vashem, establishment of numerous centers for Jewish-Catholic dialogue and chairs in Jewish Studies at Catholic colleges and universities, and sponsorship of innumerable meetings and conferences intended to deepen learning about the religious other and to foster reconciliation with a people the church had estranged over the centuries. Significantly, it served as a stimulus to other Christian traditions in the arduous process of rethinking their relationship with Judaism. Various statements from the Commission for Religious Relations with the Jews, the Pontifical Biblical Commission, and bishops' conferences have refined and expanded its claims. While its effect on the larger Catholic theological scene has developed more slowly, *Nostra Aetate* has given rise to volumes of commentary. Frequently cited in pastoral resources, it became the basis for revision of religious textbooks in Europe and North America.[107]

And yet for the vast majority of the world's Catholics who will never encounter a living Jewish community, *Nostra Aetate* §4, may well seem both esoteric and irrelevant. Even Catholics in a North American, European, or Australian context who may have a greater sense of comity between their church and Jews, are unlikely to know what *Nostra Aetate* and any of the subsequent texts actually say, let alone what prompted them.

Moreover, the significance of its central assertion that the Jews should not be indiscriminately blamed for the death of Jesus is overshadowed, if not lost, amid the proclamation of the passion narratives twice-yearly on Passion (Palm) Sunday (according to one of the Synoptic Gospels) and Good Friday (according to the Gospel of John). The passion narratives, moreover, are proclaimed as part of a powerful liturgical drama. Given the importance of ritual to religious identity, the Gospel lections about the death of Jesus occupy a central place in how Christians understand their faith.[108] Year after year, congregants hear, generally without commentary to the contrary, that Jews were responsible for the death of Jesus, whether the "chief priests, scribes, and elders," as rendered in the Synoptic Gospels, or, simply, "the Jews," as in the Fourth Gospel. Jewish responsibility for the death of Jesus is reiterated on a number of the Sundays after Easter in which excerpts from the Acts of the Apostles are read.[109]

Two relatively recent cases are indicative of both the progress since Vatican II and the work still to be done. The first involves the 1998 statement from the Vatican's Commission on Religious Relations with the Jews, *We Remember: A Reflection on the Shoah*. On the one hand, the statement bears considerable significance as a condemnation of anti-Judaism and antisemitism, asserting that they "must never again be allowed to take root in any human heart." It also expresses the "deep sorrow" of the Catholic Church for the "failures of her sons and daughters in every age." On the other hand, the claim that the pagan ideology of the Nazis had its "roots outside of Christianity" obscures the ways in which Christian teaching served as a precondition and enabler of Nazism. A footnote in *We Remember* (n. 16) defending Pope Pius XII has been widely criticized.[110] Less attention, however, has been paid to the document's claim that the "Church in Germany replied [to race science and extreme German nationalism] by condemning racism. The condemnation first appeared in the preaching of some the clergy, in the public teaching of the Catholic Bishops, and in the writings of lay Catholic journalists." In light of the distinction in some Catholic theologies between racist and "moderate" or "acceptable" antisemitism, this statement is disingenuous. So too is this claim:

Already in February and March 1931, Cardinal [Adolf von] Bertram of Breslau [President of the German Bishops' Conference], Cardinal [Michael von] Faulhaber and the Bishops of Bavaria, the Bishops of the Province of Cologne and those of the Province of Freiburg published pastoral letters condemning National Socialism, with its idolatry of race and of the State....[There were the] well-known Advent sermons of Cardinal Faulhaber in 1933, the very year in which National Socialism came to power, at which not just Catholics but also Protestants and Jews were present, [that] clearly expressed rejection of the Nazi anti-Semitic propaganda.

The bishops' pastoral letters did criticize National Socialism and initially forbade membership in the Nazi party, but primarily because it had championed race over religion, rejected the Old Testament, denied the primacy of the pope, and proposed an "undogmatic" National German Church. The bishops were silent then about treatment of the Jews—and this silence, with only a few exceptions, characterized their pronouncements during the Third Reich. Moreover, in 1933 they ended their prohibition against membership in the Nazi party.[111] Apparently, even years later, Cardinal Bertran did not recognize the full extent of Hitler's evil: After learning of *der Führer's* death in May of 1945, he instructed the parish priests of the Breslau archdiocese to "hold a solemn requiem in memory of the Führer and all those members of the Wehrmacht who have fallen in the struggle for our German Fatherland, along with the sincerest prayers for Volk and Fatherland and for the future of the Catholic church in Germany."[112] Cardinal Faulhaber did indeed challenge the Nazi disregard for the Old Testament as a heresy and defended it as a sacred book, despite its "ethical imperfections." In his first Advent sermon of 1933, he spoke of the books of the Old Testament as indeed "worthy of credence and veneration for all time." But he followed with a distinction that would appear with frequency in the sermons: "Antagonism to the Jews of today must not be extended to the books of *pre-Christian Judaism*."[113] "Pre-Christian Judaism" prepared the way for Christ but had no further value, as this excerpt from a 1933 sermon makes clear:

> After the death of Christ, Israel was dismissed from the service of the Revelation. She had not known the time of her visitation. She had repudiated and rejected the Lord's Anointed, had driven Him out of the city and nailed Him to the cross. Then the veil of the Temple was rent, and with it the covenant between the Lord and his people. The daughters of Sion received the bill of divorce.[114]

In Faulhaber's perspective, contemporary Jews no longer had access to divine revelation, the Talmud was a mere human document, and the laws of the Old Testament were no longer valid.

More accurate is the statement's mention of Bernhard Lichtenberg, "Provost of Berlin Cathedral, [who] offered public prayers for the Jews. He was later to die at Dachau and has been declared Blessed." While *We Remember* overlooks the failure of German bishops to condemn the destruction wrought by the Nazis during *Kristallnacht*, they might well have repeated the moving words of Father Bernhard Lichtenberg. During an interrogation in October of 1941, Lichtenberg said, "I state with steadfast conviction that the National Socialist ideology is incompatible with the teaching and commands of the Catholic Church."[115] When asked at his trial in May of 1942 what had led him to offer prayers for Jews, he reported it was what he had witnessed during *Kristallnacht*:

> It was in November 1938 when the windows of Jewish-owned shops were smashed and the synagogues burned; there I walked through the streets of my parish before I celebrated Mass between 5 and 6 in the morning. As I witnessed the destruction, I saw the police standing by passively. I was outraged by the vandalism and asked myself what could be done to help and how this could happen in an ordered nation. As I thought, I said to myself that help could come only through prayer. It was on this evening that I prayed for the first time, "Let us pray for the persecuted non-Aryan Christians and for the Jews."[116]

Lichtenberg's practice of leading this prayer daily at evening prayer in the cathedral from 1938 until his arrest on October 23, 1941, was the leading cause of his imprisonment in Tegel prison and then his death on November 5, 1943, while en route to Dachau.[117]

We Remember certainly represents an advance since *Nostra Aetate*, which made no mention of the Shoah. It has been complemented by statements—many much franker—by national bishops' conferences and has become a basis for a monograph on teaching the Shoah in Catholic institutions.[118] At the same time, its lack of complete candor about the church's failures during the Third Reich, particularly at the institutional level, shows the reluctance of ecclesial authorities to take ethical responsibility for those failures. "By detaching Christianity from the crimes of its adherents, we create a Christianity above history, a Christianity whose teachings need not ultimately be investigated."[119] Kevin Spicer claims that the most potentially disruptive issue between Catholics and Jews with regard to the Holocaust is the "postwar and contemporary posture of a Holy See [the Vatican] that does not seem to comprehend what Jews have suffered and lost as a result of centuries of antisemitism culminating in the Holocaust."[120]

The second case, involving revised scripts of the Oberammergau passion play, reflects greater progress in responding to hostile Christian portrayals of Jews. In 2000 and 2010, I was part of a team of scholars, both Christian and Jewish, who reviewed the script for that year's performance. In the more recent report, available in full online, we noted that the script reflected serious attempts to ameliorate the play's history of anti-Jewish characterizations. Our analysis praised changes in the 2010 script: taking account of the diversity of the Judaism of Jesus' day, portraying Jesus as a faithful Jew, depicting Pilate as a powerful autocrat rather than as a weakling manipulated by the high priest and Jewish crowds, omitting the blood oath of Matthew 27:25, and casting Judas as a complex character, not merely as the epitome of evil.[121] Nevertheless, problems remained. As we wrote:

> While the script commendably removes the Pharisees as the traditional villains, it retains the Gospels' invective against the Pharisees by applying them to the priests.

Thus the charge of Jewish "legalism" is not eliminated, but transferred....Although the 2010 script laudably attempts to place Jesus in a more Jewish context, viewers could emerge with an erroneous portrait of a Judaism so monolithic and centralized as to allow for heresy trials, and a priesthood so jealous of criticism that it convenes an illegal nighttime, Passover trial to put a stop to it....Caiaphas, the script's principal antagonist, is described as mean-spirited, vindictive, having no peace in his heart until Jesus is dead, foaming at the mouth, and persecuting Jesus post-mortem. He is fanatically driven to see Jesus crucified. The reasons for his single-minded animosity are not clear....Past characterizations of Judas as epitomizing Jewish evil and treachery are refocused onto Caiaphas.[122]

On the one hand, this case reveals considerable development since *Nostra Aetate*: the willingness of the Oberammergau's script writers to revise their play in light of criticism, the collaboration of Christian and Jewish scholars in reviewing the script, the developments in biblical scholarship that served as a foundation for our report, and the endorsement of their report by the Council on Centers of Jewish-Christian Relations. Even more remarkable is the dialogue that has happened around the 2010 production, which I will discuss in the conclusion to Part II. On the other hand, despite the evident goodwill, in the end, the script still blames the Jewish priesthood and one priest in particular, Caiaphas.

In this chapter I have documented the major developments by which the traditional charge of "Christ killer" converged with racial antisemitism and thereby forged a link with elements of Nazi ideology. In the next chapter I examine the question of continuity and discontinuity between Christian teaching about Jewish responsibility for the crucifixion of Jesus and the Holocaust.

CHAPTER 6

Christianity's Troubling Tellings and the Holocaust

The huge problem...is that the story of the Holocaust teaches us things we really do not want to know....Christians also did not want to face the Holocaust. Outside as well as inside Germany, they quite desperately wanted to think that real Christians would have recognized the immorality of the Nazi state, would have condemned the regime in their hearts, even if they did not possess the courage or the ability to stand up in opposition. Finally, if we consider that largest category—human beings—the story of the Holocaust is also frightening, a tale of crimes and atrocities humans seemed quite willing to commit....Scholarship on Nazi Germany in the past thirty years has increasingly acknowledged the discomforting complexity of this story.[1]

Chapter 3 traces the theological narratives in the New Testament about the passion and death of Jesus, identifying passages that provided raw material for harsh depictions of Judaism. Chapters 4 and 5 document ways those raw materials were used in the long history of "troubling tellings" of the passion story. The charge that the Jews were (and in the thinking of many Christians, remain) "Christ killers" stands at the center of a largely "tormented" history between Jews and Christians.[2]

Yet the accusation functioned differently in various historical periods and thus had different effects. In the rhetoric of the early church, it served primarily to form a distinct identity, a way of separating "us" from "them." It was the North Star in a constellation of accusations that Jews were faithless, blind, carnal, and legalistic—

137

tropes that resonated throughout theological commentary and pastoral exhortation. Yet for the most part the accusation remained in the realm of rhetoric.

In the medieval period, however, Jews became increasingly demonized, often through the malevolent figure of Judas as the quintessential Jew. Jews were portrayed as less than human, as usurers, bribers, and secret killers who needed the blood of Christian children for their Passover rituals. A more affective piety, manifest in devotional works, magnified the role of Jews in the passion and death of Jesus. Greater focus on the humanity of Christ intensified focus on his suffering—and, accordingly, on those regarded as culpable for his crucifixion, the Jews. Jewish perfidy became a theme not only in Latin devotional literature (for example, Ekbert's *Stimulus Amoris* and Bonaventure's *Lignum Vitae*), but also in late twelfth-century French romances (for example, *Le Roman de l'Estoire dou Graal*); mystical literature (for example, *The Book of Margery Kempe*); hagiography (for example, *The Life and Passion of Saint William the Martyr of Norwich*); literature (for example, Chaucer's *Prioress's Tale*); and passion plays. The latter reached their apotheosis in the production of the Bavarian village of Oberammergau.

Although the Enlightenment resulted in Jewish emancipation, it also led to preoccupation with the "Jewish question" (*Judenfrage*) regarding whether Jews could be integrated into the nation.[3] Ultimately, the Nazi death camps were the "Final Solution to the Jewish Question." Moreover, large sectors of Christianity, particularly the Catholic Church, reacted defensively to the Enlightenment critique of religion. Such defensiveness was exacerbated by what Olaf Blaschke has termed the "Second Confessional Age," a period from roughly 1830 to 1970 in which Protestantism and Catholicism restored elements of former religious ages: neo-Thomism, neo-Lutheranism, and the "confessionally poisoned climate of the sixteenth-seventeenth century."[4] The association of Jews with Bolshevism and liberalism was evident in both Protestant and Catholic Christianity, but more so with the latter. This may have been in large part a reaction because anti-Catholicism played an important role in liberal thought: "Anti-Catholic intolerance was a central and inherent feature of liberalism."[5]

The chapters in this section implicitly raise the disconcerting and discomfiting question about the extent to which Christianity is complicit in the genocide perpetrated by the Third Reich. That is, what continuity exists between Christian teaching and preaching about alleged Jewish responsibility for the crucifixion and Nazi ideology? To what extent is such teaching discontinuous with it? These questions point to the tensions "between continuity and break.... Clearly, from a historical point of view, every event is rooted in the past, but at the same time, every phenomenon is at least in some way new and unique. The ongoing debate on break and continuity is thus only about correct proportions. One cannot hope to decide between the two; one can only judge their relative importance."[6]

CONTINUITIES

Although the churches have been slow and often defensive in addressing such questions, some notable admissions of culpability have been issued. One of the most forthright is the "Declaration of Repentance" by the Catholic bishops of France on September 30, 1997:

> In the judgment of historians, it is a well-proven fact that for centuries, up until Vatican Council II, an anti-Jewish tradition stamped its mark in differing ways on Christian doctrine and teaching, in theology, apologetics, preaching and in the liturgy. *It was on such ground that the venomous plant of hatred for the Jews was able to flourish.* Hence, the heavy inheritance we still bear in our century, with all its consequences which are so difficult to wipe out. Hence, our still open wounds.[7]

Certainly, the element of continuity is more complicated than might appear in the use of metaphors such as the "ground" on which the "venomous plant of hatred for the Jews was able to flourish." This metaphorical language has often given rise to similar images. For example, John Pawlikowski writes: "We cannot obfuscate the fact that traditional Christianity provided an *indispensable seedbed* for the widespread support, or at least acquiescence, on the part of large numbers of baptized Christians during the Nazi attack on the Jews....Christian antisemitism definitely had a major role in undergirding Nazism in its plan for Jewish extermination."[8] In a similar vein, I have often used terms such as "fertile seedbed" in my own writing and lectures; in a recent essay, I have claimed that it seems "undeniable that the teachings of Christianity about Judaism played their own nefarious role" in the Holocaust.[9] Marc Saperstein has criticized such language: "One often has the impression that the use of metaphors to express a relationship seems to substitute for an actual historical argument based on evidence, as if mere picturesque assertion is enough."[10] While metaphors offer a way for people to grasp a link between interpretations of Christian teaching and real consequences for Jews, Saperstein's cautions are important. Narratives that suggest a trajectory from the passion stories to Auschwitz ignore crucial context and function, distort historical complexity, and conflate the teaching of contempt with state-sanctioned genocide.

Precision in assigning culpability, however, is elusive; how precisely to assess the degree of Christian complicity is fraught with difficulty. Not surprisingly, Holocaust historians differ in their judgment about the extent of Christian responsibility, as Saperstein documents in the article cited above.

But quantification is not the issue here, as if continuity and discontinuity could be apportioned in a mathematical formula. What is at stake is the willingness of Christians to look long and hard at what our tradition taught and confront the consequences on real people. Christians have an ethical responsibility to take responsibility for the legacy of the *Adversus Judaeos* tradition of "marking out 'the Jews'—flesh and blood Jews—for ostracization, alienation, marginalization, torment, and on many occasions, death."[11] As the three previous chapters document, Christians bear responsibility for singling Jews out as "worthy of hatred."[12] This "imperious myth" is not to be conflated with the "sovereign myth," into which Nazis placed the Jews that

> shattered the ethical and sociopolitical compromises at the heart of Christian anti-Judaism—this was its very raison d'être—and destroyed, or, according to its own principles, 'redefined,' all moral norms heretofore operative in this confrontation. *Accordingly, Christianity can be fairly and accurately described, for all the voluminous violence it legitimated and unloosed, as an ambivalent, cautious, mediating,*

moral, nongenocidal program, whereas Nazism, in sharp contrast, must be described as a resolute, unhesitating, non-mediating, immoral, genocidal project. Annulling the humanity of 'the Jew,' Nazism creates gas chambers and incinerators to once and forever overcome the otherness of the Other that is 'the Jew.' As such it replaces constraint with excess, compromise with inflexibility, ethical scruples (however ignored or distorted in practice) with racial necessities, and an atemporal hope with a temporal relentlessness.[13]

In this respect, then, Christian teaching was what Steven T. Katz terms the *precondition* of Nazi ideology. Had "Christianity not irrevocably transformed 'the Jews' into mythical beings, Nazism would not have chosen to do the same."[14] But the *Adversus Judaeos* tradition as it played out in varying ways and with varying effects over the centuries was not only a precondition. It was in some sense an *enabler* insofar as its depiction of a degenerate Judaism fused with racial antisemitism in sectors of Central Europe in the nineteenth and twentieth centuries. As a result, many Christians would have found it difficult to distinguish between the antisemitism of the Third Reich and that of the church. Furthermore, a number of its members promulgated views that were deeply imbued with Nazi ideology. In terms of the Catholic Church, Kevin Spicer concludes:

> Though the Church rejected the National Socialist racist form of antisemitism that preached 'a struggle against the Jewish race' and made blood the sole determining factor of Jewish identity, it nevertheless, almost since its foundation, continued to promote a religious-based antisemitism, often referred to as anti-Judaism, by blaming Jews for Jesus' crucifixion. Regardless of the theological logic underlying antisemitism, the negative portrayal of Jews facilitated discrimination and persecution. Even when Catholics tried to distance themselves from antisemitism or at least demonstrate moral sympathy toward Jews, it was very difficult for them to show any theological sympathy.[15]

Consequently, Spicer argues, this lack of theological sympathy led Catholics to a "reductive appraisal of Jews as persistent non-believers, too alien and obstinate for the Church's leaders to include in the gospel mandate to 'love thy neighbor.'" Thus, Catholics had only to translate what they heard in church into common and every-day antisemitic language. For ordinary Catholics, lines between different forms of antisemitism—racial, theological, economic, and cultural—became not only "indistinguishable but mutually reinforcing."[16]

Recent research, such as that of Richard Steigmann-Gall cited in the previous chapter, also reveals that the Nazis were neither so "pagan" nor so anti-Christian as many had assumed. At least some of their leading figures were shaped by Christian teaching. "For every Protestant who expressed misgivings privately, there was another who believed Nazism meant a return to Christianity."[17] Moreover, Nazi perpetrators, and in many cases, their wives as well, believed themselves forgiven by the merciful God of Jesus Christ—in contrast to the vindictive God of Judaism.[18]

The extent to which references and allusions to the Christ-killer charge became part of German culture may be seen in issues of the weekly tabloid *Der Stürmer*, published from 1923 to 1945. "The Jews are our misfortune" (*Die Juden sind unsere Unglück*) ran along the bottom of each front page. During Holy Week in April of 1927, an article, "Golgotha," appeared:

The Galilean Jesus Christ was an avowed mortal enemy of the Jews, before the entire world. He told them flat out what he thought of them: "You are children of the devil! Your father is a murderer from the very beginning. And you seek to act according to your father's desires." His [Jesus'] struggle was for liberation. The liberation of a native agricultural people out of indentured servitude under the bloody dominion of the racially foreign Jews. This is why Christ had to die. Death on the cross. Because he was not a trader and Pharisee and perverter of the Scripture. Because he had the courage to confess himself to his people and against the Jews. The Promised Land was going to ruin. What was left remained a gravestone.

But the murderers of Christ live. They live in the midst of the German people. And strive for its collapse. The hand of Judah lies heavily upon it [the German people]. It [the German people] has been driven into debt. Eroded and maltreated in body and spirit. The German people [are] on the path to Golgotha. All Judah wants its death. Because his [Judah's] father is a murderer from the very beginning. And because the Jew wants to act according to its father's desires. Germany is to go down in a racial chaos of humanity. Is to be wiped out, out of the heroism of its history.

Germany awake! It is almost midnight![19]

Similarly, on Easter Sunday 1933, the paper has a sketch of a Nazi soldier and a German woman standing together, gazing at the crucified Jesus; a church steeple is visible in the background. The caption reads: "The Jews nailed Christ onto the cross and thought he was dead. He is risen. They nailed Germany to the cross and thought it was dead, and it is risen, more gloriously than ever before."[20]

The notion of a fusion between Christian teaching over the ages about Jews and Judaism with the growing antisemitic ideology in early twentieth-century Germany (with parallels in Austria) is an important one. Particularly after the devastating defeat in World War I, many Germans sought redemption in a regeneration of its people through a resurgent nationalism in which radical antisemitism became identical with the campaign against the Weimar Republic (1919–1933).[21] Various "patriotic" groups coalesced around the need to "purify" the German people. By the end of the 1920s, many were demanding that Jews be excluded from citizenship, and the boycott against Jewish businesses widened. In the final years of the Weimar Republic, no significant social or political groups existed to counter radical antisemitism. By the 1930s, the liberals, who had championed Jewish emancipation in the nineteenth century, were no longer a potent political force. The workers' movement, less influenced by antisemitism, was preoccupied by class issues and gave short shrift to the ideology of the National Socialists. Moreover, antisemitism, Peter Longerich notes, was "rife" among Catholics: Although radical, racist antisemitism was incompatible with Catholicism, such incompatibility did not lead the church to stand up to a form of anti-semitism rooted in opposition to liberalism and Bolshevism. Rather, "[the Catholic Church] was by no means hostile to a certain weakening of the Jews' position in society so that in the end, both variants, religious and racist, were mutually supportive."[22] German Protestantism, more allied with the power of the state, was equally vulnerable to Nazi ideology. Thus, we see in Germany in the 1930s how little institutional power existed to counter the growing anti-semitism that was so integral to Hitler and the NSDAP (National Socialist German Workers' Party).

Although we lack detailed knowledge of how the faith formation of European Christians in the 1930s and 1940s affected their view of Nazi propaganda, we have ample documentation of the lack of forthright criticism of Nazi ideology with regard to the "Jewish question" by ecclesiastical authorities. Both Catholics and Protestants protested about issues of concern, particularly about the so-called "Euthanasia" program in which some 200,000 mentally and/or physically handicapped persons were gassed in various clinics and installations throughout Germany. They were far more vociferous, however, regarding the killing of the handicapped than in opposing brutal policies against the Jews.[23] The authorities challenged Nazi strictures on the churches, but they were largely silent in the face of the Nuremberg Racial Laws, Kristallnacht, and the concentration/death camps.[24]

In fact, the churches played a key role in the management of the Nuremberg Laws of 1935, the "Law for the Protection of German Blood and German Honor" and the "Reich Citizenship Law." The latter law denied Jews citizenship, and the former mandated that anyone who had three or four Jewish grandparents be considered a Jew, regardless of religious affiliation.[25] Ironically, the system the Nazis designed to assess whether a person was a "true" German (that is, an Aryan) or a Jew required a signed and stamped document proving (or not) that a person's grandparents had been baptized. Thus, the Christian churches became the "single most important site for the implementation of Nazi racial segregation."[26] With millions of Germans seeking four baptismal records, the staff of the churches carried an extra workload, "but there is no record of complaint about being made complicit in the racist process."[27]

A 1938 religious education booklet for Catholic adults, *Nathanaelfrage* (Nathanael's Question), took issue with the notion of an Aryan Christ, but "warned that [although] Christ might have been part of the Jewish people and a Jew through his birth and adherence to Jewish customs,...this would not mean he was racially a Jew....Christ became less and less 'Jewish.' His manner [*Wesen*], his word and work, were not Jewish but divine. All his life he had stood against the Pharisees and the 'voice of [Israel's] blood and the longings of its national ambitions.'"[28] The same booklet admitted that Christ's "blood link" with the Jewish people arose from his birth by the virgin Mary, "who was engaged to Joseph....[But] everything that was rotten in the Jewish people's blood has not...touched him....A wall was erected in Mary [through the Immaculate Conception] against the unholy bloodstream of the Jewish people."[29] Both texts reveal increasingly racialized discourse and emphasize the distance between Judaism and Christianity. The hierarchy also engaged in racialized discourse. In a Lenten address of 1939, Archbishop Konrad Gröber of Freiburg objected to portraying Jesus as an Aryan, but insisted that he was Jewish "only on His Mother's side, since He was conceived of the Holy Ghost."[30] The distinction discussed in chapter 5 between a "permissible," moderate antisemitism and the immoral, national-political antisemitism that Gustav Gundlach (and others) had proposed appeared in catechetical form as the difference between "often degenerate Jews who live today dispersed all over the world" and the Jews of the old covenant.[31]

As historian Ulrike Ehret concludes, "National Socialist race theory was no longer rejected out of hand (criticism was reserved for 'race religion'), as the Church had done since the late 1920s; this was now taken as a given category including the racial image of the Jews. *This essentially abandoned the Jews to anti-Semitic vilification and persecution.*"[32] Similarly, John Connelly has premised an inextricable link between racism and antisemitism among some leading Catholic thinkers, who argued that the difference of Jews from non-Jews made Jews both threatening and inferior:

> What made this Catholic racism confounding was that it claimed to recognize the supremacy of the spiritual while in fact espousing the existence of heritable traits among

supposed racial groups like the Jews or the Germans....*To them alleged failings of the spirit among particular groups of people—for example, the Jews' rejection of Christ—came to appear historically indelible.*...Catholic thinkers were especially prone to modern racism in German-speaking Central Europe, where they desperately sought cultural relevance beyond their ghetto. For many of them, the scientific discovery of race seemed to reconcile spirit to matter and Catholicism to the German nation.[33]

As Yehuda Bauer says, although Christian teaching had resulted in the dehumanization of Jews over the centuries, the prevalent, non-genocidal antisemitism in the general population "prevented any serious opposition to the Nazis once they had decided to embark on the murder of the Jews."[34] Although in some instances German theologians offered an explicit authorization for Nazism and the Holocaust, "for the most part, they provided no religious basis for refusing to participate in the Holocaust."[35] It was not so much that antisemitism in the churches inevitably led to the Final Solutions, but rather that it "predisposed" many not to act.[36] As Robert Ericksen provocatively asks, "Is it possible, however, that ordinary Germans who became killers for the Nazi state felt they had received permission from their churches or from their universities?"[37]

Thus, while it is impossible to quantify Christian complicity, we have ample evidence of the churches' feeble response to Nazi ideology. And in some cases, we see active, even enthusiastic support. Although "Hitler's priests" were relatively few in number (though many priests supported Hitler), their sense of the compatibility of Catholic Christianity with Nazi racial theory is chilling. So, too, is the activity of the Institute for the Study and Eradication of Jewish Influence on German Church Life. Protestants and Catholics were separated by differences in beliefs and practices but united in their opposition to Jews. As historian Doris Bergen concludes, "Two traditions had shaped the life of the churches in Germany since the time of Luther and even before. One was hostility toward Jews and Judaism, the other confessional strife. Both of them thrived in the Third Reich."[38]

A few church figures stand out for their protest of the Nazi regime. Particularly notable was Bernhard Lichtenberg, Provost of Berlin's St. Hedwig Cathedral, who, among other defiant acts, prayed for the Jews from the pulpit each evening for three years. Arrested in October of 1941, Lichtenberg responded to his prosecutors in December of 1941: "I think I am not only authorized but obliged, to preach to the Catholic believers, that they may not let themselves be confused by unchristian dispositions but live by Jesus Christ's commandment: 'Thou shall love thy neighbor as thyself.' That includes Jews."[39] Lichtenberg organized the office of the Special Relief of the Diocese of Berlin (*Hilfswerk beim Ordinariat Berlin*) and drew Dr. Margarete Sommer, a member of the Berlin Catholic resistance circle, into the organization. After Lichtenberg's death, she became the organization's director. Lichtenberg also worked with resister Dr. Gertrud Luckner, who led actions on behalf of Jews in Berlin and Munich through the German Catholic charity Caritas.[40] At the behest of Lichtenberg's bishop, Konrad Graf von Preysing of Berlin, Sommer composed a "Draft for a Petition Favoring the Jews" in August of 1943:

> With deepest sorrow—yes, even with holy indignation—
> have we German bishops learned of the deportation of
> non-Aryans in a manner that is scornful of all human
> rights. It is our holy duty to defend the unalienable rights
> of all men guaranteed by natural law....The world would
> not understand if we failed to raise our voice loudly
> against the deprivation of rights of these innocent people.
> We would stand guilty before God and man because of our
> silence.[41]

The German bishops as a body, however, rejected Sommer's draft: "The combination of [Cardinal Adolf von] Bertran's accommodating attitude and the 'fatherland first' attitude of many bishops made it impossible for Preysing to win over his colleagues at a time when the war had begun to go badly for Germany."[42]

One of the most disturbing aspects of Catholic postwar activity is the way in which high church officials, clerics, agencies, and monasteries, along with the collusion of various governments, facilitated the escape of Nazi war criminals. This is a complicated story, part of the church's extensive efforts to ameliorate the situation of the hundreds of thousands of displaced persons amidst the chaos of postwar Europe. The efforts of agencies such as the Vatican's Relief Commission for Refugees were marred by the assistance also extended to Nazis, apparently justified by a twofold rationale: Aiding the anti-communist Nazis would prevent the spread of communism, and offering forgiveness and assistance to Nazis and their collaborators provided the possibility of conversion or return to the practice of Catholicism.

Austrian bishop Alois Hudal (1885–1963) played an especially disedifying role. Well known for his desire to "Christianize" National Socialism in order to counter communism, Hudal had written a book in 1937, *The Foundations of National Socialism*; he sent a copy to Hitler with the inscription, "To the Siegfried of German greatness."[43] Working from Rome after the war, Hudal enabled a number of notorious Nazis to escape Europe via his "ratline" (escape route). Among Hudal's beneficiaries were Adolf Eichmann, who oversaw the deportation and extermination of Jews; Franz Stangl, the commandant of the Sobibior and Treblinka death camps; and Dr. Josef Mengele (the "Angel of Death"). Eichmann and Mengele made it to Argentina and Stangl to Brazil by way of Damascus. "We do not believe in the eye for an eye of the Jews," Hudal said, but he was not alone in his thinking:

> Pius XII and the Catholic bishops repeatedly asked for mercy and even amnesty for war criminals and Holocaust perpetrators. They believed that the responsibility for the crimes lay only with a handful of leaders; foremost among them were Hitler, Himmler and Goebbels. All others, including SS men, were not responsible, and were, perhaps, victims too....The lost sheep had to be brought back to the fold, they thought. The Catholic Church celebrated its moral victory over National Socialism.[44]

Similarly, Croatian priest Krunoslav Dragonovic operated a large ratline that enabled many Ustaši war criminals who had committed atrocities against some 300,000 to 400,000 Orthodox Serbs and 50,000 Jews. Among Dragonovic's beneficiaries were the Croat fascist leader Ante Pavelić and Klaus Barbie, the infamous "Butcher of Lyon." Barbie lived in Bolivia for nearly thirty years before being exposed and extradited to France in 1983.[45]

Whatever certain churchmen of the 1940s and 1950s may have believed, Christians had no moral victory over National Socialism to celebrate.

DISCONTINUITIES

However extensive, shameful, and sinful Christianity's complicity in the Shoah, it alone does not bear the blame. Christianity's legacy of denigrating Judaism (and too often vilifying Jews) never, even its most extreme voices, sanctioned state-sponsored genocide, the so-called "Final Solution." In the succinct formulation of Jewish historian Yosef Hayim Yerushlami, even if "Christian teaching was a necessary cause leading to the Holocaust, it was surely not a sufficient one."[46] Thus, it is important to sketch out the larger context in which interrelated developments in science, nationalism, colonialism, fascism, and World Wars I and II were causal factors. Racism and antisemitism were integral to all.

In the realm of science and medicine, eugenics and racial hygiene held many in thrall in the late nineteenth and early twentieth centuries, not only in Germany but also in Great Britain and the United States.[47] Because heredity was considered to be determinative and immutable, the only recourse was to prevent the decay by such methods as compulsory sterilization, the killing of persons disabled by mental or physical deficiencies, and the destruction of foreigners (especially Jews, but also the Roma). By the end of World War II, some 200,000 "deficient" children and adults had been put to death in killing centers overseen by medical personnel. The importance of cleanliness and purity of blood was most effectively conveyed by designating others—especially Jews—as the foil. When Joseph Goebbels, head of the Nazi Ministry of Propaganda and Enlightenment, described how Jews would take over the world, he depicted them as "international carriers of bacilli" whose "workers are infected."[48] The Jew as a racial pariah became a fundamental theme of the curriculum in German schools. A document for teachers, "3000 Years of Jewish

Hatred," prepared by the Main School Office of the NSDAP in 1943 (when about 75 percent of Jews murdered in the Shoah were already dead), declared:

> The Jewish question is, however, in the first line not an economic, but rather a racial one. That means that the individual Cohn or Levi are not our enemies, but the race....The visible opponent is never so dangerous as the invisible. Known are the most dangerous enemies of our physical existence, the bacillae, and these are invisible. We do not see them, but sense them intuitively. Therefore, the battle against them will be led. This is exactly so with the Jew: We do not see him anymore, but we *sense him intuitively* [spüren ihm]. We sensed him for years in his malicious agitation, we sense him now in the war. The war is his work.[49]

Moreover, in the various concentration camps, medical professionals oversaw the selection process and the gassing of victims, and engaged in unethical (and often gruesome) medical experiments. Most of the scientists and physicians involved in these barbarous actions were "integrated members of one of the world's preeminent scientific communities."[50]

The "Jewish question" was central to nationalist movements as nations-in-formation worked out the constituency of their citizenry. When Germany became a unified nation-state in 1871, Jews held full legal equality, but tensions raised by rapid urbanization and antisemitic societies gave rise to more exclusionary perspectives. Germany's expansionist policies under Kaiser Wilhelm II led to Germany's colonization of Southwest Africa (now Namibia) and East Africa (now Tanzania), as well as in Cameroon, Togo, and Samoa. Anti-black racism on the part of German colonists rationalized exploitative and cruel treatment of natives, who revolted and were in turn viciously suppressed. Germans pursued a campaign of "deliberate annihilation" against Southwest Africa's Herero and Nama peoples. Between 1904 and 1908 large numbers died, whether in combat, in concentration camps, or from starvation and thirst in the Omaheke desert to which Germans had driven them: "Germany's first racial state and society took shape, not under the Third Reich, but under Imperial

Germany in its prime African colony. The German army, colonial administrators, and settlers learned that against Africans they could practice the most brutal measures possible, and could do so with active support of the very center of German state power, the Kaiser, the military staff, and the civilian government."[51] Organizations such as the Pan-German League, formed at the end of the nineteenth century, exacerbated the racialization of national identity. Obsessed with racial "mixing," they believed European norms of war were not applicable to the inferior Africans, and that Jews were "colonizing" Germany.[52] Insofar as Africans and Jews were judged to be a threat to their culture and way of life, Germans must subjugate them.

World War I accentuated the desire to dominate others, but after defeat and the Treaty of Versailles in 1919, which stripped Germany of its colonies, many in Germany gave way to the "pathos of victimization"—and the Nazis cleverly exploited both the aspiration of domination and the misery of loss.[53] The defeat in the Great War taught Hitler the importance of totally destroying enemies, within and beyond Germany's borders. As the enemy within, during this war Jews had been, in Heinrich Himmler's words, "secret saboteurs, agitators and troublemakers." For the Nazis, the loss of World War I "served as a call to world domination, a threat, and a rationalization for murder of the Jews and anyone else cast in the role of shirker, traitor, or defeatist."[54]

Antisemitism and racism were foundational to the fascist ideology of National Socialism and Italian Fascism, as well as to the various fascist movements in the 1920s and 1930s in the wake of the perceived failure of European civilization. Fascist leaders made use of race science to justify authoritarian means of binding a nation into a single people by means of an aggressive foreign policy, militarism, and exaltation of the nation-state. Jews in particular were pariahs because as foreigners they detracted from the purity of a nation's people. Other peoples as well were regarded as threats: some Slavic peoples, most notably Russians; ethnic Poles, the Roma and Sinti peoples ("Gypsies"), and homosexuals. The Jews alone, however, "were thought to pose an evil going beyond the evidence of the senses."[55]

The complexity of the Shoah has given rise to extensive scholarship, of which only a limited review is possible here. My intent is simply to establish the broad outline of contributing causes—certainly not to exculpate Christianity, but rather to indicate the multifaceted character of this event that in the end defies comprehension.

INTERSECTIONS

As a heuristic, the categories of "continuities" and "discontinuities" provide a way of organizing thinking. Though distinguishable, they obviously intersect in complicated ways. Here I note a few of those complicating factors.

The linkage of Christianity with antisemitism is painfully clear. The centuries of hostility toward Jews, the people accused of responsibility for the death of Jesus Christ, meant that phenomena such as antisemitic societies and publications that developed late in nineteenth-century Europe were not so outlandish. The ghettos the Catholic Church imposed on Jews beginning in the mid-sixteenth century may have been rationalized by theology rather than the Nazi ideology that gave rise to the ghettos of Warsaw or Łódź. Fewer Jews may have died of starvation or brutality in the ghetto of Rome than those of Poland, but the differences are primarily of degree rather than nature.

We should not overlook the horror that Nazi rule inspired, particularly in the late 1930s and early 1940s. This reign of terror makes all the more significant and heroic those who resisted in various ways, including providing safe havens for Jews, smuggling Jews across borders, and falsifying passports and baptismal certificates.[56] German Christians of sufficient courage and will to resist "had to place their own sense of moral values above obedience and loyalty to their national government, perhaps even to the point of juridical treason." [57] Though their number is few, it is important to recognize that odious opinions might nevertheless be contradicted by courageous actions. Perhaps best known in this regard is Dietrich Bonhoeffer, who in his early career held traditional views on the Jewish question but at considerable cost spoke out against the church's capitulation to Nazi views.[58] Bonhoeffer's involvement in resistance circles ultimately cost him his life in April of 1945. Perhaps, speculates Robert Ericksen, "Bonhoeffer learned to oppose Adolf Hitler because he did not attend church as a child, because most church-going Protestants tended to think Hitler was wonderful."[59] Less well known is the case of Zofia Kossak-Szcucka, a Polish author who likewise held conventional views, seeing Jews as a foreign race, and was supportive of an economic boycott against them. During the German occupation, however, she risked her life in opposition. Working with a few other Poles, she helped to organize a Polish underground movement, known as *Żegota*, dedicated to rescuing Jews from the Nazis. She also wrote appeals in the underground press, urging more Poles to become involved in rescuing Jews: "Whoever remains silent in the face of murder becomes an accomplice of the murder."[60] *Żegota* was ultimately able to rescue some four thousand Jews.[61]

Furthermore, within early twentieth-century Catholic circles, the traditional disparagement of Judaism took on new layers as Judaism was conflated with communism, liberalism, Freemasonry, the modern secular state, and democracy. Popes and various Catholic publications railed against Freemasonry because of its religious "indifferentism" (in many lodges, Protestants, Catholics, Jews, and nonbelievers associated as equals), its alleged responsibility for the French Revolution and other liberalizing movements, and its supposed corruption of morals. A long line of papal condemnations beginning in 1738 and continuing through the interwar period forbade Catholics to belong, a censure often ignored in practice. The Vatican's criticism of Freemasonry and of liberalism, however, paled in the light of its horror of communism. Furthermore, the stereotype of Jewish solidarity provided the foundation for identifying Jews with communism. This was especially evident in Poland, despite the relative paucity of Jewish communists.[62]

In light of communism's decline in recent years in so many parts of the world, it is difficult to imagine what a powerful grip anti-communism had for much of the twentieth century. Yet without recognition of the tremendous fear of communism that gripped many, particularly in the interwar and postwar years, we will assign the church's anti-Jewish teachings too much influence in shaping behavior during the Holocaust. Clearly, Popes Pius XI and Pius XII held traditional theological positions on Judaism that contributed to their willingness to "make a pact with the devil."[63] Their timidity in the face of Nazism is appalling. Pius XII, for example, played the role of diplomat when the world needed a prophet. Yet they deserve to be read in the full complexity of their times and, in particular, to be acknowledged as failing to act on behalf of Jews in large measure because of their horror of communism. Michael Phayer, for example, argues that Pope Pius XII's "obsession" with communism is the most important element of his papacy. [64] Phayer writes:

> Doing battle with the evils of modernity became endemic to the Vatican. Pope Pius XII took up the battle against communism as his special mission. It defined his papacy. As Jacques Maritain perceived, Pius believed his mission in life was to save western civilization from communism. After World War II, the struggle between religion and communism took on the magnitude of a final showdown in the pope's eyes. It became the purpose of the Catholic religion to do battle with communism....In Pius XII's eyes, communism constituted an insidious enemy that had fifth columns all over the world....To a considerable extent, Pius XII isolated ethical considerations from the decision-making process. This divorce of practice from theory took place across the board, from diplomacy to finance to politics, and resulted in a misalignment of the Vatican's ethical compass. We first took note of this during the interwar period when Cardinal Pacelli and Pius XI decided to take a strong position against communism rather than against Nazi racism, although the Holy Office had advised to the contrary.[65]

Seeing Christianity, particularly my own Catholic Church, in the tarnished mirror of history is deeply disturbing. If, however, we are to do more than lament—a necessary response—then it is incumbent upon us to commit ourselves to contribute to the continuing process of reconciliation between Jews and Christians. Moreover, if we are to reclaim the "power in the story" of the death of Jesus after the Holocaust, then we must begin by repudiating the "Christ killer" charge. In Part III, "A Transformed Telling," I will turn to ways in which Christians might draw upon their sacred story of the passion and death of Jesus in ways that do justice and deepen prayerfulness.

As a prelude to this transformed telling, it seems appropriate to revisit the 2010 Oberammergau production and reassess the judgments my colleagues and I made in our evaluation of the script (see chapter 5). In July of 2010 I had opportunity to hear from three rabbis who had viewed the play, as well as a Catholic scholar who had seen it in the company of Jews. While recognizing that the script still has problems, they urged me to recognize the remarkable changes for the 2010 performances. The play's director, Christian Stückl, has made considerable effort to learn about Judaism (there are no Jews in Oberammergau). He has led cast members in a trip to Israel, where, in addition to visiting the sites associated with Jesus, they also went to Jerusalem's Holocaust memorial, *Yad Vashem*, and met with Holocaust survivors. And even once the production was underway, he made adjustments in view of conversations with knowledgeable Christian and Jewish leaders. For example, after discussion with some Jewish leaders in May, he adjusted the crucifixion scene so that the audience heard not only the cry, "Crucify him," but also the voices of Jesus' supporters.[66]

One story sheds light on the effects of dialogue. In early July of 2010, at the invitation of the American Jewish Committee, a delegation of New York Catholics, led by Archbishop Timothy Dolan (then moderator for Catholic-Jewish relations for the United States Conference of Catholic Bishops, and now Cardinal Dolan), went to Oberammergau in the company of Rabbis Gary Greenebaum and Noam Marans.[67] They not only viewed the play, but also had an opportunity to meet with Stückl , deputy director Otto Huber, community leaders, and some of the principal members of the cast. Archbishop Dolan, while mindful that further changes are necessary, reflected on the "good news" in Oberammergau: "as two rabbis and an archbishop were inspired by the 2010 Play; as major progress in the ongoing noble goal of removing any hint of inaccurate and unjust caricaturing of Jews has been made; and as the three of us agreed that continued dialogue about the renowned Play could indeed be a boost to Jewish-Catholic friendship."[68] Rabbis Greenebaum and Marans had a similar judgment:

> Few places on earth have tested progress in Catholic-Jewish relations more than Oberammergau....No one

should take for granted the considerable advances in Catholic-Jewish relations since *Nostra Aetate*. But regarding Oberammergau, although the mission of reforming the Play is not complete, we are no longer in pre-Stueckl 1984, and we are certainly not in 1934. It is time for the Jewish community to recognize the good which has been done.[69]

On that note of hope, I turn to consider what is involved in a "transformed telling."

PART III

A TRANSFORMED TELLING

CHAPTER 7

New Perspectives on Troubling Texts I

The Roman Empire as a Backstory to the Crucifixion

Jesus was crucified; he was accused of violating Roman law; he was put to death on orders of the Roman governor, Pontius Pilate. The role of the Jews in the death of Jesus was minimal and limited to a few leading priests acting on behalf of the Romans. Thus, it is historically inaccurate to claim that Jews were responsible for Jesus' death.[1]

We might imagine interpretation of Scripture as a banquet at which we twenty-first-century interpreters are by no means the first ones to arrive. We pull our chairs over to the table where the meal has already been in progress for generations—some three thousand years since the first biblical texts were written. Those around us are engaged in lively discussion; if we wish to join them, we must break into well-established conversations. We may not like those with whom we are seated; we may well have other preferences for the seating arrangements. Generations of interpreters have come before us, both individuals and communities, leaving behind persistent traditions and meanings that have been applied to a variety of texts. "To read the Bible is also to sit at table in the company of all…some of whom brought bitter offerings to the feast."[2]

In Part II, "A Troubling Telling—and Its Tragic Consequences," we have indeed witnessed some of the bitter offerings many of our ancestors have brought to the feast by using New Testament texts to justify vilification of Jews: Jews were no longer regarded as God's chosen people but rather as a perfidious people whom God rejected because they had murdered Jesus Christ. The "crucifying Jew" came to personify evil. The "Christ killer" charge was (and is) the theological core of antisemitism.

Understandings of the Apostle Paul complemented that charge. Over the centuries, many have regarded Paul as a convert to Christianity; they have interpreted his experience on the road to Damascus (see Acts 9:1–22; 22:4–16; 26:9–18) as his abandonment of Judaism. They have construed passages such as Galatians 2:16 to mean that the works of the Jewish Law were of no value because persons were justified in God's eyes only through faith in Jesus Christ. Thus, the Torah lacked salvific power. Furthermore, many read Paul's letters as contrasting the grace and freedom of the Gospel with the burden and "curse" of the Law (Galatians 3:13a). Paul seemed to be saying not only that Jesus Christ had superseded the Torah, but that Christianity was the antithesis of Judaism, which was a religion of works righteousness, of law rather than love. In short:

> Paul seems able to proclaim his gospel of grace only against the dark foil of Jewish legalism. The Judaism which many see reflected in Paul's polemics is thus a joyless, hypocritical, nationalistic means of earning salvation by mechanically doing the works of the law. The God of the Jews is seen as a remote, gloomy tyrant who lays the burden of the law on people, and their response is twofold: they either become proud and self-righteous hypocrites who are scrupulous about food but ignore justice, or they are plunged into guilt and anxiety, thinking themselves accused for breaking a single commandment.[3]

Thus, the hostility engendered by the "Christ killer" charge was heightened by a characterization of Judaism as oppressively legalistic and Jews as cursed by God for rejecting Jesus Christ. Together, these claims provided biblical legitimization for denigration of Judaism and condemnation of Jews.

In our time, however, the immense resources of biblical and theological scholarship enable us to read these troubling texts differently. This scholarship is an essential component in transforming the raw materials of texts so that they no longer justify opposition to Judaism but rather serve as portals to the immensely complex world of antiquity. An important foundation is the recognition that Scripture is a vast and disparate anthology with a long tradition of varied interpretations; it is a classic text that thus invites interpretation from many points of view. As our horizon of knowledge and experience expands, new readings of troubling texts not only become possible—they become obligatory.

In particular, three central claims of biblical scholarship call us to reinterpret New Testament texts about alleged Jewish responsibility for the death of Jesus. The first, the focus of this chapter, highlights the way the Roman Empire operated as the critical backstory to the passion accounts. For the Roman rulers, crucifixion functioned as a mode of state terrorism to intimidate peasants and slaves into passivity.

A second area of scholarship explores new insights about the identity and mission of the Apostle Paul, thereby resituating him in his Jewish milieu and reinterpreting his perspectives on the Law. The third claim demands our reassessment of "Judaism" and "Christianity" as distinctive religions in the first three centuries of the Common Era; the boundaries between them were far more complicated and permeable than has traditionally been understood. These topics are the focus of chapter 8.

Collectively, these three claims challenge conventional readings of familiar New Testament texts. Because of the detail devoted to substantiating the claims, they are divided into two chapters.

CRUCIFIXION IN THE ROMAN EMPIRE

When the Gospels are read as straightforward reportage—that is, as factual accounts of the life and teaching of Jesus of Nazareth— they leave the clear impression that Jews (or groups of Jews, such as the "chief priests, scribes, and elders") are responsible for the death of Jesus. Nonetheless, reading texts in this manner is a misreading because it overlooks the social, historical, and literary contexts crucial for understanding biblical accounts. *Knowledge of the contexts not only immeasurably enriches understanding of Scripture, it is imperative if we are to interpret the texts in salutary ways.*

In short, we must make the plot line more complex. Rather than explain the conflict as one between Jesus and Jews, we more accurately might speak of a conflict between, on the one hand, Jesus and his preaching of God's reign, and on the other, Rome imperial rule. *We will tell the passion story correctly only when we situate it in the backstory of the Roman Empire.* Mary Rose D'Angelo argues that the Gospels, by assigning the motivation and initiative for the crucifixion to the Jewish leaders, seriously misrepresented the role of Jews. Despite their portrait of a Pilate besieged by the demands of the priests and Jewish mobs, in fact Pilate held the reins of power; the priests held office and officiated liturgically only at his sufferance.[4]

We must situate the cross of Christ under the Roman arch, and inquire into the disparity between the New Testament accounts and first-century history.

The Cross of Christ under the Roman Arch

Authors necessarily make certain assumptions about the world of their readers. Their assumptions, however, may not be evident to another generation or culture. For the New Testament writers, the oppressive power of imperial Rome seems to have been one such assumption. Yet their taken-for-granted world is much less transparent to modern readers. The Roman Empire does make an occasional explicit appearance; this is most evident in the two works ascribed to Luke, the Gospel and Acts of the Apostles. The Gospel refers to Emperor Augustus and the Syrian governor Quirinius (2:1–2). Acts has sixteen references to Rome and Roman, while the rest of the New Testament has a mere four references. In addition to the frequent mention of Caesar (seventeen times in Luke-Acts), Luke names various officials in Acts, including King Herod (Agrippa I) (12:1); the governor of Judea (Antonius) Felix (23:24); his successor, Porcius Festus (24:27); and King (Herod) Agrippa (II) (25:13).[5] Various rulers named Herod, client-kings (non-Romans who ruled by virtue of Roman patronage) also make an appearance in all the Gospels, as does Pontius Pilate, the Judean governor, who not only

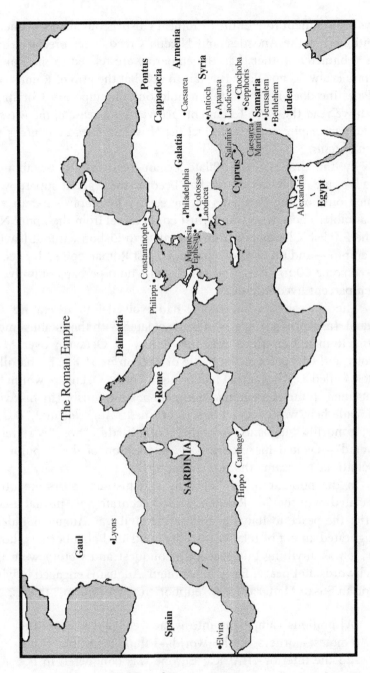

Map of Roman Empire

plays a prominent role in the canonical Gospels but also is explicitly mentioned in the Apostles' and Nicene Creeds.[6] Yet precisely how these characters (other than the emperor) are related to the Roman Empire is always not clear. It is fair to say that the grip of Rome's rule in Palestine does not have much hold on contemporary Christians when we read the New Testament. *Yet without a sense of the ways of the Roman Empire, we misinterpret the New Testament accounts of the death of Jesus.*

By the time Pontius Pilate began what would be about a decade's rule in 26 C.E., Rome had become the regnant superpower, rivaled only by the Parthians to the east.[7] The empire's extent was remarkable. Those with wanderlust could travel from the upper Nile to the English Channel or from Jerusalem to Lisbon without leaving the empire—and no need of a passport, just Roman coins.[8] It encompassed some 60 to 70 million people, of whom perhaps only five to seven percent lived in cities.[9]

The process by which Rome had evolved into an empire was gradual. Insofar as a single event is associated with the establishment of the Roman Empire, it was the victory of Octavian over Marc Antony and Cleopatra at the Battle of Actium in 31 B.C.E. that ultimately ended a civil war that had brought chaos. Octavian, whom his great-uncle Julius Caesar had adopted posthumously (in his will) and made heir, was declared *Imperator Caesar Augustus* in 27 B.C.E. The honorific *Augustus—meaning* "dignified," "holy," "stately," "revered"—evoked his program of "restoration of the Republic,"[10] which, in fact, became the Roman Empire.

In the popular mind Augustus and his successors are often associated with the *Pax Romana*. This is accurate only insofar as we restrict the peace to Italy. By ending the civil war, Augustus indeed inaugurated an era of relative stability. Outside Italy's borders, however, it was anything but peaceful. Conquest and victory were the watchwords, not peace. Early in his reign, Augustus engaged in what historian Susan Mattern terms "euphoric expansionism," that is:

[A]mbitious campaigns into what were perceived as the remotest corners of the world—Ethiopia, Arabia Felix, and the interior of Africa; Europe was conquered to the Danube, the last remaining corner of Spain was subdued

164

and annexed and there was talk of invasions into Britain and Dacia....Armies were committed to the pacification of the Alps and to campaigns across the Rhine.[11]

Rome's foreign policy was intended to dominate and humiliate the enemy—to inspire fear and awe in those it conquered. The barbarian "must be terrified at all times."[12] Rome celebrated its victories by various means: collecting and publicizing lists of peoples and lands it had conquered, creating sumptuous displays of the spoils of their expeditions, humiliating leaders of enemy peoples, and engaging in triumphal processions. Some three hundred triumphal arches survive (or appear on coins or inscriptions), testifying to the glory of conquest.[13]

Meanwhile in Rome, Augustus embarked on an unprecedented cultural renewal, building temples, theaters, and magnificent public buildings. Drawing upon classical Greek visual forms, Augustus created what Paul Zanker calls a "completely new pictorial vocabulary, changing the outward appearance of Rome, in interior decoration and furniture and clothing."[14] Around the time he took on the title *Augustus,* one of his supporters (or perhaps Augustus himself) commissioned a sculpture, known as *The Augustus of Prima Porta.* It depicts Augustus in classic form as a young, noble warrior in an elaborate cuirass (body armor), with scenes of the Roman victory over the Parthians. The sculpture is the visual equivalent of his title in which all who viewed it would think of Augustus as ageless, dignified, striking, and thoughtful. The portrait was widely reproduced throughout the Empire.[15]

Such triumphal art—sculptures, coins, buildings, and decorative art—exemplifies Roman imperial ideology by employing gendered and ethnic differences. As Davina Lopez argues, the figures on the breastplate of Augustus are a "stand-in for the masculine triumphalism of the Roman Empire itself. The emperor bears a gospel of imperial salvation worn on his perfectly chiseled chest."[16] On the cuirassed Augustus, a Roman soldier is shown receiving the military standards from a Parthian soldier; the former is a noble figure, the latter a barbarian, even effeminate figure. Two women, crouching, represent the conquered northern territory of Gallia/Gaul and the western territory of Spain. The various visual representations depict

Romans as the fittest race to rule the world and its conquered nations as vanquished peoples.

Augustus also reconstituted the priesthood, revived cultic shrines, increased the offering of sacrifices, and purchased or commissioned images of gods to display through the city of Rome. On his deathbed, according to Cassius Dio, Augustus boasted, "I found Rome of bricks. I leave it to you of marble."[17] He was regarded as a god, as his poet laureate Horace wrote in his "Third Ode": "Because you are servants of the gods, you rule on earth."[18] Submission to Rome was submission to the will of the gods.[19] The emperors bore titles of "Divine, Son of God, and God from God; Lord, Redeemer, Liberator, and Savior of the World."[20]

By 17 B.C.E., Augustus had inaugurated what poets lauded as the Golden Age. As the poet Ovid wrote in his *Ars Amatoria* (The Art of Love):

> There was a rude simplicity before, now Rome has turned
> to gold,
> For she possesses the great treasures of a conquered world.[21]

Ovid's observation is revealing: Rome's Golden Age was fashioned from the labor and tribute of those it ruled. Augustus and his successors oversaw an aristocratic empire, one with a great gulf between rich and poor. The Empire was a pyramid in which wealthy elites, perhaps two to three percent of the population supported by a retainer class of bureaucrats of about five percent, ruled over vast lands and peoples.[22] The peasants they ruled and taxed supported Rome, with its population of more than a million people—the largest city in the western world until London surpassed a million people in the eighteenth century.[23] The tribute from the provinces was vital to Rome's survival, enabling the emperor to placate the populace with "bread and circuses."[24] Rome imported between 200,000 and 400,000 tons of wheat annually, most of it from subject peoples in North Africa and Egypt.[25] The ruling elite also extracted between 30 and 70 percent of the production of peasants and artisans.[26] After all, "to rule in aristocratic empires is, above all, to tax."[27] Taxes and tributes, forced labor and slave labor funded the splendors of Rome; the urban ruling elite regarded peasants as inferiors, "rustics" whom they could exploit. The Empire's military enforced their privileges and made rebellion very dangerous.

Rome's military might lay less in the extent and number of its forces than in its ability to deter rebellion by terror.[28] Occupying armies were stationed to contain revolts. Campaigns were always fought on the enemy's territory, and should the enemy manage a victory, a reprisal would follow. Mattern argues that image was the central aspect of Roman strategy. Even if troop deployments were "astonishingly small," it "did not matter in the Roman system as long as the enemy believed that he would suffer massive retaliation for a breach of faith and as long as the Romans were both willing and able to enforce this principle at whatever cost." The Romans understood the psychology of fear.[29]

Augustus and his successors also grasped the power of spectacles that provided public entertainment while drawing spectators into the mythos of imperial rule. Conventional games—athletic contests, plays, chariot races, and gladiatorial combats—continued. Augustus' innovation was the construction of amphitheaters throughout the expanse of the empire where thousands of viewers watched brutal fights with wild beasts in the morning, the public execution of criminals by fire, crucifixion, or by being eaten by wild animals at noon, and gladiatorial contests (mainly between slaves, criminals, or prisoners of war) in the afternoon.[30] The spectacles that took place in the arenas and the expensive gifts of animal and human victims were the emperor's gift, his benefaction or "good works" to the people, that is, the "works of the law" in Paul's vocabulary.[31] The cruelty of what transpired in the arenas dehumanized those to be tortured and killed. The spectators, no matter how lowly, were nonetheless superior to those being punished, who were not regarded as human but as bestial and treacherous:

> The righteous brutalization of the civic body in the arena is an essential requirement of warfare and is reflected in the cruelty of cities plundered and their people tortured, slaughtered and raped. The mass consumption of the emperor's games, together with his bread, was metabolized into political compliance with the rules of battle and victory, conquest and subjugation, competition and vio-

lence, domination and distinction as codified and sanctioned by Roman law for the inside and toward the outside
of the Roman Empire....[T]he arena not only exposed but
also veiled, covered, softened with its bloody sand all the
deadly tension, violence, and injustice that in reality were
at the core of Roman society itself. It transformed privileged and nonprivileged members into a common Roman
subjectivity of one-self, lifting up even the lowest ranking
members of the plebs, the socially others inside society,
but putting them above someone lower—the outcast
dying in the arena....The blood of the other drenching the
sand of the arena becomes the magical substance that
gives birth to the civic self.[32]

In this context of brutality and dehumanization, we begin to
grasp the function of crucifixion. What greater mechanism to inspire
fear and keep order than crucifixion? The first-century orator
Quintilian observed, "Whenever we crucify the guilty, the most
crowded roads are chosen, where the most people can see and be
moved by this fear. For penalties relate not so much to retribution as
to their exemplary effect."[33] We best understand crucifixion as
"highly organized, massive state terrorism, intended to intimidate
the vast peasant and slave populations of the empire into passivity."[34]
Or, in Fredriksen's blunt description, crucifixion was a "spectacle for
the edification of those watching."[35] As a public humiliation—the
naked body hanging for all to see, sometimes for days—it was torture designed as the ultimate deterrent. Not even the dignity of burial was given. Remains of the crucified were piled with other corpses,
left to ravens and dogs.[36] Rome reserved crucifixion only for peasants, foreigners, and slaves it deemed guilty of heinous crimes, such
as fomenting rebellion, treason, and murder. Roman citizens were
not subject to crucifixion. Tens of thousands of Jews suffered death
by crucifixion under Roman rule.

Perhaps we might better understand the effect of crucifixion
upon the populace though the lens of a contemporary analogy. A day
after the death of the Libyan leader, Colonel Muammar el-Qaddafi,
on October 20, 2011, *The New York Times* published a lengthy analy-

sis of his regime, including a graphic description of the violence he fomented in order to control the Libyan people:

> In the late 1970s and early '80s, he [Qaddafi] eliminated even mild critics through public trials and executions. Kangaroo courts were staged on soccer fields or basketball courts, where the accused were interrogated, often urinating in fear as they begged for their lives. The events were televised to make sure that no Libyan missed the point.
>
> The bodies of one group of students hanged in downtown Tripoli's main square were left there to rot for a week, opposition figures said, and traffic was rerouted to force cars to pass by.[37]

According to the Libyan writer Hisham Matar, Colonel Qaddafi "deliberately tried to create a campaign that would terrorize the population, that would traumatize them to such an extent that they would never think of expressing their thoughts politically or socially."[38] Similarly, the Romans used crucifixion to terrorize the populace into submission.

Rome neither invented crucifixion nor was alone in employing it on a large scale.[39] Crucifixion seems to have been a widespread form of torture in antiquity, attested at least as early as the seventh century B.C.E. Alexander the Great was said to have crucified two thousand Tyrians, and Antiochus IV, the Syrian king, crucified Judeans in 167 B.C.E. The Hasmonean king Alexander Jannaeus crucified eight hundred rebellious Pharisees in 88 B.C.E. Whatever the precedents, however, Rome used crucifixion to great effectiveness. Its great orator Cicero (106–43 B.C.E.) called it "a most cruel and disgusting penalty," the "extreme and ultimate penalty for a slave" (*In Verrem*, 2.5.64, 66). The Jewish historian Josephus later called it "the most pitiable of deaths" (*Jewish War*, 7.6.4).

The emperor delegated the power of capital execution, as well as other responsibilities of rule. Augustus (emperor from 31 B.C.E to 14 C.E.) and his successor Tiberius (14–37 C.E.) oversaw their widespread empire through various subordinates, such as the ruthless Herod ("the Great"), client-king of Roman Palestine (37–4 B.C.E.).

After Herod's death, his three sons split the considerable territories his father had amassed and beautified in honor of his Roman patrons.[40] Archelaus, however, so mismanaged Judea that he lasted just two years, until 6 C.E. Herod Antipas, in contrast, remained as tetrarch of Galilee and Perea until the emperor Caligula banished him to Gaul in 37 C.E., and he figures prominently in the Gospel accounts. His brother Herod Philip also enjoyed a lengthy rule in the Northern Territories (Iturea, Gaulanitis, Trachonitis, Batanea, Auranitis) until 34 C.E.

Archelaus was such an inept and brutal ruler that a delegation of Judeans went to Rome to plead with the emperor for his removal. Augustus eventually deposed him in favor of Roman-appointed prefects or governors; successive emperors continued with this administrative arrangement until the Jewish War (66–73 C.E.).[41] Governors typically held equestrian rank (below that of senators), had some military background, and were moderately wealthy. Their principal responsibilities involved keeping order and settling disputes; collecting taxes and overseeing fiscal matters; engaging in public works and building projects; commanding troops; and administering Roman-style justice, including capital execution.[42]

In the case of Judea, regarded as a backwater, a governor such as Pontius Pilate would be answerable to the senatorial legate of the province of Syria as well as to the emperor. The Syrian legate controlled four Roman legions (about twenty thousand men) and about five thousand cavalry. The Judean prefects, who lived on the Mediterranean at Caesarea Maritima (not to be confused with Caesarea Philippi in the north on the headwaters of the Jordan River), commanded only three thousand or so troops. Some troops also watched over fortresses and around the temple in Jerusalem.

With relatively few troops at his command and minimal centralized bureaucracy, prefects like Pilate had to form alliances with what social scientists call the retainer class, about five percent of the population who served the needs of the ruler and governing class: Sadducees and leading scribes and Pharisees, as well as bureaucratic government officials, and various kinds of officials.[43] These officials were not simply religious leaders, as most readers of the New Testament tend to assume, but participants in the Roman imperial system with a limited measure of social and political power. Civic, religious, and imperial powers were inextricably linked.

Of particular note is the relationship between prefects and chief priests. Augustus decreed that the prefect would exercise the same power as had Herod the Great: the appointment (and removal) of the high priest and supervision of the priestly vestments. In his *Antiquities of the Jews* (18.93–94) Josephus writes:

> When the Romans took over the government, they retained control of the high priest's vestments and kept them in a stone building, where they were under seal both of the priests and of the custodians of the treasury and where the warden of the guard lighted the lamp day by day. Seven days before each festival the vestments were delivered to the priests by the warden. After they had been purified, the high priest wore them; then after the first day of the festival he put them back again in the building where they were laid away before. This was the procedure at the three festivals each year and on the fast day.[44]

Since Caiaphas was high priest for the entirety of Pilate's rule (18–36 C.E., in fact), we may infer that together high priest and prefect formed a powerful alliance. His longevity contrasts sharply with that of the five high priests during the prefecture of Pilate's predecessor, Valerius Gratus (15–25 C.E.). Certainly Caiaphas had excellent family connections; he was the son-in-law of Annas, who was high priest from 6–15 C.E., and five of his brothers-in-law also served as high priests.[45] Yet gaining a clear sense of the precise role Caiaphas played in the passion and death of Jesus is difficult to ascertain, as is the specific role of the chief priests and elders of the people. As Adele Reinhartz shows, the various contradictions and ambiguities in the four Gospel accounts of the passion imply that the evangelists themselves did not know the exact role (if any) Caiaphas might have played. Clearly, they do not regard him as a hero, but neither do they portray him as the wicked arch villain he became in later Christian tradition, history, and culture.[46] Once the layers of narrative and tradition are removed, first-century sources "reveal almost nothing about Caiaphas except the facts of his existence, his service as high priest, and perhaps the ossuary in which his bones may have rested."[47]

In addition to his cultic duties, most notably on Yom Kippur (see Leviticus 16:1–30), the high priest in the Roman period represented the people to the governor and the governor to the people. The ability to get along with the secular power was indispensable; because the governors and many of their troops lived much of the time in Caesarea, it is likely that the high priest had considerable influence in overseeing Judea.[48] The high priest also supervised a guard force of several thousand to keep order in Jerusalem, especially in the precincts of the temple, which meant he oversaw the payment of the tribute Rome exacted.

The chief priests, most likely men from the aristocracy who belonged to four or five families from whom high priests were selected, served alongside the high priest.[49] Their precise role depended on circumstances as well as on their character. Aristocratic lay people, whom the New Testament terms "elders" (*presbyteroi*), also exercised power and influence.[50] The sources do not permit clarity about how the people regarded this power class (that is, the high priest, chief priests, and elders). Warren Carter, for example, argues that they were in essence agents of the interests of the Roman governors, co-opted by their access to wealth and power, and thus despised by the majority of Judeans.[51] In contrast, E. P. Sanders suggests a more complicated perspective, in which respect for the office of the high priesthood mixed with disdain for those who were "corrupt, out for their own gain and that of their sycophants."[52] Nonetheless, because of the significant gap in wealth and influence between the power class and the peasantry, it is reasonable to suspect considerable disparagement by the latter toward the former.

However one assesses the power class, Roman rule engendered the people's resistance. There were periodic outbreaks of violence, with social bandits seeking to redress the imbalance between the wealthy and the vast majority who lived in a subsistence economy. At certain junctures, particularly around the time of instability at the death of Herod in 4 B.C.E. and later during the Jewish War of 66–73

C.E. and the Bar Kochba Revolt of 132–135, messianic movements moved through the countryside.[53]

The chasm between the retainer class that enjoyed a relatively elite status because of its alliance with Roman officials and the vast majority of Judeans and Galileans suggests the problem in using terminology such as "Jews" without additional qualification. A few Jews belonged to the privileged and powerful families of the high priests or were of Herodian lineage. Under Roman rule they flourished, while the overwhelming majority of Jews were overtaxed peasants. Galilean Jews lived at a distance from the temple in Jerusalem and thus had different experiences from Judean Jews, who were more affected by the alliance between governors and the power class. Many Jews lived in the Diaspora, dispersed throughout the Roman Empire and in Babylonia. Richard Horsley claims that the "people of Palestine at the time of Jesus appear as a complex society full of political conflict rather than a unitary religion (Judaism)."[54] Yet Paula Fredriksen argues that Jews, however differently they experienced political rule, were nonetheless "united through kinship and through cult." Jews throughout the world paid the half-shekel temple tax or two drachmas and cared about what happened to Jews outside their own region.[55]

Granted Fredriksen's point, those who seek to understand the historical forces at work in the death of Jesus must keep in mind that the term *Jew* encompasses people in starkly different social and economic realities. This was all the more the case during the chaos of the Jewish War and Bar Kochba Revolt.

In sum, the historical record is far more complicated than the New Testament accounts indicate.[56] Jesus was crucified by the authority of the Roman governor Pontius Pilate, likely in collaboration with the Jewish high priesthood. Although the precise charge cannot be established, it is probable that Pilate viewed Jesus as guilty of sedition. It may be that Luke has a historical kernel of truth for such an accusation: "Then the assembly rose as a body and brought Jesus before Pilate. They began to accuse him, saying, 'We found this man perverting our nation, forbidding us to pay taxes to the emperor, and saying that he himself is the Messiah, a king'" (23:1–2).

The Backstory and the New Testament Accounts

If the Roman Empire was implicated in the death of Jesus, why do the New Testament texts assign blame principally to Jews? In short, why blame the Jews?

Yet even to pose the question in such terms is anachronistic, since "Jews" and "Christians" were not clearly definable, separable groups in the latter part of the first century when the Gospel narratives were composed. And the term for Jew—*Ioudaios*—carried various levels of meaning in the first century. These complications of identity will be discussed in greater detail in the subsequent section. In more nuanced fashion, we might ask why believers-in-Jesus, many of whom we would think of as "Jewish," placed blame on other Jews and seemingly ignored the brutality and dehumanization of imperial Rome and its mode of execution.

No scholarly consensus exists with regard to this provocative question, and the motivations of the Gospel writers lie beyond our ken. A popular and not unreasonable hypothesis is that the Gospel writers, as well as Paul, were acutely conscious of Rome's might vis-à-vis their fledgling movement. Fashioning narratives in which Rome was blamed for the death of the one they called Lord would have been dangerous under the rule of those who regarded the emperor as lord. Perhaps this was the case, although the animosity toward Rome evident in coded fashion (as the "whore of Babylon") in the Book of Revelation raises doubts. Moreover, the Gospels show no undue respect for Roman officials.

The varying judgments of scholars lie principally in their differences with regard to the degree of historical reliability of the passion narratives. In his massive and meticulously detailed two-volume study, *The Death of the Messiah*, Raymond E. Brown concludes that the evangelists—neither eyewitnesses nor mere reporters of eyewitness accounts—had "historical raw material" available to them. In turn, they reshaped that material, drawing upon a trove of Old Testament citations, allusions, and midrash.[57]

In contrast, John Dominic Crossan argues that the passion narratives arose from "prophecy historicized" rather than from "history remembered."[58] That is, the disciples of Jesus, in trying to understand what had happened to Jesus, searched their Hebrew Scriptures, particularly the prophetic texts. Those texts gave rise to and were eventually embedded in the passion narratives.

Yet even if one were able to prove beyond a shadow of a doubt that the passion narratives are overwhelmingly literary-theological constructs with a minimal historical basis, the fact is that nearly two thousand years of a largely tormented history stand between us and the New Testament. To claim that a text lacks solid historical basis does not alone solve the problem that our "bitter offerings" caused. One needs ethical commitments and reading strategies to deal with troubling texts—an issue addressed in the final section of this book. As Amy-Jill Levine writes, "The only resolution to the question of New Testament anti-Judaism cannot come from historians. The elimination of anti-Jewish readings must come from theologians, from those members of the church who conclude that anti-Judaism is wrong and who insist on Christian sensitivity to the issue."[59] In view of how these troubling texts have functioned over the centuries, it imperative that Christian theologians present alternative interpretations of the death of Jesus.

Ultimately, the question of historicity cannot be solved, as the sources do not permit us certainty. It seems highly plausible that a few Jewish leaders, most likely from the high priestly family, were involved. Without question, the Roman Empire had no compunction about crucifying a Jew like Jesus who drew crowds, particularly when Jerusalem's population was swollen with pilgrims for the Passover feast.[60]

Gerard Sloyan argues that the historical substratum of the passion narratives may well be only that of Luke 23:1–2 in which Jesus was accused of "perverting our nation, forbidding us to pay taxes to the emperor, and saying that he himself is the Messiah, a king." He concludes that this text offers a sort of "hard core of reminiscence" of the last day (or days) of Jesus. It may be that "all the remaining details in the Gospels could have been elaborations of that remembered fact." He argues that after the resurrection the disciples of Jesus reconstructed the events of that Friday "on the basis of the fact that Roman justice disposed of him, after successful priestly efforts to counter his mounting popularity by bringing him up on a charge of sedition."[61] Then the evangelists developed these reminiscences in dramatic narratives that later centuries misinterpreted as historical documentation.[62] He concludes that it is impossible to know from the Gospels what sequence of events brought Jesus to the cross because "ambiguity is the hallmark of all four accounts."[63]

Sloyan uses the term *power class* to describe the opponents of Jesus in the passion, rather than Jewish authorities or Jewish leaders. Sloyan's nomenclature is crucial because it points to the alliance between the high priestly families and the Roman Empire, as represented by the office of the governor, Pontius Pilate. But, of course, this is not the term used by the Gospel writers. Why did they shift blame onto Jews? Sloyan offers a hypothesis. He notes that the evangelists would have assumed that Rome would engage in repressive behavior—this was the air they breathed, what they took for granted. The evangelists viewed the involvement of the high priest and Jerusalem council, both considered by many people as collaborators because of their allegiance to the Roman authorities, as another matter altogether. He speculates that as the movement grew beyond the borders of Palestine, what was perceived to be the "betrayal of God's just one, Jesus, by the highest religious authority in Judea would still have rankled." Continuing debates took place between the "Jesus Jews, with their admixture of Samaritan and gentile believers, and the bulk of Jews, undoubtedly far more law-observant in their ethnic homogeneity than this new band claiming to be Israel."[64] As a result, a polemic permeated the Gospel accounts "by means of exchanges reported as having taken place in Jesus' lifetime." For believers in Jesus, "he was the one great Jew who should have been accepted." The story of his rejection by religious authorities in Judea grew in their minds, and eventually four dramatizations were written. "In any event, this emphasis on the part played by the priests and 'the whole people' (Matt 27:25) has led to terrible consequences for Jews."[65]

Unless some as-yet-unknown first-century source were to be discovered, we lack sufficient evidence to know for certain why the New Testament writers assign blame to Jews. *What we do know is that we have compelling warrants for situating those texts in a wider horizon and for rethinking their theological meaning.*

176

Having established the historical context critical for understanding Jesus' crucifixion—and that of thousands of his fellow Jews—we turn now to new perspectives on the Apostle Paul and on the complexities of the terms *Jew* and *Christian* in the early centuries of the Common Era.

CHAPTER 8

New Perspectives on Troubling Texts II

Complicated Identities

We not only need to understand one another, we need
one another to understand ourselves.[1]

THE APOSTLE PAUL: IDENTITY AND MISSION

The review in chapter 3 of the texts used as source material for
hostility to Jews gave only brief attention to Paul's letters. Aside
from the troubling text in 1 Thessalonians 2:14–16, in which Paul
speaks of the Jews "who killed both the Lord Jesus and the
prophets," he manifested little interest in the events of the passion
and death of Jesus. Yet Paul's letters have been used as the primary
source of "misplaced caricaturistic opposites" such as legalism/faith,
flesh/spirit, fear/love, Law/Gospel, and Law/grace.[2] How we understand Paul in relationship to Judaism, therefore, becomes an important aspect of reworking our understanding of troubling texts.

Who was this Saul of Tarsus who became known as Paul? Was
he "Saint Paul," the zealous persecutor of Christians who converted
to Christianity after a mystical encounter with the Risen Christ on
the road to Damascus? Was he the passionate advocate for a Law-free
Gospel and the critic of the "works-righteousness" of Judaism? Or
was he so grounded in pagan mystery religions that he misinterpreted and misrepresented Rabbi Jesus, distorted Judaism, and

became the "inventor" of a mythical Christianity?[3] Or was Paul an "example of total dedication to the Lord and to his Church"?[4] Or was he not a Christian?[5] Or was he a "radical Jew" who "lived and died convinced that he was a Jew living out Judaism."[6]

Even the writer of 2 Peter found Paul's letters a challenge. "There are some things in them hard to understand, which the ignorant and unstable twist to their own destruction, as they do other scriptures" (3:16).

Understanding Paul situates us in the complex realm of religious identity in the Roman Empire in the middle of the first century, a time when boundaries between Jesus-believing Jews, Jesus-believing non-Jews, and Jews who did not believe in Jesus were very much in flux. Scholars today increasingly acknowledge that this fluidity complicates a simple identification of the post-Damascus Paul as a "Christian." Particularly in the last thirty years, Paul's relation to Judaism has taken center stage in biblical studies. Today, two opposing streams of thought about Paul coexist. The traditional view, which has been the prevailing paradigm, is that Saul was an educated and fervent Jew whose experience on the road to Damascus changed him irrevocably. Paul's mystical encounter with Christ formed him in a view of Christianity in which the "demands of Torah [Jewish legalism] had yielded to [Christ's] grace."[7] When we combine this characterization of Paul—Paul the convert to Christianity liberated from the works-righteousness and legalism of Judaism—with a reading of the canonical Gospels that attributes the death of Jesus to Jews (whether "the Jews," as in the Fourth Gospel, or groups of Jews, such as in the Synoptics), we have identified a critical element of what the Jewish historian Jules Isaac would centuries later term the "teaching of contempt."[8]

In contrast, a "new perspective on Paul" portrays him as faithful to Judaism, committed to thinking theologically about the relationship of non-Jews to the God of Israel and about the relationship of Jewish and non-Jewish followers of Jesus.[9] When read in tandem with the scholarship reviewed in the previous chapter situating the evangelists' telling of the passion and death of Jesus within the context of the Roman Empire, this portrait of Paul requires us to rethink his mission and meaning.

Within these broad streams of scholarship on Paul, many different rivulets flow. To trace all their varying directions, however, would take us far afield. What is most important is to see how standing in one broad stream or another shapes how we interpret Paul's writings on the passion.

Christ and the Law: Radical Incompatibility?

The view of Paul in which the "demands of Torah had yielded to grace" has long dominated Pauline scholarship, and thus has generated abundant literature.[10] Its premises are evident in an essay by the eminent scholar Jerome Murphy-O'Connor, "'Even Death on a Cross': Crucifixion in Pauline Letters" (2000).[11]

Murphy-O'Connor takes his title from the hymn in Philippians 2:6–11 (v. 8: "he humbled himself and became obedient to the point of death—even death on a cross"), which he sees as an indication that Christ chose to die by this mode of execution: "Christ chose death by crucifixion in order to demonstrate in the most radical way possible the completeness of his love for humanity."[12] Christ's self-sacrificial love has deeply affected Paul. In writing to the Galatians, Paul claims, "For through the law I died to the law, so that I might live to God. I have been crucified with Christ; and it is no longer I who live, but it is Christ who lives in me. And the life I now live in the flesh I live by faith in the Son of God, who loved me and gave himself for me" (2:19–20). As Murphy-O'Connor reads Paul, this means that the apostle no longer leads a life governed by the rules and regulations of the law, but rather by Christ's love, expressed most profoundly in the crucifixion. The cross of Christ is the "instrument that redefines Paul's relationship to the world."[13]

Similarly, in commenting on Galatians 6:14 ("May I never boast of anything except the cross of our Lord Jesus Christ, by which the world has been crucified to me, and I to the world"), Murphy-O'Connor looks to the larger context in which that boast is situated: the question of whether Jesus' male followers should be circumcised.[14] On that issue, Murphy-O'Connor writes:

> Manifestly, for such people [Jews and Judaizers] circumcision retains all its value as the symbol of belonging to the Chosen People, the channel of salvation. It is the defining

feature of their "world." Galatians 6:15–16 asserts the complete irrelevance of such symbolism, "Neither circumcision or uncircumcision counts for anything." *We have to do with a different world, another Israel, a new creation.*[15]

Thus, says Murphy-O'Connor, there is no word more appropriate than crucifixion to "bring out fundamental devaluation of all that the pre-Christian Paul had inherited from his Jewish 'world.'"[16] Crucifixion is the "decisive objection to any attempt to reconcile Christ and the Law"; there is a "radical incompatibility" between them: "Law inexorably bred legalism. To follow a pattern of external observances was infinitely easier than living the sacrificial love of the Crucified."[17] The crucifixion of Jesus "made the Law meaningless" (Galatians 3:13). Similarly, "acceptance of circumcision makes his sacrifice irrelevant. Once again, it was the modality of Christ's death that revealed the inherent powerlessness of any other channel of salvation."[18]

Murphy-O'Connor concludes:

> For Paul the will of God is very simple, and this lack of ambiguity terrifies us. It mandates the following of Christ who is defined by the cross. This is the revealed will of God. We must exhibit the self-sacrificing, empowering love that Christ showed in his crucifixion. We must bear in our bodies the dying of Jesus in order that the life of Jesus may be manifest to the world. Crucifixion is what makes a Christian.[19]

Although this brief summary of Murphy-O'Connor does not do justice to the rich detail of his essay, the principal lines of his arguments reveal widely held assumptions about Paul and Judaism. In fact, Murphy-O'Connor's reading is typical of a long line of interpreters.

In sum, the reading of Paul that has dominated both academic and pastoral interpretation until recently is as follows: "Judaism" and "Christianity" have clear lines of demarcation, and Paul has left the former for the latter; after his conversion on the road to Damascus, he stood outside Judaism and within Christianity. As Murphy-O'Connor and generations of interpreters have understood Paul, the

Apostle viewed Judaism as a religion of external observances. Under the influence of such interpreters, so have most Christians understood Paul and regarded Judaism as legalistic. Similarly, Paul's traditional interpreters have claimed that following the law's rules and regulations is burdensome; Judaism neither inspires nor requires the sacrificial love Christ showed on the cross and asks of his followers. Moreover, by his death on the cross, Jesus has brought salvation to the world and shown the ineffectiveness of Judaism—symbolized by circumcision—as a channel of salvation.

A comparable understanding of Paul on Judaism developed out of Martin Luther's distinction between the "active righteousness of the Law" and the "passive righteousness of Christ."[20] When in Galatians, for example, Paul challenges the "works of the law" (2:16 and 3:10; see also Romans 3:2), Luther and a long stream of well-known interpreters in his wake (for example, Rudolf Bultmann, Ernst Käsemann, and Günther Bornkamm) read this as a critique of self-righteousness. That is, following the Law entailed "earning" God's love through engaging in good works. Rather, these Lutheran scholars stressed, we are saved not by our good works but only by God's grace in Christ.

Scholars across a broad range of national and denominational boundaries have constructed an image of Paul and Christianity as the antithesis of Judaism. Even in the current era, many New Testament scholars and most preachers assume that Paul's theology resulted in his abandoning Judaism.[21] Each year Catholics celebrate the feast of the "Conversion of St. Paul" on January 25.

A Jesus-Believing Jewish Paul in His Roman Context

Paul, however, may be read through a different set of assumptions, such as the following: Paul was principally addressing non-Jews, not humankind in general. Accordingly, his major theological concerns focused on non-Jews, even with regard to Torah. His remarks on circumcision, for example, were not directed to Jews, but counsel to Gentiles. Paul showed little interest in how Jesus-believing Jews followed Torah. He understood himself as remaining within Judaism or the people Israel, while called to envision new ways of thinking about identifying and instructing non-Jewish believers in Jesus.

These assumptions rest on a prior claim: *Paul belonged to first-century Judaism.* This argument constitutes the common ground for what Magnus Zetterholm classifies as "radical new perspectives" on Paul.[22] By no means is this school of thought in complete agreement, although a clear consensus exists that Paul addressed Gentile followers of Jesus. Accordingly, he was not preoccupied with interpretations of Torah among Jews, nor did he consider that the Law constituted a "plight" for Jews. Paul's mystical encounter with the risen Christ, moreover, led him to take issue with Roman imperial ideology: *Jesus, not Caesar, was lord and savior—a dimension of Pauline thought largely obscured by traditional readings of Paul.*

The Cross: A Doctrine of Divine Justice and Partiality toward the Oppressed

New perspectives on Paul require engaging his enigmatic statements in Galatians, such as the apostle's claim that he had died to the Law (2:19–20; see citation above in discussion of Murphy-O'Connor). Then there is his famous charge that the Law was a "curse":

> For all who rely on the works of the law are under a curse; for it is written, "Cursed is everyone who does not observe and obey all the things written in the book of the law." Now it is evident that no one is justified before God by the law; for "The one who is righteous will live by faith." But the law does not rest on faith; on the contrary, "Whoever does the works of the law will live by them." Christ redeemed us from the curse of the law by becoming a curse for us—for it is written, "Cursed is everyone who hangs on a tree"—in order that in Christ Jesus the blessing of Abraham might come to the Gentiles, so that we might receive the promise of the Spirit through faith. (Galatians 3:10–14)

Murphy-O'Connor is only one in a long line of scholars who have read such passages as asserting that Paul is no longer *constricted* by Judaism's rules and regulations. Neil Elliott, however, offers a counter reading. Elliott argues that traditional interpretation has rested on the notion that Paul is describing Judaism's "plight," that is, that Jews are trapped insofar as they can neither keep all of the Law's commandments nor justify themselves. In the conventional reading, Christ's death is the "solution" to their plight. The plight/solution paradigm is inadequate, he says, for three reasons: (1) it rests on an erroneous understanding of Judaism that did not equate perfect observance of the commandments with righteousness before God; (2) it mistakenly assumes that for Jews faith and the Law (see Galatians 3:11–12) were opposed; and (3) it assumes that the covenant relationship symbolized by Torah was inherently defective from the beginning. Rather, Elliott says, Israel's "plight" rests in its failure as a people to live according to the covenant.[23]

In the citation above from Galatians 3, Paul twice refers to Deuteronomy—the "book of the law." But Paul here is not thinking primarily about the transgressions of individuals but rather of the covenant between God and the people, the emphasis of the latter chapters of that book.[24] In the perspective of the Deuteronomist, blessings come to those who keep the covenant, and curses to those who abandon it—including being uprooted from the land and exiled. In Paul's day, Roman occupation and lordship were a curse, a state of exile: "As long as Herod and Pilate were in control of Palestine, Israel was still under the curse of Deuteronomy.[29] This was not a matter of private theological judgment or insight....It was publicly observable fact."[25] Insofar as the people of the covenant had been enticed by Rome's values and benefactions—the "works of the law"—they had committed idolatry.

By saying that Christ "redeemed us from the curse of the law," Paul may be read as presenting Jesus as the representative of Israel who takes on Israel's curse and exhausts it: "Jesus dies as the King of the Jews, at the hands of the Romans whose oppression of Israel is the present, and climactic, form of the curse of exile itself."[26] Thus, in Galatians 3 Paul is not focused on the nature of Torah. His emphasis, rather, lies on what God has brought about in the death and resurrection of Jesus Christ.

Paul is passionate in his attempts to dissuade the Gentiles in Galatia from taking on Jewish practices ("judaizing") such as male circumcision or observance of the dietary laws. He even accuses judaizing Gentiles of being "foolish" (Galatians 1:1). But Paul's reasoning is not based on the belief that the Torah is no longer valid or that by adopting Torah the Gentiles will, like Jews, be under the law's curse. Rather, from Paul's point of view, *all* nations ruled by Rome fell under the "curse of the [Roman] law." Thus, "the region where the curse pertains is not Judaism as such."[27] Paul, rather, seeks to persuade the Gentiles that they should not pursue their own way with Torah because they will not be able to find a path to righteous living apart from the historical course of the covenant between God and Israel.

Elliott speaks of Paul's "doctrine" of the cross as one of "God's justice and God's partiality toward the oppressed":

> In the crucifixion of the Messiah at the hands of the Roman oppressors, God has recapitulated the history of Israel's exile and brought it to a decisive climax; indeed, in a slave's death on a cross (Phil 2:8) the enslavement of the whole creation is embodied (Rom 8:20–22). Thus, for Paul...the most important aspect of Jesus' humanity is the "*partisan* quality of this humanity," revealed for Paul precisely in the Messiah's embodying the fate of a crucified people.[28]

Paul understood the crucifixion less as a miscarriage of Roman justice and more as an apocalyptic event that revealed the hostility of the "rulers of this age" (1 Corinthians 2:6, 8) to God's reign. Thus, the death and resurrection of Jesus inaugurated God's final "war of liberation" against those powers who ruled by violence and oppressed the poor. For the Roman elite—among the "rulers of this age"—talk about the torturous death of the crucified was distasteful. Paul, however, insisted on talking about it; he placed the cross at the center of his rhetoric because the death of Jesus meant the beginning of the dissolution of Roman rule. And when Paul spoke about baptism as a dying and rising with Christ that enabled persons to "walk in newness of life" (Romans 6:4), he was thinking on a grand scale: "Through baptism, the death *and resurrection* of Christ transfers men and women from the cosmic sphere of sin and death to the sphere of God's justifying, sanctifying and life-giving power."[29] Similarly, when Paul spoke of Jesus' followers as free from the condemnation of the

Law, it was not that the crucifixion had invalidated the Law, but that it no longer applied to the baptized, who had died to sin.[30]

Paul and Judaism

Common to those whom Zetterholm classifies under the rubric of a "radical new perspective" on Paul is a deeper and more adequate understanding of Judaism than had been held by traditional theorists. Scholars such as E. P. Sanders opened up fresh ways of thinking about the role of Torah in Second Temple Judaism. In his impressive analysis of an array of texts in his 1977 *Paul and Palestinian Judaism*, Sanders revealed the importance of the covenantal relationship and overturned the conventional conclusion that Judaism was a legalistic religion of works-righteousness. Today, a number of scholars argue for views that transcend the new perspectives, including situating Paul within Hellenistic Judaism or even, as Mark Nanos argues, claiming that the Apostle was Torah-observant.[31] Among those who "return" Paul to Judaism, Pamela Eisenbaum contends that Paul's mystical encounter with the risen Christ on the road to Damascus may have altered the "constellation of his theological universe," but not his universe itself, that is, the realm of Judaism.[32] What was new was how he understood the moment of history of which he was a part. The end of time was drawing closer. So also was the epoch when all the nations (the Gentiles) would go up to Zion in acknowledgement of the one, true God, the God of Israel in fulfillment of Isaiah's vision:

> In days to come the mountain of the LORD's house shall be established as the highest of the mountains, and shall be raised above the hills; all the nations shall stream to it. Many peoples shall come and say, "Come, let us go up to the mountain of the LORD, to the house of the God of Jacob; that he may teach us his ways and that we may walk in his paths. For out of Zion shall go forth instruction and the word of the LORD from Jerusalem." (Isaiah 2:1–3)

Paul's utopian, monotheist vision of the gathering of the varied nations shaped his perspective on what he taught about the Law—the Torah—to the Gentiles. In condemning Gentile observance of

Torah with regard to circumcision and dietary laws, for example, Paul is not condemning the Torah's prescriptions of Jewish boundary markers. Rather, Paul regarded *Gentile* attempts to take on such practices after the death-resurrection of Jesus as doubting God's promises. If, at the end of days God were to be recognized as God of the entire world, then it would be necessary for the different nations of the world to gather as the nations—not as part of the Jewish people. Yet this created an anomaly at the core of the controversy in Galatia. Paula Fredriksen observes:

> By insisting both that the Gentiles *not* convert to Judaism (thus maintaining their public and legal status as pagan) and that they nonetheless *not* worship the gods (a protected right only of Jews), Paul walked these Gentiles-in-Christ into a social and religious no-man's-land. In the time before the Parousia, they literally had no place to be. And in the long run, their position would prove untenable: It is precisely this Gentile group who fall victim to anti-Christian persecutions in the long centuries until the conversion, in 312, of Constantine.[33]

Paul's insistence that the Galatians remain unmarked by circumcision yet refuse to participate in the rituals of imperial religion upset the civic arrangement. They belonged to Christ, not to Caesar, an identity the Roman rulers could not tolerate. Jews, too, likely would have had reservations about this anomalous situation, since it endangered the status quo regarding the agreement they had forged with the Empire in order to preserve their monotheism.

As the Apostle to the Gentiles, it is Paul's call to integrate non-Jews into the family of Abraham, regarded in Jewish tradition as the first monotheist. Like Abraham, called to abandon what was familiar so as to witness to the one true God among foreigners, Paul was the "new Abraham," living among Gentiles so as to instruct them in the futility of idolatry and the wisdom of worshipping the one true God.[34] According to Eisenbaum, Paul's notion of "justification by faith" principally concerns the way in which the faithfulness of Jesus, "obedient to the point of death—even death on a cross" (Philippians 2:8)—atoned for the sins of Gentiles, thereby making them "right" with God and incorporating them into the Abrahamic family. He was not preoccupied with the question of how individuals were "saved," but rather with how God would reconcile all people, Jew and Gentile. "All will be kin; none will be strangers, but the Gentile will not become Jew, and the Jew will not become Gentile."[35]

Paul and the Roman Empire

Two recent studies utilize material culture as a complement to textual analysis to situate Paul within the world of the Roman Empire, and thereby to offer a new lens on the Jewish Paul. Through analysis of visual representations of Roman conquest—typically of a virile Roman subduing a defeated woman—and of textual representations of Roman destiny and superiority, Davina Lopez portrays Paul as a Jewish critic of the ideology in which Caesar was lord and savior. Paul was sent to the conquered nations to witness to a different sort of power, God's wisdom.[36]

Lopez argues that Paul's experience on the road to Damascus resulted in his becoming a different kind of Jew—and a different sort of man, even one characterized by a kind of gender instability. In persecuting followers of Jesus, Paul had been replicating the Roman mode of violent domination.[37] After "God…set me apart before I was born and called me through his grace, [and] was pleased to reveal his Son to me so that I might proclaim him among the Gentiles [en tois ethnesin]" (Galatians 1:15–16), Paul changed. It was then said of him: "The one who formerly was persecuting us is now proclaiming the faith he once tried to destroy" (Galatians 1:23). Like Jeremiah (1:5) and Isaiah (49:1), Paul had been called from the womb; in being sent to the nations, he, too, had become a "prophet to the nations" (Jeremiah 1:5). He had become Israel, sent to be a "light to the nations" (Isaiah 49:6) who are all connected through their common creator (Genesis 10).

Paul's call leads to a heightened awareness that the Jews are among the nations ravaged by Rome. It is this consciousness that gave rise to Paul's crucifixion language in Galatians (2:19; 3:1; 3:13; 4:12; 6:14, 17).[38] In contrast to traditional interpretations of "Christ is revealed in Paul," Lopez says that God has revealed to Paul that "he has Christ in him, that he has the dynamic of defeat by the Romans within him."[39] Thus, Paul considers himself dead to the world and crucified with Christ (2:19); he bears the marks of Christ on his body (6:17), and boasts only in the cross (6:14). This she calls "Christ in Paul," a phrase that "signifies awareness of that theo-political imagery [of Roman violence], its pervasiveness, and his role in affirming the world order it naturalizes. Persecution is not something Paul should do to others, since he himself is persecuted by the very dynamics he duplicates."[40] In other words, "Christ in Paul" has led to a "shift in consciousness" in which he has become more conscious of the particularity of his Jewishness and of his commonalities with members of others nations in the Roman Empire. Paul has "come to consciousness as a marginalized person."[41]

Paul's awareness that he is among the marginalized can be discerned from his self-description of being worn down by the trauma of bodily injury.[42] Unlike the Roman conquerors, he models a "defeated, and not heroic, male body. His defeated body is identified with slavery and with Christ, who is in him and crucified alongside him."[43]

Lopez's mentor (and my colleague), Brigitte Kahl, analyzes key images of imperial rule—for example, sculptures of conquered peoples, the Great Altar of Pergamon, and Virgil's description of the shield of Aeneas in Book 8 of the *Aeneid*—to meticulously construct a case that Paul's denunciation of the "works of the law" (*erga tou nomou*) should be read as a critique of Roman law (*nomos*) rather than of Torah observance.[44] Paul's insistence, moreover, on the image of the crucified Christ was the messianic counter-vision to the images of the divine Caesar.

Precisely because the equation of "works of the law" with Jewish observance of Torah has played such a crucial role in Protestant biblical theology, Kahl's analysis of imperial religiosity, manifest in public rituals and performances that were the "benefactions" of the emperor and priests that kept the conquered nations as obedient subjects, is of great importance. By becoming soldiers in the empire's war machine, and by participating in empire-sponsored festivals, banquets, and competition, as well as beholding the spectacles of torture and execution in the amphitheaters, Galatians engaged in "upholding and reproducing the 'combat order' of the imperial world constructs with the victorious self at the top."[45] This may have "justified" the Galatians in the empire's perspective, but not in God's new creation: In Christ, the hierarchy of conqueror/conquered dissolves.

"All are one in Christ Jesus" (Galatians 3:28). Having been crucified with Christ (Galatians 2:19b), the Galatians—the vanquished, conquered nations—receive the blessings of Abraham and the promise of the Spirit through faith (see Galatians 3:14):

> To see the image of the crucified not as the image of an evil other to be lawfully destroyed but as the image of the world savior and divine life-giver, shatters all the images of power that were the embodiment of imperial ideology....To substitute "works of the (imperial) law" by faith in the crucified, as Paul urges...destroys the very foundations of warfare, victory, and the imperial power establishment built on it. It dismantles the self/other perceptions that are produced in the public spectacles of the arena as rigorously as the basic notions of godhead and supreme power ingrained in the observances of imperial religion.[46]

So how, then, does Kahl understand Paul's insistence in Galatians that "in Christ neither circumcision nor uncircumcision counts for anything" (5:6)? In contrast to Murphy-O'Connor, for whom circumcision symbolized the ineffectiveness of Judaism, Kahl reads Paul here as advocating for the Galatians' "disorderly identity." That is, unlike the Jews, the (male) Galatians were to retain their foreskins. In so doing, they were fulfilling the eschatological vision of Isaiah (2:2–3) and Zephaniah (3:9) in which at the end of time the nations went up to Jerusalem. By refusing circumcision they retained their status as "the nations," non-Jews called to worship the one God of Israel. Kahl regards Paul's denial of "legible identity markers in the age of the Messiah" as the core of the Galatian controversy. In her view, going against a well-established body of scholarship, the Galatian conflict was less about Jewish religion than about the "precarious status of Jewish and non-Jewish communities alike when they stepped outside of conformity with the law and religion of the Roman city and the Roman Empire."

Kahl continues:

> In practical terms, Paul destroys the flexibility pagan adherents to the synagogue would normally have enjoyed

with regard to their civic obligations and requires them to observe what he sees as the chief commandment of Torah: not to worship any deity except God alone. But he refuses them circumcision because, for him, in the resurrection of Jesus as apocalyptic turning point, God has reclaimed his visible sovereignty over Jews and nations alike. What is called for is nothing less than a new type of "transnational" obedience, including Jews and non-Jews, self and other alike with all their differences, in one messianic community that worships God alone. Emperor Claudius might describe it differently as a "general plague infecting the whole world."[47]

In Kahl's judgment, Paul is a radical Jew who adheres to strict monotheism, in contrast to the imperial theology in which Caesar was worshipped as god. He places the new messianic community at the core of his argument in Galatians, insisting that God's oneness means that both self and "other" have become one in Christ. In Caesar's reign, one consumes the other as a commodity. In God's reign, however, self and other are reconciled in a "noncompetitive and nonhierarchical body of 'new life.'"[48]

Situating Paul within the context of the Roman Empire—"a militarily created hegemony of immense land mass that harboured hundreds, if not thousands of different societies"[49]—also permits a new perspective on the passage from 1 Thessalonians 2:14–16 in which Paul speaks of "the Jews, who killed both the Lord Jesus and the prophets, and drove us out" (briefly discussed in chapter 3). An extensive literature bears witness to the various controversies the text has spawned.[50] Without entering into the complexities of the various commentaries, attentiveness to the ways in which many in Thessalonica, particularly among its aristocratic members, cultivated and profited from Roman beneficence opens new perspectives on this passage. Just as some among the Jewish ruling elite in Judea, particularly the high priestly family, had accommodated themselves to imperial mores, so, too had elites in Thessalonica.[51] Given the pro-Roman atmosphere that had brought suffering to Paul's assembly in Thessalonica, and the similarities with pro-Roman Judean rules against other Jewish groups, "it seems likely that in 1 Thess 2:13–16

Paul is criticizing the pro-Roman aristocracy in Thessalonica by way of an analogy with the pro-Roman rulers of Judea."[52]

In sum, a rich body of scholarship offers us a new context in which we might view Paul's identity and mission: as a Jesus-believing Jew whose gospel of the Lord Christ contrasted dramatically with the Roman imperial order of hierarchy, power relations, and salvation by the "rulers of this age."[53] Jesus is Lord, not Caesar. Caesar, represented by Pontius Pilate in Judea, could not tolerate a messianic figure who proclaimed "release to the captives" and letting the "oppressed go free" (Luke 4:18). Roman rulers had little forbearance for Jewish prophets whose followers considered the reign of the one true God to be the only kingdom that mattered.

COMPLICATED BOUNDARIES

Today we tend to think of Judaism and Christianity as well established, relatively homogeneous, and distinct religious traditions. Typically, the firm boundaries between these traditions are assumed when we read about Jews (*Ioudaioi*) in the New Testament, often to the point of erasing the Jewishness of Jesus and his disciples. It is likely that many, if not most, people assume that Christianity began with Jesus or shortly after the death and resurrection of Jesus Christ ca. 30 or 33 C.E. Others date its inauguration to the mid-50s, attributing the distinctiveness of Christianity—and its separation from Judaism—to the Apostle Paul. Yet as scholars have proposed a "more complex and capacious" understanding of Judaism, they have similarly revealed an extended and complex separation between "Jews" and "Christians."[54] The new perspectives on Paul, discussed above, result from that scholarship. Particularly in the last several decades, numerous studies have challenged conventional assumptions about terminology and described new contours of the process by which Judaism and Christianity became separate religions. Rethinking our assumptions will pay rich dividends for understanding the New Testament texts about the passion and death of Jesus as we consider: (1) the fluidity of "Jewish" and "Christian" identity in the early centuries, (2) the protracted process by which the two traditions eventually separated, and (3) the relationship between the

"rhetoric of invidious contrast" in Christian writings and social realities of everyday life between Jews and Christians.[55]

Fluidity of Identity

In the late 1980s, the title of the anthology *Judaisms and Their
Messiahs at the Turn of the Christian Era* signaled the necessity of
honoring diverse ways of Jewish practice and belief. The argument
was that the varied ways in which Jews lived and understood themselves in the period of Second Temple Judaism (from the rebuilding
of the temple in Jerusalem ca. 520 B.C.E to its destruction by the
Romans in 70 C.E.) constituted a plurality of "Judaisms":

> In ancient times, as in every age of the history of the
> Jewish people, diverse groups of Jews have defined for
> themselves distinctive ways of life and world views. A
> Judaism therefore constitutes the world view and the way
> of life that characterize the distinctive system by which a
> social group of Jews works out its affairs. True, these sev-
> eral systems produced by different groups of Jews
> assuredly do exhibit traits in common. For example, they
> universally appeal to the same Hebrew Scriptures. But in
> fact points in common underline the systems' essential
> diversity. For if we ask a group to specify those verses of
> Scripture it finds critical and to explain their meaning, we
> rarely hear from one a repertoire of verses found equally
> central in the system of some other distinct group.[56]

Although the terminology of "Judaisms" has not been widely
adopted, the underlying premise has been accepted: the heterogene-
ity of Second Temple Judaism is well established. James Charlesworth,
for example, suggests the era encompassed as many as twenty Jewish
groups—not only the better known ones, such as the Pharisees,
Sadducees, Essenes, and Zealots, but also Samaritans, Boethusians,
Baptist, and Enoch groups. Among these groups was the Palestinian
Jesus Movement. What we have typically called early Christianity
should be regarded as a Jewish phenomenon.[57]

But then, what precisely makes a phenomenon "Jewish"? It is
now clear that the term *Jew—Yehudi* in Hebrew, *Ioudaios* in Greek

[feminine, *Ioudaia*; plural, *Ioudaioi*]—had a range of meanings that changed over time.[58] Before about 100 B.C.E., it meant a Judean, a member of the people of the homeland, Judea; it was both a geographic and ethnic designation. This meaning never completely disappeared, but after the clash with Greek culture during the Maccabean revolt and Hasmonean period, it came to be complemented by a political meaning as well as religious/cultural one. A *Ioudaios* was a citizen or ally of the Judean state; the *Ioudaioi* formed a political community, and membership could be extended even to those outside of Judea, such as to the Idumaeans and Ituraeans. Around the same time, a third meaning emerged. A *Ioudaios* [or *Ioudaia*] was someone who believed in certain distinctive tenets and followed certain distinctive practices, such as worshipping the one God, offering sacrifice in the temple in Jerusalem, and observing dietary and purity norms. In this usage, "Jew" denotes culture, way of life, or "religion," rather than an ethnic or geographic origin.

The first use of the term *Ioudaismos*—normally translated as "Judaism"—occurs in 2 Maccabees (for example, 2:21 and 14:37–44). Shaye J. D. Cohen, among others, argues this translation is too narrow because it does not yet designate a religion. Rather, here *Ioudaismos* means the:

> aggregate of all those characteristics that make Judaeans Judaean (or Jews Jewish). Among these characteristics, to be sure, are practices and belief that we would today call "religious," but these practices and beliefs are not the sole content of the term. Thus, *Ioudaismos* should be translated not as "Judaism" but as Judaeanness. Its antonym is the adoption of foreign ways or "paganness," and more particularly, *Hellenismos*, the adoption of "Greek" ways.[59]

This shifting range of semantic meanings for *Ioudaios* suggests that when the New Testament speaks of "the Jews," particularly in the Acts of the Apostles and the Gospel of John, the term may not carry precisely the same meaning in each use.[60] Perhaps translators might better speak to the range of meanings were they to qualify the text, such as "certain Judeans" or "some Judean leaders," or "certain Jewish authorities."[61] Another important implication may be found in Daniel Boyarin's argument that *Ioudaismos* was transformed into a "religion" with national, ethnic, and cultural components only after the emergence of *Christianismos,* that is, "Christianness." Only in Christian literature does *Ioudaismos* come to refer to a religiously Jewish way of life.[62] In Boyarin's analysis, the eventual formation of Christianity led to the formation of religion as a discrete category of human experience.

The fluid boundaries in early antiquity between what later became Judaism and Christianity suggest that historical imagination is a prerequisite when approaching texts from this period, lest we impose categories from our own experience. Boyarin offers two linguistic metaphors by which we might more imaginatively approach the relation of Jews and Christians in the second and third centuries. In his 1999 *Dying for God*, he used the analogy of dialects: While French is today the official language on the French side of the border separating it from Italy (where Italian is spoken), such distinctiveness has not always been the case. In the Early Middle Ages, one Romance dialect would have been spoken in Paris, and another in Rome. As a person traveled from Paris southward toward the current border with Italy, no sudden change from one language to the other would have transpired. Instead, more and more elements of the Roman dialect would become apparent, while the Parisian elements would gradually fade.[63] Thus, we should think of Jews and Christians as more like dialects than as separate languages. Boyarin offers a second metaphor, a "wave theory" of relationship. If we think of Judaism and Christianity as points in the middle of a continuum, with Marcionites (followers of Marcion, d. 160, who rejected the Old Testament entirely) on one extreme and Jews for whom Jesus meant nothing on the other extreme, we would find many gradations in the middle. The similar beliefs and practices in the middle disseminated and interacted "like waves caused by stones thrown in a pond," both converging and diverging. Shared cultural and religious innovations flowed in both directions, thereby offering "social contiguity and contact and even cultural continuity."[64]

The Protracted Process of Separation

Another significant contribution to a more precise understanding of the relations of "Judaisms" and "Christianities" may be found in the work of biblical scholar James D. G. Dunn in the early 1990s. He offered language that dominated scholarship for some time when he spoke of three "partings of the ways" that eventuated in separate Jewish and Christian communities. The first parting had to do with the development of a critique of the temple and its sacrificial system. The second arose from the erasure of boundary markers (for example, dietary laws and circumcision for males) as more and more Gentiles were drawn into following the Way of Jesus. Dunn attributes the third parting to the post-resurrectional Christology that developed in the early second century and appeared to challenge the boundaries of Jewish monotheism. After the failed Bar Kochba rebellion in 135 C.E. against Rome, Dunn claims that Jewish followers of Jesus could no longer consider themselves both Jews and Christians.[65]

Without question, Dunn considerably advanced the question by identifying multiple factors and a lengthier process in the eventual separation. More recently, however, numerous scholars have taken issue with the very notion of *the* partings of the ways, as is evident in the title of a 2003 collection of essays entitled *The Ways That Never Parted*. The ways, of course, did eventually part, but at different times, under different circumstances, and in different locations—and never completely, since Jews and Christians have interacted continuously over the centuries. Perhaps the fourth century C.E. was *a* decisive turning point (for example, the Council of Nicea in 325), but, given the many variant forms of Judaism and Christianity, no single, definitive turning point can be accurately identified:

> For example, the essential difference between Judaism and Christianity continued to be asserted and reasserted and reasserted again by proto-orthodox and orthodox church leaders, thereby suggesting that the incompatibility of Jewish and Christian "ways" remained less clear for others in their midst....Jews and Christians (or at least the elite among them) may have been engaged in the task of "parting" throughout Late Antiquity and the early Middle Ages, *precisely because* the two never really "parted" during that period with the degree of decisiveness or finality needed to render either tradition irrelevant to the self-

definition of the other, or even to make participation in both an unattractive or inconceivable option.[66]

In brief, the complex process by which Judaism and Christianity came to define themselves in mutually exclusive terms developed over the course of several centuries. In this period, church leaders tended to speak the language of "invidious contrast," whereas the boundary lines for many of the more "ordinary" followers of Jesus were more fluid (for example, John Chrysostom's diatribes against "Judaizing Christians" who participated in the worship of both church and synagogue).[67]

A key implication is that we must acknowledge the complications of the term *Christian* in the first three centuries. Some, particularly among religious leaders who gained ascendancy, understood following the Way of Christ as a path separate from and superior to Judaism. For many others, the boundary was blurred; the Way of Christ did not preclude connection to Jewish beliefs and practices.

Rhetoric and Reality

Over the centuries, the New Testament texts examined in chapter 3 became fundamental components of anti-Jewish rhetoric. In the early church an entire literature developed among the literary elite that a later age categorized as *Adversus Judaeos* (Against Jews).[68] In this rhetorical realm, certain themes formed a constellation of charges. The north star of the constellation was the claim that the Jews as a people are Christ-killers; surrounding this were accusations of their faithlessness, blindness, carnality, and legalism. These claims resonated through theological commentary, pastoral exhortation, and popular culture. They have not entirely disappeared, though they appear less often now, especially in the churches of the West that have sought to repair relations with Jews.

The rhetorical realm, however, should not be regarded as a mirror of social reality. Even in the second, third, and fourth centuries, when the anti-Jewish rhetoric flourished, there is "abundant and continuous evidence of intimate social interaction" between Jews and Christians.[69] Moreover, the complexities of changing societies and cultural variations lay veiled beneath the consistent anti-Jewish invective. As Judith Lieu observes, ideological or doctrinal literature tends to stress differentiation. The realm of social and religious experience, however, tends to be less tidy.[70] Anti-Jewish attitudes varied in tone, intensity, and effect. The anti-Jewish literature of the second century, for example, constructed images of Jews that shifted with author, context, and literary genre.[71] More hostility became evident in the fourth century as post-Constantinian Christianity gained political power: "In the Christianized empire, Judaism came to be perceived as the only remaining major negation of the universally proclaimed truth. What had been a family argument now came to be perceived as a permanent and public insult to God and His true faith."[72]

Anti-Jewish rhetoric was not primarily about the religious other. It served a significant function in the formation and maintenance of Christian identity as the church developed from its origins as an illegal religious minority. Struggling to find its niche in Roman society, Christianity appeared to be an "upstart cult no longer covered by the respected antiquity of Judaism."[73] Christians needed to justify their existence and to explain its teachings both to a skeptical culture and to its own adherents. As Paula Fredriksen writes, "polemics ostensibly directed against outsiders work rhetorically to establish definitions of community for insiders." Jews were the crucial "other" against which orthodox Christian belief and practice might be calibrated.[74] Polemics may seem to be directed against the other, but a prime function is to strengthen the religious identity of believers.

The linkage of polemics with religious identity rests on the recognition of the role that binary oppositions play in the construction of identity. Forming clear boundaries of "us" and "them" constitutes a common and powerful way in which individuals and groups express their self-understanding.[75] In the case of Christianity, rivalry with pagans and Jews was crucial to its development. Yet oppositional identity was (and is) destructive, particularly when complemented by a vast power differential and differences exaggerated in ways that dehumanized the other.

Jewish Characterizations of the "Christian" Other

The struggle for self-definition and characterization of the other was an issue for Jews as well. Israeli historian Israel Jacob Yuval locates the confrontation with Christianity at the heart of Midrashic and Talmudic Judaism, but it was a confrontation done in a "very circuitous and complex conversation."[76] Against the dominant reading in which Christian literature and ritual are regarded as having their origins in Judaism, Yuval argues for a two-way street in which Christianity also shaped Jewish expression. While no extant Jewish polemical works against Christianity existed prior to the ninth century, he argues that those who tune their ears to listen to "more hidden tones" will hear "rustlings of subtle hints intended to counter the claims of 'heretics.'"[77] For example, Yuval argues that the Passover Haggadah should be regarded as a Jewish "countergospel." He suggests that in the early centuries, it was "story against story, Haggadah against Haggadah."[78] After the destruction of Jerusalem and its temple in 70 C.E., both the followers of Jesus and (other) Jews drew upon the Exodus event to make meaning of their existence, albeit in varying ways. Jews who had not followed Jesus told the story that began as slavery and ended in deliverance as a narrative of hope for their future liberation (from Rome, initially). The followers of Jesus told the story that began with the "enslavement" of the passion and death of Jesus and ended with his liberation at Easter as a narrative of hope for the second coming of Jesus (the *Parousia*).

Yuval claims that while the Passover Haggadah makes no explicit mention of Christianity, two complementary processes were at work: an external polemic and a redefinition of identity. This can be seen, among other places, in the Jewish liturgical poem (*piyyut*), the *Dayyenu* ("We should have been contented" or "We should have thought it enough"):

> God has bestowed many favors on us.
> Had he brought us out of Egypt
> And not punished the Egyptians,
> *Dayyenu,...*
> Had he sustained us in wasteland,
> And not fed us with manna,
> *Dayyenu,...*
> Had he brought us to Mount Sinai,
> and not given us the Torah,
> *Dayyenu*

Had he given us the Torah,
and not brought us to Israel,
Dayyenu,

Had he brought us to Israel,
And not built the Temple for us,
Dayyenu.[79]

While the earliest known text of the Dayyenu is from the tenth century, it was likely created considerably earlier. Yuval reads it as a response to Christian accusations in the second century that Jews, by killing Christ, were ungrateful to God—precisely the charge that Melito of Sardis had leveled in his *Homily on the Passover:*

> Come, ungrateful Israel, be judged before my face for your ingratitude.
> What value have you set on his guiding you? What value have you set on his election of your fathers? What value have you set on the descent into Egypt and your being nourished there by that good man, Joseph?…What value have you set on the gift of manna from heaven and the possession of water from the rock and the giving of the Law on Horeb?…You, however, without honoring him, have repaid him with ingratitude. You have repaid him evil for good and affliction for joy and death for life—to him on whose account you ought to have died.[80]

By ending the *Dayyenu* with the temple, Yuval claims that its author evoked the atoning sacrifices of temple worship, in contrast to Jesus' atoning sacrifice on Calvary. The Passover Haggadah does not explicitly reject Christianity but it does contest its validity of its theological and eschatological interpretations. It was a "covert dialogue with a rival liturgy."[81] Yuval concludes that the literature of the Talmudic Sages should be regarded both as a source for Christian ideas and ceremonies and as a "response to the challenge posed by Christianity to Judaism, for the Oral Torah is, in the deepest sense, a Jewish answer to the Christian Torah, the New Testament."[82]

Adiel Schremer adds an important perspective on the complicated boundaries of the first centuries of the Common Era. He
regards rabbinic discourse about heresy—*minut*—and heretics—
minim—as more about aloofness from those deemed a threat to the
fragile post–Bar Kochba community, with its "frantic sensitivity to
identity and difference."[83] Schremer claims that the polemics found
in the sayings of the second-century Palestinian rabbis (the *Tannaim*)
were principally directed against the Roman Empire. He speculates
that the followers of Jesus eventually became *minim* because they
were known to have established their own congregations. This sepa-
ratism was regarded as a threat to the unity and social identity of the
Jewish community. Labeling them as *minim* ultimately transformed
them into a social other, that is, Christians. Schremer concludes:
"The ways of Judaism and Christianity did not 'part'; the followers of
Jesus were labeled as *minim*, viewed as separatists who joined the
nations of the world, marginalized, placed beyond the pale, excluded
from the Jewish community."[84]

One further instance of Jewish characterizations of the other,
the *birkat haminim*, deserves mention. As the twelfth of the Eighteen
Benedictions (the *Amidah*) to be recited in weekday Jewish liturgies,
it expresses the hope that the "*minim* immediately perish" (or "be
blotted out of the Book of Life," etc.; the wording varied). A once-
influential stream of Christian scholarship claimed that the *birkat
haminim* lay behind the assertion in John 9:22 (see also 12:42 and
16:2) that the parents of the man born blind were "afraid of the Jews;
for the Jews had already agreed that anyone who confessed Jesus to
be the Messiah would be put out of the synagogue" (*aposynagogos*).[85]
Thus, the *birkah haminin* became a hypothesis to explain the hostility in the Fourth Gospel to "the Jews": John's (Jewish-Christian)
community had been excommunicated from the synagogue. Among
a number of Christian students of the New Testament, it became a
commonplace understanding in the 1980s that by about 90 C.E.,
Jews had expelled Christians from their synagogues via the *birkat
haminim*, since the followers of Christ would not be able to recite it
in good conscience.

But such a boundary construction could not be sustained under
more rigorous analysis of the *birkat haminim*.[86] As Ruth Langer documents in her extensive study of the *birkat haminim*, we have neither

a reliable reconstruction of the original text nor a grasp of who the *minim* originally were. Nor can we be certain that the *birkat haminim* became a part of the Jewish liturgy as a specific response to Christianity.[87] Lacking indisputable evidence that Christians knew of or reacted to it until the end of the fourth century, the *birkat haminim* does not substantiate a firm boundary between Jews and Christians in the late first or early second century. The fluidity of identity in the first three centuries of the Common Era requires us to be cautious in speaking of "Judaism" and "Christianity" as if each was a fully established and separate religious tradition.

The scholarship reviewed in chapters 7 and 8 holds vital implications for how we interpret the New Testament's troubling texts on the passion and death of Jesus because it fundamentally reorients how we construe the conflicts that gave rise to those events, Paul's identity and mission, and the boundaries between "Christians" and "Jews."

1. Jesus stands not in primary opposition to Judaism but to the Empire over which Caesar rules as lord and savior. Responsibility for his death falls not to "the Jews" but to the Roman governor, Pontius Pilate, in alliance with the power class. Jesus, the Jew from Nazareth, suffers the excruciating death by crucifixion not as the lone victim of Jewish hostility to the Son of God, but as one of thousands of Jews (and others) whom the Empire tortured as a deterrent, lest they resist its rule.

2. Living under the "curse" of Roman domination, Paul viewed the death and resurrection of Jesus as the beginning of the dissolution of its rule. Paul was neither a critic of Torah nor a "convert" to "Christianity," but a Jew whose mystical encounter with Christ called him to integrate non-Jews into the family of Abraham. Called to preach Christ crucified and risen from the dead beyond the boundaries of Judaism, Paul regarded Gentile attempts to take on the Torah's boundary markers of dietary practices and circumcision as questioning God's promises and mimicking Roman order and law.

3. The process by which Judaism and Christianity became separate religions took several centuries. Until well into the third

century, "Christians" and "Jews" were more like dialects of a single language (for example, Spanish speakers in Cuba and Mexico) than separate languages. There was no single and definitive point of separation; the "dialects" became separate "languages" at different times, under different circumstances, and in different locations. The protracted process of separation included polemical exchange, but this rhetoric principally concerned the formation and maintenance of a community's identity. Yet while the writings of the literary elite tended to stress differentiation, evidence attests to extensive social interaction among Jews and Christians.

In view of this evidence, reinterpretation of troubling texts is a fundamental responsibility of Christians in our religiously diverse world. The next chapter continues the exploration of this responsibility.

CHAPTER 9

Turn It and Turn It Again

Turn it [Torah] and turn it again, for everything is in it, and
contemplate it and grow grey and old over it and stir not
from it, for thou canst have no better rule.

THE HOLY WORK OF SEEKING UNDERSTANDING

The aphorism cited above appears in the tractate *Pirke Avot*
(Ethics of the Fathers, 5.25) of the Mishnah, a compendium of
rabbinic commentaries and law from the early third century C.E.[1]
Attributed to the memorably named Rabbi Ben Bag-Bag, the saying is
also a salutary dictum for interpreting New Testament texts about
the death of Jesus. The counsel to "turn it and turn it again" suggests
that the process of seeking meaning in our sacred texts requires us to
pursue meanings from varied angles. It implies that because the texts
are intricate and complicated works, readers should resist premature
conclusions about meaning. Meanings should arise out of study, contemplation, and from living the text. In this turning, we ask not only
about meanings, but what consequences various interpretations have
had on the lives of real people and societies. To search for meanings
is work; it is the holy work of seeking understanding.

An insightful perspective on the complexity of the interpretive
process comes from biblical scholar Barbara Green, who has developed at length an analogy likening interpretation of the Bible to the
PBS television show "This Old House." This PBS program takes
viewers into homes under renovation and shows the artistry and
complexity of home improvement.[2] Renovation encompasses a wide

variety of tasks. It involves investigating the history of a house—its givens, such as the period in which it was built, the architectural style and construction materials, building codes, changes made by various owners, and the topography of its location. Similarly, interpreting the Bible also involves studying what is often termed the *worlds behind the text*: its language and textual variations, and the evidence of archaeology, history, and social science. Chapters 7 and 8 are precisely a study of the *worlds behind the text*. Investigation of the worlds behind the text is vital, but insufficient because it is inherently "incapable of making contact with the eternal."[3] Other modes of interpretation must build upon and complement it.

Renovation, while necessitating knowledge of a house as it has been, is very much about the present, particularly the aesthetic vision of the inhabitants as shaped by their desires, values, needs, and resources. So, too, understanding the *worlds within the text* requires sensitivity to the rhetoric, style, characterization, and texture of Scripture. For example, narrative criticism, which examines traits such as time and space, plot, characterization, the narrator's position, and the governing values discernable within a text, "has generated wonderful insights into the artistry of the gospel texts… [and made] freshly visible the narrative beauty and even complexity of the text."[4]

Discernment of genre is a fundamental dimension of *the worlds within the text*. The four canonical Gospels, for example, are narratives about the life, work, and teachings of Jesus of Nazareth. They bear semblance to ancient biographies, albeit with differences in literary style and language.[5] Yet, insofar as biography includes a historical element, it is crucial to recognize that ancient biographers did not construct history as do modern writers. Rather, "history writing in the Bible is less concerned with what actually happened in the past and is more a creative activity" than readers today assume. Genuine historical information lies behind the Gospels, but their primary goal lies in theological presentation rather than in historical accuracy.[6] To regard the Gospels as historically reliable documentaries is to misunderstand their genre.

Intertextuality, which involves investigating the relationship a text has with other texts, is another significant aspect of *worlds within the text*.[7] In the passion narratives, for example, citations and allusions to Old Testament texts abound. It is clear that the evangelists drew upon a variety of Old Testament texts in order to draw meaning from the appalling death of Jesus. Passover imagery permeates the passion accounts in the depiction of the Last Supper, of Jesus as the Lamb of God who was slain at the same hour as the Passover lambs in the temple, and of the vinegary wine offered to Jesus on hyssop. Paul, too, makes use of the image as he tells the community in Corinth: "Clean out the old yeast so that you may be a new batch, as you really are unleavened. For our paschal lamb, Christ, has been sacrificed" (1 Corinthians 5:7). Indeed, the "drama of Jesus' passion week is painted on the canvas of Passover, its memories of a past deliverance and its hopes for a future one."[8]

Similarly, behind Matthew's portrayal of the fate of Judas lies the story of Ahithophel in 2 Samuel. An advisor to King David (2 Samuel 15:12) and esteemed for his wisdom ("as if one consulted the oracle of God," 2 Samuel 16:23), Ahithophel betrayed David and aligned himself with Absalom. When their revolt came to naught, Ahithophel hanged himself (2 Samuel 17:23). Similarly, Luke fashioned his dramatic account of Judas' end (Acts 1:16–25) on the lurid account of the death of the wicked Antiochus Epiphanes in 164 B.C.E. in 2 Maccabees 9:1–29 (see also 1 Maccabees 6:1–17 and 2 Maccabees 1:13–17). The plot to put the prophet Jeremiah to death, led by the priests and officials of Judah, including Jeremiah's protest that such action would bring "innocent blood upon yourselves and upon this city and upon its inhabitants" (Jeremiah 26:15), foreshadows Matthew's use of innocent blood (Matthew 27:24).

The Psalms provided especially rich resources for composing the passion narratives. Raymond E. Brown detected a total of thirty-two psalm parallels to the passion narratives; the laments of Psalms 31 and 69 provide rich resources. It is Psalm 22, however, that has been the most significant influence, contributing twelve of the allusions or citations.[9] Its vivid poetry offers a way of expressing the forsakenness of the Crucified One, the division of his garments, and the jeering of those who mock him. Both Mark (15:34) and Matthew (27:46) cite the opening outcry of Psalm 22 as they depict Jesus as crying from the cross, "My God, my God, why have you forsaken me?"[10] These are the only words Jesus speaks from the cross in these two Gospels. All four Gospels, however, draw upon the psalmist's protest, "They divide my clothes among themselves, and for my clothing they cast lots" (22:18), albeit in varying ways. The Synoptic writers compress the two verses: "...and divided his clothes among them by casting lots..." (Mark 15:24, Matthew 27:35, and Luke 23:34b are similar). The Fourth Gospel, however, elongates the process of division, and explicitly notes the citation:

> When the soldiers had crucified Jesus, they took his clothes and divided them into four parts, one for each soldier. They also took his tunic; now the tunic was seamless, woven in one piece from the top. So they said to one another, "Let us not tear it, but cast lots for it to see who will get it." This was to fulfill what the scripture says, "They divided my clothes among themselves, and for my clothing they cast lots." (19:23–24)

The evangelists also draw upon the psalmist's lament that he is being derided: "All who see me mock at me; they make mouths at me, they shake their heads; Commit your cause to the Lord; let him deliver—let him rescue the one in whom he delights" (22:7–8). In the passion narratives, Jewish authorities, Roman soldiers, Herod and his cohort, passersby, and even the two criminals with whom Jesus is crucified mock him, often using vocabulary closely corresponding to the Septuagint (the first Greek version of the Scripture).[11] Clearly, the New Testament accounts of the death of Jesus, particularly the Gospels, regard the Old Testament—that is, the Scripture of their day—as a profound way of grappling with the meaning of the death of Jesus Christ. The New (or Second) Testament, James Sanders observes, is "largely about Jews in the first century searching Scripture to try to understand what was happening to them in their experience of the Christ in their lives, and what God was doing through Christ and themselves."[12]

Investigating the *worlds behind the text* and the *worlds within the text* pay rich dividends; they allow readers to attain greater depth and breadth of knowledge about biblical texts. There is, however, another world to explore: the *worlds of the readers*.

Returning to Green's analogy, an old house bears the residue of the values and circumstances of its owners. A house built by a wealthy family might have grand rooms on the ground and second floors and small rooms on the top floor—suggestive of their having had servants. This house might occupy several acres, while nearby homes sit on smaller plots. Once we acknowledge the way a house reflects the values and situation of those who owned it, we are able to recognize the social record of factors such as class, race, ethnicity, and gender in a house. This is true as well in biblical studies, where the *worlds of the readers* challenge us to be more conscious of who we are and what we bring to the interpretative process. It calls attention to and makes explicit the various worlds of "owner-users" who have "constructed and inhabited our biblical text during its long life, particularly in the present." This third dimension of reading texts seeks to make visible the generations of "'ghosts' who have had and continue, in a sense, to have an impact on what is extant and in use—whether we acknowledge them or not!"[13]

> As we think about our "old biblical text," whose story does it tell? We may think of it as a thick book, but of course it records just a sliver of what it might, covering hundreds of years as it does. Who sponsored it and why? and how?…In short, the biblical text embeds, subtly or not, value systems which were part of the culture when the narratives were written. The most notable of these in current study are the ideologies surrounding sex and gender, race and ethnicity, caste and class, nature and the body. It is not as if writers could have avoided such matters; clearly, they could not. But we need to be alert to the presence of what is there—ranging from obvious to subtle.[14]

And even as we become aware of the "ghosts" that inhabit biblical texts—most notably, in the New Testament texts that became raw materials for hostility to Jews—we begin to realize that certain perspectives shape our own readings as well. This is a relatively new development in interpreting texts: "The thumb of the reader has been part of the interpretative picture taken from his or her angle, but that thumb was not always recognized by the photographer as local!"[15] Or to put it another way: "Where we stand determines what we see. And where we stand is in itself determined by a lot of things…with the color of our skin, the degree of our financial security or insecurity, and whether our last name is Armstrong or Zablocki. It has a lot to do with class."[16] Thus, we must be mindful of where we stand:

> But by becoming aware of ourselves as we live within the text, we will be more likely to take proper responsibility for our readings of it, which are properly from our own idiosyncratic particularity—though they are ideally and importantly, shaped within the many communities of other readers who share the text with us.…Again, a caveat: That we are aiming to take responsibility does not mean that we know fully what we are doing; we must know that our desires are complex and ultimately non-factorable. That those on whose shoulders we stand did not, for the most part, recognize clearly their own participation in reading should caution us against any smugness that we know our own minds and hearts fully. But since we are reading selectively, with many filters in place, the more self-aware we can be the better. We will read for particular projects, and with distinctive interest, and with multiple purposes. But since no reader now can begin to imagine that she can do all readings and claim anything like a complete or fully adequate reading, we need to choose what we are doing.[17]

Among the implications we might draw from the *world of the readers* are two claims. We are readers accountable to history, and readers confronted with disturbing truths about the Christian tradition.

Readers Accountable to History

In her extraordinary first novel, *The Archivist,* Martha Cooley portrays a couple in which Christian and Jewish identities play a complicated role. The husband, Matthias Lane (named after the disciple who replaces Judas Iscariot as one of the Twelve in Acts 1:26), is an archivist at a university library where he oversees rare books

and manuscripts of prominent writers, such as T. S. Eliot. Judith
Rudin, his wife, is Jewish and a poet who works as a legal secretary.

Judith is an intense woman who suffers a nervous breakdown.
Eventually, Matthias—Matt—hospitalizes her. She is haunted by the
stories emerging from the camps of Europe, but Matt fails to recognize the ironclad grip these reports have on her. Nor can he deal with
the God in whom she believes:

> I shouldn't have tried to take her God from her—the pas-
> sionate, demanding God of the Old Testament, the God
> who spoke to the desert tribes as if they were his children
> or his lovers, capable of wounding him as much as he
> could hurt them. I found this God unacceptably proxi-
> mate. The One I had known all my life was believable in
> direct proportion to the distance he took from all the par-
> ticulars of my life; His force as well as my faith lay in this
> remove.[18]

Matt had an excellent memory for his work, yet for him the
postwar years were a blur. "I went to school, graduated, worked, read
books. I didn't pray or attend church, although I persisted in a
belief—unarticulated, unquestioned—that Christ's intercession
would govern the course of my days. I did not wish to know how, or
why" (57).

In contrast, Judith became obsessed with theodicy, seeking
"proof of a beneficent God" (58), poring over the mystical Jewish literature of the Kabbalah. Her obsession awakens in Matt memories of
"my mother's urgent, alienating faith" (59). A gap opens between
them, "a rift in feeling, experience, perception." Once institutional-
ized, Judith scrutinizes and saves back issues of the *New York Times*
her uncle Len brings her. Obsessively hunting for stories about the
camps, she becomes an archivist of the Shoah. Meanwhile, Matt,
thinking to protect her, destroys all her files.

Matt's inability to truly understand Judith, whom he loves in
his removed sort of way, lies in large measure in his reluctance to face
history. Judith longs for Matt to reveal a "certain kind of hunger: to
know what happened and at least ask why. Because the *tikkun*

(mending or repair) can't start until everyone asks what happened—not just the Jews but everybody" (118).[19]

In contrast, Matt thinks that Jews ask too many questions and take doubt too far (28); they focus too much on their exile, which "seems arrogant to me" (144). Judith sees Christianity as taking grace too far (28) and as "a lie of consolation" (60). Yes, Matt does feel her suffering, she tells Dr. Clay, her therapist. "But he does nothing. It's all in Christ's hands" (202). She writes in her journal: "Matt's been terribly afraid all his life, and Christ is a cage for the fear that he knows will escape some day. His faith is like that line in Frost, *a momentary stay against confusion*" (163).

We might say that one of Matt's failures is his inability to mourn and to be affected by grief. He remembers what has happened in Europe, but that memory doesn't jolt him into doing anything.

Like him, we who are Christian know *about* the Holocaust—but does its memory make any difference to the way we interpret the Scriptures? To the way we live? A few may know vaguely about the long, largely troubled history with Jews that preceded the Shoah: the forcible baptisms, the charges of blood libel and ritual murder, and, above all, the centuries-long accusation that the Jews were/are Christ killers. But such knowledge generally has not jolted us into changing our self-understanding vis-à-vis Jews. Perhaps in our "astounding resistance to being disconcerted in the face of the Shoah," we are, like Matt, guilty of "cultural amnesia."[20] It may be that our theology has covered up all too quickly the "historical injuries, all the gaping wounds, all the collapses and catastrophes," avoiding the pain of remembering in its God-talk. "Must not the Shoah, at least, work as an ultimatum to an all-too-easy theological intercourse with history?"[21]

Personal encounter with survivors or a reflective visit to a Holocaust memorial or museum can be profoundly unsettling. The architecture of the Jewish Museum in Berlin, for example, seems to be designed to disconcert those who visit it, as I did in July of 2009. Three intersecting axes of the German-Jewish experience form the pathways through the new building. The longest, the axis of continuity, leads from the old building of 1735, which is the museum's only entrance, into the new building designed by Daniel Libeskind that opened in 2001. The axis of the holocaust leads to a dead end—

the Holocaust Tower. The axis of emigration provides the only path to the outside world—and thus to freedom—but with its sloping floors and slanted walls, it is a walkway of disequilibrium that leads to a heavy door opening onto the Garden of Exile. Libeskind said he designed this garden to "completely disorient the visitor."[22] Indeed, it does. Lying on a twelve-degree gradient with narrow stone paths running through forty-nine concrete stelae on a square plot, the constricted space between its columns and the uneven ground literally throw one off balance.

Yet I have never felt that Christianity has never been profoundly shaken by the Shoah. Will memory of this history in which our churches are complicit make a difference? Or is our faith but a momentary stay against confusion? To put it another way: "Ask yourselves," Johann-Baptist Metz says, "if the theology you are learning is such that it could remain unchanged before and after Auschwitz. If this be the case, be on your guard."[23] The Holocaust is an interruption, a "frightening disclosure of the real history within which we have lived." Theology "cannot face that interruption in history without facing as well the anti-Semitic effects of its own Christian history."[24]

So, too, with our reading of Scripture: as readers with an ethical obligation to face history, we are compelled to theologize differently about the New Testament texts that have had such a tragic effect upon Jews.[25] This requires clarity about the nature of the Bible as the word of God in human language, that is, as a text that *mediates* divine revelation but is not to be equated with it. This means situating texts in their contexts as artifacts of human culture, and being attentive to literary genre and structure, to the customs of ancient cultures, to issues of language and translation. It also implies reading biblical texts in a discerning manner because they bear the limitations and wounds of human finitude.

But more than that: We must pursue the consequences of our interpretation of texts. In the realm of biblical scholarship, this has given rise to a method known as *Wirkungsgeschichte*, the history of the effect produced by a book or a passage of Scripture, or the history of a text's influence over time. In Dorothee Sölle's terms, this is a "hermeneutic of consequences."[26] Attentiveness to the consequences of how the Bible has been used by real people in concrete circumstances grounds the church in space and time. It involves searching for the "fruits" of the text in the course of history as a criterion for truth. The interpretational process is deficient if it involves only "Lord, Lord," but bears no fruit.[27] Even more is it lacking when texts have borne spoiled fruit—or the "strange fruit" about which Billie Holiday sang in that 1939 song of the same name. In the case of the passion narratives, the history of effects makes for a potent cautionary tale. Interpreting our sacred texts must necessarily include acknowledgment of the violence—whether rhetorical, physical, or both—they have helped to inspire, sustain, or justify. Christians in particular are myopic about ways their tradition has been a source of lethal violence.[28] As Leo D. Lefebure claims, "[T]he concrete, violent content of some scriptural demands and the later history of violence of the Christian tradition itself demand that we scrutinize carefully what is claimed to be revelatory of God's will."[29]

Consider, for example, Christian readings of the so-called "Servant Songs" of Isaiah (42:1–8; 49:5–6; 50:4–9; 52:13—53:12), which early followers of Jesus interpreted as prophesying about his suffering and ignominious death on a cross. This is evident in the Acts of the Apostles (8:26–40); Luke tells about Philip's meeting with an Ethiopian eunuch who, while riding in his chariot en route home from Jerusalem, was reading the prophet Isaiah, specifically 53:7–8 ("Like a sheep he was led to the slaughter, and like a lamb silent before its shearer, so he does not open his mouth"). Hearing him, Philip asked whether he understood what he was reading. The Ethiopian, in turn, asked Philip to guide his interpretation. Philip, "starting with this scripture...proclaimed to him the good news about Jesus" (verse 35). Following the Ethiopian's request to be baptized, Philip did so.[30]

This connection between the fourth of the Servant Songs (52:13—53:12) and the death of Jesus is familiar to Christians. In fact, it is one of the Good Friday lections in many traditions. In tandem with the passion narrative from the Gospel of John, and until recently, prayers for the "perfidious Jews" and the singing of "Reproaches," the Good Friday service in Catholicism emphasized Jewish culpability for the suffering and death of Jesus. What all too few Catholics realize is that in sectors of medieval Europe our ancestors in faith left their Good Friday services and attacked Jews as

Christ killers.[31] Moreover, because Passover often occurs in proximity to Holy Week, this antagonism toward Jews was intensified by the charges that during this season Jews drank the blood of Christian children.[32] Given the association of Isaiah 52:13—53:12 with violence against Jews, it is not surprising that this powerful text is given far less emphasis in the synagogue. For example, when Jews remember the destruction of the first and second temples on Tisha B'Av, the readings include many passages from this section of Isaiah—but not 52:13—53:12.[33]

Readers Confronting Disturbing Truths about Christianity

As readers in a globalized world, we have a responsibility not to perpetuate the linkage of religion and violence. Whenever a text appears to give divine sanction to violence, we must interpret it in light of the tradition's fuller understanding of God. Martin Buber, in his discussion of the notion of "holy war" in ancient Israel in the context of 1 Samuel 15:3 (the prophet Samuel's demand that Saul kill all the Amalekites, including women and children), asserts that "Samuel has misunderstood God." He continues: "[A]n observant Jew of this nature, when he has to choose between God and the Bible, chooses God....[I]n the work of the throats and pens out of which the text of the Old Testament has arisen, misunderstanding has again and again attached itself to understanding....Nothing can make me believe in a God who punishes Saul because he has not murdered his enemy."[34] Following Buber, we might assert that nothing can make us believe in a God who wreaks vengeance on Jews because a few Jewish authorities played a role in the crucifixion of Jesus.

It is mortifying to discover the depth and breadth of the violence against Jews, both rhetorical and physical, that has shadowed preaching and teaching about our crucified Lord. The "troubling tellings" of the passion and death of Jesus weigh heavily on the spirit. They may intensify disillusionment with the institutional church, which may account in part for defensiveness of certain church officials. The bitter offerings we Christians have brought to the banquet of biblical interpretation haunt us, requiring us to fast from triumphalism.

Thus, *grieving* is one essential dimension of transforming Christian tellings of the passion and death of Jesus. "Taking proper responsibility for our readings," as Barbara Green exhorts, involves more than intellectual knowledge—although it certainly requires careful thought.[35] It also necessitates letting ourselves *be affected by the wounds of history that Christianity has inflicted.*

In short, redeeming our sacred story requires a willingness to be *attentive to disturbing truths about one's own tradition.* This attentiveness is similar to what Raimon Panikkar has called "intrareligious dialogue": "an inner dialogue within myself, an encounter in the depth of my personal religiousness, having met another religious experience on that very intimate level." Panikkar premised this inner dialogue as a crucial accompaniment to interreligious dialogue. He envisioned a rhythm between the two forms of dialogue as that from "exteriority to interiority, from the condemnation of others to the examination of one's own conscience, from the problem of political power to personal issues, from dogma to mysticism."[36]

One aspect of this inner dialogue is a kind of vulnerability that refuses defensiveness in the face of disquieting truths. For this we need the virtue of humility, as Elizabeth Groppe writes in a moving essay. Drawing on Augustine's *Confessions*, she suggests that human pride (*superbia*) is a fundamental misdirection of human desire. Augustine believed that the antidote to pride was God's love as mediated by the humility of the crucified Christ; Christ is the *medicus humilis*, the doctor of humility. Yet, while walking the streets of Jerusalem in 2007 in the company of Jewish and Muslim scholars, Groppe mused about what the Bishop of Hippo would say of a "history in which *crucesignati* (crusaders, those signed by the cross) murder Jews in an archbishop's palace [in Mainz in 1096] and kill Muslim women and children seeking sanctuary in a mosque [Jerusalem's al-Aqsa mosque in 1099]." Such atrocities mean that the cross that served as such a meaningful symbol of humility for Augustine has today become a symbol associated with Christian violence. In response, she suggests, we follow Augustine in practicing theology in the mode of confession. Furthermore, we need to scrutinize Christian teaching and worship to discern whether they "contain elements that may legitimate or even sacralize humiliation and violence."[37]

One example of this in the Catholic Church was the service of repentance that Pope John Paul II led on the first Sunday in Lent 2000 (March 12) marking the beginning of a new millennium. In a series of seven prayers, he and leading Vatican officials asked God's forgiveness for sins committed against a variety of peoples. Amidst the grandeur of St. Peter's Basilica, they prayed, for example, for forgiveness for sins "committed in action against love, peace, the rights of peoples, and respect for cultures and religions":

> *Archbishop Stephen Fumio Hamao:* Let us pray that contemplating Jesus, our Lord and our Peace, Christians will be able to repent of the words and attitudes caused by pride, by hatred, by the desire to dominate others, by enmity towards members of other religions and towards the weakest groups in society, such as immigrants and itinerants. [Silent prayer.]
>
> *The Holy Father:* Lord of the world, Father of all, through your Son you asked us to love our enemies, to do good to those who hate us and to pray for those who persecute us. Yet Christians have often denied the Gospel; yielding to a mentality of power, they have violated the rights of ethnic groups and peoples, and shown contempt for their cultures and religious traditions: be patient and merciful towards us, and grant us your forgiveness! We ask this through Christ our Lord. R. Amen. R. *Kyrie, eleison; Kyrie, eleison; Kyrie, eleison.*[38]

The seven prayers of Pope John Paul II explicitly named sins that those in the church have committed over the course of centuries: enmity toward others, violation of the rights of ethnic groups and people, contempt for other cultures and religious beliefs, intolerance, causing Jewish suffering, failure to acknowledge the equality of men and women, discrimination on the basis of race and ethnicity, and trust in wealth and power while manifesting contempt toward the marginalized and poor. While recent church documents have in part acknowledged such sins, the liturgical context and solemnity of this "purification of memory" provided a stark admission of the ways in which the Catholic Church had failed to live the Gospel of love it proclaims.[39] The church's repentance, however, lies not only in formal confession but especially in transformed ways of acting.

Facing our history—being responsive to it—involves dying to notions of Christianity that see it *only* as a force for good in the world. If, as William Burrows says, the death of Jesus on the cross is the "paradigmatic revelation of God," then the "dynamic of finding new life through death is the ultimate paradigm of Christian existence." Thus, he reasons, the "death of Jesus is key to a Christian hermeneutic of mission in the contemporary world."[40] The connection of a dying to self as an integral element of Christian spirituality vis-à-vis the religious other is best developed by Michael Barnes, a British Jesuit and scholar of the religions of India. Barnes writes of the importance of allowing ourselves to be changed by the encounter with the religious other. Speaking of the post-Shoah encounter with Jews, he writes:

> The disturbing return of the irreducible reality of continuing Jewish faith has done more than awaken ethical sensitivity; it has also shown that the Church's history is by no means a record of straightforward progress toward the eschaton....In recognizing the Jewish matrix of all their theology, a matrix which continues to exist independently of ecclesiastical control, Christians may no longer presume to speak as if they are in perfect possession of a panoptic vision. They must learn to live with the strangeness of the other—what is new, what has been occluded, or what has been simply forgotten.[41]

On a number of occasions, Barnes advocates the importance of "passivity"—a willingness to be affected by the other—for Christian faith and practice in a pluralistic world. He describes it as the "experience of limitation imposed by otherness of all kinds," a form of "contemplative apophasis" (a "not knowing") that is intrinsic to the Christian vocation.[42] In encountering the strangeness of the other, we must resist the temptation to formulate a grand strategy that fits the other into our scheme of meaning. Rather, we are called to foster a contemplative sensitivity: "a God-given grace which enables human beings to reach beyond themselves, to imagine the unimaginable, to live with the provisional, to enter into a demanding engagement with others."[43] To reach beyond ourselves involves us in the heart of Christian spirituality: "The question is not, therefore, how Christians can find a way of including the other within a single story, still less a theological scheme, but whether they can discern in their own experience of *being altered*—made other—something of the mystery of Christ's Death and Resurrection."[44]

Aware that Christianity, especially Catholicism, runs the risk of seeking a "premature finality," Barnes suggests that the experience of Christians learning how to relate to the religious other mirrors Christ facing death.[45] In the language of Christian spirituality, inter-religious encounter is an experience of the paschal mystery, a dying to self in order to live a transformed life. The "turning and turning and turning" of our troubling texts until we find more just interpretations is an act of asceticism.

The transformation of our tellings of the passion and death of Jesus involve our own life of faith. They must not, however, end there, lest our faith be but a "momentary stay against confusion." As Groppe writes, "Our bloodstained history has altered the meaning of the cross of Christ, but the true meaning of the symbol may be restored by the lives of Christian communities authentically living out the compassion and active nonviolence of Christ the good physician."[46] Redeeming our sacred story involves not only reading troubling texts differently, but living into their transformed meanings.

TURNING THOSE TROUBLING TEXTS: ALTERING FOR THE ALTAR

If indeed our bloodstained history has altered the meaning of the cross of Christ, what might be said from the altar? In particular, given the prominence of the death of Jesus in Christian liturgical life, in what ways might we "turn and turn again" troubling texts so that new interpretations might contribute to a more profound understanding of his death? In what ways might new readings of troubling texts do greater justice to the Christian relationship with Judaism?

By way of prelude, three contextual matters are important. The first involves timing; consideration of the manner and meaning of the death of Jesus should be integrated throughout the liturgical year, not limited merely to Lent or Holy Week. How preachers and teachers speak about the relationship between the Testaments, the Jewish Jesus and the Judaism of his time, the development of the church out of Jesus' Movement, the nature of the Gospels, and Paul's identity and mission provide a fundamental ground for interpreting the passion and death of Jesus.

Second, it is vital to speak directly to the various troubling texts in the Scriptures—for example, those texts that appear to condone violence, denigrate Judaism, demean women, and uphold slavery—whenever they occur. This does not mean belittling the Bible, nor does it suggest berating our ancestors in faith for their misuse of texts. Rather, it involves a frank admission that biblical texts and their interpreters bear the limitations and wounds of human finitude. Texts, therefore, must be read in a discerning manner. Too often in the churches the impression is unintentionally left that the Bible is something like a transcript of God's voice emanating from the heavens. In contrast, it is important to recognize it as the "word of God expressed in human language."[47] As Timothy Radcliffe says, the Word "does not come from outside but gestates within our human language. The Word of God does not come down from heaven like a celestial Esperanto."[48] Texts need to be situated in their context as artifacts of human culture, lest we bypass the human reality in the search for spiritual meaning.[49] Moreover, because of sinfulness, human interpretation always has a provisional character: The Scriptures "witness to people's interpretations of God's self-communication to them....Since God enters people's lives in the historical conditions and limitations of real life, their interpretations are colored by these circumstances and shaped by their myopia and blind spots. The human authors of the scriptures are at the same time virtuous and sinful."[50]

Consideration of the role of polemics in antiquity helps to enlarge the context in which we interpret troubling biblical texts and early church literature. This is not to justify the "blood curse" of Matthew 27:25 or the oratorical excesses of Melito of Sardis or John Chrysostom. Rather, it is vital to situate these claims in their broader historical-cultural-literary framework. This requires mindfulness of our propensity for anachronism, such as thinking of "Judaism" and

"Christianity" in the New Testament era as settled and separate traditions. It also requires recognition of the internal disputations involved in any diverse group, as well as the function of rhetoric in identity formation. As Luke Timothy Johnson shows, the believers in Jesus (or messianists) were part of a much larger debate within Judaism over the correct meaning of Torah. Their "rhetoric of slander" was part of the language of disputation in Judaism, evident in the Dead Sea Scrolls, Josephus, and Philo. It also must be understood as part of the conventional language of recrimination and debate in Hellenistic philosophical schools.[51] Thus, regarding the "blood curse" of Matt 27:25, Johnson says, "We cannot view with the same seriousness the 'curse' laid on Jews by Matthew's Gospel when we recognize that curses were common coinage in those fights and there were not many Jews and Gentiles who did not have at least one curse to deal with."[52]

Johnson's argument is crucial for recognizing the polemical context in which the New Testament was forged. Yet it falters once the followers of Jesus no longer understood themselves to be a part of Israel. As "Christianity" came to be understood as a distinct religion, Christian readers of the New Testament lost the ability to recognize the genre of slander as a language of disputation *within Judaism*. Instead, they interpreted the polemic as an accurate depiction of Judaism—with tragic consequences. Although acknowledgment of the conventional nature of New Testament polemic frees us from its mythic force and potential for harm, we must be mindful of the immense damage that has been done by generations of interpreters who misread the messianists' polemic as a factual portrayal of Jewish attitudes, practices, and beliefs.

Third, it is necessary to be attentive to what is deeply embedded in the religious imagination: "To 'imagine redemption' is to discover the difference that the death of Jesus makes right here and now."[53] Patrick Evans evoked the importance of this sensitivity in the course of leading a session on hymnody in April of 2011. He shared about a hymn that had deeply affected him since his childhood, "There Is a Fountain":

> E'er since by faith I saw the stream
> Thy flowing wounds supply,

Redeeming love has been my theme,
And shall be till I die.
And shall be till I die.
And shall be till I die.
Redeeming love has been my theme,
And shall be till I die.[54]

He observed that whatever complex theological understandings we may hold, on our deathbeds we will be far more consoled by the hymnody we carry deep in our memories than we will be by more abstract formulations. His remarks serve as a vivid reminder of the importance of learning what role hymns, poetry, prayer, ritual, and visual testimony about the passion and death of Jesus play in the lives of congregants or students. Whatever new perspectives we offer need to be in conversation with understandings already embedded. Think of this as the "redeeming love" principle.

PUTTING INTERPRETIVE STRATEGIES TO WORK

With that larger context established, I offer eight guidelines for interpreting New Testament texts about the passion and death of Jesus. These offer both a partial summary of this book and an invitation to integrate its arguments into preaching and teaching.

1. **Call attention, as appropriate, to the numerous and varied ways the New Testament speaks about the passion and death of Jesus.** The passion narratives constitute a densely textured fabric, with strands of history and theology, drama and myth intricately interwoven. Each of the canonical Gospels has lengthy narratives that attributes responsibility for the death of Jesus primarily to Jews rather than to the Romans, stresses Jesus' innocence and the injustice of his opponents, works with tropes about martyrdom and noble death, and draws upon the Scriptures—what Christian would later term the "Old Testament," both by way of allusion and fulfillment citations in fashioning their accounts. Paul also gives great significance to the death of Jesus, but does so in ways rich with metaphor. He has a "dazzling array of colors in

the mural of...[his] theology of the cross."[55] We will better comprehend his multihued theology if we situate Paul as embedded in Judaism while called to be Apostle to the Gentiles.

2. **Present the passion narratives as stories intended to deepen faithful living rather than as historically reliable reports.** They are retrospective reflections, not documentaries. As Stephen Patterson says, "The important question was not what really happened. The questions—the truly important questions—were now, 'Were we right about him or not? Were we right to follow him? Was his cause just?'"[56]

3. **Situate the New Testament accounts in the larger context of the Roman Empire. Rome's rule is the crucial "backstory."**

   3.1 Jesus was crucified by the authority of the Roman governor, Pontius Pilate, likely in collaboration with the Jewish high priesthood. This was the "power class," though the power of the high priests was controlled by the Roman governor.

   3.2 Although the precise charge cannot be established with absolute confidence, it is likely that Pilate viewed Jesus as guilty of sedition for having preached about the counter-kingdom, that is, the reign of God. It may be that Luke has a historical kernel of truth for such an accusation: "Then the assembly rose as a body and brought Jesus before Pilate. They began to accuse him, saying, 'We found this man perverting our nation, forbidding us to pay taxes to the emperor, and saying that he himself is the Messiah, a king'" (23:1–2).

   3.3 Crucifixion was "highly organized, massive state terrorism, intended to intimidate the vast peasant and slave populations of the [Roman] empire into passivity."[57] It was a "spectacle for the edification of those watching"[58]

4. **Connect the passion accounts to the ministry of Jesus.** Jesus died as a consequence of what he lived for and how he embodied God's merciful justice. Jesus was a *victim* of imperial Rome, a threat to the cult of the emperor and to the theology of empire. His utopian teaching suggested another order of things, that those who were "expendables" in the Roman

Empire were important in God's eyes. Jesus imagined another kind of imperial order: that of God's reign (or, as Patterson puts it in *Beyond the Passion*, "God's empire").

5. **Use language that depicts the complexity of the early centuries.**

   5.1 "Jews" and "Christians" are complex and capacious terms, both historically and in the present. "Jewish" and "Christian" identities were fluid in the early centuries, and "Jew" encompassed people in starkly different social, economic, political and geographic realities.

   5.2 In speaking about New Testament texts, we might speak more accurately of "Jesus-believing Jews" and "non-Jesus-believing Jews," rather than of Christians and Jews. Granted, this is linguistically awkward, but it does help to deconstruct the conventional understanding of Jesus and his followers as over against "the Jews."

   5.3 We might think of "Christians" and "Jews" in the second and third centuries more as dialects of a single language (for example, Spanish speakers in Mexico and Puerto Rico) than as separate languages—and with many gradations.

   5.4 "Jesus-believing Jews" became outnumbered by "Jesus-believing Gentiles." "Christians" gradually became separate from "Jews" as a religious entity over a lengthy period of time. There was no single turning point of separation: the "dialects" became the "separate languages" at different times, under different circumstances, and in different locations. By the fourth century, the separation seemed in most places to have taken place.

   5.5 The separation affected how the New Testament was understood. "Yet once Jesus' words became placed in the Gospel narratives and addressed to Christian churches, comments spoken *to* Jews became perceived by the church as well as the synagogue as comments spoken *against* Jews."[59]

6. **Inquire into what the accounts of the passion and death of Jesus inspired, sustained, and/or rationalized over the centuries.** Be willing to confront the shadow side of Christian his-

tory. In what specific ways have the accounts functioned to bear witness to the Gospel imperative to love God and neighbor? In what ways have the accounts functioned to betray this imperative? It is particularly important to learn and tell the "other half of the story"—the animosity between Christian and Jew fueled by alleged Jewish responsibility for the crucifixion.

6.1 The anti-Jewish rhetoric of the literary elite in early "Christian" circles served a significant function in the formation and maintenance of ecclesial identity. Jews were the crucial "other" against which Christian belief and practice might be calibrated. Certain themes of this literature formed a constellation, of which the North Star was the claim that "the Jews" are Christ-killers. Accompanying this central claim were accusations of faithlessness, blindness, and carnality. Yet the polemics of the rhetorical realm were not matched by the social reality: there was abundant social interaction at least until well into the fourth century.

6.2 In post-Constantinian Christianity, when the church acquired political power, the lines of separation hardened and what had been a family argument became that of two different religions.

6.3 In the eleventh century, a virulent anti-Judaism emerged among the populace, particularly in northern Europe, and the "Christ killer" charge lay at the heart of violence against Jews—in the Crusades, in the dehumanization of Jews in religious literature and the popular imagination, in myths such as ritual cannibalism and blood libel. Passion plays, most notably at Oberammergau (first performed in 1634 and performed virtually every decade since then), heightened emphasis on Jewish villainy.

6.4 In the nineteenth century, particularly in central and northern Europe, the anti-Jewish attitudes disseminated in the churches merged with a growing societal antisemitism. Jews were associated with Bolshevism and liberalism. The church's anti-Jewish teaching merged with growing antisemitism in the culture.

6.5 Christian teaching and preaching about the Jews—partic-

ularly their alleged responsibility for the death of Jesus—
was both a precondition and an enabler of Nazi ideology.
6.6 "Ask yourself if the theology you are learning is such that
it could remain unchanged before and after Auschwitz. If
this be the case, be on your guard."[60]

7. **Reject the authority of intrinsically oppressive texts while
claiming their larger vision of God's concern for the flourishing of life and salvation of all.** The accusation that "the
Jews" crucified Jesus may be considered an "intrinsically
oppressive" text, that is, an authoritative text that human sinfulness has touched to the core.[61] It is not compatible with the
Gospel, and does not carry authority for Christians in our
time. At the same time, we should not reduce texts to their
anti-Jewish (or patriarchal) dimensions, as two Belgian scholars write:

> For us, admitting the potential of anti-Jewish elements in
> the fourth gospel by no means leads us to reject the
> gospel, as if it excluded the possibility of authentic
> Christian faith on principle. To the contrary, we are con-
> vinced that one may not overlook the universal concern
> of God's saving love, expressed so eloquently by the
> fourth evangelist. The Johannine Jesus says about him-
> self, "I came that they may have life and have it abun-
> dantly" (John 10:10). God's ultimate concern is life and
> salvation for the world in an inclusive sense. We under-
> stand God's desire of salvation for all to be so strong that
> the rejection of Christ as mediator of salvation is not nec-
> essarily a reason for excluding people from salvation.[62]

8. **Connect the cross of Jesus to the crosses of history.** That
Jesus was crucified is important because it reminds us that he,
through whom we Christians see God revealed, is one with
the marginal peoples of this world—all those whom brutal
rulers, whether Pontius Pilate, Hitler, or Pol Pot, considered
expendable, of nonhuman status. The following of Christ
obligates us to respond to the sufferings of people in our time.
We "deny his death when we turn our backs to the death on
our streets."[63] Assessing the truthfulness of an interpretation

of a biblical text requires us to ask what our interpretation leads to. Does our interpretation bring forth love? "By 'love' I mean the limitless dedication to the human cause that finally led Jesus to his death in spite of the fact that he had the opportunity to avoid this destiny."[64]

Contemplating Jesus' prophetic witness enables us to make connections to our broken world in which people at the margins of society suffer. We know people in our own day who, despite opposition and danger, nevertheless carry on their advocacy for a more just society, even if they suffer death because of it. Their memory inspires and sustains us because, like Jesus, they were willing to carry on for a cause greater than themselves, a cause furthering God's reign on earth. In their passionate commitment to counter evil in its varied and powerful manifestations, they mediate the divine care for creation. These "saints" exemplify God's desire for the flourishing of all, human and non-human. They are participants in the divine drama of salvation.

9. **Reclaim the "power of the story."** This includes communicating more vividly how walking the Way of Jesus saves us. Claims that Christians alone will be saved obscure the powerful message of the Gospel. Certain texts have been read in ways that exclude others from God's salvific love. Perhaps the best known of these allegedly exclusionary texts is John 14:6 ("I am the way, and the truth, and the life. No one comes to the Father except through me"). Ulrich Luz, however, paraphrases it as follows: "The history of Jesus is a way and enables a way. It is a criterion, not in the sense of limiting the truth but in the sense of making the search for it possible. It is the point from which Christians in their search for truth depart and to which they return."[65] To say that God saves us through Jesus Christ is in part to claim that Jesus calls us to a way to God that patterns our daily lives. God has given us in Christ a way of living that saves us from excessive self-absorption, fear, and enslavement. In living as disciples, we not only experience salvation but also act in ways that contribute to the world's sal-

vation. Discipleship calls us to turn away from the destructiveness of sin.

Graced by his Spirit, we are enabled to experience salvation. By striving to love our enemies, we lessen the world's violence and the violence within our own being. By engaging in acts of foot-washing and table service, we are redeemed from the constriction of selfishness and become part of activity larger than ourselves—an activity that partakes of the coming reign of God. By forgiving others (and ourselves), we experience deliverance from an anger that can so easily corrode us by sapping our psychic energy. By responding to those in need, we mediate God's healing.

Were we to lay claim to the "everyday" character of salvation, we might begin to connect salvation to taking up our cross, that is, that God asks us to participate in the world's salvation by giving freely of our lives to others, to engage in "salvific activity" in innumerable ways. "There is no salvation apart from being in relation with other human beings."[66] Such understandings of salvation help Christians connect their belief in Christ with the world in which they live rather than lifting their eyes only to the heavenly realm.

CHAPTER 10

The Cross as the Tree of Life
for the Healing of the Nations

Then the angel showed me the river of the water of life, bright as crystal,
flowing from the throne of God and of the Lamb through the middle of
the street of the city. On either side of the river is the tree of life with
its twelve kinds of fruit, producing its fruit each month; and the leaves
of the tree are for the healing of the nations. (Revelation 22:1–2)

The symbol of the Tree of Life spans cultures and millennia. The
peoples of ancient Egypt, Persia, and Mesopotamia considered it
a sacred symbol. In Judaism it became a metaphor for Torah as wisdom: "She [wisdom] is a tree of life [etz chayim] to those who lay hold
of her; those who hold her fast are called happy" (Proverbs 3:18). In
Christianity the wood of the cross of Jesus became the tree of life in
which suffering is ultimately redeemed and new life emerges from
death. In the above citation from the Book of Revelation, we find a
vision of a restored world, with a new heaven and a new earth in
which the leaves of the tree of life heal the nations.

In a book that has underscored what Christians have perpetrated on Jews for their alleged responsibility for the crucifixion, it is
imperative to highlight the "power of the story" for good. It is necessary to redeem the stories that were used to justify such violence,
both rhetorical and physical. Simply put, the stories of the passion
and death of Jesus Christ are indispensable to Christianity. If the
cross is to be the tree of life that contributes to the healing of the
nations, then Christians must cultivate new shoots of understanding,

228

living, and telling. It is my hope that by transforming our telling, we might both breathe new life into our relationship with the Jewish people and reanimate the understanding and practice of our own Christian vocation in the world.

In chapters 7 and 8, I argued for reading New Testament accounts of the crucifixion in light of the "backstory" of the Roman Empire, and explained the complexity of "Christianity" and "Judaism" in the early centuries of the Common Era. In chapter 9, I reflected on our moral obligation to be affected by our history vis-à-vis Jews—not so as to wallow in shame but to be jolted out of indifference. Understanding ourselves as accountable to history impels us to rethink teachings that inspired and rationalized the "Christ killer" charge. Accordingly, I offered principles to guide how we make meaning of ancient texts today. These chapters constitute important intellectual resources for redeeming our sacred story.

In this final chapter, I explore possibilities for letting the power in the story transform us, both personally and communally. As a framework, I will draw upon two "tellings" of the passion and death of Jesus that have influenced Christian spiritualities. I will first engage with the *Spiritual Exercises* of St. Ignatius of Loyola (1491–1556), a sixteenth-century manual of practical directives for deepening one's Christian identity. Although the Exercises originated in the context of the Catholic Counter-Reformation and constitutes the core of the spirituality of the religious order of men Ignatius founded (the Society of Jesus, or the Jesuits), its possibilities transcend the particularities of its origins. Inspired in part by the affective piety characteristic of the late medieval period, his own intense search for holiness, and his experience in guiding people in prayer, Ignatius fashioned the Exercises as a means of deepening intimacy with God and growing into greater interior freedom.

I then turn to the so-called "Seven Last Words" of Jesus that the Gospels attribute to him as he is dying on the cross. This devotional practice has played an important role in Christian spirituality since its origins in the twelfth century. It has also inspired numerous musical compositions, most notably those by Heinrich Schütz (ca. 1648), Franz Joseph Haydn (1785), Charles François Gounod (1858), and, more recently, James MacMillan (1993). Many Protestant and Catholic churches have services of the Seven Last Words during Holy

Week, usually on Good Friday, and the Seven Last Words continue to inspire reflection, as a spate of recent publications attests.[1] Writer Mary Gordon regards them as utterances of "radical honesty, radical porosity."[2]

THE PASSION AND DEATH OF JESUS IN THE *SPIRITUAL EXERCISES*

For a number of reasons, the *Spiritual Exercises* offer a useful heuristic for exploring a "transformed telling" of the passion story. Since their publication in Rome in 1548, they have been and remain an influential spirituality in Catholicism, particularly in the West. Increasingly, they have become a resource in Protestant Christianity. Contemporary interpretations of the Exercises and variant ways of following them are widely available, including online formats—even an "Ignatian wiki."[3] Of particular importance, the Exercises lend themselves to new approaches to biblical texts because they invite persons to place themselves within the New Testament stories. They foster reflecting on the Scriptures with imagination; biblical scholarship today offers many resources for imaginative reconstruction. Moreover, the Exercises are organized into a four-week movement in which the third week focuses on the passion and death of Christ, thereby providing a text to test my arguments.[4]

Most significantly, the meditative techniques that Ignatius recommended emphasized affective knowing: "For, what fills and satisfies the soul consists, not in knowing much, but in our understanding the realities profoundly and in savoring them interiorly."[5] Affective knowing is critical to integrating the intellectual resources of biblical studies into one's life. Yet while Ignatius drew upon the meditative style of his medieval predecessors, particularly the Spanish translation of *Vita Christi* by Ludolphus of Saxony, the Exercises lack the preoccupation with Jewish treachery so characteristic of his predecessors and contemporaries.[6] This significant difference has not been sufficiently noted, although others have pointed to Ignatius's respect for Judaism, which went against the grain of the antisemitism of Spanish society of his day, including its obsession with "blood purity" (*limpieza de sangre*).[7]

By stressing imaginative reconstruction of biblical scenes, he invited those making the Exercises to enter into the narrative, to be present in each scene. In his book on the Exercises, the influential Jesuit theologian Karl Rahner noted that by joining concrete images with ideas, Ignatius desired to move the whole person in ways that resulted in a "conversion to history."[8] This phrase more economically expresses what I wrote in the previous chapter: the need "to be affected by the wounds of history that Christianity has inflicted."

The Exercises provides a repertoire of ways of praying intended to form contemplatives in action. The first week stresses discursive meditation that creates an awareness of what may have gone astray in our lives. It invites those meditating to recognize their need for healing and for turning away from sin; they are to see themselves as "loved sinners," forgiven by a merciful God. The second week focuses on contemplating Jesus in the Gospels; entering imaginatively into the mission of Jesus is intended to evoke a desire to follow him more intensely. The third week involves dwelling with Jesus as he undergoes his passion and death. By entering empathically into the suffering of Jesus, the person making the Exercises is called to a greater realization of Christ's profound love for humankind and, in response, to become more compassionate in the face of his suffering. In the fourth week, this sharing of Jesus' grief is intended to give way to the joy of the resurrection and to elicit a response of love for God, who did not permit death to have the final word.

Although Ignatius designated the third week for contemplation of the passion and death of Jesus, it assumes a prominent place in the initial meditation of the first week. In this meditation, Ignatius invited persons to imagine "Christ our Lord suspended on the cross before you," and he suggested they "converse with him in a colloquy," dying in this way for "my sins." He instructed them to look at themselves, asking what they have done for Christ, what they are currently doing for Christ, and what they might do in the future for Christ. "In this way, too, gazing on him in so pitiful a state as he hangs on the cross, speak out whatever comes to your mind."[9]

Two techniques of prayer that emerge in weeks one and two are fundamental to the third week. One is the frequent instruction to create a "composition, seeing the place." That is, in approaching a biblical scene, those making the Exercises are invited to bring it to life by filling in the details of geography, architecture, environment, and interplay of characters: using the imagination, one puts herself or himself there in a scene. In a sense, Ignatius anticipated what the slaves would later sing, "Were You There When They Crucified My Lord?"

Complementing the composition of place is the instruction to pray with the five senses, or "application of the senses." Ignatius instructs:

> **First Point.** By the sight of my imagination I will see the persons, meditating and contemplating in detail all the circumstances around them, and drawing some profit from the sight.
>
> **Second Point.** By my hearing I will listen to what they are saying or might be saying; and then, reflecting on myself, I will draw some profit from this.
>
> **Third Point.** I will smell the fragrance and taste the infinite sweetness and charm of the Divinity, of the soul, of its virtues, and of everything there, appropriately for each of the persons who is being contemplated. Then I will reflect upon myself and draw profit from this.
>
> **Fourth Point.** Using the sense of touch, I will, so to speak, embrace and kiss the places where the persons walk or sit. I shall always endeavor to draw some profit from this.[10]

The Gospel narratives provide ample material for composition of place and application of the senses. Yet without attentiveness to insights from historical-critical methods, the Ignatian techniques may simply reinforce troubling tellings. For example, when biblical scholar Maria Anicia Co uses Ignatius in her reading of the Fourth Gospel, she seems to leave behind important insights from the scholarship. For example, in reflecting on the cleansing of the temple (2:13–22), her interpretation lacks sufficient encounter with the world behind the text. Co writes:

> I hear so much noise, the sound of the oxen and bleating sheep being driven out of the temple. I hear the clatter of

coins and the shattering sound of overturned tables of the money-changers. I observe the angry and pained face of Jesus as he speaks to the sellers of pigeons. "Take these things away; you shall not make my Father's house a house of trade." The Jews react with a challenge, "What sign have you to show us for doing this?" Jesus answers, "Destroy this temple and in three days I will raise it up." I perceive that the Jews think he is silly....The religious authorities of his day who refuse to give him a hearing reveal themselves to be resisting God himself. The consequence is fatal: they no longer deserve to act as God's representatives before the people....Yes, the story of Jesus goes on not only in the text of John but in the text of my life. I cannot forget Jesus's passionate action and his face displaying anger, grief and compassion. I have the same feelings as I look at the realities affecting the lives of the majority of our people.[11]

Co seems to have been caught up in the Johannine technique of depicting "the Jews" as opponents of Jesus—what Adele Reinhartz terms the "rhetoric of binary opposition."[12] Yet everyone in this episode in the temple is Jewish, including Jesus, of course. Moreover, she has generalized beyond the text to the "religious authorities of his day" and accused them of resisting God. So composition of place and application of the senses are no panacea to readings hostile to Judaism. In this case, they require the correction of scholarship.

But when used in tandem with scholarship, the details generated by composition of place and application of the senses can enrich meditation. For example, we know that in Second Temple Judaism the Jewish practice of wearing inscribed biblical texts—*tefillin*—came into use. *Tefillin* (from the Hebrew *tefillah*, a prayer) are two small leather containers containing tiny parchment scrolls of scriptural texts; they are attached to leather straps and wound around the arms, hand, and fingers, as well as around the head and one shoulder.[13] *Tefillin* came to be associated with the injunction in Deuteronomy 6:6, 8–9 to "Keep these words that I am commanding you today in your heart....Bind them as a sign on your hand, fix them as an emblem on your forehead, and write them on the doorposts of your house and on your gates." They were worn while praying.

So when we are meditating on Jesus at prayer, we might imagine him putting on *tefillin*. Similarly, while we know virtually nothing about Jesus' home life, we can imagine him touching the *mezuzah* ("doorpost") on his home—the literal fulfillment of writing them "on the doorposts of your house and on your gates."[14] We may stand alongside the woman with the twelve-year hemorrhage (Matthew 9:20–21), who *touched* the fringes (*tzitzit*) of Jesus' cloak. The *tzitzit* fulfilled the commandment to the Israelites in Numbers 15:37–40 to "make fringes on the corners of their garments....You have the fringe so that, when you see it, you will remember all the commandments of the LORD and do them, and not follow the lust of your own heart and your own eyes."[15] Of this latter practice, Amy-Jill Levine argues:

> The reminder of the fringes has a practical payoff for Christians. The Gospels' preservation of this detail indicates that the Old Testament must be acknowledged as more than just an anticipation of the coming of the messiah, after which it can be discarded or, more respectfully, put on the shelf next to the other antiques, to be admired but not used. By preserving the detail that Jesus wore fringes, the New Testament mandates that respect for Jewish custom be maintained and that Jesus's own Jewish practice be honored, even by the gentile church, which does not follow those customs.[16]

For many years, we Christians have barely touched the fringes of Jesus' Jewishness, that is, the humanity of Jesus. The *Spiritual Exercises*, amplified by contemporary biblical studies, provide us with a way of entering more deeply into his world, and it is in the third week that Ignatius accents his humanity. Visualizing Jesus praying with *tefillin*, touching the *mezuzah* with Jesus, and standing alongside the hemorrhaging woman as she reached for his *tizizit* in hope of healing become concrete embodiments of the life of Jesus, the Jew from Nazareth.

The techniques of application of the senses and composition of place also figure prominently in the third week, when Ignatius emphasizes the humanity of Jesus, that is, the Jewish Jesus.[17] Ignatius invites those meditating to see the road from Bethany to Jerusalem, the room of the Last Supper, and then the road from Mount Zion to the Valley of Josaphat (Kidron Valley) to Gethsemane. He invites them to visualize the persons at the Last Supper, to hear what they are talking about, and to gaze at what they are doing. In every case, he says, benefit from applying the senses. Similarly, apply the senses to Jesus in Gethsemane; follow him from the garden to the house of Annas, to the house of Caiaphas, to Pilate, to Herod, and then back to Pilate. Then be with him at the crucifixion—recreate the entire scene in the imagination—and follow his descent from the cross and entombment. Finally, go to the house "where Our Lady went after the burial of her Son....Consider, too, Our Lady's loneliness along with her deep grief and fatigue; then, on the other hand, the fatigue of the disciples."[18]

Throughout this third week, persons making the Exercises are to ask for the grace of "heartfelt sorrow and confusion because the Lord is going to his Passion for my sins."[19] They are instructed to "Consider how he suffers all this for my sins, and so on; and also to ask, 'What ought I do for him?'" Further: "Hear what is proper for the Passion: sorrow with Christ in sorrow; a broken spirit with Christ so broken; tears; and interior suffering because of the great suffering which Christ endured for me."[20] After contemplating these scenes, Ignatius recommends returning to the events by spending a day on the first half of the passion, a subsequent day on the second half, and then an entire day for its entirety. William Meissner, a Jesuit psychotherapist, summarizes the logic of the Exercises:

> They [the first and second weeks] provide the intellectual and affective substratum for [the third week's] entering into and identifying with Christ suffering and dying, for recognizing that the basic cause of that suffering is in ourselves, in our sinfulness. Christ embraced that sinfulness in order to change the sorrow and despair of the human condition to life and joy. Therefore, in terms of this logic, Christ's suffering becomes our own, and only through

union with his suffering does love deliver us from evil and make our suffering redemptive. The election [deciding to abandon that which draws us away from God] itself involves a conversion, a turning from sin to grace, from self-absorption to love, from sinfulness to forgiveness.[21]

The third week of the Exercises is premised on the notion that "sharing in the passion of another leads to communion with them and praying the passion of Jesus will inevitably lead to compassion for those most in need."[22] The empathy engendered by the Exercises is meant to overflow into self-transcendence.

TURN IT AND TURN IT AGAIN: THE *SPIRITUAL EXERCISES*, CONTEMPORARY BIBLICAL SCHOLARSHIP, AND THE SPIRITUALITY OF CHRISTIANS

Ignatius's sixteenth-century world differs radically from ours. Thus, many of the assumptions that shaped his classic work are no longer widely held, whether the Ptolemaic cosmology of the times; his understanding of the historicity of the Gospels; his theological anthropology, with its scrupulosity about sin; his uncritical obedience to the institutional church; or his hierarchical thinking, in which women and children played a lesser role. An abundant literature reinterpreting and "reclaiming" the Exercises for our time has developed, providing rich resources.

My own exploration of the Exercises here is far more modest: to reread aspects of Ignatius's perspectives on the passion and death of Jesus in light of the biblical scholarship and sensibilities explored in chapters 7 through 9. In turn, I will make use of his recommendations about composition of place and application of the senses, suggesting that they complement scholarly ways of approaching texts. This chapter merely *hints* at some of the possibilities in the hopes that readers will pursue implications more extensively.

Approaching the passion narratives some 460 years since the publication of the Exercises necessitates working within a different horizon of interpretation. Conscious of the literary, historical, and sociocultural contexts that shaped their composition, we neither

236

assume their historicity nor conflate the various accounts. Each of the Gospels offers its own lens on the ministry, passion, death, and resurrection of Jesus of Nazareth. So rather than harmonize the accounts, as Ignatius does, it may be beneficial to stay with a particular evangelist's rendition in the full context of his Gospel. Similarly, Ignatius paid no attention to the way passion narratives drew upon Old Testament texts, whether by allusion or direct citation. Reflecting on these texts, particularly the use of the Psalms and Isaiah, invites entry into the many layers of the narratives. The emotive language of the Psalms encourages application of the senses.

Ignatius wisely links the ministry of Jesus (second week) with the passion and death (third week). Unlike the Nicene Creed, in which one passes with barely a breath from "he was born of the Virgin Mary and became man" to "for our sake he was crucified under Pontius Pilate," Ignatius has us linger over the ministry of Jesus, seeing with the eye of our imagination the "synagogues, villages and towns through which Christ our Lord preached."[23] This connection between the ministry and the passion is crucial to interpreting the passion narratives: "One of the great mistakes of Christian theology has been our attempt to understand the death and resurrection of Jesus apart from his life."[24] *The ministry of Jesus must permeate reflection on his passion and death.*[25]

For example, in meditating on the Last Supper—whether in the Synoptic accounts with the words of institution (Mark 14:22–25; Matthew 26:26–29; Luke 22:15–20) or in the Fourth Gospel's footwashing (John 13:1–20)—persons might enter imaginatively into those scenes by remembering how important meals were (and are) in Jewish tradition. When Ignatius instructs those making the Exercises to "bring to memory the narrative" of the Last Supper, we might first recall the memorial meal that serves as a backdrop for all of the events of the passion: the Passover. New Testament writers saw in the Passover a way of interpreting Jesus' passage from death to life: "The drama of Jesus' passion week is painted on the canvas of Passover, its memories of a past deliverance and its hopes for a future one."[26]

Scripture scholars have devoted considerable attention to the question of whether the Last Supper was a Seder, as depicted in the Synoptic Gospels.[27] Like many questions about events and practices in antiquity, insufficient evidence precludes a definitive answer. The

Seder itself has evolved over the centuries. How Jesus and his disciples might have celebrated Passover before the destruction of the temple in 70 C.E. would in any case differ from the Seder as specified by the rabbis in later Jewish texts, such as the Mishnah and Talmud. Post-70, Jews celebrated the Seder at home and no longer sacrificed a lamb, since the sacrificial system ended with the demise of the temple.

Rather than recreating and imagining ourselves at the scene of a Seder meal, we might more fittingly enter into the symbolic realm, recalling instances when we have experienced deliverance that the Seder celebrates. Passover celebrates redemption. It is the paradigmatic salvific event for the Jewish people. By entering into the story of the Exodus, we remember when we, too, were slaves in Egypt, and recall those instances when we experienced liberation. We also begin to understand how the imagery of Passover enabled Jesus' disciples to make meaning of his death and to ritualize this in a meal in remembrance of him. Just as God had heard the groaning of the Israelite slaves in Egypt and remembered his covenant with Abraham, Isaac, and Jacob (and Sarah, Rebekah, Leah, and Rachel [Exodus 2:24]), so God was delivering his people through the death and resurrection of Jesus.

Given the importance of the Passover meal in Jewish tradition, it is not surprising that much of Jesus' ministry involved meals. Eating with people on the margins of society was a distinctive characteristic of his public ministry, even to the point of scandal: "This fellow welcomes sinners and eats with them" (Luke 15:2). As the eminent preacher and writer Barbara Brown Taylor puts it, "He thought nothing of sitting down to eat with filthy people whose lives declared their contempt for religion."[28] His inclusive meals witnessed to the wideness of God's mercy; they, too, were salvific events. As well, the meal tradition points to the importance of access to food; sufficient bread for the day was a matter of justice. In teaching his disciples how to pray, Jesus instructed them to ask, "Give us this day our daily bread." The disciples carried on the tradition of gathering at meals. Meals were a central way in which early Christians spent time together: making decisions about their communal life and relations with the broader world; teaching and learning from each other;

singing, praying, and worshipping. The meal was "a central community event."[29]

Reflection on meals as occasions of redemptive experiences and communal identity invites us to connect our own experience of being redeemed. Brazilian theologian Ivone Gebara observes that while we may speak of various difficulties in our lives as a "cross," we tend to be more reticent about noting times of redemption. She observes that "there is a whole spirituality focused on the elemental things of life, in friendships, in the little joys of every day that lead to feelings of gratitude and gratuitousness."[30] Gebara, who lives and works with some of Brazil's poorest, speaks of the necessity of searching each day for salvation—"a process of resurrection, of recovering life and hope and justice along life's path even when these experiences are frail and fleeting." She speaks about salvation as redemption in the here and now of our bodies and daily routines. It is everywhere—even in the hell of suffering—and present everywhere "under different forms, inviting us to go beyond the evil or despondency that torments us."[31] Gebara rightly says that claiming the "dailiness" of salvation does not deny the perspective of "the beyond of history." There is always a tension, so we must take care not to "affirm the beyond at the expense of actual history."[32]

Without question, familiarity with current biblical scholarship can considerably enhance our composition of place and application of the sense. Without that familiarity, however, it is all too easy to impose inadequate understandings of Judaism on imaginative reconstructions of the narratives of the passion. For example, Jesuit priest and spiritual director Monty Williams comments on Simon of Cyrene carrying the cross of Jesus:

> Simon, a Jew, had come to Jerusalem to celebrate the Passover and the Feast of the Unleavened Bread, as was required by law for all Judean males. He would have had no desire to carry the cross of a criminal: in doing so he would have become ceremonially unclean and thus unfit to eat the Passover meal. To be drafted to do this by Roman force was, for him, not only demeaning, it broke the ethical taboos of his religion. Although his act is not one of gratuitous kindness, it has interesting results.

Simon's family is mentioned later in the Scriptures as being Christian and helping Paul in his works. The power of his act of humiliation changes the path of his life. It carries him beyond the safe, established confines of his religion to an encounter with a broken man. But instead of being destroyed by that encounter, Simon is transformed. He becomes part of the living force of redemption.[33]

There are a number of discordant notes in this commentary. Simon, in Williams's rendering, *had* to come to Jerusalem for the Passover and Feast of Unleavened Bread because Jewish Law required it of all *Judean* males. Simon, however, is not from Judea but from Cyrene, the capital city of the district of Cyrenaica in North Africa (roughly, the area of Libya). Moreover, Williams implies that such a pilgrimage was an onerous requirement—an obligation imposed by the Law. In contrast, a contemporary of Jesus, Philo of Alexandria (ca. 20 B.C.E.–40 C.E.), describes the pilgrimage to Jerusalem:

And the most evident proof of this may be found in the events which actually took place. For innumerable companies of men from a countless variety of cities, some by land and some by sea, from east and from west, from north and from the south, came to the temple at every festival, as if to some common refuge and safe asylum from the troubles of this most busy and painful life, seeking to find tranquility, and to procure a remission of and respite from those cares by which from their earliest infancy they had been hampered and weighed down, and so, by getting breath as it were, to pass a brief time in cheerful festivities, being filled with good hopes and enjoying the leisure of that most important and necessary vacation which consists in forming a friendship with those hitherto unknown, but now initiated by boldness and a desire to honor God, and forming a combination of actions and a union of dispositions so as to join in sacrifices and libations to the most complete confirmation of mutual good will. (*Special Laws,* I:69–70).

240

As to the required nature of the pilgrimage, it was indeed decreed in Torah (Exodus 23:17 and 34:23; Deuteronomy 16:16) that males go up to Jerusalem for the three annual festivals, but there was no system of enforcement. Furthermore, the claim that Simon would have been in a state of impurity because Roman authorities forced him to help Jesus carry his cross is dubious.[34] Purity norms required a state of cleanliness for offering sacrifice at the temple and for eating the Passover meal; touching corpses made one unclean. The Lukan text, however, does not situate Simeon in any of those contexts. Moreover, what we can reliably claim about this Simon is problematic. In the Acts of the Apostles, we find a number of associations with Cyrene: Cyrenians are among those who argue with Stephen and stir up false witnesses against him in Acts 6:9–15. Peter's vision at Joppa includes mention of a Simon (11:9–20), and the church at Antioch included among its prophets and teachers "Simeon who was called Niger" (13:1). It is virtually impossible to know with certainty who Simon was; "it seems as if imaginations abound about NT figures in inverse proportion to what the NT tells us about them."[35]

What is disturbing is that Williams finds it necessary to establish a contrast between "the safe confines of his [Jewish] religion" and the "redemption" Simon experiences in his encounter with Jesus. In so doing, Williams has erased Jesus' Jewishness and considerably shortened the complex process by which "Christian" became distinct from "Jew." My point is not that every director of the Exercises needs to be a biblical scholar. Rather, my claim is that we must take care not to let outmoded and inadequate understandings of Judaism contaminate our meditation on the passion accounts. To set the "Christian" way of Jesus over against the "ethical taboos" of Judaism falsifies the mission and ministry of the Jewish Jesus.

Knowledge of Second Temple Judaism and of the Roman Empire enhances the process of recreating scenes of the ministry, passion, and death of Jesus. Consider the two meditations in the second week: the Two Standards and Jesus' Entry into Jerusalem. In the former, Ignatius, shaped by his years as a soldier, proposed that those making the Exercises meditate on whether they followed the standard—the flag that rallied the troops—of "Christ, our Commander-in-chief and Lord" or of the standard of "Lucifer, mortal enemy of our human nature." The scene he has set is a vivid one, filled with mythic imagery. Lucifer, seated in a great chair of fire and smoke in a large field of Babylon, is issuing summons to "innumerable demons," scattering them from city to city throughout the world. In stark contrast, Christ is situated in a great field in the region of Jerusalem, speaking to those he calls and sends throughout the world, asking them to choose poverty over riches, contempt over worldly honor, and humility against pride. This meditation on the two standards reflects an understanding of a conflict Ignatius saw as endemic to humankind: the struggle between our desire for God and our desire for gratification and ego control.[36]

Nevertheless, its military imagery, evocation of Lucifer and demons, and valorization of poverty, contempt, and humility can be alienating to the modern mind. Reinterpreting this today, some speak, for example, of "forces, habits, and dimensions in our lives that turn us away from the love that desires us," noting that, for Ignatius, "narcissism keeps us from being fully human": "In the meditation on the Two Standards, evil is shown to operate by terrorizing us and then offering us a way of coping with our terror by seductive techniques of ego-maintenance. This meditation offers us a way of discovering how our own personality dynamics respond to being presented with situations that elicit our fear."[37]

Biblical scholarship offers another way of making meditation on Jesus' entry into Jerusalem come alive. Two contrasting processions might be imagined—the one of the Gospel narratives, the other in the world behind the text. The biblical texts, familiar from Palm Sunday liturgies, speak of Jesus processing into Jerusalem from the eastern villages of Bethphage and Bethany. It is a simple procession of people of lowly status. Jesus is riding on a colt, with crowds shouting, "Hosanna! Blessed is the one who comes in the name of the Lord! Blessed is the coming kingdom of our ancestor David! Hosanna in the highest heaven!" (Mark 11:9–10).[38] His is the "standard" of the reign of God, symbolized by the cross he will take up in Jerusalem. Or, in the prophet's poetry: this king "will cut off the chariot from Ephraim and the warhorse from Jerusalem; and the battlebow shall be cut off, and he shall command peace to the nations" (Zechariah 9:10).

Another procession into the city, however, would have taken place about the same time: The governor, Pontius Pilate, would have entered Jerusalem from the west, processing with a retinue from his splendid seaside residence in the west, Caesarea Maritima, to oversee a city swollen fourfold with Passover pilgrims. In light of what we know about Roman triumphal imagery, we can readily imagine his imperial procession. It invites application of the senses:

> A visual panoply of imperial power: cavalry on horses, foot soldiers, leather armor, helmets, weapons, banners, golden eagles mounted on poles, sun glinting on metal and gold. Sounds: the marching of feet, the creaking of leather, the clinking of bridles, the beating of drums. The swirling of dust. The eyes of the silent onlookers, some curious, some awed, some resentful.[39]

All this display enacted the imperial theology represented by Pilate. It conveyed the glory of Rome and evoked the divine status of the emperor in whose name the governor ruled. After all, it was the emperor who bore the titles of "Divine, Son of God, and God from God; Lord, Redeemer, Liberator, and Savior of the World."[40] Pilate's procession followed the standard of Caesar: dominion over the nations.

Here the "backstory" of the Roman Empire invites us to engage in a composition of place in which we situate ourselves alongside each of the processions. Are we dazzled by the splendor of Pilate's entourage? After all, which of us doesn't long now and then for a little glory for ourselves, some recognition and honor? Are we apprehensive about joining Jesus' ragtag procession, which seems so utopian and difficult? By reflecting on the contrasting values of Jesus and the Empire—two opposing standards—we confront our own issues of truth and power. We discover our own inner conflicts and are challenged to name our doubts, fears, and denials. It also invites us to name the communities with which we stand in solidarity and to assess our willingness to dedicate ourselves to the struggle for justice.[41]

Just as our world speaks in different cadences about the two standards of Christ and Lucifer, so too does it speak of sin differently from Ignatius and his contemporaries. The Exercises focus primarily on personal sin "because for my sins the Lord is going to the Passion." Grief for one's sinfulness is intended to lead to identification with Christ's grief—and ultimately to develop one's compassion. Contemporary interpreters of the Exercises speak of personal sin as "whatever lessens humanity, decreases the capacity to love, or gets in the way of developing her potential as an image of God." They suggest that the Exercises "invite the seeker to engage prayerfully in the graced and sinful moments of the larger human story," leading to a dialogue "between the past cosmic story and personal stories of sin and grace…personal sin has social and planetary repercussions."[42]

Linking personal sin with social or structural sin moves the one making the Exercises away from self-absorption and toward more communal accountability. This might mean, for example, experiencing both sorrow for my own transgressions as well as grief for the sufferings of the Jewish people that resulted from Christian accusations that they were "Christ killers." It might require meditating on Gospel scenes from a Jewish perspective. For example, the Jewish New Testament scholar Adele Reinhartz writes of her own "profound discomfort" with the rhetoric of binary opposition in the Gospel of John. She is troubled by the "totalizing" perspective of this Gospel in which humankind is consigned to one of two opposing and mutually exclusive groups, believers and non-believers, without allowing for mediating possibilities. Even beyond the troubling anti-Judaism she sees as inherent in John, Reinhartz objects to this Gospel "not just because it marginalizes the Johannine Jews, a group with which I identify…but because the ethical model that it implies allows no room for a different model."[43] Given certain political and historical circumstances, totalizing perspectives can be used to justify expulsion or even annihilation of the "other":

> This is not to lay the Crusades, the Spanish Inquisition, and the Holocaust on the Beloved Disciple's shoulders, but rather to draw some comparisons between his worldview and other totalizing views whose consequences can be measured directly. I would not be standing alone in making such a claim; the Beloved Disciple's exclusive truth

claims are troubling not only to Jewish readers but also to many Christian interpreters of this gospel.[44]

The "troubling tellings" that I have traced in part II invite not only personal grief but also consideration of what it would mean for the church to repent. Experiencing shame at the church's disparagement of Judaism and vilification of Jews is at least a prelude to a conversion to history. We need to stay with this shame long enough for it to serve as a catalyst for change.

Moreover, understanding how the Roman Empire used crucifixion as the ultimate deterrent—as "highly organized, massive state terrorism, intended to intimidate the vast peasant and slave populations of the empire into passivity"—suggests that we might grieve not simply for the suffering of the crucified Christ, but for all the world's peoples who have suffered torturous deaths through the centuries and in our own time, including the thousands of Jews crucified by Rome.[45] Thus, it is not so much that we should focus solely on Jesus' suffering, as Ignatius recommends, but rather to reflect on the power of evil: the "sin of the world, and in particular political situations, in the hearts of human beings, in the ability to destroy another human being, and in a whole world of innocent suffering."[46]

Yes, Jesus had to die, because mortality is part of the human condition, not because he had to avenge God for humanity's sinfulness. It was not necessary, however, that he had to die violently in a crucifixion. That was the consequence of the politics of first-century, Roman-ruled Judea, in which thousands, if not hundreds of thousands, of Jews were crucified. Pontius Pilate would have had no scruples about doing away with a Jewish teacher from the Galilee who attracted crowds and seemed to fear no human power. Knowledge of crucifixion's function in the Empire reminds us that Jesus, through whom we Christians see God's salvation revealed, must be seen along with the many nameless of the world who suffer from unjust rule:

Mentioning the cross, then, means mentioning crosses. And when we speak of crosses, or more precisely of sufferings inflicted by some on others, or simply of suffering as the lot of every human life, we always need to speak in the plural....I think of the crosses that development has imposed on different ecosystems, the cross of the destruction of the ozone layer, the cross of nuclear war, the cross of a national missile defense system. We are being invited to look beyond the cross of Jesus so that we may think also of a broader and more specific salvation for all creation.[47]

Thus, contemplating the events of the passion and death of Jesus opens us to the world's pain. It is a call to live out our belonging to what Douglas John Hall calls a "community of suffering":

> The point is: the suffering of the church is not the goal but the consequence of faith. For faith, we said, is that trust in God that frees us sufficiently from *self* to make us cognizant of and compassionate in relation toward the other—in particular, the other who suffers, who is hungry and thirsty, who is imprisoned; the other who "fell among thieves"; the other who knocks at our door at midnight in need. The church is a community of suffering because it is a community whose eyes have been opened to the suffering that *exists*. The first assumption of this ecclesiology is not that the church should suffer, but that it should be (in Simone Weil's sense) "attentive"—namely, attentive to the suffering that is simply there and that is usually bypassed by the world, as in the parable of the Good Samaritan. The Bible assumes that human and creaturely suffering is perennial and manifold. If the church does not see this suffering and if, seeing it, it does not take the burden of it upon itself, then its whole life must be called into question.
>
> Surely, the only survival in which the church as *Christ's* body can be interested ultimately is the survival of God's groaning creation.[48]

Hall's argument that suffering is not a goal but a *consequence of faith* is vital if we are to avoid viewing Jesus' suffering as having intrinsic meaning and thereby glorifying victimization. Rather, we might understand his passion as a "radical commitment to covenant life that retains the power to heal and transform even in the face of rejection and death."[49] Excessive emphasis on the crucifixion as the singular salvific act removes it from its historical matrix in Second Temple Judaism and Roman-ruled Palestine, and obscures the salvific dimension of Jesus' teachings and resurrection:

> Herein lies the saving power of this event: death does not have the last word. The crucified one is not annihilated but brought to new life in the embrace of God, who remains faithful in surprising ways. Thereby the judgment of earthly judges is reversed and Jesus' own person, intrinsically linked with his preaching and praxis, is vindicated.[50]

Ignatius of Loyola had a profound insight in linking meditation on the life and ministry of Jesus with his passion and death. What biblical scholarship helps to reveal is the inextricable relationship between them. Jesus' death recapitulated his life insofar as it actively drew his ministry and life to a close; he died as a consequence of his mission to counteract suffering and death. His total commitment to God's reign was "intensified when confronted by the highest possible challenge, the voluntary surrender of one's life.... Jesus' kenotic self-emptying, in the sense of complete self-dedication to the kingdom, is climaxed by God's exaltation of him, and this resurrection transforms even such a death, which is in itself meaningless and evil, into something meaningful, not in itself, but in his being raised by God."[51]

THE "SEVEN LAST WORDS"[52]

In the passion accounts of the canonical Gospels, Jesus speaks from the cross. The Gospels of Luke and John each contain three of these sayings, and Mark and Matthew one. Each of the seven words is a pathway into the drama of an evangelist's rendering of the death of Jesus. The seven, typically placed in this order, are given below; I have included a fragment of context and placed the words themselves in boldface:

Two others also, who were criminals, were led away to be put to death with him. When they came to the place that is called The Skull, they crucified Jesus there with the criminals, one on his right and one on his left. Then Jesus said, **"Father, forgive them; for they do not know what they are doing."** (Luke 23:34)

One of the criminals who were hanged there kept deriding him and saying, "Are you not the Messiah? Save yourself and us!" But the other rebuked him, saying, "Do you not fear God, since you are under the same sentence of condemnation? And we indeed have been condemned justly, for we are getting what we deserve for our deeds, but this man has done nothing wrong." Then he said, "Jesus, remember me when you come into your kingdom." He replied, **"Truly, I tell you, today you will be with me in Paradise."** (Luke 23:43)

Meanwhile, standing near the cross of Jesus were his mother, and his mother's sister, Mary the wife of Clopas, and Mary Magdalene. When Jesus saw his mother and the disciple whom he loved standing beside her, he said to his mother, **"Woman, here is your son."** Then he said to the disciple, **"Here is your mother."** And from that hour the disciple took her into his own home. (John 19:26–27)

When it was noon, darkness came over the whole land until three in the afternoon. At three o'clock Jesus cried out with a loud voice, *"Eloi, Eloi, lema sabachthani?"* which means, **"My God, my God, why have you forsaken me?"** When some of the bystanders heard it, they said, "Listen, he is calling for Elijah." And someone ran, filled a sponge with sour wine, put it on a stick, and gave it to him to drink, saying, "Wait, let us see whether Elijah will come to take him down." Then Jesus gave a loud cry and breathed his last. (Mark 15:33–36)[53]

After this, when Jesus knew that all was now finished, he said (in order to fulfill the scripture), **"I am thirsty."** (John 19:28)

A jar full of sour wine was standing there. So they put a sponge full of the wine on a branch of hyssop and held it to his mouth. When Jesus had received the wine, he said, **"It is finished."** (John 19:30)

It was now about noon, and darkness came over the whole land until three in the afternoon, while the sun's light failed; and the curtain of the temple was torn in two. Then Jesus, crying with a loud voice, said, **"Father, into your hands I commend my spirit."** Having said this, he breathed his last. (Luke 23:46)

My intent in working with the "Seven Last Words" is similar to what I have attempted to do with the *Spiritual Exercises*: to *begin* a conversation with a classic practice of Christian spirituality. Following the lead of contemporary biblical scholarship, I have endeavored to situate each "word" in its particular Gospel account, and to suggest interpretations grounded in respect for Jewish tradition. I hope the three "words" I have chosen to engage will provide a glimpse of possibilities for all seven.

"Father, forgive them; for they do not know what they are doing."

In Luke—from whom we hear the first two of the "Seven Last Words"—we see how even on the cross Jesus continues to speak the word of reconciliation that has characterized his ministry. In a word, the message of Jesus in Luke is "Be merciful, just as your Father is merciful" (6:36). On the cross Jesus acts in accord with what he had preached: "Love your enemies, do good to those who hate you, bless those who curse you, pray for those who abuse you" (verses 27–28). Luke's Jesus not only says, "Forgive and you will be forgiven" (6:38), but goes so far as to say, "The one to whom little is forgiven loves little" (7:48).

Not that this word of reconciliation was readily accepted. Luke portrays some as thinking that Jesus forgave far too freely; his word of forgiveness scandalized many of his hearers, especially the dutiful and respectable. The expanse of God's mercy threatened their narrow worlds. For example, in a story only Luke narrates (7:36–50), a certain Simon, a Pharisee, entertained Jesus for dinner in his home, only to have a woman of the city—a sinner—interrupt the dinner party with an embarrassing emotional display: bathing Jesus' feet with her tears, drying them with her hair, kissing his feet and anointing them with ointment. Simon was incensed. If Jesus truly were the prophet people claimed he was, then he should have known immediately what sort of woman this was and not let her go on so extravagantly. In Simon's perspective, Jesus should have treated her with the disdain due a sinner.

But Jesus turned the tables on his host. He bluntly told Simon that it was precisely this nameless, sinful woman who had shown "great love"; so her sins, though many, were forgiven. Simon, on the other hand, who apparently thought he had little to be forgiven for, is rebuked as one who "loved little."

Luke has another well known tale, that of the prodigal son (15:11–32). It is a touching story of a father's generous embrace of a rogue son, followed by a grand feast to celebrate the rascal's return. But this parable ends on a decidedly somber note: the grumbling elder brother who so resents his father's lavish celebration of the prodigal that he sulks, refusing to join in the feast: "For all these years," he whines, "I have been working like a slave for you, and I have never disobeyed your command; yet you have never given me even a young goat...but when this son of yours [note not "my brother"] came back you killed the fatted calf" (verses 29–30). The father's largesse has revealed the elder brother's constricted outlook on the world.

Luke, I suspect, knew his hearers very well; he knew that it had Simons and resentful older brothers as well as repentant sinners and returned prodigals. It is likely that all of those characters lurk in us as well.

Forgiveness does not come easily. In fact, it appears that this word of forgiveness spoken by Jesus on the cross scandalized some in the early church, since it was not included in all the manuscripts. Already by the early second century some otherwise reliable manuscripts of Luke's Gospel omit this word of forgiveness.[34]

Why the omission? Considerable evidence exists in the writings of early churchmen that this text, read as extending forgiveness to Jews, troubled those such as Melito of Sardis, who interpreted the Roman conquest of Jerusalem in 70 C.E. as divine retribution for the crucifixion: "You [Jews] cast the Lord down, you were cast down to earth. And you—you lie dead" (*Homily on the Passover*, 99). John Chrysostom suggested that the forgiveness Jesus extended on the cross was heard for forty years; but because Jews remained in their disbelief, forgiveness was no longer extended: "For he [God] did not immediately bring the punishment and retribution on them, but he waited for longer than 40 years after the cross. For the Savior was crucified under Tiberius, but their city was taken under Vespasian and Titus....He desired to give them time to repent...but since they remained incurable, he led the punishment and retribution to them."[55]

The copyists in the early church who apparently decided to excise this saying from their manuscripts reveal to us just how challenging this word of forgiveness is. Even they had a hard time accepting the breadth and depth of God's mercy that Jesus extended.

And yet this mercy may be just what our church needs when we face the tragic consequences of our troubling tellings—not as a cheap grace, but as a call to repent. For much of our history we Christians have not grasped the full extent of what we were doing vis-à-vis Jews. But now that our sinfulness is laid bare, we seek divine mercy to grace us with the courage to redeem our sacred story.

"My God, my God, why have your forsaken me?"

This fourth word from the cross comes as something of a shock. Not only does its tone contrast with the words of forgiveness in Luke, it goes against our sensibilities. How is it that Jesus Christ, whom the Nicene Creed describes as "the Only Begotten Son of God, born of the Father before all ages, God from God, Light from Light, true God from true God, begotten, not made, consubstantial with the Father," should, as Mark and Matthew put it so baldly, "*scream* out," "My God, my God, why have you forsaken me?"

Over the course of history, the tendency has been to want to explain it away. This is the first verse of Psalm 22. Though Jesus cries out only this initial verse, many in the church have reasoned that he knew the final stanzas, which proclaim that God neither "despises nor abhors the affliction of the afflicted": "He did not hide his face from me but heard when I cried to him" (verse 24). So really Jesus was not as desolate as this fourth word would suggest.

But might not Mark and Matthew intend for us to hear this word precisely as a moment of deep desolation? They would want us to wrestle with it, not explain it away as simply the first note of a psalm that begins in lament and ends in praise. I have no doubt that Jesus knew Psalm 22 in its fullness. In fact, I believe it was precisely his knowledge of his religious tradition that gave him both the vocabulary and the "permission," as it were, to cry out in anguish.

Mark and Matthew in particular show us a Jesus who comes to know God's will only through struggle. Their accounts of the passion vividly portray the way in which Jesus feared death, experienced betrayal, and felt pain. This is nowhere more apparent than in their account of Jesus in Gethsemane. Jesus feels the need for human support in his God-wrestling, so he takes with him Peter, James, and John. The evangelists tell us Jesus began to be "grieved and agitated." He tells the disciples, "I am deeply grieved, even to death; remain here, and stay awake with me."

We know that the disciples failed Jesus miserably; three times Jesus rose from prayer only to find them sleeping. The focus properly belongs not on those drowsy disciples, but on Jesus, who spent the entire night in prayer, anguishing over what he should do. Presumably, he could have gone underground, or muted his message or in some way given himself more breathing space. He chose not to only after a long night of seeking what God was calling him to do.

It's vital to hear the import of Gethsemane: Jesus did not know what he should do. He had to listen in his inmost depths to come to a sense of what was right. Jesus, "like us in all things but sin," had no infused sensibility, no automatic line to the Father. He had to grapple with his own fears. Only after a night of prayer could he say, "My Father, if this [cup] cannot pass unless I drink it, your will be done" (Matthew 26:42b). As the Letter to the Hebrews says, "In the days of the flesh, Jesus offered up prayers and supplications with loud cries and tears" (5:7).

Jesus inherited a tradition where one could do this. In Judaism, intimacy with God is precisely what allowed the people of the covenant to challenge God, and to give voice to anger and pain. Think of Abraham boldly bargaining with God about the fate of Sodom and Gomorrah (Genesis 18:23–33). It was the "groaning" of the Hebrew slaves that led to the Exodus: God heard their groans, remembered the covenant, looked upon the Israelites, and took notice of them (Exodus 2:23–25). Moses persuaded God to let divine anger pass, lest the Egyptians be scandalized by the impropriety of the Holy One's temper (Exodus 32:11–14). Even Jonah's "funk" (see Jonah 4:1–11) when Nineveh repented tells us something about how Israel understood God. A person, even a prophet, could sulk before the Divine Presence. The Psalms testify that no emotion need be censored; one could say anything to God, even curse one's enemies or question God's apparent absence. As Kathleen Norris says about the psalms, they "do not deny your true feelings but allow you to reflect on them, right in front of God and everyone."[56]

From Israel we learn that we need not edify God with our prayer; trusting God means being able to say anything from our depths and believing, sometimes despite ourselves, that God hears. From Israel we also learn that the people of the covenant can question God's apparent absence. During the years of forced captivity in Babylon, Jews lamented: "Why have you forgotten us completely? Why have you forsaken us these many days?" (Lamentations 5:20). Job cries, "God gives me up to the ungodly, and casts me into the hands of the wicked…he slashes open my kidneys, and shows no mercy; he pours out my gall on the ground. He bursts upon me again and again; he rushes at me like a warrior" (16:11–15).

So when Jesus screamed out, "My God, my God, why have you forsaken me?" his cry followed a long tradition. It also challenges us to follow in that same tradition. If we are to love God as we are commanded, with "all your heart, and with all your soul, and with all your might" (Deuteronomy 6:5), then we come before God with everything that is in us. That means not just with our "nice" qualities, but also with our doubts and questions and misgivings and anger and bitterness.

God invites us to touch into the world's pain, to feel with those who are desolate. All of us experience grief and loss, and we are meant to let God know what this sorrow does to us. But the cry from the cross also summons us to listen to the desolation of those beyond the borders of our own lives. We have brothers and sisters who live in the most unimaginable conditions, whether in refugee camps in war-torn areas of the world or in the squalor of cities. We have brothers and sisters deranged by mental illness, who seem to live in worlds beyond our imagining. We have brothers and sisters who seem to have little chance to make it in this world, and children left to fend for themselves, who too often are victims of violence and abuse in their own families.

We are meant, I believe, to stand in Israel's tradition, to cry out with Jesus, "My God, my God, why have you forsaken us?" We are meant to long passionately for a world that will be different, for the time when God "will wipe away every tear and death will be no more; mourning and crying and pain will be no more" (Revelation 21:4).

God will not be silent forever. God hears the groaning of those who cry out. This was Israel's faith. It is the faith of Jesus who screams out, "My God, my God, why have you forsaken me?" It is the faith that gives depth and resonance to Easter's alleluias.

"It is finished."

This is the last word Jesus speaks from the cross in John's Gospel. As in all the sayings of Jesus in John, the phrase evokes multiple meanings. Yes, the life of Jesus of Nazareth is ending; death is imminent. But this is not a medical report of his death, as if we are meant simply to note that the deceased breathed his last at 3 o'clock in the afternoon of April 7 in the year 30 (or possibly April 3, 33). Jesus does not merely stop breathing. Rather, he "gives over" or "hands on" his spirit because his life is "brought to completion" (*tetelestia*). He has drunk from the cup given to him by God.

This sixth word from the cross closely relates with the previous one, Jesus' cry of thirst (John 18:28). Between the two sayings is a curious detail: "A jar full of sour wine was standing there. So they put a sponge full of the wine on a branch of hyssop and held it to his mouth" (verse 29).The kind of hyssop that grew in first-century Palestine was a sort of marjoram that wasn't strong enough to bear the weight of a sponge. So why did the Fourth Gospel add the detail about hyssop?

Apropos of the principle that John is more interested in symbolic meaning than literal, the evangelist is not reporting botanical facts but evoking a memory deep in Israel's tradition. Hyssop was used to sprinkle the blood of the paschal lamb on the doorposts so that the Lord would pass over the houses of the Israelites (see Exodus 12:22). This association of Passover with the death of Jesus becomes more evident in view of John's chronology: Jesus' judgment before Pilate takes place at the same hour as the slaughter of the lambs for Passover (19:14). This association of Jesus' death with Passover preceded John, because some thirty years earlier Paul had written to the community at Corinth: "For our paschal lamb, Christ, has been sacrificed. Therefore, let us celebrate the festival, not with the old yeast, the yeast of malice and evil, but with the unleavened bread of sincerity and truth" (1 Corinthians 5:7b–8).

Thus we have one of the deep metaphors of Christian life: Just as Israel passed through the waters from slavery to freedom, so, too, Jesus passes from death to new life. We recapitulate this journey: Like Jesus, we undergo death in the waters of baptism in order to be raised to newness of life. This transformation exacts a cost, however. As Paul puts it, our old selves are crucified so that we might no longer be enslaved to sin (Romans 5:5–8). And just as death no longer has dominion over Jesus, it no longer has dominion over us.

What might this mean in the realm of our everyday existence when it appears that sin and evil still enslave us, and death beckons? What power lies in the metaphorical journey from death to new life?

At the heart of the metaphor is this: any life-giving change in our lives, any meaningful transformation, is costly. Authenticity and integrity are the graced achievements of a lifetime of work. Maturity doesn't happen simply by growing older; it entails facing our fears, acknowledging our limits, and dealing with those things in our lives that block growth, whether addictions or harsh memories or deeply rooted insecurities. Facing the "demons" in our lives is an arduous task. Learning to love more wholeheartedly is literally excruciating; we have to "die" to putting our own desires and needs front and center.

"It is finished" has another layer of meaning: the church's resolve to end its negative depiction of Judaism. The work of transformation is demanding and graced: acknowledging the church's complicity in the Shoah, rethinking core teachings, learning with and from Jews about Judaism, paying close attention to ways in which troubling texts are proclaimed and preached, and renouncing triumphalism. In so doing, the church is in the process of replacing the old yeast of malice and evil with the "unleavened bread of sincerity and truth." Or, to change the metaphor, by coming to terms with what we see in the tarnished mirror of history, the wood of the cross might thereby become the tree of life for the healing of the nations.

Epilogue

I would like to begin again by stressing the often-neglected notion
of an *intrareligious* dialogue, that is, an inner dialogue within myself, an
encounter in the depth of my personal religiousness, having met
another religious experience on that very intimate level. In other
words, if *interreligious* dialogue is to be real dialogue, an *intrareligious*
dialogue must accompany it; that is, it must begin with my
questioning myself and the *relativity* of my beliefs (which does not
mean their *relativism*), accepting the challenge of a change, a
conversion, and the risk of upsetting my traditional patterns.[1]

The seeds of this book were sown in a question asked in the
course of an evening of Jewish-Christian dialogue in the late
1990s at B'nai Jeshurun Synagogue in New York City. While I have
no recall of many specifics of that event, including the overall topic,
I have a keen recollection of one exchange. The discussion had
turned to how the Jews were presented in the New Testament. I
explained as lucidly as I could the problems raised by some of the
texts and the commitment in many Christian traditions to interpret
these texts in a new light. Immediately a questioner responded, "But
if these texts present negative images of Jews, why keep reading
them? Why *do* you continue to read the passion narratives?"

Why *do* we continue to read them? In many respects, it is this
question that lies at the core not only of this book, but of my own
immersion in Christianity. It has inspired me to rediscover the
"power in the story," even as I confronted the depths of hostility to
which those texts contributed.

The grace of interreligious exchanges lies not simply in what
happens when people of different traditions come together to under-

257

stand their differences but also in what happens later "in the depth of my own personal religiousness."

I conclude *Redeeming Our Sacred Story* with some personal reflections about writing a book that has been challenging, disedifying, intriguing, and enriching. In short, a brief word about a manuscript that has evoked a gamut of emotions for many years.

CHALLENGING

> I think we ought to read only the kind of books that wound and stab us. If the book we're reading doesn't wake us up with a blow on the head, what are we reading it for? So that it will make us happy...? Good Lord, we would be happy precisely if we had no books, and the kind of books that make us happy are the kind we could write ourselves if we had to. But we need the books that affect us like a disaster, that grieve us deeply, like the death of someone we loved more than ourselves, like being banished into forests far from everyone, like a suicide. A book must be the axe for the frozen sea inside us. That is my belief.[2]

Truth be told, in the process of research, I read about as many books "that wound and stab" as I could stomach. Many days I simply had to set them aside and walk away, taking refuge in lighter fare, in the pleasure of quotidian demands of teaching, and in the necessities of daily living. When friends would ask what I was working on, my response often elicited silence—clearly, I was at work on a book unlikely to increase the happiness quotient.

Other challenges arose as well. For a long time the "big picture" eluded me. I would start in one place and end up in another. Once I finally decided upon the framework, the demand of creating a responsible synthesis weighed upon me. Traversing biblical, hermeneutical, and historical studies led to a keen awareness of the perils of synthesizing complex fields of study, even as I persevered in the belief that synthesis is the proper work of a "practical" theologian. I confess I had to tear myself away from the research in virtually every chapter, resisting the temptation to refashion myself as a New Testament scholar or a medievalist or a historian of the Holocaust. There is a great deal I have yet to learn. Yet I believe an author who works on a broad canvas also has her or his place in the realm of scholarship.

Two further challenges presented themselves throughout. One is perennial: making complex ideas accessible to readers with less specialized knowledge. I doubt I have entirely succeeded in this, but it has not been for lack of effort. The second involves moral judgments. On the one hand, I have documented serious ethical failures of Christians across time. I think especially of those Christians in Europe who remained bystanders as their Jewish neighbors were derided, dispossessed, and destroyed in the ovens of Auschwitz. I rage at their behavior and regard it as a betrayal of everything I believe Christianity to stand for. But would I have done differently? Of course, I hope so, but I know myself well enough to confess I stand on no moral high ground here. Dietrich Bonhoeffer, Bernhard Lichtenberg, Margarete Sommer, Alfred Delp, Gertrude Luckner: Would that I might live with their integrity and courage. *Kyrie, eleison.*

I have walked on numerous occasions in the Garden of the Righteous among the Nations in Israel's memorial to the Holocaust, *Yad Vashem*.[3] I consider those so honored to be among the communion of saints.

DISEDIFYING

Conversation with Jews is indispensable to understanding
the Christian faith....The historical evidence massively attests
to the fact that apart from listening and talking with Jews,
we will misunderstand the Christian faith and act on our
misunderstandings.[4]

Perhaps had I been an outsider to Christianity, or no longer a practicing Catholic, this would have been a far less emotionally draining book to write. Not that I am innocent of the shadow side of my Catholic tradition, but confronting the extent of its hostility to Judaism over the ages has been overwhelming. I have long been interested in questions about interpreting troubling biblical texts, and am aware that every religious tradition has problematic passages

259

in its sacred literature. All of us are obliged to reinterpret them, lest pernicious readings inspire hostility toward the religious other in our time. But what struck me with new force was the way in which a dominant Christianity, particularly my own Roman Catholic Church, has again and again exercised its power over against Jews, its quintessential "other."

Yet facing this history in the complexity of its contexts has been easier than witnessing the apathy among so many in our contemporary church who seem to feel no serious moral obligation to engage in concrete acts of penitence and reconciliation with Jews. I see few, especially among our leaders, who are truly disconcerted in the face of the Holocaust or who are willing to confront candidly the shadow side of our tradition's conduct vis-à-vis the "other." Thankfully, the enmity of previous epochs has passed. But I see too little resolve to be "jolted" by history, to commit to a theology truly changed by Auschwitz. Instead, we often get platitudes, photo ops, and "tea and sympathy."[5] Or we get a tamed narrative, testifying to the opposition of certain church figures to the Nazis while passing over their silence with regard to the situation of Jews.

The lack of candor is evident in the 1998 document from the Vatican's Commission for Religious Relations with the Jews, *We Remember: A Reflection on the Shoah*. Even as I appreciate its general tenor, this important text conflates the church's condemnation of racism with opposition to Nazi persecution of Jews. It also exaggerates the degree of resistance to the Third Reich in its claim that "many" Christians gave "every possible assistance to those being persecuted, and in particular to the persecuted Jews." To say that "many did, but others did not" is simply not borne out by the facts, even if we wish it were.[6]

I can only speculate about the causes. Perhaps in the wake of secularism, church officials are wary of confessing the church's failures vis-à-vis Jews, lest more persons turn away from religious practice. Perhaps, too, they feel compelled to be beacons of moral certainty in the chaos and ambiguities of postmodernism, without recognizing that moral certainty "ignites every inquisition and then feeds it with oxygen."[7]

Another example may be seen in Pope Benedict's address at the "Day of Reflection, Dialogue, and Prayer for Peace and Justice" in

Assisi, Italy, in October of 2011. Responding to the post-Enlightenment critique that religion causes violence, he said:

> As a Christian I want to say at this point: yes, it is true, in the course of history, force has also been used in the name of the Christian faith. We acknowledge it with great shame. But it is utterly clear that this was an abuse of the Christian faith, one that evidently contradicts its true nature. The God in whom we Christians believe is the Creator and Father of all, and from him all people are brothers and sisters and form one single family. For us the Cross of Christ is the sign of the God who put "suffering-with" (compassion) and "loving-with" in place of force. His name is "God of love and peace" (2 Cor 13:11). It is the task of all who bear responsibility for the Christian faith to purify the religion of Christians again and again from its very heart, so that it truly serves as an instrument of God's peace in the world, despite the fallibility of humans.[8]

Perhaps this was not the occasion for a more probing analysis. But the passive voice ("force has also been used") and claim that violence contradicts the "true nature" of Christian faith seem to move away all too quickly from what the tarnished mirror of history reveals. Yes, the God revealed in the cross of Jesus Christ is loving and compassionate—in stark opposition to "Hitler's God [who] promised salvation to the many through mercilessness towards others."[9] Yet Christians need more frank acknowledgment of how the cross also became a symbol of our violence toward the "other," particularly Jews. I suspect that many in the leadership of our churches—Catholic, Orthodox, and Protestant—have never truly *grieved* for Christianity's role in antisemitism. We need services of lament that allow us all to mourn the ignorance, the misplaced zeal, the violence, and the triumphalism that so scarred the preaching of the gospel of Jesus Christ—and in too many places, still do.

Writing this in proximity to Holy Week, I am mindful of how many in our churches will regard the Gospels' depiction of Jewish responsibility for the death of Jesus—"Crucify him!" (John 19:15)—

as historically reliable. Do we not have an obligation after the Holocaust to rethink how the passion narratives are proclaimed? If we were truly to face Auschwitz, would we not alter the liturgy of Good Friday? Pay more attention to the lyrics of our hymns?[10] In too many other liturgical and educational settings, we hear the "same old, same old" canards about Pharisees, Jewish failures to recognize the messiah, and Jewish responsibility for the death of Jesus. I long for preachers and teachers to "turn and turn again" the Scriptures; I long for them to learn with and from Jews about Judaism, rather than continue to hand on oversimplifications and distortions of this tradition. We desperately need Christians to feel obliged to honor the commandment "You shall not bear false witness against your neighbor" when they speak about the religious other.[11]

Finally, I believe that Christians need to practice what British Jesuit Michael Barnes terms a "healthy and humble reticence," to counter our tendencies to triumphalism. *This does not mean turning away from its proclamation of the gospel.* To the contrary: The church "speaks of what it knows in faith—that God raised Jesus from the dead and thereby transformed the whole of creation." This is our deep and abiding conviction. Yet the church does not know the "total reality of what always remains other and utterly mysterious. Christians must, therefore, acknowledge this possibility: God may act in the world in ways of which the Church does not know."[12] Had Christian leaders, in particular, practiced this healthy and humble reticence, the history of our relations with Jews would have been dramatically different.

However disedifying my journey through our church's history, I conclude this section on an edifying note. In the years since 2001, many Christians (and others) have come to regard Muslims rather than Jews as the ultimate religious other. The instances of Islamophobia, grounded in ignorance and bias, are indeed "disedifying." Thus, it is important to learn from those whose experience not only teaches us otherwise, but who edify us by their understanding of the meaning of the death of Jesus for their lives. I speak of the French Trappist monks of the monastery of Notre-Dame de l'Atlas in the Algerian village of Tibhirine, memorably portrayed in the 2010 film *Of Gods and Men (Des hommes et des dieux)*, that was based in large part on the 2002 book, *The Monks of Tibhirine*.[13]

The eight monks were deeply ingrained in the life of the village. Its only Christians, they refrained from missionizing the Muslim villagers, instead "proclaiming" the gospel by their commitment to the well-being of the people. The medical clinic they conducted was vital to the villagers, and they and the monks had developed ties of respect and friendship. But all in Tibhirine came under threat from the violence between various factions that roiled Algeria in the 1990s and ultimately resulted in the deaths of some 60,000 to 100,000 Algerians. As French citizens, the monks debated: Should they leave, particularly after terrorist threats and the subsequent urging of government officials that they flee to safety? Or should they remain, in recognition that their life was with the villagers? As the film so movingly portrays, the monks were deeply ambivalent and frightened—with good reason. In 1996, an armed group forced their way into the monastery and took seven of them hostage. Two months later, the severed heads of the monks were discovered; the rest of their remains were never found. "Yet the monks were not martyrs to their faith. They did not die because they were Christians. They died because they would not leave their Muslim friends, who depended on them and who lived in equal danger."[14]

As the threats to the monastery intensified, Prior Christian de Chergé wrote a final testament, a letter to his youngest brother, Gerard, sometime after Christmas 1995. After the monks' deaths, it was widely published in French and Algerian newspapers. He wrote:

> If the day comes, and it could be today, that I am a victim of the terrorism that seems to be engulfing all foreigners living in Algeria, I would like my community, my Church, and my family to remember that I have dedicated my life to God and Algeria.
>
> That they accept that the Lord of all life was not a stranger to this savage kind of departure; that they pray for me, wondering how I found myself worthy of such a sacrifice; that they link in their memory this death of mine with all the other deaths equally violent but forgotten in their anonymity.
>
> My life is not worth more than any other—not less, not more. Nor am I an innocent child. I have lived long enough

to know that I, too, am an accomplice of the evil that seems to prevail in the world around, even that which might lash out blindly at me. If the moment comes, I would hope to have the presence of mind, and the time, to ask for God's pardon and for that of my fellowman, and, at the same time, to pardon in all sincerity he who would attack me.

I would not welcome such a death. It is important for me to say this. I do not see how I could rejoice when this people whom I love will be accused, indiscrimately, of my death. The price is too high, this so-called grace of the martyr, if I owe it to an Algerian who kills me in the name of what he thinks is Islam.

I know the contempt that some people have for Algerians as a whole. I also know the caricatures of Islam that a certain [Islamist] ideology promotes. It is too easy for such people to dismiss, in good conscience, this religion as something hateful by associating it with violent extremists. For me, Algeria and Islam are quite different from the commonly held opinion. They are body and soul. I have said enough, I believe, about all the good things I have received here, finding so often the meaning of the Gospels, running like some gold thread through my life, and which began first at my mother's knee, my very first church, here in Algeria, where I learned respect for the Muslims.

Obviously, my death will justify the opinion of all those who dismissed me as naïve or idealistic: "Let him tell us what he thinks now." But such people should know my death will satisfy my most burning curiosity. At last, I will be able—if God pleases—to see the children of Islam as he sees them, illuminated in the glory of Christ, sharing in the gift of God's Passion and of the Spirit, whose secret joy will always be to bring forth our common humanity amidst our differences.

I give thanks to God for this life, completely mine yet completely theirs, too, to God, wanted it for joy against, and in spite of, all odds. In this Thank You—which says everything about my life—I include you, my friends past and present, and those friends who will be here at the side of my mother and father, of my sisters and brothers—thank you a thousandfold.

And to you, too, my friend of the last moment, who will not know what you are doing. Yes, for you, too, I wish this thank-you, this "A-Dieu," whose image is in you also, that we may meet in heaven, like happy thieves, if it pleases God, our common Father. Amen! Insha Allah![15]

While it is true that the monks were not killed because they were Christians but because of their fidelity to their Muslim friends, note the allusion in the final paragraph of de Chergé's testament to Jesus' word spoken on the cross to the thieves: "Father, forgive them for they do not know what they are doing" (Luke 23:34). The monks' deep attachment to the way of Jesus Christ is what sustained them even in their fear.

INTRIGUING

On the practical level in particular, Christians must therefore strive to acquire a better knowledge of the basic components of the religious tradition of Judaism; they must strive to learn by what essential traits Jews define themselves in the light of their own religious experience....To tell the truth, such relations as there have been between Jew and Christian have scarcely ever risen above the level of monologue. From now on, real dialogue must be established. Dialogue presupposes that each side wishes to know the other, and wishes to increase and deepen its knowledge of the other. It constitutes a particularly suitable means of favoring a better mutual knowledge and, especially in the case of dialogue between Jews and Christians, of probing the riches of one's own tradition. Dialogue demands respect for the other as he [she] is; above all, respect for his [her] faith and his [her] religious convictions.[16]

Among the factors that sustained my writing was the endlessly fascinating material I encountered: the ways various Christian communities have discovered "power in the story," the myriad (if often disillusioning) ways in which my ancestors in faith drew upon New Testament texts in the formation of their religious identity vis-à-vis Jews, the vast literature on the Shoah, and the immense resources of biblical scholarship. I became absorbed in the project of reclaiming classic modes of Christian devotional practice—the Spiritual Exercises and Seven Last Words—even as I recognized I was only hinting at possibilities.

In the course of research came a discovery both surprising and ironical: Jewish artistic representations of the passion and death of Jesus. I knew that depictions of Jews in Christian art mirrored much of our tormented history, particularly in Europe.[17] The substantial body of work on the crucifixion by Jewish artists, however, was new to me.

Since the late nineteenth century, Jewish artists have on occasion depicted Jesus as a Jew. How and why they have fashioned paintings and sculptures of the crucifixion is revealing. Complex and intense debates among European Jews after the Enlightenment about reclaiming Jesus as a Jew foreshadowed these representations. The cross figured prominently in these debates. Some, such as the writer Sholem Asch, thought of Jesus as a Jewish martyr and tragic hero; his sympathies lay with Jesus, though not with Christians. Others, such as in Lamed Shapiro's Yiddish short story *Der tseylem* (The Cross), give a far more negative portrayal. His story centers on a violent pogrom in Russia; the protagonists "carve the sign of the cross on their Jewish victim's forehead in an attempt to 'save his Yid soul from hell.'"[18] In a 1920 Yiddish play by Moyshe Leyb Halpern, the central character speaks about Jesus: "...he who hangs on the cross belongs to us. He is ours, our martyr...."[19]

The cross became a way some Jews told their own passion history of persecution, most notably, the pogroms and the Shoah. Sholem Asch memorably describes the liquidation of the Warsaw Ghetto:

> Battalions of people dragged themselves across the streets
> of the ghetto, singing, praying, crying out to God with the
> same prayers which accompanied victims in former days
> on their way to the stakes of the Inquisition, the same out-

cry heard on the cross from him who gave his life to save the world, "Eli, Eli, lama sabachtani"—"My God, my God, why hast thou forsaken me?" That same cry was heard on the streets of Warsaw from hundreds of souls who, with their crosses, were being whipped on the way to Golgotha.[20]

A number of Marc Chagall's paintings testify to his long fascination with the crucified Christ, beginning with his 1912 "Golgotha/Dedicated to Christ." Two of his most famous works, "White Crucifixion" of 1938 and "Yellow Crucifixion" of 1943, juxtapose Jesus, covered with a tallith, on the cross surrounded by scenes of violence and chaos. David Roskies describes the "recognizably Jewish Christ" of "White Crucifixion." A prayer shawl serves as his loincloth. Although Jesus on the cross dominates the canvas, "all the scenes clustered around him are unaffected by his presence. Revolutionary mobs attack from the left, the matriarchs and patriarchs weep up above, a synagogue burns on the right, Jews flee the destruction on foot and by boat, the Torah scroll is in flames, a mother clutches her baby, an old Jew weeps."[21] Chagall composed a poem in Yiddish in 1938, "My Tears" (*Mayne trern*):

I carry my cross every day,
I am led by the hand and driven on,
Night darkens around me,
Have you abandoned me, my God? Why?[22]

Another use of crucifixion imagery recurs in Samuel Bak's many paintings based on the famous photo of the boy from the Warsaw ghetto held at gunpoint by SS officers in 1943.[23] The boy, about eight years old, stands with his hands held up in surrender, amid a group of frightened Jews being herded from the ghetto. Bak, born in Poland in 1933 and a survivor of the Vilna ghetto, sees himself in the photo: "In the Vilna ghetto, I was his age and I looked— as did thousands of other children destined for the same fate— exactly like him. Same cap, same out-grown coat, same short pants. I always considered this picture a kind of portrait of myself in those times."[24] It became for him "the most poignant image of Jewish crucifixion: [A]rms that reach for the sky are also a gesture of surrender, of giving up. When you superimpose the image of a crucified Son on the image of the little Warsaw boy with his uplifted arms, you wonder where is God the Father?"[25] In the many paintings based on the Warsaw boy, Bak always depicts the cross, albeit with intriguing variations.

The plot of Chaim Potok's novel, *My Name Is Asher Lev*, centers on a young Hasidic Jew who paints two crucifixion scenes, much to the horror of his family:

> My name is Asher Lev, *the* Asher Lev, about whom you have read in newspapers and magazines, about whom you talk so much at your dinner affairs and cocktail parties, the notorious and legendary Lev of the *Brooklyn Crucifix*.
>
> I am an observant Jew. Yes, of course, observant Jews do not paint crucifixions. As a matter of fact, observant Jews do not paint at all—in the way that I am painting. So strong words are being written and spoken about me, myths are being generated: I am a traitor, an apostate, a self-hater, an inflictor of shame upon my family, my friends, my people; also, I am a mocker of ideas sacred to Christians, a blasphemous manipulator of modes and forms revered by Gentiles for two thousand years.
>
> Well, I am none of those things. And yet, in all honesty, I confess that my accusers are not altogether wrong: I am indeed, in some way, all of those things.[26]

Potok, a rabbi who died in 2002, also painted his own "Brooklyn Crucifixion I." Among the most recent Jewish artistic works on the crucifixion is Argentine composer Osvaldo Golijov's *La Pasión segun San Marcos*, commissioned for the 250th anniversary of J. S. Bach that premiered in 2000.

My encounter with these works suggests the importance of Marina Hayman's argument that the multifaceted dimensions of interreligious dialogue mean that if we restrict dialogue to the realm of "words and verbal interchange," we will hamper its development.[27]

ENRICHING

And Christians must rediscover the truth that the Cross is the
sign of life, renewal, affirmation and joy, not of death, repression,
negation and the refusal of life.[28]

Redeeming Our Sacred Story is by no means intended as an adequate theology of the cross. It is primarily an exegetical and historical study, yet along the way I have given thought to the numerous
theological understandings of the death of Jesus and to their implications for Christian spirituality. Long after the final pages of my
manuscript are in the publisher's hands I will continue to reflect on
this great mystery of Christian life. Here I offer only a few thoughts
from the riches of my research.

In Christian teaching and preaching, the death of Jesus is often
evoked in terms of enduring suffering. As I indicated in the first
chapter, some of this has taken us in a "deadly direction" insofar as
it has valorized suffering. Among those to whom I am indebted for a
more adequate articulation is the Canadian theologian Douglas John
Hall. His insights are worth citing at length:

> [Jesus] is not simply born to suffer: he is born as one
> whose gift for compassion and justice will probably in the
> natural course of events lead to great suffering, but he is
> not presented as one following a script written by
> Another....Jesus' decision for the cross, which he makes
> only with the greatest difficulty precisely because he is
> perfectly free *not* to make it, is a voluntary decision on his
> part, and this same volition belongs, in some real measure,
> to the community that Jesus calls the body of Christ (*soma
> Christou*)....The church does not *have* to suffer, as if there
> were no other possibility—indeed, the fact that the his-
> toric church has so regularly and characteristically man-
> aged to *avoid* suffering ought to set to rest any insistence
> that Christians always and necessarily suffer. *However*,
> whenever the church has made good its claim to Christ's
> discipleship, it has at least known the *call* to suffer. And
> again let me repeat (because it can never be said often

enough): called to suffer not because suffering is good or beneficial or ultimately rewarding...but called to suffer *because there is suffering*—that is, because God's creatures, including human beings, are already suffering, because "the whole creation groans."[29]

Another insight inviting a lifetime of contemplation is the formulation of Michael Barnes; cited in chapter 9, it bears repeating because of its importance in reorienting Christians in the face of the religious other. Barnes suggests that the call for Christians is to discern the "seeds of the Word," the "image of the unseen God" in those of a different tradition of faith. This entails a refusal to seek to encapsulate the other within a single story or theological scheme. Rather, it involves discerning how one has been altered in the process of engaging with the other. To be "altered" is to be made other, that is, to experience "something of the mystery of Christ's Death and Resurrection."[30]

Barnes points to the altering experience of dialogue. In my case, being with the Jewish "other" has altered my immersion in the mystery of the death and resurrection of Jesus. As I complete this book, I am mindful of the call to discover anew the depth of Christianity's sacred story, living daily the process of redeeming it—and, in that process, rediscovering the cross of Jesus amid the crosses of history.

Notes

INTRODUCTION

1. Michael A. Signer, "*Speculum Concilii*: Through the Mirror Brightly," in *Unanswered Questions: Theological Views of Jewish-Catholic Relations*, ed. Roger Brooks (Notre Dame, IN: University of Notre Dame Press, 1988, 105–127. The Latin original of the citation is "*Omnis mundi creatura quasi liber et pictura nobis est in speculum*," from *De Planctu Naturae*. A preeminent scholar of Jewish-Christian dialogue, Rabbi Signer died in January of 2009 after a brief illness. See *Transforming Relations: Essays on Jews and Christians Throughout History in Honor of Michael A. Signer*, ed. Franklin T. Harkins (Notre Dame, IN: University of Notre Dame Press, 2010).

2. Signer, *Speculum Concilii*, 109. The allusion is to 1 Corinthians 13:12 ("For now we see in a mirror, dimly, but then we will see face to face. Now I know only in part; then I will know fully, even as I have been fully known").

3. Edward H. Flannery, *The Anguish of the Jews: Twenty-three Centuries of Anti-Semitism* (New York: Macmillan, 1964), xi. The second edition, 1985, does not have this vignette.

4. The phrase "tarnished mirror of history" comes from the national foundation Facing History and Ourselves, founded on the belief that confronting history's tarnished mirror, particularly the Armenian Genocide and the Holocaust, offers invaluable perspectives on contemporary moral choices regarding violence, racism, antisemitism, and bigotry. See http://www.facinghistory.org.

5. See Christopher Hitchens, *God Is Not Great: How Religion Poisons Everything* (New York: Twelve, 2009).

6. Kevin J. Madigan and Jon D. Levenson, *Resurrection: The Power of God for Christians and Jews* (New Haven, CT: Yale University Press, 2008).

7. Also known as the Catechism of the Council of Trent, intended as a handbook for parish priests. This excerpt is taken from the online Modern

History Source Book, Article IV, http://www.fordham.edu/halsall/mod/
romancat.html.

CHAPTER 1

1. Gerard S. Sloyan, *The Crucifixion of Jesus: History, Myth, Faith*
(Minneapolis: Fortress, 1995), 2.

2. For analysis of the Yiddish version and its significant differences
with *Night*, see Naomi Seidman, *Faithful Renderings: Jewish-Christian
Difference and the Politics of Translation* (Chicago: University of Chicago
Press, 2006), 220–224.

3. Elie Wiesel, *A Jew Today*, trans. Marion Wiesel (New York:
Random House, 1978), 16. Of course, at age 27, 70 seems ancient.

4. Wiesel, *A Jew Today*, 18.

5. Ibid., 19.

6. Wiesel refers to *Night* as "testimony" and as a "deposition." See
Wiesel, *All Rivers Run to the Sea: Memoirs* (New York: Schocken Books,
1995), 79.

7. François Mauriac, "Foreword," in Elie Wiesel, *Night*, trans. Stella
Rodway (New York: Avon Books, 1969), 10–11. Emphasis added. See Eva
Fleischner, "Mauriac's Preface to *Night*: Thirty Years Later," *America* 159/15
(November 19, 1988): 411, 419.

8. *All Rivers Run to the Sea,* 271.

9. Perhaps Mauriac had in mind Paul's formulation: "For Jews
demand signs and Greeks desire wisdom, but we proclaim Christ crucified
a stumbling block [*skandalon*] to Jews and foolishness to Gentiles, but to
those who are the called, both Jews and Greeks, Christ the power of God
and the wisdom of God" (1 Corinthians 1:22–24).

10. *Faithful Renderings*, 227. Emphasis added. See also Eva Fleischner,
"Mauriac's Preface to *Night*: Thirty Years Later," *America* 159/15
(November 19, 1988): 411–412.

11. This image of the cornerstone functions in two principal ways in
the New Testament. The first usage occurs in Ephesians, where Paul (or,
more likely, a writer in the Pauline tradition) exhorts them to realize that
they are "no longer strangers and aliens, but…citizens with the saints and
also members of the household of God, built upon the foundation of the
apostles and prophets, with Christ Jesus himself as the cornerstone. In him
the whole structure is joined together and grows into a holy temple in the
Lord; in whom you also are built together spiritually into a dwelling place
for God" (Ephesians 2:20–22). The second usage draws upon Psalm 118:22,

alluding to Jesus as the cornerstone initially rejected by the builders. See Mark 12:10, with parallels in Matthew 21:42 and Luke 20:17; see also Acts 4:11 and 1 Peter 2:6.

12. French Catholic philosopher Jacques Maritain, then his country's ambassador to the Vatican, was not able to attend the conference but played an important role behind the scenes. He and Dr. Gertrude Luckner, a German Catholic whose anti-Nazi activity landed her in the Ravensbrück concentration camp for two years and who pioneered postwar reconciliation with Jews, assisted the French Jewish scholar Jules Isaac in writing a background paper for the conferees. Mauriac wrote to the secretary of the Seelisberg gathering, urging "battle against anti-Semitism...[as] a fundamental obligation for the conscience and a primordial duty of moral health for what is left of our civilization." Cited in Robert A. Ventresca, "Jacques Maritain and the Jewish Question: Theology, Identity and Politics," *Studies in Christian-Jewish Relations* 2/2 (2007): 58–69; citation, 69. See also Christian Rutishauser, "The 1947 Seelisberg Conference: The Foundation of the Jewish-Christian Dialogue," *Studies in Christian-Jewish Relations* 2 (2007): 34–53; see also Victoria J. Barnett, "Seelisberg: An Appreciation," *Studies in Christian-Jewish Relations* 2 (2007): 54–57. This journal is available at http://escholarship.bc.edu/scjr/vol2/iss2. For details on the important roles Maritain and Luckner played both during and after the Shoah, see Michael Phayer, *The Catholic Church and the Holocaust, 1930–1965* (Bloomington: Indiana University Press, 2000), esp. 176–182.

13. This statement, generally referred to as the "Ten Points of Seelisberg," is available in full on a number of websites. See, for example, http://www.jcrelations.net/en/?item=983.

14. Section 1 of *Nostra Aetate* is a general introduction, and §2 discusses relations with non-Christian religions (Buddhism and Hinduism are named explicitly); §3 deals with the relationship with Islam; and §4, with the church's relationship with Judaism. The concluding §5 offers a hortatory word about the dignity of all peoples created in God's image and, therefore, the impermissibility of "any discrimination against persons or harassment of them because of their race, color, condition of life, or religion." It is widely available online and in various languages; see, inter alia, http://www.vatican.va/archive/hist_councils/ii_vatican_council/documents/vat-ii_decl_19651028_nostra-aetate_en.html (accessed January 20, 2010).

15. Much of the criticism of *Nostra Aetate* has centered on its somewhat tepid statement "deploring" rather than condemning antisemitism. Subsequent documents have been more forceful, though elements of defensiveness may be seen in texts such as the 1998 Vatican statement "We Remember: A Reflection on the Shoah." For one analysis of what *Nostra*

Aetate inaugurated, see my "The *Nostra Aetate* Trajectory: Holding Our Theological Bow Differently," in *Never Revoked: Nostra Aetate as Ongoing Challenge for Jewish-Christian Dialogue,* Louvain Theological and Pastoral Monographs 40, ed. Maryanne Moyaert and Didier Pollefeyt (Leuven, Belgium: Peeters Publishers, 2009), 133–157.

16. Elizabeth A. Dreyer, "Behold, the One You Seek Has Been Lifted Up," in *The Cross in Christian Tradition: From Paul to Bonaventure,* ed. E. A. Dreyer (New York and Mahwah, NJ: Paulist, 2000), 236–258; citation, 238.

17. Barbara E. Reid, O.P., *Taking Up the Cross: New Testament Interpretations through Latina and Feminist Eyes* (Minneapolis: Fortress, 2007), 15.

18. On the ways in which theologies are at work in artists' interpretation of the passion, see Richard Viladesau, *The Beauty of the Cross: The Passion of Christ in Theology and the Arts, from the Catacombs to the Eve of the Renaissance* (New York: Oxford University Press, 2006) and *The Triumph of the Cross: the Passion of Christ in Theology and the Arts from the Renaissance to the Counter-Reformation* (New York: Oxford, 2008).

19. See Colleen Carpenter Cullinan, *Redeeming the Story: Women, Suffering, and Christ* (New York and London: Continuum, 2004). Other critiques include Joanne Carlson Brown and Carole R. Bohn, eds., *Christianity, Patriarchy and Abuse: A Feminist Critique* (New York: Pilgrim Press, 1990); JoAnne Marie Terrell, "Our Mothers' Gardens: Rethinking Sacrifice," *Cross Examinations,* 33–49; Catherine Clark Kroeger and James R. Beck, eds., *Women, Abuse, and the Bible: How the Bible Can Be used to Hurt or Heal* (Grand Rapids: Baker, 1996).

20. See Joel B. Green and Mark D. Baker, *Recovering the Scandal of the Cross: Atonement in New Testament and Contemporary Concerns* (Downers Grove, IL: InterVarsity Press, 2000).

21. Brian Mavis, "The Passion of the Christ: True or False?" (Vista, CA: Outreach, Inc, 2003), pp. 5–6; a pdf of the book is available online at http://www.sermoncentral.com/images/The%20Passion.pdf.

22. Brian Mavis, "Experience the *Passion of the Christ*," in *The Passion of the Christ Sermon Series* (Vista, CA: Outreach, Inc., 2003), p. 5; a pdf of the the book is available online at http://www.sermoncentral.com/images/The%20Passion.pdf.

23. One exception: Rita Nakashima Brock and Rebecca Ann Parker, to whose work I refer in the next section, examine anti-Judaism in the Gospel of John; see their article, "Enemy and Ally: Contending with the Gospel of John's Anti-Judaism," in *Walk in the Ways of Wisdom: Essays in Honor of Elisabeth Schüssler Fiorenza,* ed. Shelly Matthews, Cynthia

Kittredge, and Melanie Johnson (Harrisburg: Trinity International Press, 2003), 161–180.

24. Roberta C. Bondi, *Memories of God: Theological Reflections on a Life* (Nashville: Abingdon, 1995), 112–113.

25. Ibid., 139.

26. Ibid., 141.

27. Ibid.

28. Rita Nakashima Brock and Rebecca Ann Parker, *Proverbs of Ashes: Violence, Redemptive Suffering, and the Search for What Saves Us* (Boston: Beacon, 2002), 158. The title comes from Job 13:12: "Your maxims are proverbs of ashes, your defenses are defenses of clay."

29. *Proverbs*, 53.

30. Ibid., 248.

31. Ibid., 250–251.

32. Delores S. Williams, "Black Woman's Surrogacy Experience and the Christian Notion of Redemption," *Cross Examinations: Readings on the Meaning of the Cross Today*, Marit A. Trelstad, ed. (Minneapolis: Fortress, 2006), 19–32. This critique is developed more fully in her *Sisters in the Wilderness: The Challenge of Womanist God-Talk* (Maryknoll, NY: Orbis, 1993).

33. "Black Women's Surrogacy," 26–27.

34. Ibid., 27.

35. Ibid., 30–31. Cf. James H. Cone, *The Cross and the Lynching Tree*, 149.

36. Sally A. Brown, *Cross Talk: Preaching Redemption Here and Now* (Louisville: Westminister John Knox, 2008), 49–55.

37. Ibid., 61.

38. *Taking Up the Cross*, 67. Reid also speaks of "dangerous directions," 29.

39. Marian Ronan, while acknowledging that *Proverbs of Ashes* is a "brave and much-needed denunciation of the misuse of the cross," criticizes Brock and Parker's "broader claims about the cross and the Christian theological tradition as a whole." I share Ronan's assessment that their attempt to "expel the cross from Christianity and to divorce the suffering and death of Jesus from his resurrection [is] deeply troubling." See her "Coming Closer to the Cross: New Feminist Perspectives on the Passion of Jesus," a paper presented to the Protestant Akadamie at Bolder, Zurich, Switzerland, January 2008).

40. *Taking Up the Cross*, 182–183.

CHAPTER 2

1. Sally B. Purvis, *The Power of the Cross: Foundations for a Christian Feminist Ethic of Community* (Nashville: Abingdon, 1993), 92.

2. Although the death and resurrection of Jesus are distinct events, and the facticity of his death more empirically verifiable than that of the resurrection, from a theological perspective they might be regarded as a single event, the passage from death to new life. See chapter 3 for an analysis of the differences in the passion narratives of the canonical Gospels.

3. Barbara E. Reid, O.P., *Taking Up the Cross: New Testament Interpretations through Latina and Feminist Eyes* (Minneapolis: Fortress, 2007). Reid uses the heuristic of "deadly directions" and "liberating possibilities" (67).

4. Karyn Carlo, *The Cross and the Women of Galilee: A Feminist Theology of Salvation* (PhD Dissertation, Union Theological Seminary in the City of New York, 2009), 11.

5. Howard Thurman, *Deep River: Reflections on the Religious Insight of Certain of the Spirituals*, rev. and enlarged ed. (New York: Harper and Brothers, 1955), 23.

6. Thurman, *Deep River*, 24.

7. James H. Cone, *The Spirituals and the Blues: An Interpretation* (New York: Seabury, 1972), 53–54.

8. James A. Noel, "Were You There?" in *The Passion of the Lord: African American Reflections,* ed. Noel and Matthew V. Johnson (Minneapolis: Fortress, 2005), 39.

9. Ibid., 49.

10. Precise statistics about how many were lynched cannot be determined. Although the numbers were significant—perhaps as many as 5,000 persons lynched—more powerful testimony comes from photographs. See in particular http://www.withoutsanctuary.org. This website is a sobering witness to the unspeakable cruelty; see also the book, James Allen et al., *Without Sanctuary: Lynching Photography in America* (Santa Fe: Twin Palms Publishers, 2000).

11. James H. Cone, "Strange Fruit: The Cross and the Lynching Tree," *Harvard Divinity Bulletin* 35/1 (Winter 2007): 46–54; citation, 53–54.

12. Ibid., 54.

13. Ibid., 52.

14. Ibid., 54.

15. The lyrics originated from a poem by a Jewish teacher in the Bronx, Abel Meeropol, who published it in a 1936 issue of *The New York Teacher* under the name Lewis Allen. He wrote the poem in response to a

photograph of the 1930 lynching of Thomas Shipp and Abram Smith in Marion, Indiana, and later put it to music. See David Margolick and Hilton Als, *Strange Fruit: Billie Holiday, Café Society and an Early Cry for Civil Rights* (Philadelphia: Running Press, 2000).

16. James Cone, *The Cross and the Lynching Tree* (Maryknoll, NY: Orbis, 2011), 18.

17. Christopher Pramuk, "'Strange Fruit': Black Suffering/White Revelation," *Theological Studies* 67/2 (June 2006): 345–377; citation, 347.

18. Ibid., 347.

19. Ibid., 364. "You killed him" alludes to Acts 5:30: "The God of our ancestors raised up Jesus, whom you had killed by hanging him on a tree." This "you," of course, has traditionally been read as referring to Jews. See chapter 4 for discussion of the consequences of this accusation.

20. Pramuk, "Strange Fruit,'" 362.

21. Cited in Demetrius K. Williams, "Identifying with the Cross of Christ," in *The Passion of the Lord*, 106. See Cone's excellent chapter on King in *The Cross and the Lynching Tree*, 65–92.

22. Nicholas C. Criss and Jack Nelson, "Dr. King Slain by Sniper in Memphis," *Los Angeles Times* (April 5, 1968), http://encarta.msn.com/sidebar_761593843/dr_king_slain_by_sniper_in_memphis.html (accessed September 23, 2009).

23. Composed in 1968 and first performed by the National Symphony in February 1974, *The Passion of Martin Luther King* is available in a recording from Koch International Classics. Paired with it is a musical setting of King's words composed by Joseph Schwantner in 1982, *New Morning for the World.*

24. Translated in the score as "He saw Jesus tortured for the sins of his people and subjected to the scourge, and he saw him give up the Ghost." How one interprets "for the sins of his people" bears further discussion. The standard translation by Edward Caswall (1814–1868) reads: "For the sins of his own nation / Saw him hang in desolation / All with bloody scourges rent. / Bruised, derided, cursed defiled, / She beheld her tender child / 'Til his spirit forth he sent."

25. It is not clear precisely what actions young Emmett Till engaged in vis-à-vis the white woman, twenty-one-year-old Carolyn Bryant, the wife of store owner Roy Bryant. When her husband heard that a black child had allegedly made overtures toward his wife, he was outraged, and conspired with his half brother, J. W. Milam, to make an example of Till. Bryant and Miliam were acquitted by an all-white jury in 1955, but later admitted that they had beaten and killed Till.

26. Cited in Carlo, *The Cross and the Women of Galilee*, 110.

27. Emmett Till's death has inspired plays (for example, Toni Morrison's *Dreaming Emmett,* and James Baldwin's *Blues for Mister Charlie*); poetry (for example, Gwendolyn Brooks's "The Last Quatrain of the Ballad of Emmett Till"; Langston Hughes's "Mississippi–1955," and his "Money Mississippi Blues," with music by Jobe Huntley; and Audre Lorde's "Afterimages"); music (for example, Bob Dylan's "The Death of Emmett Till"); and fiction (for example, Lewis Nordan's novel *Wolf Whistle*).

28. Cone, *The Cross and the Lynching Tree*, 156.

29. Diana L. Hayes, *Were You There? Stations of the Cross*, Art by Charles S. Ndege (Maryknoll, NY: Orbis, 2000).

30. Ibid., xi.

31. The story of Veronica may be a sort of midrash on the story of the woman who was cured from her hemorrhage as she touched the cloak of Jesus (Luke 8:43–48). She is given a name in the mid-fourth-century apocryphal *Acts of Pilate*. The legend grew in the eleventh century as the detail of Christ's image on her cloth was added, and by the late fourteenth century this was linked to the passion of Jesus.

32. Hayes, *Were You There?* 40–41.

33. Ibid., 41.

34. See http://www.okcatholicsforlife.org/pax-christi-poster-exhibit.htm (accessed January 4, 2010).

35. See http://www.paxchristiusa.org/StationsoftheCross.pdf.

36. Its mission statement:

Pax Christi USA strives to create a world that reflects the Peace of Christ by exploring, articulating, and witnessing to the call of Christian nonviolence. This work begins in personal life and extends to communities of reflection and action to transform structures of society. Pax Christi USA rejects war, preparations for war, and every form of violence and domination. It advocates primacy of conscience, economic and social justice, and respect for creation.

Pax Christi USA commits itself to peace education and, with the help of its bishop members, promotes the gospel imperative of peacemaking as a priority in the Catholic Church in the United States. Through the efforts of all its members and in cooperation with other groups, Pax Christi USA works toward a more peaceful, just, and sustainable world.

Pax Christi is a section of Pax Christi International, the Catholic peace movement.

See http://paxchristiusa.org/about/our-mission/ (accessed February 24, 2012).

37. See http://stationsofcross.blogspot.com/ (accessed January 5, 2010).

38. Available in various modes on the website of Scottish scholar and activist Alastair McIntosh: http://www.alastairmcintosh.com/general/1992-stations-cross-esquivel.htm. CIDSE, an alliance of sixteen member-organizations for human development from various European and North American countries, published these paintings with a commentary in a 1992 handbook, *Way of the Cross from Latin America*; English version edited by Toni Bernet-Strahn and Erwin Mock by CAFOD (Catholic Agency for Overseas Development, the British member-organization of CIDSE).

39. See Marguerite Feitlowitz, *A Lexicon of Terror: Argentina and the Legacies of Torture* (New York: Oxford University Press, 1999); Jo Fisher, *Mothers of the Disappeared* (Boston: South End Press, 1999); and Jacobo Timmerman, *Prisoner without a Name, Cell without a Number,* trans. Toby Talbot (Madison: University of Wisconsin Press, 2002).

40. Statistics from LISC/Chicago, an agency that stimulates comprehensive neighborhood development; see http://www.newcommunities.org/communities/pilsen/about.asp (accessed January 6, 2010).

41. Karen Mary Davalos, "The Real Way of Praying: The Via Crucis, *Mexicano* Sacred Space, and the Architecture of Domination," in *Horizons of the Sacred: Mexican Traditions in U.S. Catholicism*, ed. Timothy Matovina and Gary Riebe-Estrella (Ithaca, NY: Cornell University Press, 2002), 41–69; citation, 47.

42. Constanza Montaña, "Passion Play Unites Pilsen," *Chicago Tribune,* March 26, 1991, 11. http://pqasb.pqarchiver.com/chicagotribune/access/7868915.html?dids=7868915&FMT=ABS&FMTS=ABS&type=current&date=Mar+26%2C+1991&author=Montana%2C+Constanza&pub=Chicago+Tribune&edition=&startpage=11&desc=Passion+Play+Unites+Pilsen (accessed January 6, 2010).

43. Davalos, "The Real Way of Praying," 63.

44. Ibid., 60–61.

45. See Margaret M. Nava, "Via Crucis," *Commonweal* 136/6 (March 27, 2009): 6. Ironically, a white supremacist website criticizes the Pilsen Via Crucis because there's "not a Jew involved, only 'Romans.'" See http://www.stormfront.org/forum/showthread.php?t=590380&s=a530532923644dea73e7a2dbfe4283d2& (accessed August 16, 2010).

46. Hayes, 88.

47. Rita Nakashima Brock and Rebecca Ann Parker, *Proverbs of Ashes: Violence, Redemptive Suffering, and the Search for What Saves Us* (Boston: Beacon, 2001), 39.

48. Serene Jone, *Feminist Theory and Christian Theology: Cartographies of Grace*, Guides to Theological Inquiry (Minneapolis: Fortress, 2000), 53. For advocacy of a "self giving that is not easy, that is not glamorous, that offers few immediate rewards" drawn from the image of Christ as a nursing mother, see Jeannine Hill-Fletcher, "Christology between Identity and Difference," in *Frontiers in Catholic Feminist Theology: Shoulder to Shoulder*, ed. Susan Abraham and Elena Procario-Foley (Minneapolis: Fortress, 2000), 79–96, esp. 88–89.

49. Following many who have studied Romero's life, I call him a martyr, although he is not considered a martyr by the Vatican, for which one must have been killed for her or his unambiguous profession of faith by a killer who is motivated by *odium fidei* ("hatred of the faith"); moreover, there must be witnesses to testify to the steadfastness of the martyr. Pope John Paul II expanded the definition when he canonized Maximilian Kolbe, who gave up his life for another prisoner at Auschwitz in 1941, as a "martyr of charity." Kenneth L. Woodward argues that the witness of the Latin American church should give rise to a new definition of martyr as one who dies for the sake of God's reign. Martyrs are witness to the "absolute claims of the kingdom over all other values, including the value of life itself" (*Making Saints: How the Catholic Church Determines Who Becomes a Saint, Who Doesn't, and Why* [New York: Simon and Schuster, 1990], 127–155; citation, 154). Elizabeth A. Castelli defines *martyrdom* as "willing and self-sacrificing death on behalf of one's religion, one's political ideals, or one's community"; see her *Martyrdom and Memory: Early Christian Culture Making* (New York: Columbia University Press, 2004), 33.

50. Renny Golden, "Oscar Romero: Bishop of the Poor," http://www.uscatholic.org/culture/social-justice/2009/02/oscar-romero-bishop-poor (accessed January 25, 2010).

51. For example, in §17 of the final document promulgated on September 6, 1968, the Latin American bishops wrote: "We wish to confirm that it is indispensable to form a social conscience and a realistic perception of the problems of the community and of social structures. We must awaken the social conscience and communal customs in all strata of society and professional groups regarding such values as dialogue and community living within the same group and relations with wider social groups (workers, peasants, professionals, clergy, religious, administrators, and so on). This task of 'concientización' and social education ought to be integrated into joint Pastoral Action at various levels" (*The Church in the Present-Day Transformation of Latin America in Light of the Council*, vol. 2 (Bogotá: CELAM, 1970). Several years later, the international synod of Catholic bishops issued the document "Justice in the World." Its thesis is

frequently cited: "Action on behalf of justice and participation in the transformation of the world appear to us as a constitutive dimension of the preaching of the Gospel, or, in other words, of the Church's mission for the redemption of the human race and its liberation from every oppressive situation." See *The Gospel of Peace and Justice: Catholic Social Teaching Since Pope John*, ed. Joseph B. Gremillion (Maryknoll, NY: Orbis, 1976), 514.

52. See William Reiser, "The Road from Aguilares," *America* 201/14 (November 16, 2009): 13–15; citation, 14.

53. Michael Campbell-Johnston, "Very Ordinary Saints," *The Tablet*, November 14, 2009, 14.

54. Michael Campbell-Johnston, "Martyrdom and Resurrection in Latin America Today," in *Truth and Memory: The Church and Human Rights in El Salvador and Guatemala*, ed. Michael A. Hayes and David Tombs (Leominster, UK: Gracewing, 2001), 44–58; citation, 48.

55. Jon Sobrino, *Archbishop Romero: Memories and Reflections*, trans. Robert R. Barr (Maryknoll, NY: Orbis Books, 1990), 10. Sobrino suggests other factors in Romero's transformation: the realization that conservative elements in the church ceased to offer support when he became more identified with the poor, and the poor themselves, whose suffering "must have shaken Archbishop Romero to his depths as he watched their oppression swell to such intolerable proportions" (13). Moreover, in his earlier assignment as the bishop of Santiago de Maria, Romero had been deeply moved by the harsh realities of the people's lives.

56. Carter refused Romero's request. After the rape and murder of four American churchwomen—Maryknoll sisters Maura Clarke and Ita Ford, Ursuline sister Dorothy Kazel, and lay missionary Jean Donovan—on December 2, 1980, Carter suspended the aid. But, bowing to pressure, he reinstated it. During the administration of Ronald Reagan, more money and advisers were sent to the ruling junta in El Salvador. Over the course of ten years, the U.S. government sent some seven billion dollars in foreign and military aid to that nation. The assassination of six Jesuits of the University of Central America, their housekeeper, and her daughter by a military death squad on November 16, 1989, was so shocking to many in the United States that it led to an outcry against the aid.

57. Campbell-Johnston, "Very Ordinary Saints," 14.

58. Cited in Sobrino, *Archbishop Romero*, 41.

59. Sobrino, *Archbishop Romero*, 20.

60. Cited in Sobrino, *Archbishop Romero*, 40.

61. Cited in Anna L. Peterson, *Martyrdom and the Politics of Religion: Progressive Catholicism in El Salvador's Civil War* (Albany: State University of New York Press, 1997), 144.

62. John Dear, "Oscar Romero, Presente!" See http://www.commondreams.org/views05/0324-21.htm (accessed January 25, 2010).

63. Stations of the Cross in the chapel of the University of Central America in San Salvador commemorate the "crucified peoples" of El Salvador's civil war. See http://www.edow.org/spirituality/lent/ElSalvador/stations.html (accessed November 9, 2010).

64. Cited in Peterson, *Martyrdom*.

65. Cited in Jeannette Rodriguez and Ted Fortier, *Cultural Memory: Resistance, Faith and Identity* (Austin: University of Texas Press, 2007), 69 and 71.

66. Ibid., 72.

67. The citation is from Carlos Bravos, in Peterson, *Martyrdom*, 132.

68. Peterson, *Martyrdom*, 133.

69. Ibid., 142.

70. Ibid., 149–150.

71. Ibid., 151.

72. Jones, *Trauma and Grace*, 82.

73. Alexander Schmemann, *Of Water and the Spirit: A Liturgical Study of Baptism* (Crestwood, NY: St. Vladimir's Seminary Press, 1974), 39.

74. Ibid., 39.

75. See Mark Searle, *Christening: The Making of Christians* (Collegeville, MN: Liturgical Press, 1980), 91.

76. Tom Grufferty, "Through Death to Life," *The Tablet*, April 19, 2003, pp. 20–21.

77. Sara Lee, with whom I went to Auschwitz, and I have written about this in our coauthored book, *Christians and Jews in Dialogue: Learning in the Presence of the Other* (Woodstock, VT: Sky Light Paths Publishing, 2006), 114–138.

78. Teresa and Henryk Świebocki, *Auschwitz: The Residence of Death*, trans. William Brand (Krakow and Oświęcim: Auschwitz-Birkenau State Museum and Bialy Kruk, 2003). Photographs are by Adam Bujak.

79. These were primarily Polish dissidents and intellectuals, but also housed at Auschwitz I were Soviet prisoners of war. Some Germans and others arrested for criminal acts against the Nazis were also at this camp.

80. Gerard S. Sloyan, *The Crucifixion of Jesus: History, Myth, Faith* (Minneapolis: Augsburg Fortress, 1995), 217.

CHAPTER 3

1. Sandra M. Schneiders, "Feminist Ideology Criticism and Biblical Hermeneutics," *Biblical Theology Bulletin* 19 (1989): 3–10; citation, 9. Note that "the Christ-killer charge" is my addition.

2. *Dei Verbum*, §8.

3. The passion narratives are generally identified as Mark 14:1— 15:41; Matthew 26:1—27:66; Luke 22:1—23:56; and John 18:1—19:42.

4. See Richard J. Powell, *Homecoming: The Art and Life of William H. Johnson* (New York: Rizzoli, 1991), 185. Powell dates this painting to 1939–1940, and says that it "demonstrates Johnson's first serious attempt at creating a black analogue for a standard biblical theme" (182). Around 1944 Johnson painted another crucifixion theme, *Mount Calvary*. Grünewald's *The Crucifixion of Christ* is dated ca. 1510–1515.

5. Available on a compact disk from Koch International Classics, *The Passion of Martin Luther King*, performed in 1974 by the Oregon Symphony.

6. In Matthew's version of this story (15:21–28), she is described as a Canaanite woman.

7. See, for example, John 9:14–15.

8. See Proverbs 27:6: "Well meant are the wounds a friend inflicts, but profuse are the kisses of an enemy." In cheating Esau of his blessing, Jacob kisses Isaac (Genesis 27:26–27). David's son Absalom kissed all the Israelites who came to do obeisance to him; "so Absalom stole the hearts of the people of Israel" (2 Samuel 15:5–6).

9. Mark here uses the term *lēstēs* for bandit (as also in 11:17 and 15:27); it connotes a more violent form of robbery than does another Greek term *kleptes*, "thief" (see Luke 12:23). Bandits were sometimes highway robbers seeking personal gain, but the term also was used of guerilla fighters, seeking to right the wrongs of Roman rule. As to fulfilling the Scriptures, see the three predictions of the passion in Mark 8:31, 9:12, and 14:21.

10. See Psalm 38:12–14: "Those who seek my life lay their snares; those who seek to hurt me speak of ruin, and meditate treachery all day long"; see also Psalm 39:9: "I am silent; I do not open my mouth."

11. See Daniel 7:13: "As I watched in the night visions, I saw one like a human being [Son of Man] coming with the clouds of heaven. And he came to the Ancient One and was presented before him"; see also Psalm 110:1: "The LORD says to my lord, 'Sit at my right hand until I make your enemies your footstool.'"

12. See Psalm 31:13: "For I hear the whispering of many—terror all around!—as they scheme together against me, as they plot to take my life";

Psalm 54:3 "For the insolent have risen against me, the ruthless seek my life; they do not set God before them"; Psalm 71:10: "For my enemies speak concerning me, and those who watch for my life consult together"; Psalm 86:14: "O God, the insolent rise up against me; a band of ruffians seeks my life, and they do not set you before them."

13. See Psalm 22:18 "They divide my clothes among themselves, and for my clothing they cast lots."

14. In Mark, this cry is in Aramaic, and in Matthew it is in Hebrew. See Psalm 22:1: "My God, my God, why have you forsaken me?"

15. In Luke 9:41, Jesus speaks of "You faithless and perverse generation...."

16. See Acts 4:26–28: "'The kings of the earth took their stand, and the rulers have gathered together against the Lord and against his Messiah.' For in this city, in fact, both Herod and Pontius Pilate, with the Gentiles and the peoples of Israel, gathered together against your holy servant Jesus, whom you anointed, to do whatever your hand and your plan had predestined to take place."

17. This is the third time in Luke that Pilate has declared Jesus innocent of the charges: 23:4, 23:14, and 23:22.

18. See Psalm 31:5: "Into your hand I commit my spirit; you have redeemed me, O LORD, faithful God." On God as Father, see Luke 2:49, 11:2, 10:21, 23:34, and 22:42.

19. The term is dikaios, or "righteous." See Luke 1:6, 17, 75; 2:25; 5:32; 12:57; 14:14; 15:7; 18:9; 20:20; 23:47, 50.

20. The Greek term for a "detachment" [of soldiers] is a speira, that is, a "cohort." A Roman cohort consisted of 600 soldiers.

21. References: John 4:26; 6:35, 41, 48, 51 (bread of life/living bread come down from heaven); 8:12; 10:7, 9, 11, 14, 25 (gate for sheep, good shepherd); 14:6; 15:1, 5.

22. See John 6:39, 10:28, and 17:12.

23. The term the Jews (hoi Ioudaioi) occurs some 61 times in John. Although occasionally used neutrally, it more often functions negatively.

24. Was the sister of the mother of Jesus Mary, the wife of Clopas, or simply unnamed? See the discussion in Raymond E. Brown, The Gospel According to John, XII–XXI (Garden City: Doubleday, 1970), 904–906.

25. Luke seems to portray the Pharisees more favorably in Acts than in his Gospel; not only does the Pharisee Gamaliel show tolerance, but Luke identifies him as Paul's teacher (22:3); Paul describes himself, of course, as a Pharisee (26:5). In 15:5, Pharisaic believers in Jesus maintain that Gentile believers in Jesus must be circumcised and observe the Torah. Paul and Barnabas represent the opposite point of view.

26. See John T. Carroll, Joel B. Green, et al., *The Death of Jesus in Early Christianity* (Peabody, MA: Hendrickson, 1995), 114.

27. Neil Elliott, *Liberating Paul: The Justice of God and the Politics of the Apostle* (Minneapolis: Fortress, 2006), 93.

28. In the Greek original, "handed on" (*parédka*) and "betrayed" (*paredídeto*) are from the same word, *paradídmi*.

29. For a succinct review of the question of authorship of 1 Thessalonians 2:14–16, see Raymond E. Brown, *The Death of the Messiah*, vol. 1 (New York: Doubleday, 1994), 378–381.

30. *The Gospel of Judas from Codex Tchacos*, ed. Rodolphe Kasser, Marvin Meyer, and Gregor Wurst (Washington, DC: National Geographic Society, 2006). The text is from a third- or fourth-century papyrus codex in Coptic, though many speculate it was originally written in Greek. Discovered in the 1970s, the badly damaged manuscript was restored in 2001, though sections remain difficult to decipher. The portrait of Judas differs markedly from the canonical Gospels. Here Judas understands Jesus far better than the other disciples because, in part, Jesus reveals himself more fully to Judas. He asks Judas to hand him over to his death. Thus what in the canonical Gospels is "betrayal" (or "handing over," a translational issue to be discussed below) is in this text obedience. Other scholars have taken issue with the translation. For example, biblical scholar April D. DeConick argues that Judas is not a hero, as the National Geographic-sponsored translation has it, but rather a demon. See her op-ed "Gospel of Truth," *New York Times* (December 1, 2007). See http://www.nytimes.com/2007/12/01/opinion/01deconink.html?r=18&oref-slogin (accessed January 22, 2009). See also her book, *The Thirteenth Apostle: What the Gospel of Judas Really Says* (New York and London, Continuum, 2007).

31. See Kim Paffenroth, *Judas: Images of the Lost Disciple* (Louisville: Westminster-John Knox, 2001).

32. See Mark 3:19, Matthew 10:4, and John 6:71. John calls Judas the "son of Simon Iscariot." The meaning of Iscariot is unclear. For analysis of various hypotheses regarding its meaning, see Brown, *Death of the Messiah*, vol. 2, 1413–1416.

33. See especially William Klassen, *Judas: Betrayer or Friend of Judas?* (Minneapolis: Fortress, 1996). On the varied meanings of *paradidomai* in the passion narratives, see Brown, *Death of the Messiah*, vol. 1, 211–212.

34. The same Greek term, *prodotēs*, is used in Stephen's speech: "Which of the prophets did your ancestors not persecute? They killed those who foretold the coming of the Righteous One, and now you have become his *betrayers* and murderers" (Acts 7:52).

35. See Jeremiah 32:6–15, in which the prophet buys a field at Anathoth for seventeen shekels of silver as a symbolic act: "For thus says the LORD of hosts, the God of Israel: Houses and fields and vineyards shall again be bought in this land" (verse 15). For the reference to a potter in Jeremiah, see 18:2–3.

36. It appears that Luke's dramatic account of the death of Judas bears a resemblance to other accounts of the death of evil persons. Compare, for example, his description of the death of Herod Agrippa, also in Acts of the Apostles (12:21–23): "On an appointed day Herod put on his royal robes, took his seat on the platform, and delivered a public address to them. The people kept shouting, 'The voice of a god, and not of a mortal!' And immediately, because he had not given the glory to God, an angel of the Lord struck him down, and he was eaten by worms and died." Luke may well have had source material from earlier descriptions of retributive deaths. Wisdom 4:18–19 speaks of the unrighteous as becoming "dishonored corpses," "an outrage among the dead forever," who "will suffer anguish and the memory of them will perish. Second Maccabees (9:5–9) graphically describes the death of the malevolent Antiochus IV Epiphanes: "But the all-seeing Lord, the god of Israel, struck him with an incurable and invisible blow. As soon as he stopped speaking he was seized with a pain in his bowels, for which there was no relief, and with sharp internal tortures—and that very justly, for he had tortured the bowels of others with many and strange inflictions….And so the ungodly man's body swarmed with worms, and while he was still living in anguish and pain, his flesh rotted away, and because of the stench the whole army felt revulsion at the decay."

37. Paffenroth, *Judas*, 14–15.

38. Adrian Thatcher, *The Savage Text: The Use and Abuse of the Bible*. Blackwell Manifestos (Oxford: Wiley Blackwell, 2008), 4.

CHAPTER 4

1. Leo D. Lefebure, *Revelation, the Religions and Violence* (Maryknoll, NY: Orbis, 2000), 77.

2. See the text (fragments, rather than a complete work) and discussion in Christian Mauer and Wilhelm Schneemelcher, "The Gospel of Peter," in *New Testament Apocrypha*, vol. 1, rev. ed. by W. Schneemelcher, trans. R. McL. Wilson (Louisville, KY: Westminster, 1991), 216–227. The date of this text and whether it influenced the composition of the passion narratives of the canonical Gospels is debated. Cf. J. Dominic Crossan, *The Cross that Spoke* (San Francisco: Harper & Row, 1988), who argues that a

shorter form of the *Gospel of Peter* (the "Cross Gospel") was a source for the
passion narratives of the canonical; also Raymond E. Brown, *The Death of
the Messiah*, vol. 2 (New York: Doubleday, 1994), 1317–1349, for a detailed
refutation of Crossan's thesis and an argument that the author of *Gos. Pet.*
likely had access to the oral tradition stemming from the Gospels of Luke
and John.

3. Dating of the *Acts of Pilate* is uncertain. The oldest extant copy is
a twelfth-century Greek manuscript, and there are two basic editions (with
the older edition translated into many languages), and a number of variations. One section may have been composed by the late second century. For
an English translation, see F. Scheidweiler in *New Testament Apocrypha*, vol.
1, 444–484.

4. *Acts of Pilate* in *New Testament Apocrypha*, vol. 1, 477–478; cf.
Matthew 28:11–15.

5. Ibid., 482.

6. Ibid., 483.

7. Ibid., 484.

8. Daniel R. Schwartz, "Pontius Pilate," in *Anchor Bible Dictionary*,
vol. 5, ed. David Noel Freedman et al. (New York: Doubleday, 1992), 400.
The apocryphal Pilate lingers in the Ethiopic and Coptic churches, since
they consider Pilate a saint.

9. Cf. 2 Corinthians 3:14–16. St. Justin Martyr, *Dialogue with Trypho*,
trans. Thomas B. Falls, ed. Michael Slusser (Washington, DC: Catholic
University of America Press, 2003). See Graham N. Stanton, "Justin Martyr's
Dialogue with Trypho: Group Boundaries, 'Proselytes' and 'God-fearers,'" in
Tolerance and Intolerance in Early Judaism and Christianity, ed. Graham N.
Stanton and Guy G. Stroumsa (Cambridge: Cambridge University Press,
1998), 263–279.

10. It is "highly improbable" that the *Dialogue* summarizes a "real historical conversation between Justin and some historical Jews." Trypho is
neither a "historical person [nor]...a representative member of an 'orthodox' Jewish community." So Michael Mach, "Justin Martyr's *Dialogus cum
Tryphone Iudaeo*," in *Contra Iudaeos: Ancient and Medieval Polemics between
Christians and Jews*, Texts and Studies in Medieval and Early Modern
Judaism 10, ed. Ora Limor and Guy G. Stroumsa (Tübingen: Mohr-Siebeck,
1996), 27–48; citations, 34–35. Judith Lieu suggests Justin might have cre-
ated a sort of composite character based on a number of debates with Jews.
Because "he has a character rather more flesh than blood," it may be that
Justin has drawn him from real life. See her *Image and Reality* (Edinburgh:
T&T Clark, 1996), 104, 113. In contrast, Miriam Taylor argues that the
Jewish oppressors portrayed in early church literature represent an intellec-

tual rather than literal reality. See her *Anti-Judaism and Early Christian Identity: A Critique of the Scholarly Consensus* (Leiden: E. J. Brill, 1995).

11. Paula Fredriksen and Oded Irshai, "Christian Anti-Judaism: Polemics and Policies," *Cambridge History of Judaism*, vol. 4, ed. Steven T. Katz (Cambridge: Cambridge University Press, 2006), 977–1033; citation, 983.

12. Ibid., 977 and 984.

13. All excerpts are from the translation of Richard A. Norris, Jr., *The Christological Controversy* (Philadelphia: Fortress, 1980).

14. Eric Werner, "Melito of Sardis, the First Poet of Deicide," *Hebrew Union College Annual* 37 (1966): 191–210.

15. Lieu, *Image and Reality*, 234.

16. See Nicholas deLange, *Origen and the Jews,* University of Cambridge Oriental Publications (Cambridge: Cambridge University Press, 1976), 75–123.

17. See Dennis D. McManus, "Origen," in *A Dictionary of Jewish-Christian Relations*, ed. Edward Kessler and Neil Wenborn (Cambridge: Cambridge University Press, 2005), 323.

18. de Lange, *Origen*, 76.

19. Robert Wilken, *Judaism and the Early Christian Mind: A Study of Cyril of Alexandria's Exegesis and Theology* (New Haven, CT: Yale University Press, 1971), 19.

20. Robert Wilken, *John Chrysostom and the Jews: Rhetoric and Reality in the Late 4th Century*, The Transformation of the Classical Heritage (Berkeley: University of California Press, 1983), 70.

21. Personal communication with the author, February 11, 2009.

22. All citations from these homilies are from the translation of Paul W. Harkins, *St. John Chrysostom: Discourses against Judaizing Christians* (Washington, DC: Catholic University of America Press, 1979).

23. See Carl H. Kraeling, "The Jewish Community at Antioch," *Journal of Biblical Literature* 51/2 (1932): 130–160.

24. See Robert L. Wilken, "The Jews and Christian Apologetics after Theodosius I *Cunctos Populos*," *The Harvard Theological Review* 73/3–4 (July–October 1980): 451–471, esp. 464. For the legislation, see http://www.fordham.edu/halsall/jewish/jews-romanlaw.asp (accessed August 22, 2011).

25. For an account of Julian's determination to weaken the social and religious standing of Christianity and a summary of Gregory of Nazianzus' *Invectives Against Julian,* see John McGuckin, *St. Gregory of Nazianzus: An Intellectual Biography* (Crestwood, NY: St. Vladimir's Seminary Press, 2001), esp. 115–130. Many other Christian writers attacked Julian as well.

26. The destruction of Jerusalem as punishment was prominent in Chrysostom's homilies. See, for example, "You Jews did crucify him. But after he died, he then destroyed your city; it was then that he dispersed your people; it was then that he scattered your nation over the face of the earth" (Discourse V.1.7). See also "So also now, if God had not deserted you once and for all, your enemies would not have had the power to destroy your city and leave your temple desolate. If God had not abandoned you, the ruin of desolation would not have lasted so long a time, nor would your frequent efforts to rebuild the temple have been in vain" (Discourse VI.3.7).

27. Wilken, "The Jews and Christian Apologetics," 453.

28. Wayne A. Meeks and Robert L. Wilken, *Jews and Christians in Antioch in the First Four Centuries of the Common Era*, Sources for Biblical Study 13 (Missoula, MT: Scholars Press, 1978), 30. Chrysostom explicitly mentioned Julian as one who "surpassed all the emperors in irreligion, invited the Jews to sacrifice to idols in an attempt to drag them to his own level of ungodliness" (*Discourse* V.11.4). He also wrote two apologetics works to pagan critics in which he condemned Julian.

29. On mob violence and forced conversion of the Jews of Clermont, France, in 576, see Brian Brennan, "The Conversion of the Jews of Clermont in AD 576," *Journal of Theological Studies* 36 (1985): 321–337.

30. Citations from Letters XL, ##14, 18, 26, from *Ambrose: Selected Works and Letters*, ed. Philip Schaff; see http://www.ccel.org/ccel/schaff/npnf210.html (accessed January 5, 2009).

31. Gavin Langmuir, *Toward a Definition of Antisemitism* (Berkeley: University of California Press, 1990), 74.

32. See Garry Wills, *Saint Augustine*, Penguin Lives Series (New York: Viking, 1999), 30: "Manicheism had the glamour of fashion with an edge of danger (as a heresy, it was formally banned in the Christian Empire)."

33. Paula Fredriksen, *Augustine and the Jews: A Christian Defense of Jews and Judaism* (New York: Doubleday, 2008), 183.

34. Ibid., 236. Faustus ("Blest"), like Augustine, was North African; an Elect of the Manichees (the Elect were the elites of the Manichean hierarchy who vowed celibacy, poverty, and intense abstinence; below them in the hierarchical structure were the "Hearers," among whom Augustine had been during his Manichean years), a bishop and a professor of rhetoric.

35. Typological interpretation was typical of many early church writers, most frequently in connecting the "Old" and "New" Testaments. Melito's "Homily on the Passover" is a classic example. The sermon is based on the Jewish Passover as a type of Jesus, the "Passover of our salvation."...He is the one who was murdered in the person of Abel, bound in the person of Isaac, exiled in the person of Jacob, sold in the person of Joseph,

exposed in the person of David, dishonored in the person of the prophets" (#69), in Norris, *Christological Controversy.*

36. Fredriksen's summary of salient points may be found in *Augustine and the Jews*, 316–319. For detailed exposition, see 260–289.

37. Fredriksen, *Augustine and the Jews*, 320–321.

38. Theodosius had issued the edit *Cunctos populous* in 380: "Our Will that all the peoples who are ruled by the administration of Our Clemency shall practice that religion which the divine Peter the Apostle transmitted to the Romans...this is the religion that is followed by Pontiff Damascus and by Peter, bishop of Alexandria, a man of apostolic sanctity; that is, according to the apostolic discipline and the evangelic doctrine, we shall believe in the single Deity of the Father, Son, and Holy Spirit, under the concept of equal majesty and of the Holy Trinity. We command that those persons who follow this rule shall embrace the name of the Catholic Christians. The rest, however, whom We adjudge demented and insane, shall sustain the infamy of heretical dogmas, their meeting places shall not receive the name churches" (*Theodosian Code* XVI.1.2).

39. For a summary of imperial and canonical legislation, see Louis H. Feldman, *Jew and Gentile in the Ancient World* (Princeton: Princeton University Press, 1993), 383–396.

40. Letter of Gregory to Virgilius, Bishop of Arles, and to Theodorus, Bishop of Marseilles, June 591 in Jacob R. Marcus, *The Jew in the Medieval World: A Source Book, 315–1791* (New York: Atheneum, 1981), 111–112.

41. Paula Fredriksen, "What Partings of the Ways?" in *The Ways That Never Parted*, ed. Adam H. Becker and Annette Yoshiko Reed (Tübingen: Mohr Siebeck, 3003), 35–63; citation, 61.

42. Ibid, 62–63.

43. Gavin Langmuir, *Toward a Definition of Antisemitism* (Berkeley: University of California Press, 1990), 58–60.

44. The Internet Medieval Sourcebook provides five versions of Urban's speech (http://www.fordham.edu/halsall/source/urban2-5vers.html (accessed August 23, 2011); all five were authored considerably after the Council of Clermont. See also Christopher Tyerman, who defines a crusade as a "war answering God's command, authorized by a legitimate authority, the pope, who, by virtue of the power seen as vested in him as Vicar of Christ, identified the war's object and offered to those who undertook it full remission of the penalties of confessed sins and a package of temporal privileges, including church protection of family and property, immunity from law suits and interest repayments on debt" (*Fighting for Christendom: Holy War and the Crusades* [Oxford: Oxford University Press, 2004], 30). Jonathan Riley-Smith considers the Crusades as "particularly theatrical manifesta-

tions" of holy war, and cautions that they were not a departure from some norm in Christian history. Rather, he claims, "The Crusades themselves were deeply embedded in popular Catholic ideas and devotional life. They were not thoughtless explosions of barbarism. The theory of force that underlay them was relatively sophisticated and was considered theologically justifiable by a society that felt threatened. It is hard now to conceive of the intensity of the attachment felt for the holy places in Jerusalem, the concern aroused by heresy and physical assaults on the church, and the fear Westerners had of Muslim invaders, who reached central France in the eighth century and Vienna in the sixteenth and again in the seventeenth. The men and women who took the cross seem mostly be have been pious and well intentioned" (*The Crusades, Christianity, and Islam* [New York: Columbia University Press, 2008], 79–80). He reminds his readers that secular ideological violence has recently manifested itself in wars waged in the "names of imperialism, nationalism, Marxism, fascism, anticolonialism, humanitarianism, and even liberal democracy" (80).

45. From Guibert's *Gesta Dei per Francos*, 1102, cited in Tomaž Mastnak, *Crusading Peace: Christendom, the Muslim World, and Western Political Order* (Berkeley: University of California Press, 2002), 55.

46. A Jewish chronicler of the persecutions of 1096 attributed these motives to the crusaders: "They said to each other: 'Look now, we are going to a distant land to make war against mighty kings and are endangering our lives to conquer the kingdoms which do not believe in the crucified one, when it is actually the Jews who crucified him.' They stirred up hatred against us in all quarters and declared that either we should accept their abominable faith or else they would annihilate us all, even infants and sucklings. The noblemen and common people placed an evil symbol—*a vertical line over a horizontal one*—on their garments." From the Hebrew, cited in Jeremy Cohen, *Christ Killers: The Jews and the Passion from the Bible to the Big Screen* (Oxford: Oxford University Press, 2007), 121. Emphasis in Cohen.

47. Marc Saperstein, *Moments of Crisis in Jewish-Christian Relations* (London: SCM and Philadelphia: Trinity Press International, 1989), 19.

48. Riley-Smith, *The Crusades, Christianity and Islam*, lists the wearing of crosses as one of the unchanging elements of crusading; among other consistent features was that warfare was believed to be simultaneously holy and penitential, crusades were sanctioned by papal authority, and the crusaders took vows. See Riley-Smith, *The Crusades*, 52. A significant argument in his book is that until the late nineteenth century, the Muslim world had largely lost interest in the Crusades. Their heightened interest from the 1890s to the present was influenced by European imperialism and growing

Arab nationalism. It was framed through the lens of two Western constructs: that of culturally inferior crusaders in the face of liberal and civilized Muslims (for example, the novels of Sir Walter Scott) and that of a continuing Western assault (for example, the patriotic fervor of French historian François Michaud's *Histoire des croisades*); see especially chapter 4, "Crusading and Islam," 63–78. On the term *crucesignati*, see Michael Markowski, "*Crucesignatus*: Its Origins and Early Usage," *Journal of Medieval History* 10/3 (1984): 157–165. He defines the term as "a person signed by the cross" (157).

49. Cited in Jonathan Riley-Smith, "The First Crusade and the Persecution of the Jews," in *Persecution and Toleration*, ed. W. J. Sheils (Oxford: Oxford University Press), 51–72; citation, 68–69. The charge is attributed to Baldric of Bourgueil.

50. Riley-Smith, *The Crusades, Christianity and Islam*, cites the atrocities against the Jews in the Rhineland as the earliest example of introspective violence associated with crusading; he interprets this violence against Jews as a means of creating a "uniformly Christian society by eliminating their religion" (26–27). Robert Chazan argues that, while the popular crusading assaults in the Rhineland were predicated on identifying Jews as the historical enemies of Christ, in the second half of the twelfth century another anti-Jewish theme developed: Jews as "embittered and aggressive, eager to take action against Christian contemporaries" (*Medieval Stereotypes and Modern Antisemitism* [Berkeley: University of California Press, 1977], 79).

51. James Carroll, *Jerusalem, Jerusalem: How the Ancient City Ignited our Modern World* (Boston: Houghton, Mifflin, Harcourt, 2011), 139.

52. Christopher Tyerman, *God's War: A New History of the Crusades* (Cambridge, MA: Harvard University Press, 2006), 104.

53. Langmuir, *Toward a Definition*, 306. The "Jews," Langmuir argues, functioned as symbols that allowed Christians to repress fantasies about crucifixion and cannibalism, repress doubts about the real presence of Christ in the Eucharist, and "unbearable doubts and fears about God's goodness and the bubonic bacillus that imperceptibly invaded people's bodies. By attacking 'Jews,' individuals who were poorly integrated in their societies and within themselves could express the tensions they felt as a conflict between good and bad people, between Christians and Jews" (306).

54. Thomas H. Bestul, *Texts of the Passion: Latin Devotional Literature and Medieval Society* (Philadelphia: University of Pennsylvania Press, 1996), 69.

55. Ludolph of Saxony (d. 1378), cited in Richard Kieckhefer, "Major Currents in Late Medieval Devotion," in *Christian Spirituality: High Middle*

Ages and Reformation, vol. 17, World Spirituality, ed. Jill Raitt (New York: Crossroad, 1987), 105.

56. See Ewert Cousins, "The Humanity and the Passion of Christ," in *Christian Spirituality,* 375–391. Cousins concludes that the extent to which the passion of Christ permeated the religious psyche of Western Christians as the Middle Ages progressed was problematic psychologically, reflecting at times a "morbid fascination with pain and humiliation." It was also problematic in terms of doctrine and spirituality insofar at Christians lost sight of other aspects of their faith, not in the least to a forgetfulness of the resurrection (87). Cousins, however, does not take note of the hostility directed toward Jews.

57. Cited in Bestul, *Texts of the Passion,* 94.

58. Canons 3 and 67–70 of the Fourth Lateran Council; see http://www.fordham.edu/halsall/basis/lateran4.html (accessed December 18, 2008).

59. Michael Camille, *The Gothic Idol: Ideology and Image-Making in Medieval Art* (Cambridge: Cambridge University Press, 1989), 180.

60. R. I. Moore, *The Formation of a Persecuting Society: Power and Deviance in Western Europe 950–1250* (Oxford: Basil Blackwell, 1987).

61. Latin original and translation in Bestul, *Texts of the Passion,* 102.

62. This prayer is discussed in chapter 5.

63. Bestul, *Texts of the Passion,* 103.

64. The Gospels of Mark and Matthew include the detail that after the arrest of Jesus, the high priest and the whole council sought false testimony against him. Dissatisfied with Jesus' response, Mark says that "Some began to spit on him, to blindfold him, and to strike him, saying to him, 'Prophesy!' The guards also took him over and beat him" (14:65). Matthew's account is similar: "Then they spat in his face and struck him; and some slapped him" (25:67).

65. Examples are from Latin texts and translations in Bestul, *Texts of the Passion,* 87, 96, 108. Ludolphus was writing in the context of the plague ("Black Death"), for which Jews were often made the scapegoats.

66. Bestul, *Texts,* 157.

67. Bestul, *Texts,* 159. Emphasis added.

68. Bestul, Texts, 160–161.

69. From his *Contes du Graal,* in Chrétien de Troyes, *Arthurian Romances,* trans. William W. Kibler, cited in Maureen Boulton, "Anti-Jewish Attitudes in French Literature," in *Jews and Christians in Twelfth-Century Europe,* ed. Michael A. Signer and John Van Engen (Notre Dame, IN: University of Notre Dame Press, 2001), 26.

70. All references to de Boron's work are from Boulton, "Anti-Jewish Attitudes," 246–250.

71. Vespasian was a Roman military commander who led the siege against Jerusalem in the Jewish War of 66–73 C.E.; he was the Roman emperor 69–79. Vespasian was not, however, the son of an emperor, though his two sons Titus and Domitian succeeded him as emperor from 79–81 and 81–96, respectively.

72. "Cruel Jews laid down his precious body....Alas, you cruel Jews, why fare you with my sweet son, and did he ever do you any harm? You fill my heart with sorrow." From the Book of Margery Kempe, I.80.lines 4554, 4564–4565. See *The Book of Margery Kempe*, ed. Lynn Staley (Kalamazoo, MI.: Medieval Institute Publications, 1996). See also http://www.lib.rochester. edu/camelot/teams/kemp2frm.htm (accessed December 16, 2008).

73. Judith Rosenthal, "Margery Kempe and Medieval Anti-Judaic Ideology," *Medieval Encounters* 5/3 (1999): 409–420; citation, 414. Ellen M. Ross situates Kempe, whom she calls "this Jeremiah of medieval England" in the larger realm of the literature and iconography of the suffering Christ of late medieval England. Ross argues that the heightened emphasis on the passion of Jesus inspired spiritual transformation; compassionate response to the anguish of the crucified engendered "sorrowful recognition of their own implication in the sins for which Jesus suffers. Jesus' body is a text of flesh inscribed by the bloody marks of human transgressions....The intensified corporeality of the wounded Jesus transforms hearers and spectators, and moves them to repentance" (*The Grief of God: Images of the Suffering Jesus in Late Medieval England* [New York: Oxford University Press, 1997], 123 and 132).

74. Robert C. Stacey, "Jews and Christians in Twelfth-Century England: Dynamics of a Changing Relationship," in *Jews and Christians in Twelfth-Century Europe,* 340–354; citation, 342.

75. Cited in Langmuir, *Toward a Definition*, 210.

76. Thomas of Monmouth, *The Life and Passion of Saint William the Martyr of Norwich,* in Jacob Marcus, *The Jew in the Medieval World: A Sourcebook, 315–1791,* rev. ed. (Cincinnati: Hebrew Union College Press, 1999), 135–141. All further references to the *Life and Passion* are from Marcus. For analysis of the dating and complex composition of the *Life and Passion,* see Langmuir, *Toward a Definition,* 209–216. The full Latin text (with English translation, as used in the Marcus anthology) is available in *The Life and Miracles of St. William of Norwich,* ed. Augustus Jessopp and Montague Rhodes James (Cambridge: Cambridge University Press, 1896).

77. Langmuir also distinguishes between the accusation of ritual crucifixion made in the account of "St." William of Norwich and that of ritual

cannibalism or blood libel, which he dates to 1235 in Fulda, Germany. Of the latter, he writes: "A new fantasy, the medieval libel of Jewish ritual cannibalism, was created by some people at Fulda in 1235. It caused the death of thirty-four Jews immediately; it attracted the attention of the highest authorities throughout Europe immediately after; it was soon responsible for the death of more Jews; and, directly or indirectly, it was responsible for the death of many more in the centuries to come" (*Toward a Definition of Antisemitism*, 281). In 1943, Heinrich Himmler, Reich Führer for the Establishment of the German People, instructed Ernst Kaltenbrunner, chief of the Reich Main Office for Security, to spread the charge of ritual murder as propaganda in Hungary so that the Nazis could more easily capture Hungarian Jews. See Michael Phayer, *The Catholic Church and the Holocaust 1930–1965* (Bloomington: Indiana University Press, 2000), 8.

78. Ibid., 225.

79. Chaucer, "The Prioress's Tale," trans. Gerard NeCastro. See http://www.umm.maine.edu/faculty/necastro/chaucer (accessed December 11, 2008). See Sheila Delany, "Chaucer's Prioress, the Jews and the Muslims," *Medieval Encounters* 5/2 (1999): 198–213, who argues that the Asian setting evokes the symbiosis of Jews and Muslims in Asian lands. She notes also Dante's influence on Chaucer. In his *Inferno*, Dante (1265–1321) memorably placed Judas Iscariot (Giuda Scariotto) in the ninth and lowest circle of hell, the circle of treachery. Having begun their descent into the *Inferno* on Good Friday, Dante and his guide Virgil ended their journey in Judecca (Giudecca), the innermost zone of the ninth circle where they found Judas being eternally eaten by Lucifer; his head inside Lucifer's central mouth (Brutus and Cassius are in his two other mouths) and his back raked by the devil's claws. See Canto 34.

80. The church "had awakened to the reality that Judaism did not cease to develop on the day of Jesus' crucifixion, on that day when the New Testament presumably replaced the Old. If this New Testament charted the only legitimate direction in which the religion of biblical Israel could develop, and if the Jews had survived solely to testify to that Old Testament which had given birth to Christianity, then a postbiblical or talmudic Judaism was an impossibility....The value of the Jews in a Christian world depended on their blindness, their ignorance of Christian truth, their testifying to that very truth unknowingly, despite themselves." Jeremy Cohen, *Christ Killers*, 88–89.

81. *Summa theologica* 3.47.5. See http://www.newadvent.org/summa/4047.htm.

CHAPTER 5

1. Jeremy Cohen, *Christ Killers: The Jews and the Passion from the Bible to the Big Screen* (Oxford; Oxford University Press, 2007), 119.

2. James Shapiro, *Oberammergau: The Troubling Story of the World's Most Famous Passion Play* (New York: Vintage Books, 2000), 11.

3. Cited in Shapiro, 76–77.

4. Cited in Shapiro, 151–152.

5. Michael J. Cook, in a review of the 1901 book *A Rabbi's Impressions of the [1900] Oberammergau Passion Play* by Joseph Krauskopf in *Review and Expositor* 103/1 (Winter 2006): 243–245; citation, 244.

6. Cited in A. James Rudin, "Oberammergau: A Case Study of Passion Plays," in *Pondering the Passion: What's at Stake for Christians and Jews?* ed. Philip A. Cunningham (Lanham, MD: Rowman and Littlefield, 2004), 102. Jewish complicity receives even greater emphasis in the text of the 1890 production. See *The Oberammergau Passion Play* 1890 (Munich: Friedrich Adolf Ackerman, 1890), 86–87.

7. See Rudin, "Oberammergau," 102. Rudin reviews changes made to the 2000 script and the assessment of Jewish and Christian scholars (including my own evaluation), 103–108. See also Gordon R. Mork, "Christ's Passion on Stage: The Traditional Melodrama of Deicide," *Journal of Religion and Society,* Supplement Series 1 (2004), http://moses.creighton. edu/JRS/pdf/2004-5.pdf (accessed January 11, 2010).

8. The villagers of Oberammergau sent Hitler a special set of mounted photographs of the play and actors with the inscription, "To our Führer, the protector of the cultural treasures of Germany, from the Passion village of Oberammergau." Cited in James Bentley, *Oberammergau and the Passion Play: A Guide and a History to Mark the 350th Anniversary* (New York: Penguin, 1984), 38.

9. Cited in Saul S. Friedman, *The Oberammergau Passion Play: A Lance against Civilization* (Carbondale, IL: Southern Illinois University Press, 1984), 117. There was no production in 1940; the play resumed in 1950.

10. See Friedman's detailed analysis of the Nazi connection, *The Oberammergau Passion Play,* 114–130.

11. Cited in Friedlander, *The Oberammergau Passion Play,* 125–126, 146. Here, as elsewhere, *Bolshevism* was synonymous with "Jewish." For the Nazis, Bolshevism was code for the accusation that the Jews were responsible for communism. In the 1920s, journalist Dietrich Eckhart, one of the most important ideologues of the Nazi movement, wrote a pamphlet, *Der Bolschewismus von Moses bis Lenin (Bolshevism from Moses to Lenin).* The

wide circulation of the forgery *The Protocols of the Elders of Zion* perpetuated this equation.

12. The Roman Missal of 1570, the prescribed text for celebrations of the Eucharist throughout the Catholic world, included a prayer for "the perfidious Jews" on Good Friday. The eighth of nine prayer intentions (for the church, pope, clergy, monarch, catechumens, those in danger, heretics, Jews, and pagans) in that day's liturgy, it began: *"Oremus et pro perfidis Judaeis: ut Deus et Dominus noster auferat velamen de cordibus eorum; ut et ipsi agnoscant Jesum Christum Dominum nostrum."* (Let us pray also for the faithless Jews: that Almighty God may remove the veil from their hearts; so that they, too, may acknowledge Jesus Christ our Lord.). Unlike the other eight prayers, in which the presider would precede the prayer with *"Flectamus genua"* (Let us kneel), and then conclude with *"Levate"* (Arise), this rubric was not followed in the prayer for the Jews. Instead, the presider went directly to chanting the Collect: "Almighty and everlasting God, from whose mercy not even the treachery of the Jews is shut out: pitifully listen to us who plead for that blinded nation, that opening at last their eyes to the true light, which is Christ, he may dispel the darkness in which they are shrouded." Cited in *The Roman Missal in Latin and English, Arranged for the Use of the Laity to Which Is Added a Collection of Usual Public Prayers* (Tournay, Belgium: Society of St. John the Evangelist and Declée & Co., 1911), 490–491. In a later English translation, the difference in rubric is explained: "By exception, in the supplication for the Jews, the early Christians neither knelt nor paused for private prayer, in abhorrence, it is said, of the Jews having in mockery knelt before and jeered the suffering Savior." See *The Roman Missal in Latin and English, Arranged for the Use of the Laity to Which Is Added a Collection of Usual Public Prayers*, 3rd ed. (New York: Benziger Brothers, 1925), 490–491. Pope John XXIII had the word *perfidis* removed in 1960.

13. "The" Enlightenment is, of course, a vast oversimplification of the many perspectives offered by philosophers of the seventeenth and eighteenth centuries. On the differences between French and German "enlightened" thinkers, see John Weiss, *Ideology of Death: Why the Holocaust Happened in Germany* (Chicago: Ivan R. Dee, 1996), 50–79. On the "Jewish Enlightenment" or *Haskalah*, see Shmuel Feiner, *The Jewish Enlightenment*, trans. Chaya Naor (Philadelphia: University of Pennsylvania Press, 2004).

14. J. Kameron Carter, *Race: A Theological Problem* (New York and Oxford: Oxford University Press, 2008), 41.

15. Ibid., 89. In a variant text, *Menschenkunde* (1781–1782), Kant identifies "four races on the earth": the American (Indian) people who "are not able to receive education...lack affect and passion...and they are lazy";

the Negro Race, "full of affect and passion...[who] can be educated, but only to be as servant"; the Hindus, [who] can be trained to the highest degree, but only to the arts, not the sciences...[and who] will never make progress"; the Race of Whites "contains within itself all motivations and talents." Cited in Carter, *Race: A Theological Problem*, 91.

16. Cited in Carter, 92. German original: "*Alle racen warden ausgerottet warden.*"

17. Ibid., 104.

18. Ibid.

19. Ibid, 107.

20. Carter cites (119) Kant's *Conflict of the Faculties,* 1778: "The euthanasia of Judaism is pure moral religion, freed from all the ancient statutory teachings, some of which were bound to be retained in Christianity (as a messianic faith). But this division of sects, too, must disappear in time, leading, at least in spirit, to what we call the conclusion of the great drama of religious change on earth (the restoration of all things), when there will be only one shepherd and one flock."

21. *Die Judenfrage als Racen-Sitten-und Culturfrage* (The Jewish Question as a Racial, Moral, and Cultural Question), cited in *Scattered Among the Nations: Documents Affecting Jewish History 49 to 1975,* ed. Alexis P. Rubin (Toronto: Wall and Emerson, 1993), 175.

22. Cited in ibid., 176.

23. *The Protocols* in particular have had a long shelf life. In 1920, the automaker Henry Ford published an Americanized version, *The International Jew*, in his antisemitic paper, *Dearborn Independent.* In 1923, Nazi theorist Alfred Rosenberg published *The Protocols of the Elders of Zion and Jewish World Policy*; widely influential, it went through numerous printings. *The Protocols* remain a staple of antisemitic propaganda in the contemporary world, thanks in large measure to their dissemination through the Internet and film. A good summary is available through the United States Holocaust Memorial Museum. See http://www.ushmm.org/wlc/en/article.php?ModuleId=10007058 (accessed August 16, 2011).

24. In December of 1926, Pope Pius XI banned Catholics from reading the newspaper.

25. Cited in Robert A. Ventresca, "Jacques Maritain and the Jewish Question: Theology, Identity and Politics," *Studies in Christian-Jewish Relations* 2/2 (2007): 58–69; citation, 67. Available online: http://escholarship.bc.edu/scjr/vol2/iss2 (accessed August 19, 2010). Over the course of his long career, Maritain (1882–1973) spoke out frequently against antisemitism; Richard Francis Crane analyzes his complex views, framed in part by two essays on the Jewish question in 1921 and 1937. See his *Passion of*

Israel: Jacques Maritain, Catholic Conscience and the Holocaust (Scranton, PA: University of Scranton Press, 2010). Crane documents Maritain's "increasing opposition to racist antisemitism...and at the same time a persistent, even intensified essentializing of Jews...exhibiting not only an undeniable 'anti-antisemitism' but also an ambivalent philosemitism based on Jewish stereotypes both positive and negative" (9).

26. Martin Rhonheimer, "The Holocaust: What Was Not Said," *First Things* 137 (November 2003): 18–28; citation, 19.

27. See the analysis of this archival material in Hubert Wolf, *Pope and Devil: The Vatican's Archives and the Third Reich,* trans. Kenneth Kronenberg (Cambridge, MA: Belknap Press of Harvard University Press, 2010).

28. See n. 12.

29. Cited in Wolf, *Pope and Devil,* 96.

30. Cited in ibid., 99.

31. Many high officials of the Catholic Church regarded modernity as a dire threat. In a series of documents issued primarily for internal consumption (addressed to "Venerable Brethren"), popes railed against perceived threats, including rationalism, indifferentism, communism, liberalism, nationalism, and theologies allegedly affected by such "errors." In 1864, Pope Pius IX issued *Syllabus Errorum* ("Syllabus of Errors"), listing eighty propositions that the church held to be false. Among them was the notion that "everyone is free to embrace and profess the religion which by the light of reason one judges to be true" (§15). Also held to be erroneous was that "We should at least have good hopes for the eternal salvation of all those who are in no way in the true Church of Christ" (§17). Similar in message and tone were the 1907 encyclical of Pope Pius X, *Pascendi Dominici gregis* ("Feeding the Lord's flock"), and the decree of the Holy Office that same year, *Lamentabile Sane exitu* ("A lamentable departure, indeed"), with its listing of sixty-five errors of those alleged to be "modernists." Among the proposition condemned was that "Christian Doctrine was originally Judaic" (§60).

32. Cited in Wolf, 103.

33. Cited in Wolf, 106.

34. Cited in Wolf, 105.

35. Cited in Wolf, 107.

36. See Wolf, 111.

37. *Acta Apostolicae Sedis* 20 (1928): 103–104. See also Jean Levie, S.J., "Décret de Suppression de l'Association des 'Amis d'Israel,'" *Nouvelle Revue théologique* (1928): 532–537; and Lieven Sarans, "The Attitude of the Belgian Roman Catholic Clergy toward the Jews Prior to Occupation," in

Belgium and the Holocaust: Jews, Belgians, Germans, ed. Dan Mikhman (Jerusalem: Yad Vashem Publications, 1998), 117–158.

38. Ibid. Emphasis added. The author of the petition from *Amici Israel*, Abbot Benedict Gariador, and the liturgical experts who had recommended that the petition be granted were summoned before the Holy Office and admonished. Abbot Schuster submitted his "abject submission" and recanted his recommendation; text in Wolf, 114.

39. Anna Łysiak, "Rabbinic Judaism in the Writings of Polish Catholic Theologians," in *Antisemitism, Christian Ambivalence and the Holocaust,* ed. Kevin P. Spicer (Bloomington: Indiana University Press, 2007), 29.

40. For a thorough analysis of Catholic racism, see John Connelly, *From Enemy to Brother: The Revolution in Catholic Teaching on the Jews, 1933–1965* (Cambridge, MA: Harvard University Press, 2012), 11–64.

41. The bimonthly journal *Civiltà cattolica* (Catholic civilization), founded by a Jesuit priest in Naples in 1850 under the advocacy of Pope Pius IX (1846–1878), became an authoritative voice of the Vatican. The Vatican's secretary of state had to approve all articles, a number of which expressed hostility to Jews. On Pius IX and Jews, see Frank J. Coppa, *The Papacy, the Jews, and the Holocaust* (Washington, DC: The Catholic University of America Press, 2006), 77–106. On the depiction of Jews in *Civiltà cattolica,* see David I. Kertzer, *The Popes against the Jews: The Vatican's Role in the Rise of Modern Anti-Semitism* (New York: Alfred A. Knopf, 2001), 133–146.

42. Cited in Wolf, 116–117.

43. Wolf, 119–120.

44. The term *moral impoverishment* is Wolf's, 121. A few changes were made to the Good Friday prayer. In 1938, a German missal translated *perfidious* as "faithless"; only in 1948 did the Congregation of Rites admit that *perfidius* was offensive to many Jews and agreed it would not prohibit translations with the connotation of "unbelieving." In the mid-1950s, Pope Pius XII inserted the genuflection in the prayer for the Jews (see n. 13); he also gave it a heading: "Pro conversione Judaeorum" (For the Conversion of the Jews). In 1959, Pope John XXIII omitted *perfidis* during the Good Friday liturgy. This omission became binding for the entire church a year later. After Vatican II, a revised prayer for the Jews ("the first to hear the word of God") was issued. It remains in effect, but more recently exists in tension with the formulation of Pope Benedict XVI. In 2008, Benedict composed a prayer for the Tridentine Rite that retains the heading of "For the Conversion of the Jews" and asks that God may "enlighten their hearts, that they may acknowledge Jesus Christ as savior...." See my essay "Does the Catholic Church Have a Mission 'with' Jews or 'to' Jews?" *Studies in*

Notes

Christian-Jewish Relations 3/1 (2008): 1–19 (http://ejournals.bc.edu/scjr/vol3).

45. Gustav Gundlach, S.J., "Antisemitismus," in *Lexikon für Theologie und Kirche*, 2nd rev. edition (Freiberg: Herder, 1930): I:504, cited by Georges Passelecq and Bernard Suchecky, *The Hidden Encyclical of Pius XI*, trans. Steven Rendall (New York: Harcourt, Brace & Company, 1977), 47–48. The concept of dual antisemitism had appeared in earlier sources. For example, the article on "Antisemitism" in the *Kirchliche Handlexicon*, an ecclesiastical dictionary published in1907, read: "It is possible to differentiate between two types of antisemitism. The first opposes Jewry as a race, together with everything which is related to it (including, therefore, the revelations of the Old Testament); this racial antisemitism is un-Christian." But then it continues: "The other variation [of antisemitism] simply calls for special laws to protect the Christian population from the harmful advance of the Jews. Catholic social politicians share this point of view. In fact, the Jewish people since their full emancipation in most European countries...have shown the extent to which they have become unfamiliar with the original purpose of Judaism...; the rapacious hunt for material goods, in particular, is part of their typical character....Jewry [*das Judentum*] wields a pernicious influence on religion and customs, the social institutions, literature, and art of Christian society through its powerful daily newspapers; this stands the radical movements (nowadays Social Democracy) in good stead. This is the purpose of Christian antisemitism: to achieve a change." Cited in Olaf Blaschke, *Offenders or Victims? German Jews and the Causes of Modern Catholic Antisemitism* (Lincoln: University of Nebraska Press/Vidal Sassoon International Center for the Study of Antisemitism, 2009), 32–33.

46. Cited in Passelecq and Suchecky, 47. Gundlach, however, offered a number of such negative appraisals of National Socialism that he had to emigrate to Rome in 1934. See Donald J. Dietrich, *Human Rights and the Catholic Tradition* (New Brunswick, NJ: Transaction Publishers, 2007), 165–166.

47. Pope Pius XI was in ill health and died; his successor, Pope Pius XII, typically avoided the more confrontational policies of his predecessor. Moreover, as it became more apparent that Europe would go to war, Pius XII took a more neutral stance in the hopes of mediating the conflict. See Michael Marrus, "The Vatican on Racism and Antisemitism, 1938–39," *Holocaust and Genocide Studies* 4/3 (Winter 1997): 378–395, especially 385–387.

48. Citations from *Humani Generis Unitas*, §§131–132 in Passelecq and Suchecky, *Hidden Encyclical*, 246–247. All further references to this draft encyclical are taken from Passelecq and Suchecky.

301

49. *Humani Generis Unitas*, §133.

50. Ibid., §135.

51. Ibid., §136.

52. Ibid, §§140–141. Marrus concludes: "The 'lost encyclical' turns out not to have been a tragically spurned instrument that might have restrained Nazism, but part of a wider cultural distaste for Jews, despite its rejection of Fascist antisemitism" ("The Vatican on Racism and Antisemitism," 392).

53. So Walter Zwi Bacharach, *Anti-Jewish Prejudices in German Catholic Sermons*, trans. Chaya Galai (Lewiston, NY: Edwin Mellen Press, 1993 [Hebrew original, 1991]), 59.

54. Passelecq and Suchecky, *Hidden Encyclical*, 167.

55. "Die Kirche Christi und die Judenfrage," *Die Erfüllung* 2 (1937): 73–101. Excerpted here from Elias H. Füllenbach, "Shock, Renewal, Crisis," in *Antisemitism, Christian Ambivalence, and Holocaust*, 204. Among the signatories was Jacques Maritain. Some of its initiators and authors did not sign it out of fear of endangering their families.

56. Connelly, *From Enemy to Brother*, provides a detailed analysis of Oesterreicher's journey from "missionary to Jews" to advocate of a "ministry of reconciliation." He situates Oesterreicher among "converts [to Catholicism] and border-walkers" who opposed racism and challenged Nazi treatment of Jews. Among the converts: Karl Thieme, Waldemar Gurian, Gertrud Luckner, Paul Démann, Gregory Baum, and Bruno Hussar. Among the "border crossers"—persons who crossed borders of language and culture, never "surrendering allegiance to one community in favor of the other" (63)—were, in addition to the above, Jacques and Raïssa Maritain, Sophie van Leer, Dietrich von Hildebrand, Leo Rudloff, Charlotte Klein, Kurt Hruby, and Irene Marinoff. Connelly argues: "Without converts to Catholicism, the Catholic Church would never have 'thought its way' out of the challenges of racist anti-Judaism....Conversion had involved not just willingness to accept but courage to refuse, and therefore a readiness to defend unpopular positions" (287, 289).

57. Connelly, "Catholic Racism and Its Opponents," *The Journal of Modern History* 79 (December 2007): 813–847; citation, 835. Oesterreicher (1904–1993) reached New York late in 1940, and founded the Institute for Judaeo-Christian Studies in 1953 at Seton Hall University in South Orange, NJ. He was also among the drafters of *Nostra Aetate*. The institute he founded continues at Seton Hall.

58. Cited in Crane, *The Passion of Israel*, 87.

59. Susannah Heschel, *The Aryan Jesus: Christian Theologians and the Bible in Nazi Germany* (Princeton, NJ, and Oxford: Princeton University

Press, 2008), 3. See also Doris Bergen, *The Twisted Cross: The German Christian Movement in the Third Reich* (Chapel Hill: University of North Carolina Press, 1996). Robert P. Ericksen, drawing on Pastor Wilhelm Niemöller, says that the Confessing Church maintained the allegiance of only 20 percent of Protestants in Nazi Germany; see his "Protestants," in *The Handbook of Holocaust Studies*, ed. Peter Hayes and John K. Roth (Oxford: Oxford University Press, 2010), 250–264; reference, 259.

60. See Wolfgang Gerlach, *And the Witnesses Were Silent: The Confessing Church and the Persecution of the Jews,* trans. Victoria J. Barnett (Lincoln: University of Nebraska Press, 2000).

61. For wording of the Barmen Declaration, see Arthur C. Cochrane, *The Church's Confession under Hitler* (Philadelphia: Westminster Press, 1962), 237–242; cited in Heschel, *The Aryan Jesus*, 140. For divisions within the Confessing Church, see Kyle Jantzen, *Faith and Fatherland: Parish Politics in Hitler's Germany* (Minneapolis: Fortress, 2008), 82–85. Jantzen concludes that Protestant pastors, including those of the Confessing Church, did virtually nothing to defend Jews. They were either too conflicted by their hopes for National Socialism as a source of revitalizing German society, too preoccupied by the struggles between the German Christians and Confessing Church—the *Kirchenkampf* (church struggle)—or too afraid of the consequences (93). See also Victoria J. Barnett, "Barmen, the Ecumenical Movement, and the Jews," *The Ecumenical Review* 61/1 (2009): 17–23. Barnett writes: "Given the escalating violence against Germany's Jewish population, given the numerous demands from the ecumenical world that the German church leadership address this and the equally numerous refusals by the Germans to do so, the silence of the church at Barmen about the Jews is quite stunning" (18).

62. There was some parallel to this within the Catholic world. For example, priest and professor of anthropology Wilhelm Schmidt (1868–1954) wrote in 1934: "This kind of transgression [that is, the rejection of Christ] can by itself distort the being of a people; yet in the case of the Jewish people, the betrayal of its high calling has made this distortion go very deep….In punishment this people, as Christ himself predicted, was driven out of its homeland. Almost two thousand years of distortion and uprooting of its essence has then had a secondary but real effect on its physical race. These racial effects…are not neutralized by baptism. For that, Jews will have to work hard on themselves. [Converted Jews] may therefore belong to our number, but not in the same way as our German racial comrades." Cited in John Connelly, "Catholic Racism and Its Opponents," 822.

63. Cited in Heschel, *The Aryan Jesus*, 140.

64. A high percentage of professors of theology held membership in the Institute, thus enhancing their careers and gaining intellectual tools to racialize their theological positions; moreover, students of theology throughout Germany were disproportionately represented in Nazi student groups by 1930, though later they were excluded from membership in the SS (*Schutzstaffel*, "Protective Echelon"), the SA (*Sturmabteilung*, "Storm Battalion," the so-called "Brownshirts"), and the Hitler Youth. The intellectual center of the Institute for the Study and Eradication of Jewish Influence on German Religious Life was the faculty of theology at the University of Jena, with which it was allied. See Heschel, *The Aryan Jesus*, 99, 126, 201–141.

65. See Susannah Heschel, "Nazifying Christian Theology: Walter Grundmann and the Institute for the Study and Eradication of Jewish Influence on German Life," *Church History* 63 (1994): 587–605; citation, 597.

66. Heschel, *The Aryan Jesus*, 108–111.

67. Cited in Heschel, *The Aryan Jesus*, 191.

68. Cited in Heschel, *The Aryan Jesus*, 183. Schlatter wrote in his 1921 *Geschichte des Christus* that "Jesus suffered the crucifixion as the act of the nation, and this understanding of events controls the entire Gospel record. Not the resistance of individual persons or parties, nor the sin of Caiaphas or the priests, nor the passion of the individual teachers or the rabbinate are singled out as the cause of Jesus' death. Israel proved to be a unified community in the decision; for it had in common the thoughts about God that led it into struggle against Jesus and the will that rejected him. Therefore the guilt for his death is not placed on Pilate, and Israel is not left with the excuse that Roman rule was guilty of injustice that led to Christ's crucifixion" (Adolf Schlatter, *History of the Christ: The Foundation for New Testament Theology*, trans. Andreas Köstenberger [Grand Rapids: Baker, 1997], 367–368). For analysis, see James E. McNutt, "Vessels of Wrath, Prepared to Perish: Adolf Schlatter and the Spiritual Extermination of the Jews," *Theology Today* 63 (2006): 176–190.

69. Cited in Heschel, *The Aryan Jesus*, 126. Catholic priest and professor Karl Adam (1876–1966) expressed a variant viewpoint. In contrast to Grundmann (and Houston Stewart Chamberlain, who had asserted in his 1899 *The Foundations of the Nineteenth Century* that Jesus was not Jewish), Adam believed that Christian faith originated with a Jew and in Jewish belief. Yet Jesus was not a "pure" Jew. He came from Galilee, a region with a history of interracial marriages. Jesus, moreover, did not possess Jewish traits; his mother had been conceived immaculately: "Jesus' mother Mary had no physical or moral connection with those ugly dispositions and forces that we condemn in full-blooded Jews. Through the miracle of the grace of God she is beyond these Jewish hereditary traits, a figure who tran-

scends Judaism. And, what had occurred in Mary took place too in the human nature of her son." Cited in Robert A. Krieg, "Karl Adam, National Socialism and Christian Tradition," *Theological Studies* 60/3 (1999): 432.

70. Heschel, *The Aryan Jesus, 49.*

71. Cited in Kevin P. Spicer, *Hitler's Priests: Catholic Clergy and National Socialism* (DeKalb, IL: Northern Illinois University Press, 2008), 117. Spicer notes that Haeuser, unlike Grundmann and his colleagues, did not deny that Jesus had been born a Jew (107).

72. Cited in Spicer, *Hitler's Priests*, 107.

73. Cited in Spicer, *Hitler's Priests*, 129.

74. Guardini wrote four books critical of Nazi ideology. See Robert A. Krieg, *Catholic Theologians in Nazi Germany* (New York: Continuum, 2004), 107–130. For a comparable study of Protestant theologians, see Robert P. Ericksen, *Theologians under Hitler: Gerhard Kittel, Paul Althaus and Emmanuel Hirsch* (New Haven, CT: Yale University Press, 1985).

75. Cited by Robert A. Krieg, "German Catholic Views of Jesus and Judaism, 1918–1945," in *Antisemitism, Christian Ambivalence, and the Holocaust,* 50–75; citation, 67.

76. See Robert A. Krieg, "Romano Guardini's Theology of the Human Person," *Theological Studies* 59/3 (1998): 457–474. Krieg notes that Guardini's book *The Lord* remains in print; Cardinal Joseph Ratzinger wrote the introduction to a 1997 edition. Krieg criticizes Ratzinger's failure to call attention to Guardini's outdated biblical scholarship and anti-Judaism (n. 9, 459).

77. Krieg, "German Catholic Views," 27.

78. Henry Smith Leiper, "Churchmen Who Defy Hitler, I: Bishop von Galen of Germany," *The New York Times,* June 8, 1942. See http://query.nytimes.com/mem/archive/pdf?res=FB0716FD3D5A147B93CAA9178DD8 5F468485F9 (accessed March 26, 2012).

79. See Beth Grieche-Polelle, *Bishop von Galen: German Catholicism and National Socialism* (New Haven, CT: Yale University Press, 2002), who includes them as an appendix, "Three Sermons in Dark Times," 171–196; citations in this paragraph, 173–175. She has reproduced an English translation found in her visit to St. Lambert's in 1994; I have retained the British spellings. The same translation of von Galen's sermons is available online: http://www.churchinhistory.org/pages/booklets/vongalen(n).htm (accessed March 28, 2012).

80. Ibid.; citations, 183, 181.

81. Ibid.; citations, 186, 191.

82. Robert Jay Lifton, *The Nazi Doctors: Medical Killing and the Psychology of Genocide* (New York: Basic Books, 1986), 94.

83. Griech-Polelle, *Bishop von Galen,* 94.

84. Kevin P. Spicer, "Bishop von Galen: German Catholicism and National Socialism" (review), *Holocaust and Genocide Studies* 18, no. 3 (2004): 492–495; citation, 495.

85. Griech-Polelle, *Bishop von Galen*, 97.

86. Ibid., 98–99. The quote within is from Stefan Rahner et al., *Treu deutsch sind wir—wir sind auch treu katholisch: Kardinal von Galen und das Dritte Reich* (Münster: WURF Verlag, 1987), 48.

87. Robert P. Ericksen, *Complicity in the Holocaust: Churches and Universities in Nazi Germany* (Cambridge: Cambridge University Press, 2012), 229.

88. Victoria J. Barnett, "The Role of the Churches: Compliance and Confrontation," *Dimensions* 14 (2000): 9.

89. Cited in Gregory Paul Wegner, *Anti-Semitism and Schooling Under the Third Reich* (New York and London: RoutledgeFalmer, 2002), 162; emphasis added.

90. Wegner, *Anti-Semitism and Schooling*, 181.

91. Richard Steigmann-Gall, "Old Wine in New Bottles?" in *Antisemitism, Christian Ambivalence and the Holocaust*, 304. Jantzen, *Faith and Fatherland*, argues that whether or not leading National Socialists formed their political views from Christian or extra-Christian sources, "by the later 1930s they had clearly abandoned such a position and were deeply antagonistic toward the faith" (13).

92. Cited in Richard Steigmann-Gall, *The Holy Reich: Nazi Conceptions of Christianity, 1919–1945* (Cambridge: Cambridge University Press, 2003), 29–30. For assessments of Steigmann-Gall's book, see the following articles, all of which appeared in *Journal of Contemporary History* 42/1 (2007): Doris Bergen, "Nazism and Christianity: Partners and Rivals?, 25–33; Manfred Gailus, "A Strange Obsession with Nazi Christianity," 35–46; Ernst Piper, "Steigmann-Gall, *The Holy Reich*," 47–57; and Irving Hexham, "Inventing 'Paganists': A Close Reading of Richard Steigmann-Gall's *The Holy Reich*," 59–78. Steigmann-Gall responds in "Christianity and the Nazi Movement: A Response," *Journal of Contemporary History* 42/2 (2007): 185–211.

93. Cited, *The Holy Reich*, 20–21.

94. Cited, ibid., 20–21.

95. Cited, ibid., 31–32.

96. Cited, ibid., 32.

97. Cited, "Old Wine," 294. Streicher spoke of Christianity as "one of the greatest anti-Jewish movements"; he also denied that Jesus and the apostles were Jewish (except Judas): "The crucifixion of Christ is the greatest ritual murder of all time" (cited, *The Holy Reich*, 125).

98. Cited, "Old Wine," 298.

99. Cited, *The Holy Reich*, 33.

100. Cited, *The Holy Reich*, 117.

101. Cited, "Old Wine," 299.

102. In October of 1964, the House of Bishops of the Episcopal Church (U.S.A.) released "Deicide and the Jews." Preceding *Nostra Aetate* by a year, it was also more candid: "The poison of antisemitism has causes of a political, national, psychological, social, and economic nature. It has often sought religious justification in the events springing from the crucifixion of Jesus. Antisemitism is a direct contradiction of Christian doctrine. Jesus was a Jew, and, since the Christian Church is rooted in Israel, spiritually we are Semites. The charge of deicide against the Jews is a tragic misunderstanding of the inner significance of the crucifixion. To be sure, Jesus was crucified by some soldiers at the instigation of some Jews. But, this cannot be construed as imputing corporate guilt to every Jew in Jesus' day, much less [to] the Jewish people in subsequent generations. Simple justice alone proclaims the charge of a corporate or inherited curse on the Jewish people to be false. Furthermore, in the dimension of faith the Christian understands that all men are guilty of the death of Christ, for all have in some manner denied him; and since the sins that crucified Christ were common human sins, the Christian knows that he himself is guilty. But he rejoices in the words and spirit of his Lord who said for the Roman soldiers and for all responsible for his crucifixion, 'Father, forgive them, for they know not what they do'" (cited in *Bridges: Documents of the Christian-Jewish Dialogue*, vol. 1, The Road to Reconciliation, 1945–1985, A Stimulus Book, ed. Franklin Sherman [New York: Paulist, 2011], 59).

103. See subsequent chapters for discussion of advances in biblical scholarship that provide a different interpretation of New Testament passages that seem to blame only Jews for the death of Jesus.

104. Cited in John M. Oesterreicher, "Declaration on the Relationship of the Church to Non-Christian Religions," in *Commentary on the Documents of Vatican II*, vol. 3, ed. Herbert Vorgrimler (New York: Herder and Herder, 1969), 1–136; citation, 122.

105. Michael Barnes, *Theology and the Dialogue of Religions*, Cambridge Studies in Christian Doctrine (Cambridge: Cambridge University Press, 2002), 38.

106. This is the judgment of theologian Gregory Baum, "The Social Context of American Catholic Theology," in *Proceedings of the Catholic Theological Society of America* 41 (1986): 83–100, especially 87.

107. See Claire Huchet Bishop, *How Catholics Look at Jews: Inquiries into Italian, Spanish and French Teaching Materials* (New York and Ramsey,

NJ: Paulist, 1974); Eugene J. Fisher, *Faith without Prejudice: Rebuilding Christian Attitudes toward Judaism* (New York and Ramsey, NJ: Paulist, 1977); Philip A. Cunningham, *Education for Shalom: Religion Textbooks and the Enhancement of the Catholic and Jewish Relationship* (Philadelphia: American Interfaith Institute, 1995).

108. On the power of ritual to form identity, see Paul Connerton, *How Societies Remember* (Cambridge: Cambridge University Press, 1989).

109. Two of the Eastertide Sundays in Year B have problematic readings from Acts. The Third Sunday of Easter has Acts 3:13–15, 17–19, in which Peter accuses the people: "You denied the Holy and Righteous One....The author of life you put to death." The Fourth Sunday of Easter has Acts 4:8–12, in which Peter, "filled with the Holy Spirit," addresses the "leaders of the people and elders...Jesus Christ the Nazorean, whom you crucified."

110. For a measured analysis, see Suzanne Brown-Fleming's historiographical essay on Pope Pius XII and the Holocaust in *The Holocaust and Catholic Conscience: Cardinal Aloisius Muench and the Guilt Question in Germany* (Notre Dame, IN: University of Notre Dame Press, 2006), 126–135.

111. See Donald J. Dietrich, *Human Rights and the Catholic Tradition*, 57: "With the exception of [Konrad] Preysing [of Eichstätt] and [Clemens von] Galen [of Münster], most bishops were too traditionally conservative to promote or even to think of any form of meaningful political resistance. They were unable institutionally or theologically to mobilize the faithful in any campaign beyond defending the religious interests of their administrative communities."

112. Klaus Scholder, *A Requiem for Hitler and Other New Perspectives on the German Church Struggle*, trans. John Bowden (London: SCM Press, 1989), 166. Scholder notes that this letter of instruction had been "struck through by another hand" (167).

113. Cardinal Michael von Faulhaber, *Judaism, Christianity and Germany*, trans. George D. Smith (New York: Macmillan, 1934), 14. Emphasis added. See also Mary Alice Gallin, "The Cardinal and the State: Faulhaber and the Third Reich," *Church and State* 12 (1970): 385–404.

114. Cited in George Mosse, *Nazi Culture: Intellectual, Cultural, and Social Life in the Third Reich* (New York: Grosset & Dunlap, 1966), 257–258.

115. Cited in Kevin Spicer, "Last Years of a Resister in the Diocese of Berlin: Bernhard Lichtenberg's Conflict with Karl Adam and his Fateful Imprisonment," *Church History* 70/2 (2001): 248–270; citation, 267.

116. Cited in Brenda Gaydosh, "Seliger Bernhard Lichtenberg: Steadfast in Spirit, He Directed his Own Course" (PhD dissertation, The American University, Washington, DC, 2010), 316.

117. Lichtenberg also was in trouble with Nazi authorities because of his protests against euthanasia. Reinhard Heydrich, the second-in-command of the SS, called Lichtenberg "that gutter priest from Berlin." See http://www2.facinghistory.org/Campus/weimar.nsf/Personalities/802A111C 2F05916F85256C6F00620E3D?Opendocument (accessed July 27, 2010). Note that Lichtenberg did not die "at Dachau," as *We Remember* claims, but en route there after months of imprisonment.

118. See, for example, Secretariat for Ecumenical and Interreligious Affairs of the National Conference of Catholic Bishops, *Catholic Teaching on the Shoah: Implementing the Holy See's We Remember* (Washington, DC: United States Catholic Conference, 2001). Available at http://www.nccbuscc. org/seia/we_remember.pdf (accessed July 27, 2010).

119. *The Holy Reich*, 267.

120. Kevin P. Spicer, "Catholics," in *The Oxford Handbook of Holocaust Studies*, 233–249; citation, 245.

121. "The Ad Hoc Committee Report on the 2010 Oberammergau Passion Play Script," http://www.ccjr.us/news/813-ccjr2010may14 (accessed June 18, 2010).

122. Ibid., 11–12.

CHAPTER 6

1. Robert P. Ericksen, "Christian Complexity? Changing Views on German Churches and the Holocaust," The Joseph and Rebecca Meyerhoff Annual Lecture, November 8, 2007, the United States Holocaust Memorial Museum, 5. See http://www.ushmm.org/research/center/publications/occasional/2009-11/paper.pdf (accessed January 8, 2012).

2. The 1998 statement from the Commission on Religious Relations with the Jews, "We Remember: A Reflection on the Shoah," says: "The history of relations between Jews and Christians is a tormented one." See http://www.vatican.va/roman_curia/pontifical_councils/chrstuni/documents/ rc_pc_chrstuni_doc_16031998_shoah_en.html (accessed January 10, 2012). See John T. Pawlikowski, "We Remember: Looking Back, Looking Ahead," *The Month* 33/1 (2000): 3–8.

3. See the discussion of the Jewish question in chapter 5.

4. Olaf Blaschke, *Offenders or Victims? German Jews and the Causes of Modern Catholic Antisemitism* (Lincoln: University of Nebraska Press/Vidal Sassoon International Center for the Study of Antisemitism, 2009), 43. Blaschke identifies ten arenas in which confessionalism played a key role, including denominational parties, separate organizations and

clubs, distinct media and communication, denominational schools, and everyday life in which Protestant and Catholic homes had different artifacts. He also notes that Jews had a higher level of education than did Catholics. Protestants were as a whole substantially better off economically (46–47).

5. Ibid., 48.

6. Shulamit Volkov, *Germans, Jews, and Antisemites: Trials in Emancipation* (Cambridge: Cambridge University Press, 2006), 67–68.

7. Available, inter alia: http://www.bc.edu/research/cjl/meta-elements/texts/cjrelations/resources/documents/catholic/french_repentance.htm (accessed June 29, 2010). Emphasis added.

8. John T. Pawlikowski, "Historical Memory and Christian-Jewish Relations," in *Christ Jesus and the Jewish People*, ed. Philip A. Cunningham, Joseph Sievers, Mary Boys, Hans Hermann Henrix, and Jesper Svartvik (Grand Rapids: Eerdmans, and Rome: Gregorian and Biblical Press, 2011), 14–31; citation, 22. Emphasis added.

9. See, for example, Mary C. Boys, "Facing History: The Church and Its Teachings on the Death of Jesus," in ibid., 31–63; citation, 44.

10. See Marc Saperstein, "Christian Doctrine and the Final Solution: The State of the Question," in *Remembering for the Future: The Holocaust in an Age of Genocide*, vol. 2, Ethics and Religion, ed. John K. Roth and Elizabeth Maxwell (New York: Palgrave, 2001), 814–841; citation, 826.

11. Steven T. Katz, *The Holocaust in Historical Context*, vol. 1: *The Holocaust and Mass Death before the Modern Age* (New York: Oxford University Press, 1994), 399.

12. Robert P. Ericksen, *Complicity in the Holocaust: Churches and Universities in Nazi Germany* (New York: Oxford University Press, 2012), 36.

13. Katz, *Holocaust in Historical Context*, 399–400. Emphasis added.

14. Ibid.

15. Kevin Spicer, *Hitler's Priests: Catholic Clergy and National Socialism* (DeKalb: Northern Illinois University Press, 2008), 229–230.

16. Ibid.

17. Richard Steigmann-Gall, "Christianity and the Nazi Movement: A Response," *Journal of Contemporary History* 42 (2007): 185–211; citation, 205.

18. See Katharina von Kellenbach, "God's Love and Women's Love: Prison Chaplains Counsel the Wives of Nazi Perpetrators," *Journal of Feminist Studies in Religion* 20/2 (Fall 2004): 7–24. For analysis of the pleas of Cardinal Aloisius Muench, bishop of Fargo, North Dakota who held important positions in Germany after World War II, that Germans—including Nazi perpetrators—be treated with Christian charity and love rather

than (as in the Old Testament) with the vengeance of an "eye for an eye, a tooth for a tooth," see Suzanne Brown-Fleming, *The Holocaust and Catholic Conscience: Cardinal Aloisius Muench and the Guilt Question in Germany* (Notre Dame, IN: University of Notre Dame Press, 2006).

19. See http://churchesandtheholocaust.ushmm.org/page/der-sturmer-images. I thank Victoria Barnett, Staff Director for Church Relations at the United States Holocaust Memorial Museum, and her summer assistant, Andrew Kloes, for these excerpts from *Der Stürmer*. Other examples are available at this URL (accessed August 8, 2011).

20. Ibid.

21. See Peter Longerich, *Holocaust: The Nazi Persecution and Murder of the Jews* (Oxford: Oxford University Press, 2010), 14.

22. Ibid., 26.

23. See Doris L. Bergen, "Catholics, Protestants, and Christian Antisemitism in Nazi Germany," *Central European History* 27/3 (1994): 329–348.

24. Response to *Kristallnacht* by church authorities was minimal. The only public response was from Bernhard Lichtenberg; see chapter 5. According to Günther Lewy, Archbishop Faulhaber of Munich sent a truck to rescue religious objects (*The Catholic Church and Nazi Germany* [New York: McGraw-Hill, 1964], 284).

25. Further decrees specified distinctions in a third category: *Mischlinge*, mixed- or cross-bred persons. Three classifications were made: (1) a *Mischling* with one or two Jewish grandparents who belonged to a synagogue, or was married to a Jew, or the child of a Jew (whether by marriage or out of wedlock) was considered a Jew; (2) a *Mischling* who had two Jewish grandparents, but was not a member of a synagogue, married to a Jew, or the child of a Jew was considered a *Mischling* of the first degree, and thus forbidden to marry a German or a second-degree *Mischling*; and (3) a *Mischling* with only one Jewish grandparent and who similarly did not belong to a synagogue was a *Mischling* of the second degree and could only marry a German, as it was believed that ultimately the taint of Jewish blood would be diluted.

26. Ericksen, *Complicity in the Holocaust*, 118.

27. Ibid.

28. Cited in Ulrike Ehret, "Catholicism and Judaism in the Catholic Defence against Alfred Rosenberg, 1934–1938: Anti-Jewish Images in an Age of Race Science," *European History Quarterly* 4/1 (2010): 35–56; citation at 44.

29. Ibid., 47. This bears similarity to the assertion by Catholic theologian Karl Adam: "Jesus' mother Mary had no physical or moral connec-

tion with those ugly dispositions and forces that we condemn in full-blooded Jews." See chapter 5, n. 66.

30. Cited in Bergen, "Catholics, Protestants, and Christian Anti-semitism in Nazi Germany," 335.

31. Excerpt from a 1936 booklet, *Katechismuswahrheiten* ("Truths of the Catechism"), cited in Ulrike Ehret, "Catholicism and Judaism in the Catholic Defence against Alfred Rosenberg, 1934–1938," 44.

32. Ibid., 48. Emphasis added.

33. John Connelly, "Catholic Racism and Its Opponents," *The Journal of Modern History* 79 (December 2007): 813–847; citation, 819. Emphasis added.

34. Yehuda Bauer, *Rethinking the Holocaust* (New Haven, CT, and London: Yale University Press, 2001), 105.

35. Robert P. Ericksen and Susannah Heschel, "The German Churches and the Holocaust," in *The Historiography of the Holocaust*, ed. Dan Stone (Basingstoke, Hants., UK: Palgrave MacMillan, 2004), 296–318; citation, 297.

36. So Donald J. Dietrich, *Catholic Citizens in the Third Reich: Psycho-Social Principles and Moral Reasoning* (New Brunswick, NJ: Transaction Books, 1988), 305.

37. Ericksen, *Conscience and Complicity*, 22–23.

38. Bergen, "Catholics, Protestants, and Christian Antisemitism in Nazi Germany," 348.

39. Cited in Brenda Gaydosh, "Seliger Bernhard Lichtenberg: Steadfast in Spirit, He Directed his Own Course" (PhD dissertation, The American University, Washington, DC, 2010), 311–312.

40. See Michael Phayer, "The Catholic Resistance Circle in Berlin and German Catholic Bishops during the Holocaust," *Holocaust and Genocide Studies* 7/2 (Fall 1993): 216–229. On Sommer, see also Michael Phayer, "Saving Jews Was Her Passion; Serving Survivors Was Her Agony," *Commonweal* 122/14 (August 18, 1995): 19–21.

41. Cited in Michael Phayer, *The Catholic Church and the Holocaust, 1930–1965* (Bloomington: Indiana University Press, 2000), 73.

42. Ibid., 75. On the tensions between Preysing and Cardinal Bertran, see Klaus Scholder, *A Requiem for Hitler and Other New Perspectives on the German Church Struggle*, trans. John Bowden (London: SCM, 1989), 157–160.

43. Gerald Steinacher, *Nazis on the Run: How Hitler's Henchmen Fled Justice* (Oxford: Oxford University Press, 2011), 119. See especially his chapter on "The Vatican Network," 101–158.

44. Ibid., 286.

45. Ibid., 91, 203–205. Michael Phayer discusses Dragonovic's ratline at length in his *Pius XII, the Holocaust, and the Cold War* (Bloomington: University of Indiana Press, 2008), 230–251. Both Steinacher and Phayer offer detail about the involvement of Pope Pius XII and his Secretary of State, Giovanni Battista Montini (later, Pope Paul VI), and the British and U.S. governments. After Barbie's capture in 1983, the United States apologized to the government of France (Phayer, 251).

46. Yosef H. Yerushalmi, in *Auschwitz: Beginning of a New Era? Reflections on the Holocaust*, ed. Eva Fleischner (New York: Ktav, 1977).

47. Philip R. Sloan notes the existence of a large international group of "scientists, enthusiasts for science, and social reformers from all ends of the political spectrum who were enamored with the new science of genetics and the possibilities of a genetic understanding of human beings promised for the social improvement of the human species" ("Eugenics and the Social Uses of Science: Non-religious Factors in the Genesis of the Holocaust," in *Humanity at the Limit: The Impact of the Holocaust Experience on Jews and Christians*, ed. Michael A. Signer [Bloomington: Indiana University Press, 2000], 175–179; citation, 175). Sloan's brief article introduces five excellent essays on racism and ethics in this volume.

48. Cited in Beth A. Griech-Polelle, "The Impact of the Spanish Civil War upon Roman Catholic Clergy in Nazi Germany," in *Antisemitism, Christian Ambivalence, and the Holocaust*, 121–135; citation, 124.

49. See the discussion in Gregory Paul Wegner, *Anti-Semitism and Schooling under the Third Reich* (New York: RoutledgeFalmer, 2002), 67–116; citation, 194. Wegner also documents the anti-black racism that accompanied the depiction of Jews; see 89, 105–111. Beverly Eileen Mitchell, in *Plantation and Death Camps: Religion, Ideology, and Human Dignity* (Minneapolis: Fortress, 2009), draws parallels between the Holocaust and chattel slavery. In both cases, Jews and blacks were set apart as pariahs, wrenched from their families, humiliated by degradation, brutalized by their oppressors, endured the agony of nighttime transports, and shamed and outraged by their own filth. The great commonality, Mitchell claims, is that both slaves and Jews bore witness; they left personal accounts for posterity that told the "truth from the inside of what it was like to live through a heinous assault on their dignity as children of God" (32).

50. Patricia Herberer, "Science," in *The Oxford Handbook of Holocaust Studies*, ed. Peter Hayes and John K. Roth (New York: Oxford University Press, 2010), 39–53; citation, 52.

51. Eric D. Weitz, "Nationalism," in *The Oxford Handbook of Holocaust Studies*, 54–67; citation, 62–63.

52. See A. Dirk Moses, "Colonialism," in *The Oxford Handbook of Holocaust Studies*, 68–80; reference, 71.

53. Weitz, "Nationalism," 65.

54. Doris L. Bergen, "World Wars," in *The Oxford Handbook of Holocaust Studies*, 95–110; citations, 97. The Himmler quote is from his October 4, 1943, speech to SS leaders in Posen (or Poznań)—recorded on a Nazi gramophone record. See Bauer's discussion of this speech, *Rethinking the Holocaust*, 21–22.

55. See John Connelly, "Gypsies, Homosexuals, and Slavs," in *The Oxford Handbook of Holocaust Studies*, 274–289; citation, 288.

56. See Phayer, *The Catholic Church and the Holocaust*, 111–132; Michael Phayer and Eva Fleischner, *Cries in the Night: Women Who Challenged the Holocaust* (Kansas City: Sheed and Ward, 1997); Nechama Tec, *When Light Pierced the Darkness: Christian Rescuers in Nazi-Occupied Poland* (Oxford: Oxford University Press, 1986). Also, Suzanne Vromen, *Hidden Children of the Holocaust: Belgian Nuns and Their Daring Rescue of Young Jews from the Nazis* (Oxford: Oxford University Press, 2008); Martin Gilbert, *The Righteous: The Unsung Heroes of the Holocaust* (Toronto: Key Porter, 2003); Philip P. Hallie, *Lest Innocent Blood be Shed: The Story of the Village of Le Chambon, and How Goodness Happened There* (New York: Harper & Row, 1979); *The Courage to Care: Rescuers of Jews During the Holocaust*, ed. Carol Rittner and Sondra Myers (New York: New York University Press, 1986).

57. Robert P. Ericksen, *Christian Complicity? Changing Views on German Churches and the Holocaust* (Washington, DC: United States Holocaust Memorial Museum, 2009), 10.

58. See Dietrich Bonhoeffer, "The Church and the Jewish Question," in *No Rusty Swords: Letters, Lectures and Notes 1928–1936* (New York: Harper and Row, 1965), 226: "The history of the suffering of this people, loved and punished by God, stands under the sign of the final homecoming of the people of Israel to its God. And this homecoming happens in the conversion of Israel to Christ."

59. Ericksen, *Complicity in the Holocaust*, 114.

60. Cited in Phayer, *The Catholic Church and the Holocaust*, 127. Phayer criticizes the Vatican for failing to offer financial support to Żegota and to the French rescue organization, *Amitié Chrétienne* in France (53–54, 127–128).

61. Modras, *The Catholic Church and Antisemitism*, 397.

62. Before World War II, there were 3.3 million Jews in Poland, of whom only five thousand were communist. See Ronald E. Modras, *The Catholic Church and Antisemitism: Poland, 1933–1939* (London: Routledge/

Vidal Sassoon International Center for the Study of Antisemitism, 1994), 110.

63. On May 16, 1929, Pope Pius XI said, "If it were possible to save even a single soul, to shield souls from greater harm, we would find the courage to deal even with the devil himself." The reference seems to be to Benito Mussolini, the Italian fascist leader with whom he negotiated the Lateran Pact, concluded on February 11, 1929. It may also be taken as what he and his successor perceived to be their responsibility to protect the Catholic Church from the evils of modernity in which the "devil functioned as a sort of stand-in for all modern temptations for all questioning of divine eternal truth revealed by Jesus Christ" (Wolf, *Pope and Devil*, 4).

64. See Michael Phayer, *Pius XII, the Holocaust, and the Cold War* (Bloomington: University of Indiana Press, 2008), 252–268.

65. Ibid., 264–265. Phayer cites (262) the following from a 1948 memoir of Maritain, France's ambassador to the Vatican (1945–1948): "Pius XII thinks that it is his mission to save western civilization from communism. Thus his head is taken up more and more with matters political....One is tempted to say that this attention to the political is too much considering the essential role of the church."

66. Reported by Rabbi Noam Marans in an e-mail to "scholar friends" on August 12, 2010. I thank Rabbi David J. Fine, who first contacted me in June of 2010 to urge a less critical view of the 2010 Oberammergau production.

67. At the time Rabbi Greenebaum was the Director of Interreligious and Intergroup Relations for the American Jewish Committee, and Rabbi Marans was the Associate Director; Marans is the current director.

68. Archbishop Timothy Dolan, "Two Rabbis, an Archbishop and the Oberammergau Passion Play," http://catholicexchange.com/2010/08/12/133113/ (accessed August 12, 2010).

69. Gary Greenebaum and Noam Marans, "Jews Should Recognize When Christians Change," http://www.jewishjournal.com/opinion/article/jews_should_recognize_when_christians_change_20100809/ (accessed August 12, 2010). Leonard Swidler, a Catholic theologian with long experience in interreligious affairs, including involvement with Oberammergau officials since 1979, termed the 2010 production "profoundly moving, stunningly professionally performed, esthetically sweeping—and inter-religiously triumphant" See his "Oberammergau Passion Play 'inter-religiously triumphant'" (http://ncronline.org/news/global/oberammergau-passion-play-inter-religiously-triumphant) (accessed September 15, 2010).

CHAPTER 7

1. Joseph B. Tyson, "The Death of Jesus," in *Seeing Judaism Anew: Christianity's Sacred Obligation*, ed. Mary C. Boys (Lanham, MD: Rowman & Littlefield, 2005), 44–45.

2. The image is from Mary Chilton Callaway, "Exegesis as Banquet: Reading Jeremiah with the Rabbis," in *A Gift of God in Due Season: Essays on Scripture and Community in Honor of James A. Sanders*, ed. Richard D. Weis and David M. Carr (Sheffield: Sheffield Academic Press, 1996), 219–230. I owe the reference to a former student, Rev. Jacqui Van Vliet.

3. Lloyd Gaston, *Paul and Torah* (Vancouver: University of Vancouver Press, 1987), 16.

4. Mary Rose D'Angelo, "Re-membering Jesus: Women, Prophecy, and Resistance in the Memory of the Early Churches," *Horizons* 19/2 (1992): 199–218; citation, 210.

5. See Brigitte Kahl, "Acts of the Apostles: Pro(to)-Imperial Script and Hidden Transcript," in *In the Shadow of Empire: Reclaiming the Bible as a History of Faithful Resistance*, ed. Richard A. Horsley (Louisville: Westminster John Knox, 2008), 137–156.

6. The wording of the creeds varies somewhat among Christian churches (and not all denominations and churches ascribe to creeds). The text of the Nicene Creed is more accurately the product of the Council of Nicaea (325) and the Council of Constantinople (381); the latter council added, "he was crucified for us under Pontius Pilate" (Greek original). Precise dating of the Apostles' Creed is more difficult. It bears considerable similarity to an early third-century profession of faith made by candidates for baptism and included in the *Apostolic Tradition* of Hippolytus. The candidate for baptism was asked, "Do you believe…in Christ Jesus, the Son of God, who was born of Holy Spirit and Virgin Mary, who was crucified in the days of Pontius Pilate?" See Berard L. Marthaler, *The Creed* (Mystic, CT: Twenty-Third Publications, 1987); Luke Timothy Johnson, *The Creed: What Christians Believe and Why It Matters* (New York: Doubleday, 2003); Jaroslav Pelikan, *Credo: Historical and Theological Guide to Creeds and Confessions of Faith in the Christian Tradition* (New Haven, CT, and London: Yale University Press, 2003).

7. Most scholars date Pilate's prefecture from 26 to 36 or 37 C.E., although Daniel Schwartz, based on discrepancies in Josephus, believes it is likely he began in 19 ("Pontius Pilate," *Anchor Bible Dictionary* V (New York: Doubleday, 1992), 396–397 [henceforth, *ABD*]. The Parthian Empire (ca. 238 B.C.E.–224 C.E.) succeeded the Persian Empire and thus was com-

posed of Iranian peoples; it was the chief rival to Rome. The Euphrates
River served as the main border between Roman and Parthian empires.

8. Colin West, "Roman Empire," *ABD* V, 803.

9. Warren Carter, *Roman Empire and the New Testament: An Essential
Guide* (Nashville: Abingdon, 2006), 44.

10. The Roman Senate had erected an arch in honor of the victory
ending the civil war, inscribing the legend, *res publica restituta*. By ending
the war, Octavian had saved the Republic; during his long rule, he would
oversee its restoration. See Paul Zanker, *The Power of Images in the Age of
Augustus,* trans. Alan Shapiro (Ann Arbor: University of Michigan Press,
1990), 89–100.

11. Susan P. Mattern, *Rome and the Enemy: Imperial Strategy in the
Principate* (Berkeley: University of California Press, 1999), 89.

12. Ibid., 183 and 202.

13. Ibid., 168.

14. Zanker, *The Power of Images,* 101.

15. Ibid., 98–99.

16. Davina C. Lopez, *Apostle to the Conquered: Reimagining Paul's
Mission* (Minneapolis: Fortress, 2008), 39.

17. *Roman History,* 56:30.

18. Historians recognize Augustus' brilliance as a politician while noting his cruelty. Colin West writes that he was a "brutal and difficult man,
given at times to severe delusions, and feared or disliked by those who knew
him best. Nonetheless, he proved to be a master politician and administra-
tor and, as a result, his reign marks the great watershed of Roman history"
("Augustus," *ABD* I, 527). Anthony Everitt makes a similar judgment: "The
story of his career shows that Augustus was indeed ruthless, cruel, and
ambitious for himself. This was only in part a personal trait, for upper-class
Romans were educated to compete with one another and to excel. However,
he combined an overriding concern for his personal interests with a deep-
seated patriotism, based on a nostalgic idea of Rome's antique virtues....While
fighting for dominance, he paid little attention to legality or to the normal
civilities of political life. He was devious, untrustworthy, and bloodthirsty.
But once he had established his authority, he governed efficiently and justly,
generally allowed freedom of speech, and promoted the rule of law. He was
immensely hardworking and tried as hard as any democratic parliamentar-
ian to treat his senatorial colleagues with respect and sensitivity. He suffered
from no delusions of grandeur" (*Augustus: The Life of Rome's First Emperor*
[New York: Random House, 2006], 324–325).

19. See Carter, *The Roman Empire and the New Testament,* 83.

20. John Dominic Crossan, "Roman Imperial Theology," in *In the Shadow of Empire*, 73.

21. "*Simplicitas rudis ante fuit nunc aurea Roma est/et domiti magnas possidet orbis opes.*" This third of the poems, *Ars Amatoria*, is thought to have originated ca. 1 C.E.

22. See K. C. Hanson and Douglas E. Oakman, *Palestine in the Time of Jesus: Social Structures and Social Conflicts* (Minneapolis: Fortress, 1998), 67–68.

23. Peter Garnesy and Richard Saller, *The Roman Empire: Economy, Society and Culture* (Berkeley and Los Angeles: University of California Press, 1987), 83.

24. The phrase is attributed to the poet Juvenal (late 1st c. C.E.–early 2nd c.) in *Satire X*.

25. See Richard A. Horsley, *Jesus and Empire: The Kingdom of God and the New World Disorder* (Minneapolis: Fortress Press, 2003), 25. For detail on the provinces supplying grain and other supplies, see Garnsey and Saller, *The Roman Empire*, 83–105.

26. Warren Carter, *Matthew and Empire: Initial Explorations* (Harrisburg, PA, 2001), 18.

27. John H. Kautsky, *The Politics of Aristocratic Empires* (Chapel Hill: University of North Carolina Press, 1982), 150.

28. Mattern, *Rome and the Enemy*, 119.

29. Ibid., 122.

30. The largest and most famous was the Colosseum in Rome, finished in 80 C.E.

31. See Brigitte Kahl, *Re-Imagining Galatians: Reading with the Eyes of the Vanquished* (Minneapolis: Fortress, 2010), 150. On the connection between the spectacles in the arena and crucifixions, see 156–157.

32. Ibid., 153–154. Kahl speaks of the arenas as the "megachurches of imperial religion" (156).

33. Cited in *Documents and Images for the Study of Paul*, ed. Neil Elliott and Mark Reasoner (Minneapolis: Fortress, 2011), 102.

34. Stephen J. Patterson, *Beyond the Passion: Rethinking the Death and Life of Jesus* (Minneapolis: Fortress, 2004), 8.

35. Fredriksen, *King of the Jews*, 233.

36. Patterson, *Beyond the Passion*, 9.

37. Neil MacFarquhar, "Muammar el-Qaddafi, 69, an Erratic, Brutal and Defiant Leader," *The New York Times*, October 21, 2011, A16–17; citation, A16.

38. Ibid.

39. For a comprehensive review, see David W. Chapman, *Ancient Jewish and Christian Perceptions of Crucifixion* (Grand Rapids: Baker, 2008).

40. For analysis of Herod's prowess as a builder, primarily in Judea, Samaria, and Idumea, see Peter Richardson, *Herod: King of the Jews and Friend of the Romans* (Columbia: University of South Carolina Press, 1996), 174–214.

41. There is some confusion over the terminology. Josephus, writing in Greek, uses both *epitropos* and *eparchos*; the Latin equivalents were, respectively, *procurator* (used by the historian Tacitus) and *praefectus*. In 1961, Italian archaeologists discovered a dedicatory inscription in Latin at Caesarea Maritima, from the Tiberium, a building named after Emperor Tiberius. In the English translation, the inscription reads "Pontius Pilatus, Prefect of Judea, has dedicated to the people of Caesarea a temple in honor of Tiberius." It is now part of the collection at the Israel Museum in Jerusalem, though a copy may be found at the Roman theater in Caesarea. It appears that these officials were called procurators after 44 C.E., albeit with the same general responsibilities. The New Testament uses the more general Greek term *hegemon*, which the *New Revised Standard Version* translates as governor. I use the terms *prefect* and *governor* as synonyms.

42. Carter, *Pontius Pilate: Portraits of a Roman Governor,* Interfaces, ed. Barbara Green (Collegeville, MN: Liturgical Press, 2003), 46.

43. See Anthony J. Saldarini, *Pharisees, Scribes and Sadducees in Palestinian Society: A Sociological Approach* (Wilmington, DE: Michael Glazier, 1988), 39–45. Following the work of Gerhard E. Lenski, Saldarini identifies nine classes in the Second Temple Period: ruler, governing class (for example, Pontius Pilate), retainer, merchant, priestly (except the high priestly families, part of the governing class), peasants, artisan, unclean (for example, tanners and miners), and the expendable class (for example, landless peasants).

44. The vestments—symbol of the holy office the high priest held— remained in control of the Roman governor until 36 C.E., when the Syrian legate, Vitellius, interceded with Emperor Tiberius to restore them to Jewish control. Then Fadus, the Roman governor who took office in 44 C.E., demanded the return of the vestments, but a Jewish delegation to Emperor Claudius returned them to Jewish control. The vestments then remained in Jewish hands until the destruction of the temple in 70 (*Antiquities* 15:403–405; 18:90–95; 20:6–16).

45. The high priests were Eleazar, 16–17 C.E.; Jonathan, 36 or 37 C.E.; Theophilus, 36–41 C.E.; Matthias, 42–43 C.E.; and Annas II, 62 C.E.).

46. Adele Reinhartz, *Caiaphas the High Priest,* Studies on Personalities in the New Testament, ed. D. Moody Smith (Columbia: University of South Carolina Press, 2011), 50–51.

47. Ibid., 202.

48. So E. P. Sanders, *Judaism: Practice and Belief,* 63 *B.C.E.–66 C.E.* (London: SCM Press and Philadelphia: Trinity Press International, 1992), 323.

49. Caiaphas had excellent family connections; he was the son-in-law of Annas, who was high priest from 6–15 C.E., and five of his brothers-in-law also served as high priests (Eleazar, 16–17 C.E.; Jonathan 36 or 37 C.E.; Theophilus 36–41; Matthias 42–43 C.E.; and Annas II, 62 C.E.).

50. Sanders, *Judaism,* 328–329.

51. Carter, *Pontius Pilate,* 48.

52. Sanders, *Judaism: Practice and Belief,* 323. He notes that from 59–65 C.E., there was considerable strife within the aristocracy (324).

53. Led by Simeon ben Kosiba, this second revolt against Roman rule failed, although it required some 50,000 Roman soldiers finally to subdue the revolutionaries. The results were disastrous: the razing of all Judean villages, captives sold into slavery, and Judeans seeking refuge in caves. Not only did the center of Jewish life move to the Galilee, but the Romans no longer called the region Provincia Judaea but Provincia Syria Palestina. See Hanan Eshel, "The Bar Kochba Revolt, 132–135," in *The Cambridge History of the Bible,* vol. 4, ed. Steven T. Katz (Cambridge: Cambridge University Press, 2006), 105–127.

54. Horsley, *Jesus and Empire,* 10. He speaks of "modern essentialist concepts such as 'the Jews'" (11).

55. Paula Fredriksen, *Jesus of Nazareth, King of the Jews* (New York: Vintage Books, 2000), 176–184.

56. In the second volume of his book *Jesus of Nazareth,* Joseph Ratzinger/Pope Benedict XVI gives virtually no attention to the backstory of the Roman Empire. He asserts that those who condemned Jesus to death were the "temple aristocracy" (what John's Gospel calls "the Jews") and the followers of Barabbas who had mobilized to secure the amnesty offered during Passover (the crowd or mob [*ochlos*] of Mark's Gospel). In contrast, he places little blame on Pontius Pilate and does not discuss the function of crucifixion in imperial rule. He claims that Pontius Pilate, while aware that Jesus "was not a political criminal and that the kingship he claimed did not represent any political danger," nevertheless reasoned that the "peace-building role of law" justified his judgment: "Releasing this innocent man could not only cause him personal damage…it could also give rise to further disturbances and unrest, which had to be avoided at all costs, especially at the time of Passover" (*Jesus of Nazareth. Holy Week: From the Entrance into*

Jerusalem to the Resurrection, trans. Philip J. Whitmore (San Francisco: Ignatius Press, 2001), 185–201; citations, 200–201.

57. Raymond E. Brown, *The Death of the Messiah,* vol.1, 14; see his discussion on the role of history in §1, B, 13–24. See also "Appendix VII: The Old Testament Background of the Passion Narratives," vol. 2, 1445–1491 for a close reading of Old Testament materials that "influenced heavily early Christian presentation of the passion, highlighting what should be recounted in order to expand the preaching outline into dramatic narratives" (1444).

58. John Dominic Crossan, *Who Killed Jesus? Exposing the Roots of Anti-Semitism in the Gospel Story of the Death of Jesus* (San Francisco: HarperSanFrancisco, 1995), 35. Emphases in original. An earlier work with a similar hypothesis is that of Burton Mack, *A Myth of Innocence: Mark and Christian Origins* (Philadelphia: Fortress, 1988): "Mark's Gospel was not the product of divine revelation. It was not a pious transmission of revered tradition. It was composed at a desk in a scholar's study lined with texts and open to discourse with other intellectuals....The passion narrative is simply the climax of the new storyline. The story was a new myth of origins" (322–323).

59. Amy-Jill Levine, *The Misunderstood Jew: The Church and the Scandal of the Jewish Jesus* (San Francisco: HarperSanFrancisco, 2007), 116.

60. E. P. Sanders says that the "real conflict was between Jesus and his contemporaries in Judaism." Yet it is not correct to "make a rigid distinction between 'religious' and 'political' reasons." He thinks it unlikely that even someone close to the events of the passion "knew precisely who did what" and that it is impossible that the evangelists knew the "internal motives" of those involved (*Jesus and Judaism* [Philadelphia: Fortress, 1985], 295–296 and 300). Sanders sees Jesus' "attack (both by word and deed) against the temple" as an immediate cause of his death (301–304). Paula Fredriksen refutes this view, arguing that whatever symbolic action Jesus took in the temple would have been muted by the immensity of the temple and that his predictions of the fall of the temple were composed after its destruction in 70. She writes: "Jewish pilgrims hailed Jesus as messiah in Jerusalem. Pilate killed him as a messianic pretender—not again because Jesus thought he was messiah...but because others thought and proclaimed that he was" (*Jesus of Nazareth, King of the Jews,* 225–234; citation, 234).

61. Gerard S. Sloyan, *The Crucifixion of Jesus: History, Myth, Faith* (Minneapolis: Fortress, 1995), 27–28.

62. Ibid., 29.

63. Ibid., 40.

64. Even this, however, oversimplifies the situation, since first-century Jews varied in precisely how they observed the Law. Observance of the Law varied from region to region, and there was no normative body to determine its contours.

65. Sloyan, *Crucifixion*, 43.

CHAPTER 8

1. Jean Halperin, cited in Diana Eck, *Encountering God: a Spiritual Journey from Bozeman to Banaras* (Boston: Beacon, 1993), 189.

2. The phrase appears in "Eighteen Theological Theses" from the Belgian National Catholic Commission for Relations between Christians and Jews, 1973, in *Stepping Stones to Further Jewish-Christian Relations*, ed. Helga Croner (New York: Stimulus Books, 1977), 58.

3. So Hyam Maccoby, *The Mythmaker: Paul and the Invention of Christianity* (San Francisco: HarperSanFrancisco, 1986). See the review by John Gager, "Maccoby's Mythmaker," *Jewish Quarterly Review,* New Series, 79/2–3 (1988–1989): 248–250.

4. So Joseph Ratzinger/Pope Benedict XVI, *Saint Paul* (San Francisco: Ignatius Press, 2009), 7.

5. So Pamela Eisenbaum, *Paul Was Not a Christian: The Original Message of a Misunderstood Apostle* (New York: HarperOne, 2009).

6. So Daniel Boyarin, *A Radical Jew: Paul and the Politics of Identity* (Berkeley: University of California Press, 1994), 2.

7. Magnus Zetterholm, *Approaches to Paul: A Student's Guide to Recent Scholarship* (Minneapolis: Fortress, 2009), 10.

8. See Jules Isaac, *Teaching of Contempt: Christian Roots of Anti-Semitism,* trans. Helen Weaver (New York: Holt, Rinehart and Winston, 1964).

9. In brief, the "new perspectives on Paul" originated with the work of Krister Stendahl in the 1960s, and has been developed in varying ways by E. P. Sanders and James D. G. Dunn, among others. See Stendahl, *Paul among Jews and Gentiles, and Other Essays* (Philadelphia: Fortress, 1976); Sanders, *Paul and Palestinian Judaism: A Comparison of Patterns of Religion* (Philadelphia: Fortress, 1977); Dunn, *The New Perspective on Paul,* rev. ed. (Tübingen: Mohr Siebeck, 2005).

10. For an excellent review and analysis, see Zetterholm, *Approaches to Paul,* 33–94. See also http://www.thepaulpage.com/ (accessed October 18, 2011).

11. Jerome Murphy-O'Connor, "'Even Death on a Cross': Crucifixion in Pauline Letters," in *The Cross in Christian Tradition: From Paul to Bonaventure*, ed. Elizabeth A. Dreyer (New York and Mahwah, NJ: Paulist Press, 2000), 21–50.

12. Ibid., 29.

13. Ibid., 30.

14. "It is those who want to make a good showing in the flesh that try to compel you to be circumcised—only that they may not be persecuted for the cross of Christ. Even the circumcised do not themselves obey the law, but they want you to be circumcised so that they may boast about your flesh. May I never boast of anything except the cross of our Lord Jesus Christ, by which the world has been crucified to me, and I to the world. For neither circumcision nor uncircumcision is anything; but a new creation is everything!" (Galatians 6:12–15).

15. Murphy-O'Connor, "Even Death on a Cross,'" 30–31. Emphasis added. Murphy-O'Connor observed that for the "Judaizers [that is, those who argued that Jesus' followers should observe the Law], kashrut and circumcision were the only matters of ultimate concern. They scaled the role of Christ down to irrelevance" (37).

16. Ibid., 32.

17. Ibid., 35 and 34, respectively.

18. Ibid., 36.

19. Ibid., 43.

20. See, for example, Martin Luther, "Lectures on Galatians," *Luther's Works,* vol. 26, ed. Jaroslav J. Pelikan et al. (St. Louis: Concordia, 1963), 9–10.

21. Zetterholm, *Approaches to Paul,* 84.

22. Ibid., 127–63; for a summary, see 161–163.

23. Neil Elliott, *Liberating Paul: The Justice of God and the Politics of the Apostle* (Minneapolis: Fortress, 2006), 132–139.

24. See Deuteronomy 27:26a: "Cursed be anyone who does not uphold the words of this law by observing them. All the people shall say, 'Amen!'" See also 21:23c: "for anyone hung on a tree is under God's curse."

25. N. T. Wright, *The Climax of the Covenant: Christ and the Law in Pauline Theology* (Minneapolis: Fortress, 1992), 140–141.

26. Ibid., 151.

27. Elliott, *Liberating Paul,* 137–138.

28. Ibid., 139. The citation within the quotation is from Jon Sobrino, *Jesus in Latin America,* trans. Robert R. Barr (Maryknoll, NY: Orbis, 1987), 31; parenthesis in original.

29. Elliott, *Liberating Paul,* 129.

30. Ibid., 132.

31. See Stanley Stowers, *A Rereading of Romans: Justice, Jews, and Gentiles* (New Haven: Yale University Press, 1994); Mark Nanos, *The Mystery of Romans: The Jewish Context of Paul's Letter* (Minneapolis: Fortress, 1996); and *The Irony of Galatians: Paul's Letter in First-Century Context* (Minneapolis: Fortress, 2002). N. T. Wright, *Paul: In Fresh Perspective* (Minneapolis: Fortress, 2005). Nanos has extensive resources available at his website: http://www.marknanos.com (accessed October 18, 2011).

32. Eisenbaum, *Paul Was Not a Christian*, 148.

33. Paula Fredriksen, *Jesus of Nazareth, King of the Jews* (New York: Vintage, 2000), 135.

34. Ibid., 176.

35. Ibid., 255.

36. Davina C. Lopez, *Apostle to the Conquered: Reimagining Paul's Mission* (Minneapolis: Fortress, 2008).

37. In Galatians, Paul writes: "You have heard, no doubt, of my earlier life in Judaism. I was violently persecuting the church [*ekklēsia*, assembly] of God and was trying to destroy [*eporthoun*, devaste] it. I advanced in Judaism beyond many among my people of the same age, for I was far more zealous for the traditions of my ancestors" (1:13–14).

38. Cf. Murphy-O'Connor's reading of this language with Lopez's interpretation.

39. Lopez, *Apostle to the Conquered*, 135.

40. Ibid.

41. Ibid., 137.

42. "Are they ministers of Christ? I am talking like a madman—I am a better one: with far greater labors, far more imprisonments, with countless floggings, and often near death. Five times I have received from the Jews the forty lashes minus one. Three times I was beaten with rods. Once I received a stoning. Three times I was shipwrecked; for a night and a day I was adrift at sea; on frequent journeys, in danger from rivers, danger from bandits, danger from my own people, danger from Gentiles, danger in the city, danger in the wilderness, danger at sea, danger from false brothers and sisters; in toil and hardship, through many a sleepless night, hungry and thirsty, often without food, cold and naked" (2 Corinthians 11:23–27).

43. Lopez, *Apostle to the Conquered*, 138.

44. Brigitte Kahl, *Re-Imagining Galatians: Reading Paul with the Eyes of the Vanquished* (Minneapolis: Fortress, 2010). Kahl sees the practice of benefaction or euergetism as one of the most fundamental social patterns of antiquity. It was a way of "social alchemy" because it changed a mutual exchange of gifts among coequals into a "hierarchical reciprocity that mir-

rors and cements domination and subordination" (196). It was closely connected with imperial religion and highly competitive.

45. Kahl, *Re-Imagining Galatians*, 263. Kahl offers rich detail about the identity of the Galatians, which I can only briefly summarize here. The Galatians were Celtic inhabitants of Asia Minor. Earlier, other Celtic tribes who had settled around the Alps—Gauls—had sacked Rome (387 B.C.E.). In the mid-third century B.C.E., the Galatians had been defeated and memorialized as an exemplar of the barbarian "other" ("The Dying Trumpeter") by the Kingdom of Pergamon. Ca. 180–160 B.C.E. the Great Altar of Pergamon was built in commemoration of the conquest of the Galatians. In 189 B.C.E., Romans massacred some forty thousand Galatians; Galatia was subjected to pro-Roman rule, particularly under the client king Deiotaros. In 25 B.C.E., Augustus founded the Province of Galatia. From a Roman point of view, Kahl claims, Galatia was the "region populated by the Celtic 'counternation,' that is, a peculiar species of 'universal barbarians' who, after centuries of struggle, had at last been forced into compliance with the 'world-saving' power of Roman victory, at the threshold of the era of Jesus and Paul" (33).

46. Ibid., 205.

47. Ibid., 223.

48. Ibid., 289.

49. Brent D. Shaw, "Rebels and Outsiders," in *The High Empire, A.D. 70–192*, Cambridge Ancient History 11, ed. Alan K. Bowman, Peter Garnsey, and Dominic Rathbone (Cambridge: Cambridge University Press, 2000), 361–403; citation, 361.

50. See Didier Pollefeyt and David Bolton, "Paul, Deicide and the Wrath of God: A Hermeneutical Reading of 1 Thes 2:14–16," in *Paul in His Jewish Matrix*, ed. Thomas G. Casey and Justin Taylor (Rome: Gregorian and Biblical Press, 2011), 229–257.

51. See Holland Lee Hendrix, "Benefactor/Patron Networks in the Urban Environment: Evidence from Thessalonica," *Semeia* 56 (1992): 50.

52. Abraham Smith, "Unmasking the Powers: Toward a Postcolonial Analysis of 1 Thessalonians," in *Paul and the Roman Imperial Order*, ed. Richard A. Horsley (Harrisburg, PA: Trinity Press International, 2004), 47–66; citation, 60.

53. See Richard A. Horsley, "Introduction," in *Paul and the Roman Imperial Order*, 3–5.

54. For the phrase "more complex and capacious," see Seth Schwarz, *Imperialism and Jewish Society, 200 B.C.E. to 640 C.E.* (Princeton: Princeton University Press, 2001), 4–5.

55. The phrase "rhetoric of invidious contrast" is from Paula Fredriksen, "What 'Partings of the Ways'? Jews, Gentiles, and the Ancient Mediterranean City," in *The Ways that Never Parted: Jews and Christians in Late Antiquity and the Early Middle Ages*, Texts and Studies in Ancient Judaism 95, ed. Adam Becker and Annette Yoshiko Reed (Tübingen: Mohr Siebeck, 2003), 35–63; citation, 37.

56. *Judaisms and Their Messiahs at the Turn of the Christian Era*, ed. Jacob Neusner, William Scott Green, and Ernest S. Frerichs (Cambridge: Cambridge University Press, 1987), xi–xii. The editors note that we should similarly speak of "Christianities."

57. James Charlesworth, "From Old to New: Paradigm Shifts concerning Judaism, the Gospel of John, Jesus and the Advent of 'Christianity,'" in *Jesus Research: An International Perspective*, ed. James Charlesworth and Petr Pokorný (Grand Rapids: Eerdmans, 2009), 56–72.

58. Here I am following the arguments of Shaye J. D. Cohen, *The Beginnings of Jewishness* (Berkeley: University of California Press, 1999).

59. Ibid., 106.

60. The "Jews" occurs some eighty times in Acts and sixty-seven in the Gospel of John.

61. See Franklin Sherman, "Difficult Texts: Interpreting New Testament Images of Jews and Judaism," *Covenantal Conversations: Christianity in Dialogue with Jews and Judaism* (Minneapolis: Fortress, 2008), 76–89.

62. So James Pasto, "The Origins, Expansion, and Impact of the Hasmoneans in Light of Comparative Ethnographic Studies (and Outside of Its Nineteenth Century Context), in *Second Temple Studies III: Studies in Politics, Class, and Material Culture*, ed. Philip R. Davies and John M. Halligan (London: Sheffield Academic Press, 2002), 166–201.

63. Daniel Boyarin, *Dying for God: Martyrdom and the Making of Christianity and Judaism* (Stanford: Stanford University Press, 1999), 9.

64. D. Boyarin, "Semantic Differences; or, 'Judaism'/'Christianity,'" in *The Ways that Never Parted*, 65–85; citation, 74.

65. James D. G. Dunn, *The Partings of the Ways between Christianity and Judaism and Their Significance for the Character of Christianity* (London: SCM and Trinity Press International, 2001). I summarize Dunn's argument at greater length in my *Has God only One Blessing? Judaism as a Source of Christian Self-Understanding* (New York and Mahwah, NJ: Paulist Press, 2000), 152–159.

66. Annette Yoshiko Reed and Adam H. Becker, "Introduction: Traditional Models and New Directions," in *The Ways that Never Parted*, 1–34; citation, 23.

67. See *Discourses against Judaizing Christians*, trans. Paul W. Harkins (Washington: DC: Catholic University of America Press, 1979; see also John G. Gager, "The Partings of the Ways: A View from the Perspective of Early Christianity—A Christian Perspective," in *Interwoven Destinies*, ed. Eugene A. Fisher. A Stimulus Book (New York: Paulist Press, 1986), 71–72.

68. Guy G. Stroumsa identifies ten extant texts of the *Adversus Judaeos* tradition, beginning with the *Epistle of Barnabas, Dialogue with Trypho* (Justin Martyr), *Adversus Judaeos* and *Adversus Marcionen* (Tertullian), *Evangelical Demonstration* (Eusebius of Caesarea), *Panarion* (Epiphanius of Salamis), *Homilies against the Judaizers* (John Chrysostom), *Homilies* (Aphrahat), and *Adversus Judaeos* (Augustine). He suggests that there are at least eight lost treatises. See "From Anti-Judaism to Antisemitism in Early Christianity?" in *Contra Judaeos: Ancient and Medieval Polemics between Christians and Jews*, ed. Ora Limor and Guy G. Stroumsa (Tübingen: J.C.B. Mohr, 1996), 7–9.

69. Paula Fredriksen and Oded Irshai, "Christian Anti-Judaism: Polemics and Policies," in *Cambridge History of the Bible*, vol. 4, ed. Steven T. Katz (Cambridge: Cambridge University Press, 2006), 977–1034; citation, 997.

70. Judith Lieu, *Image and Reality: The Jews in the World of the Christians in the Second Century* (Edinburgh: T&T Clark, 1996), 278.

71. Ibid., 288.

72. Stoumas, "From Anti-Judaism to Antisemitism in Early Christianity?" 20.

73. Stephen G. Wilson, *Related Strangers: Jews and Christians 70–170 C.E.* (Minneapolis: Fortress, 1994), 29. See also Robert L. Wilken, *The Christians as the Romans Saw Them* (New Haven: Yale University Press, 1984).

74. Paula Fredriksen, *Augustine and the Jews: A Christian Defense of Jews and Judaism* (New York: Doubleday, 2008), xvii, 101.

75. See Judy Yates Siker, "Unmasking the Enemy: Deconstructing the 'Other' in the Gospel of Matthew," *Perspectives in Religious Studies* 32/3 (Summer 2005): 109–123.

76. Israel Jacob Yuval, *Two Nations in your Womb: Perceptions of Jews and Christians in Late Antiquity and the Middle Ages*, trans. Barbara Harshav and Jonathan Chipman (Berkeley: University of California Press, 2006), 23 and xi. Hebrew original, 2000. Adiel Schremer, however, argues that the rabbis came to regard the followers of Jesus as "heretics" not because of a disagreement about doctrine (for example, the Trinity, Jesus' divine status) but as threats to the stability and identity of a Jewish community in despair after the crises of the temple's destruction and the Bar Kokhba demise. Contra Yuval, he claims that the significance of Christianity for the devel-

opment of rabbinic Judaism is "far too exaggerated and lacks a firm textual and historical base" (*Brothers Estranged: Heresy, Christianity, and Jewish Identity in Late Antiquity* [Oxford University Press, 2010], 10).

77. Yuval, *Two Nations in Your Womb*, 27. Also see Peter Schäfer, *Jesus in the Talmud* (Princeton, NJ: Princeton University Press, 2007).

78. Ibid., 89.

79. Translation in Philip Birnbaum, *The Birnbaum Haggadah* (New York: Hebrew Publishing Company, 1976), 89.

80. Melito of Sardis, "A Homily on the Passover," in *The Christological Controversy*, ed. and trans. Richard A. Norris, Jr. (Philadelphia: Fortress Press, 1980), §§87–88, 90–91.

81. Yuval, *Two Nations in Your Womb*, 89.

82. Ibid., 90.

83. *Brothers Estranged*, 18.

84. Ibid, 99.

85. This hypothesis is indebted particularly to J. Louis Martyn, *History and Theology in the Fourth Gospel*, 2nd ed. revised and enlarged (Louisville: John Knox, 1979), who dated the *birkat haminim* ca. 85–115 C.E. Martin reads John 9 as dramatizing the "wall of separation" between church and synagogue. He concludes: "Thus the Fourth Gospel affords us a picture of a Jewish community at a point not far removed from the end of the first century. As we get a glimpse of it, this community has been shaken by the introduction of a newly formulated means [that is, the blessing called *birkat haminim*] for detecting those Jews who want to hold dual allegiance to Moses and to Jesus as Messiah. Even against the will of some of the synagogue leaders, the Heretic Benediction is now employed in order formally and irretrievably to separate such Jews from the synagogue" (61–62).

86. See Reuven Kimmelman, "*Birkat Ha-Minim* and the Lack of Evidence for an Anti-Christian Jewish Prayer in Late Antiquity," in *Jewish and Christian Self-Definition, vol. 2: Aspects of Judaism in the Graeco-Roman Period*, ed. E. P. Sanders, A. I. Baumgarten, and Alan Mendelson (Philadelphia: Fortress, 1981), 226–244.

87. Ruth Langer, *Cursing Christians? A History of the Birkat Haminim* (New York: Oxford University Press, 2012), 4–39. Langer traces the long history of the *birkat haminim* through Jewish life under Islam, in medieval Europe—when it was indeed a curse against Christians—and in modernity, when Jews, now becoming part of Western culture, began to modify it in ways that expressed their desire for deliverance from evil. See also her "Liturgy in the Light of Jewish-Christian Dialogue," *Studies in Christian-Jewish Relations* 4 (2009): 1–13.

Notes

CHAPTER 9

1. The term *Mishnah* means "oral instruction." Various *mishnah* collections were compiled, but that of Rabbi Yehuda ha-Nasi' (Judah the Prince or Patriarch, ca. 135–220) became the authoritative compilation. Both the Babylonian Talmud (*Bavli*) and Jerusalem Talmud (*Yerushalmi*) contain the Mishnah, albeit with textual differences. See s.v., "Mishnah" in *The Oxford Dictionary of the Jewish Religion*, ed. R. J. Zwi Werblowsky and Geoffrey Wigoder (New York and Oxford: Oxford University Press, 1997), 471–472.

2. Barbara Green, "This Old Text: An Analogy for Biblical Interpretation," *Biblical Theology Bulletin* (2006/2): 72–83. The PBS website has episodes for viewing; according to this website, "This Old House's mission is to demystify the home improvement process and to celebrate the fusion of old world craftsmanship and modern technology." See http://www.pbs.org/thisoldhouse/about/ (accessed October 11, 2011).

3. Ulrich Luz, *Matthew in History: Interpretation, Influence, and Effects* (Minneapolis: Fortress, 1994), 12.

4. Green, "This Old Text," 78.

5. Willem S. Vorster, "Gospel Genre," in *The Anchor Bible Dictionary*, vol. 2, ed. David Noel Freedman et al. (New York: Doubleday, 1992), 1177–1179.

6. Steven L. McKenzie, *How to Read the Bible: History, Prophecy, Literature—Why Modern Readers Need to Know the Difference and What It Means for Faith Today* (New York: Oxford University Press, 2005), 62 and 65.

7. See Stefan Aliker, "Intertextuality and the Semiotics of Biblical Texts," in *Reading the Bible Intertextually*, ed. Richard Hayes and S. Aliker (Waco: Baylor University Press, 2009), 3–21; citation, 3. Among diverse definitions of intertextuality, James A. Sanders suggests three: the "chemistry" between two contiguous blocks of literature (for example, the two creation stories of Genesis or the Old and New Testaments); literature that draws on older texts by way of allusion, citation, phrases and/or paraphrases; readers as texts. See his "Intertextuality and Dialogue," *Biblical Theology Bulletin* 29/1 (1999): 35–44.

8. Mark Lewis Taylor, "American Torture and the Body of Christ," in *Cross Examinations: Readings on the Meaning of the Cross Today*, ed. Marit Trelstad (Minneapolis: Augsburg Fortress, 2006), 264–277; citation, 274.

9. Raymond E. Brown, *The Death of the Messiah*, vol. 2 (New York: Doubleday, 1994), 1460–1462; the entire section, "Appendix VII: Old Testament Background," is very helpful (1445–1467). Typically, the Gospel writers are using the Septuagint (that is, the Greek translation of the Hebrew Bible) for their allusions and citations. I am following the numera-

tion of the English translation (NRSV), which differs from the Hebrew when the superscription is numbered as the first verse.

10. For detailed analysis of the Markan and Matthean use of this verse, see Brown, *The Death of the Messiah*, 1051–1054.

11. See Esther M. Menn, "No Ordinary Lament: Relecture and the Identity of the Distressed in Psalm 22," *Harvard Theological Review* 93/4 (2000): 301–341. Menn shows how the rabbis in the amoraic period (third to fifth centuries), perhaps influenced in part by the way the Gospel writers used Psalm 22, began to use that Psalm to interpret the Book of Esther.

12. Sanders, "Intertextuality and Dialogue," 42.

13. Green, *This Old Text*, 78.

14. Ibid, 79.

15. Ibid., 80.

16. Robert McAfee Brown, *Creative Dislocation—The Movement of Grace* (Nashville: Abingdon, 1980), 107.

17. Green, "This Old Text," 80.

18. Martha Cooley, *The Archivist* (Boston, New York and London: Little, Brown and Company, 1998), 22. Further references are in parentheses.

19. The Hebrew word *tikkun* appears in Ecclesiastes (1:5, 7:13, 12:9), meaning "setting straight" or "putting in order." The phrase often used today, *tikkun olam*, first appeared in the *aleinu* prayer ("It is our duty to praise"; origin ca. early fourth century), and it surfaced later in the writings of medieval kabbalists. In the last century the phrase has come to mean "the betterment of the world, including the relief of human suffering, the achievement of peace and mutual respect among peoples, and the protection of the planet itself from destruction." So Karla Suomala, "Healing the World and Mending the Soul," in *Covenantal Conversations: Christians in Conversation with Jews and Judaism*, ed. Darrell Jodock (Minneapolis: Fortress, 2008), 114–115; Suomala's citation is from Arnold Wolf, "Repairing *Tikkun Olam*," *Judaism* 50/2 (1964): 479–482.

20. Johann Baptist Metz, "Between Remembering and Forgetting: The Shoah in the Era of Cultural Amnesia," trans. L. J. Penta, in *Good and Evil after Auschwitz: Ethical Implications for Today*, ed. Jack Bemporad, John T. Pawlikowski, and Joseph Sievers (Hoboken, NJ: KTAV, 2000), 21–28; citations, 21 and 23).

21. Ibid., 23.

22. See http://www.jmberlin.de/main/EN/04-About-The-Museum/01-Architecture/01-libeskind-Building.php (accessed November 10, 2010). This is the museum's website and provides those unable to visit in person a sense of the destabilizing effects of its design.

23. Johann Baptist Metz, *Emergent Church*, trans. Peter Mann (New York: Crossroad, 1981), 29.

24. David Tracy, *On Naming the Present: Reflections on God, Hermeneutics, and Church* (Maryknoll, NY: Orbis, 1994), 61–65; citation, 64.

25. The passion narratives are not the only problematic texts in the New Testament's portrayal of Jews and Judaism. The depiction of the Pharisees, particularly in the Synoptic Gospels, has contributed (and continues to contribute) to disparagement of Judaism as legalistic.

26. Dorothee Sölle, cited in Luz, *Matthew in History*, 91.

27. See Luz, *Matthew in History*, 32–33.

28. Gabriel Almond, R. Scott Appleby, and Emmanel Sivan, *Strong Religion: the Rise of Fundamentalisms around the World* (Chicago: University of Chicago Press, 2003), 3.

29. Leo D. Lefebure, *Revelation, the Religions and Violence* (Maryknoll, NY: Orbis, 2000), 202.

30. The Ethiopian eunuch was both an ethnic and a sociocultural outsider, given the hostility to eunuchs in Greco-Roman and Jewish antiquity. Significantly, in Acts he is the first Gentile outsider to be included in the new movement of followers of Jesus. Luke portrays him as a model of virtue and as an indication that the Followers of the Way can extend to every nation, even to distant Ethiopia. See Gay L. Byron, *Symbolic Blackness and Ethnic Difference in Early Christian Literature* (London and New York: Routldege, 2002), 109–115.

31. See Joanne M. Pierce, "Holy Week and Easter in the Middle Ages," in *Passover and Easter: Origin and History to Modern Times*, ed. Paul F. Bradshaw and Lawrence A. Hoffman (Notre Dame, IN: University of Notre Dame Press, 1999), 167–171. See also the analysis of the Vatican's refusal to reform the Good Friday liturgy in the late 1920s in chapter 5.

32. See the discussion in chapter 4 on ritual crucifixion and ritual cannibalism (or blood libel).

33. See David M. Carr, *An Introduction to the Old Testament: Sacred Texts and Imperial Contexts of the Hebrew Bible* (Oxford: Wiley-Blackwell, 2010), 183. See the discussion of Tisha B'Av in Irving Greenberg, *The Jewish Way: Living the Holidays* (New York: Summit Books, 1988), 283–303.

34. Martin Buber, "Autobiographical Fragments," in *The Philosophy of Martin Buber*, ed. Paul A. Schilp and Maurice Friedmann (LaSalle, IL: Open Court, 1967), 32–33. See also Adrian Thatcher, *The Savage Text: The Use and Abuse of the Bible* (Malden, MA: Wiley-Blackwell, 2008). He argues that texts can become savage in three ways: when they compromise the character of God, when they are used to justify violence, and when they desensitize us to violence (63).

35. See chapter 8, n. 8.

36. Raimon Panikkar, *The Intrareligious Dialogue*, rev. ed. (New York and Mahwah, NJ: Paulist Press, 1999), 114.

37. Elizabeth Groppe, "After Augustine: Humility and the Search for God in Historical Memory," in *Learned Ignorance: Intellectual Humility among Jews, Christians, and Muslims* (New York: Oxford University Press, 2011), 191–209; citations, 200 and 202, respectively. Groppe also suggests that fear may be as primal as pride, and cites evidence of how the crusaders were manipulated in part by fears of damnation and how Hitler was able to capitalize on a pervasive sense of insecurity in Germany in the 1930s and 1940s; see 203–204.

38. The series of seven prayers included also a confession of sins in general, sins committed "in the service of truth," sins that "have harmed the unity of the Body of Christ," sins against the "people of Israel," sins against the "rights of peoples and respect for cultures and religion," sins against the "dignity of women and the unity of the human race," and sins "in relation to the fundamental rights of the person." Archbishop (later Cardinal) Hamao of Japan was the president from 1998 to 2006 of the Pontifical Council for the Pastoral Care of Migrants and Itinerants; he died in 2007.

39. See, most notably, the 1998 statement from the Commission on Religious Relations with the Jews, *We Remember: A Reflection on the Shoah*. See chapter 5 for my discussion of this important, if flawed, document.

40. William R. Burrows, "Concluding Reflections," in *Redemption and Dialogue: Reading Redemptoris Missio and Dialogue and Proclamation*, ed. W. R. Burrows (Maryknoll, NY: Orbis, 1994).

41. Barnes, *Theology and the Dialogue of Religions,* Cambridge Studies in Christian Doctrine (Cambridge: Cambridge University Press, 2002), 59.

42. Ibid., 23. Apophatic spirituality "demands the abandonment of all concepts, thoughts, images, and symbols—even and especially those of God. God can be experienced and known only through negation, unknowing and darkness of mind....The goal of the negative way is nothing less than full union with God, that is, divinization." See Harvey D. Egan, "Negative Way," in *The New Dictionary of Catholic Spirituality,* ed. Michael Downey (Collegeville: Liturgical Press, 1993), 700.

43. Barnes, *Theology and the Dialogue of Religions,* 186.

44. Ibid., 204.

45. Ibid., 207.

46. Groppe, "After Augustine," 205.

47. Here the wording is taken from the Pontifical Biblical Commission, *Interpretation of the Bible in the Church,* 1993, §IA; see §III.D.2; see http://www.ccjr.us/dialogika-resources/documents-and-statements/

roman-catholic/vatican-curia/287-pbc-1993 (accessed January 9, 2012). Peter Williamson considers this expression the first principle of the document; see his *Catholic Principles for Interpreting Scripture: A Study of the Pontifical Biblical Commission's The Interpretation of the Bible in the Church* (Rome: Editrice Pontificio Istituto Biblico, 2001), 28–30.

48. Timothy Radcliffe, *Seven Last Words* (New York: Continuum, 2005), 73.

49. Here I draw on Williamson's wording in *Catholic Principles*, "No 'spiritual' bypassing of the human reality is possible," 30.

50. Reimund Bieringer, Didier Pollefeyt, and Frederique Vandecasteele-Vanneuville, "Wrestling with Johannine Anti-Judaism: A Hermeneutical Framework for the Analysis of the Current Debate," in *Anti-Judaism and the Fourth Gospel*, ed. Bieringer, Pollefeyt, and Vandecasteele-Vanneuville (Louisville: John Knox, 2004), 3–37; citation, 34.

51. See Luke Timothy Johnson, "The New Testament's Anti-Jewish Slander and the Conventions of Ancient Polemic," *Journal of Biblical Literature* 108/3 (1989): 419–441.

52. Ibid., 441.

53. Sally A. Brown, *Cross Talk: Preaching Redemption Here and Now* (Westminster John Knox, 2008), 47.

54. Text adapted from Zechariah 13:1; lyrics, William Cowper, 1772; "Cleansing Fountain," attributed to Lowell Mason, 1702–1872.

55. John T. Carroll and Joel Green, *The Death of Jesus in Early Christianity* (Peabody, MA: Hendrickson, 1995), 114.

56. Stephen Patterson, *Beyond the Passion: Rethinking the Death and Life of Jesus* (Minneapolis: Fortress, 2004), 45.

57. Patterson, *Beyond the Passion*, 9.

58. Paula Fredriksen, *Jesus of Nazareth, King of the Jews* (New York: Vintage Books, 2000), 233.

59. Amy-Jill Levine, *The Misunderstood Jew: The Church and the Scandal of the Jewish Jesus* (HarperOne, 2007), 111.

60. Johannes Baptist Metz, *The Emergent Church*, trans. Peter Mann (New York: Crossroad, 1981), 29.

61. Mary Elsbernd and Reimund Bieringer, "Interpreting the Signs of the Times in the Light of the Gospel Vision and Normativity of the Future," in *Normativity of the Future: Reading Biblical and Other Authoritative Texts in an Eschatological Perspective*, ed. R. Bieringer and M. Elsbernd (Leuven: Peeters Publishers, 2010), 47–90; here, 63.

62. Reimund Bieringer and Didier Pollefeyt, "Open to Both Ways...? Anti-Judaism and Johannine Christology," in *Normativity of the Future*, 121–134; citation, 134.

63. Diana Hayes, *Were You There? Stations of the Cross* (Maryknoll, NY: Orbis, 2000), 88.

64. Luz, *Matthew in History*, 94.

65. Ibid., 90.

66. Roger Haight, *Jesus: Symbol of God* (Maryknoll, NY: Orbis, 1999), 356.

CHAPTER 10

1. Among those published in recent years, see Alice Camille, *The Seven Last Words: Lenten Reflections for Today's Believers* (Chicago: ACTA Publications, 2003); Stanley Hauerwas, *Cross-Shattered Christ* (Grand Rapids: Brazos, 2004); Richard John Neuhaus, *Death on a Friday Afternoon* (New York: Basic Books, 2000); Timothy Radcliffe, *Seven Last Words* (New York: Continuum, 2005); Fleming Rutledge, *The Seven Last Words from the Cross* (Grand Rapids: Eerdmans, 2005); William H. Willimon, *Thank God It's Friday: Encountering the Seven Last Words from the Cross* (Nashville: Abingdon, 2006).

2. Mary Gordon, *Reading Jesus: A Writer's Encounter with the Gospels* (New York: Pantheon, 2009), 196.

3. See, for example, http://en.ignatianwiki.org; http://ignatianspirituality.com. Among the numerous adaptations are programs such as "The Spiritual Exercises in Everyday Life" (SEEL). See, for example, http://www.seelpugetsound.org. In the interests of full disclosure, I have made the Exercises on retreats; I claim, however, no special expertise, as I have not been trained to guide others in the Exercises.

4. In the fourth of the annotations that precede the Exercises proper, Ignatius advises that it is not necessary that each week consist of seven days; those directing persons in the Exercises should be flexible according to the needs of each person.

5. All citations from the *Spiritual Exercises* are from the translation by George E. Ganss, S.J., in *Ignatius of Loyola: Spiritual Exercises and Selected Works*, ed. Ganss, et al., Classics in Western Spirituality Series (New York and Mahwah, NJ: Paulist Press, 1991). The citation here is from Ignatius's second "Introductory Explanation." The one who directs or accompanies a person draws upon the text of the Exercises as a guide; the person making the Exercises generally does not work directly with the text.

6. On Ludolphus of Saxony's emphasis on Jewish villainy, see chapter 4. Ganss, *Ignatius of Loyola*, analyzes Ludolphus' influence on Ignatius, 19–26.

7. See also James Reites, "St. Ignatius and the Jews," *Studies in the Spirituality of the Jesuits* 13 (1981): 1–48.

8. Karl Rahner, *Spiritual Exercises* (London: Sheed and Ward, 1967), 44.

9. *Spiritual Exercises*, §53.

10. *Spiritual Exercises*, §§122–125.

11. Maria Anicia Co, "Reading and Sense-Experiencing the Gospel of John," in *The Personal Voice in Biblical Interpretation,* ed. Ingrid Rosa Kitzberger (New York: Routledge, 1999), 86–96; citation, 94.

12. Adele Reinhartz, *Befriending the Beloved Disciple: A Jewish Reading of the Gospel of John* (New York: Continuum, 2001), 25.

13. The texts in the boxes are Deuteronomy 6:4–9, Exodus 13:1–10, Exodus 13:11–16, and Deuteronomy 11:13–21; these passages contain references to the mitzvah of laying *tefillin*. For a review of the complex history, see Yehuda B. Cohn, *Tangled Up in Text: Tefillin and the Ancient World,* Brown Judaic Studies 351 (Providence: Brown University Press, 2001. Cohn argues that the Jewish practice of wearing inscribed biblical texts originated in late Second Temple Judaism after Jewish encounter with Greek culture, in which protective amulets had widespread use. The Greek term that translates *tefillin, phylakterion,* means protection. The Dead Sea Scrolls provide evidence of *tefillin* practice.

14. The *mezuzah* also contains parchment with the text of Deuteronomy 6:4.

15. See Matthew 9:20 and Mark 6:56. In Matthew 23:5, Jesus takes issue with the Pharisees and scribes who "make their phylacteries broad and their fringes long." See Jeffrey Tigay, "On the Term Phylactery (Matthew 23:5)," *Harvard Theological Review* 72/1–2 (1979): 45–53. Today many Jews use a *tallit* or prayer shawl in fulfillment of the text from Numbers; the *tzitzit* is the fringe attached to the four corners of the *tallit*.

16. Amy-Jill Levine, *The Misunderstood Jew: The Church and the Scandal of the Jewish Jesus* (San Francisco: HarperOne, 2007), 24. See Levine, 119–166, in which she critiques seven stereotypical notions of Judaism that have shaped Christian readings of the New Testament.

17. "Consider how his divinity hides itself." See *Spiritual Exercises,* §196.

18. Ibid., §§190–208.

19. Ibid., §193.

20. Ibid., §§ 197 and 203.

21. William Meissner, *To the Greater Glory: A Psychological Study of Ignatian Spirituality* (Milwaukee: Marquette University Press, 1999), 228.

22. Katherine Dyckman, Mary Garvin, and Elizabeth Liebert, *The Spiritual Exercises Reclaimed: Uncovering Liberating Possibilities for Women* (New York and Mahwah, NJ: Paulist, 2001), 224.

23. *Spiritual Exercises*, §91.

24. Stephen Patterson, *Beyond the Passion: Rethinking the Death and Life of Jesus* (Minneapolis: Fortress, 2004), 2.

25. For an insightful linkage of the passion with his ministry, see Barbara E. Reid, *Taking up the Cross: New Testament Interpretations through Latina and Feminist Eyes* (Minneapolis: Augsburg Fortress, 2007).

26. Mark Lewis Taylor, "American Torture and the Body of Christ," in *Cross Examinations: Readings on the Meaning of the Cross Today*, ed. Marit Trelstad (Minneapolis: Augsburg Fortress, 2006), 274.

27. If the Last Supper was a Passover meal as depicted in the Synoptic Gospels, then the subsequent events of the arrest, trial before the chief priests and elders of the people, trial before Pontius Pilate, flogging, and death on the cross would have taken place on the Passover. This is not likely. In the chronology of John's Gospel, the Last Supper occurs on at the more indeterminate "before the festival of Passover" (13:1). The death of Jesus, "the Lamb of God," occurs at the precise hour when the paschal lamb was sacrificed in the temple on the preparation day for Passover. See Anthony J. Saldarini, *Jesus and Passover* (New York: Paulist, 1984), and Frank C. Senn, "Should Christians Celebrate the Passover?" in *Passover and Easter: The Symbolic Structuring of Sacred Seasons*, Two Liturgical Traditions, vol. 6, ed. Paul F. Bradshaw and Lawrence A. Hoffman (Notre Dame, IN: University of Notre Dame Press, 1999), 183–205.

28. Barbara Brown Taylor, "Table Manners," *Christian Century* (March 11, 1998), 257.

29. Hal Taussig, *In the Beginning Was the Meal: Social Experimentation and Early Christian Identity* (Minneapolis: Fortress, 2009), 21.

30. Ivone Gebara, *Out of the Depths: Women's Experience of Evil and Salvation*. Ann Patrick Ware, trans.(Minneapolis: Fortress, 2002), 124.

31. Ibid., 123.

32. Ibid., 124.

33. Monty Williams, The *Gift of Spiritual Intimacy: Following the Spiritual Exercises of St. Ignatius* (Montréal: Novalis, 2009), 230.

34. On Jesus and the purity laws, see John P. Meier, *A Marginal Jew: Law and Love*, vol. 4 (New Haven: Yale University Press, 2009), 342–477. Meier argues that "Jesus' *studied indifference to ritual impurity* must be seen within this larger framework of his claim to be the charismatic prophet of the end time" (415). Emphasis added.

35. Raymond E. Brown, *The Death of the Messiah: From the Garden to Gethsemane*, vol. 2 (New York: Doubleday, 1993), 916.

36. See Meissner, *To the Greater Glory*, 191.

37. See Williams, *The Gift of Spiritual Intimacy*, 143–144. Perhaps by acknowledging the very real fears of our world, we will be less inclined to fashion scapegoats—a role so often assigned to Jews.

38. There are differences among the accounts, with John's (12:12–19) as the most distinctive. Matthew (21:1–9), in contrast to Mark (11:1–10) and Luke (19:28–40), has Jesus improbably mounted on both an ass and a colt. Matthew cites the passage from Zechariah 9:9 ("Rejoice greatly, O daughter of Zion! Shout aloud, O daughter Jerusalem! Lo, your king comes to you; triumphant and victorious is he, humble and riding on a donkey, on a colt, the foal of a donkey") that is implicit in Mark and Luke; he seems to have understood Zechariah as speaking of two animals rather than read the text as a parallelism.

39. Marcus J. Borg and John Dominic Crossan, *The Last Week: What the Gospels Really Teach about Jesus's Final Days in Jerusalem* (New York: HarperOne, 2006), 3.

40. John Dominic Crossan, "Roman Imperial Theology," in *In the Shadow of Empire: Reclaiming the Bible as a History of Faithful Resistance*, ed. Richard A. Horsley (Louisville: Westminister-John Knox, 2008), 73.

41. See Dyckman, Garvin, and Liebert, *The Spiritual Exercises Reclaimed*, 199.

42. Ibid., 162. They are writing specifically about guiding women through the Exercises, though much of what they say is applicable to men as well.

43. Reinhartz, *Befriending the Beloved Disciple*, 141.

44. Ibid., 142.

45. Stephen J. Patterson, *Beyond the Passion: Rethinking the Death and Life of Jesus* (Fortress, 2004), 8.

46. Roger Haight, *The Future of Christology* (New York: Continuum, 2005), 95.

47. Gebara, *Out of the Depths*, 120–121.

48. Douglas John Hall, *The Cross in our Context: Jesus and the Suffering World* (Minneapolis: Fortress, 2003), 151–153.

49. Henry F. Knight, *Celebrating Holy Week in a Post-Holocaust World* (Louisville: Westminster-John Knox, 2005), 112.

50. Elizabeth A. Johnson, "The Word Was Made Flesh and Dwelt Among Us: Jesus Research and Christian Faith," in *Jesus: A Colloquium in the Holy Land* (New York and London: Continuum, 2001), 157.

51. Haight, *The Future of Christology*, 102.

52. Eamon Duffy situates the Seven Last Words on the Cross in the context of late medieval English Catholic lay piety. This devotion, as well as that to the Five Wounds of Christ, reflected the "democratization of the tradition of affective meditation on the Passion which was the staple of the religious practice of the devout and the religious élite of late medieval England and Europe in general." See his *The Stripping of the Altars: Traditional Religion in England 1400–1580* (New Haven, CT: Yale University Press, 1992), 248–256; citation, 265.

53. Matthew has a nearly identical version: "From noon on, darkness came over the whole land until three in the afternoon. And about three o'clock Jesus cried with a] loud voice, "Eli, Eli, lema sabachthani?" that is, "My God, my God, why have you forsaken me?" When some of the bystanders heard it, they said, "This man is calling for Elijah." At once one of them ran and got a sponge, filled it with sour wine, put it on a stick, and gave it to him to drink. But the others said, "Wait, let us see whether Elijah will come to save him" (Matthew 27:45–49).

54. For evaluation of the variant textual evidence, see Raymond E. Brown, *The Death of the Messiah: From Gethsemane to the Grave*, vol. 2 (New York: Doubleday, 1994), 971–981; and Nathan Eubank, "A Disconcerting Prayer: On the Originality of Luke 23:34a," *Journal of Biblical Literature* 129/3 (2010): 521–536. Eubank argues that external evidence alone (that is, the various manuscripts traditions) fails to offer a decisive answer to whether the shorter or longer text was the original. He concludes that the verse is Lukan in style, and was omitted by some scribes because it was a "problem passage in early Christianity" (535–536).

55. From *In principium actorum*, Sermons for Baptism, ca. 388; cited in Eubank, "*A Disconcerting Prayer,*" 529.

56. Kathleen Norris, *The Cloister Walk* (New York: Riverhead Books, 1996), 92.

EPILOGUE

1. Raimon Panikkar, *The Intrareligious Dialogue*, rev. ed. (New York and Mahwah, NJ: Paulist Press, 1999), 73–74.

2. Franz Kafka, *Letters to Friends, Family, and Editors*, trans. Richard and Clara Winston (New York: Schocken, 1997), 16.

3. This garden in Jerusalem's *Yad Vashem* honors non-Jews who risked their lives to save Jews during the Holocaust.

4. Clark Williamson, *A Guest in the House of Israel* (Louisville: Westminster/John Knox, 1993), 9.

5. This is a phrase the late Rabbi Leon Klenicki used to describe inter-religious dialogue events that remained on the superficial level. See Leon Klenicki, "Toward the Year 2000: Memory, Reckoning, and Reconciliation," *The Month* 32/4 (April 1999): 129–139; citation, 133.

6. Text: http://www.ccjr.us/dialogika-resources/documents-and-statements/roman-catholic/vatican-curia/278-we-remember (accessed February 2, 2012). See my analysis of *We Remember* in chapter 5.

7. Cullen Murphy, *God's Jury: the Inquisition and the Making of the Modern World* (Boston: Houghton Mifflin Harcourt, 2012), 244.

8. "Address of His Holiness Benedict XVI at the Meeting for Peace in Assisi," October 27, 2011. See http://www.vatican.va/holy_father/benedict_xvi/speeches/2011/october/documents/hf_ben-xvi_spe_20111027_assisi_en.html (accessed February 3, 3012).

9. Rainer Bucher, *Hitler's Theology: A Study in Political Religion*, trans. Rebecca Pohl (New York: Continuum, 2011), 114.

10. J. Frank Henderson has done superb work for years in offering resources for rethinking liturgies in light of Jewish-Christian issues. See http://www.jfrankhenderson.com (accessed March 28, 2012). See also Gabe Huck: *The Three Days: Parish Prayer in the Paschal Triduum*, rev. ed. (Chicago: Liturgy Training Publications, 1992); Henry F. Knight, *Celebrating Holy Week in a Post-Holocaust World* (Louisville: Westminster John Knox, 2005); Theresa Sanders, *Tenebrae: Holy Week after the Holocaust* (Maryknoll, NY: Orbis, 2006); and Marilyn Salmon, *Preaching without Contempt: Overcoming Unintended Anti-Judaism* (Minneapolis: Fortress Press, 2009).

11. The late Lutheran bishop and New Testament scholar Krister Stendahl spoke often of this commandment as a fundamental norm of inter-religious exchange.

12. Michael Barnes, *Theology and the Dialogue of Religions*, Cambridge Studies in Christian Doctrine (Cambridge: Cambridge University Press, 2002), 192 and 59, respectively.

13. Xavier Beavois directed the film; the book is by John W. Kiser, *The Monks of Tibhirine: Faith, Love, and Terror in Algeria* (New York: St. Martin's Griffin, 2002).

14. Kiser, *The Monks of Tibhirine*, xiii.

15. Cited in Kaiser, *Monks of Tibhirine*, 244–246.

16. Commission for Religious Relations with the Jews, "Guidelines and Suggestions for Implementing the Conciliar Declaration *Nostra Aetate*, no. 4"; see http://www.ccjr.us/dialogika-resources/documents-and-statements/roman-catholic/vatican-curia/277-guidelines (accessed February 2, 2012).

17. See Heinz Schreckenberg, *The Jews in Christian Art: An Illustrated History*, trans. John Bowden (New York: Continuum, 1996).

18. Cited in Matthew Hoffman, *From Rebel to Rabbi: Reclaiming the Jewish Jesus and the Making of Modern Jewish Culture* (Stanford: Stanford University Press, 2007), 69. Hoffman explores the complicated reasons Jewish artists reinscribed Jesus in modern Jewish culture. Coming from a tradition that prohibited graven images, Jews who were drawn to Western culture naturally turned to its models.

19. Cited ibid., 180.

20. Cited ibid., 201.

21. David G. Roskies, *Against the Apocalypse: Responses to Catastrophe in Modern Jewish Culture* (Cambridge, MA: Harvard University Press, 1984), 294.

22. Cited in Hoffman, *From Rebel to Rabbi*, 220.

23. The photo is widely available online. See, for example, http://lens. blogs.nytimes.com/2010/10/12/the-ghetto-the-nazis-and-one-small-boy/.

24. Cited in Danna Nolan Fewell and Gary A. Phillips, "Bak's Impossible Memorials: Giving Face to the Children," in *Representing the Irreparable: The Shoah, the Bible, and the Art of Samuel Bak*, ed. D. N. Fewell, G. A. Phillips, and Yvonne Sherwood (Boston: Pucker Art Publications, 2008), 94.

25. Ibid., 95. Among the many paintings based on the photo of the Warsaw boy are his *Study J* (1995), *Self-Portrait* (1995), *Absence* (1997), *Children's Corner* (1997), and *In the Footsteps* (1997).

26. Chaim Potok, *My Name Is Asher Lev* (Greenwich, CT: Knopf, 1972), 9.

27. See Marina Hayman, "Christ in the Work of Two Jewish Artists: When Art Is Interreligious Dialogue," *Studies in Christian-Jewish Relations* 4 (2009): 1–14; citation, 2.

28. Thomas Merton, *Courage for Truth: the Letters of Thomas Merton to Writers*, Thomas Merton Letters Series, vol. 4, ed. Christine M. Bocher (New York: Harcourt Brace, 1997), 197. This letter was addressed to Argentine poet Miguel Grinberg on June 21, 1963.

29. Douglas John Hall, *The Cross in our Context: Jesus and the Suffering World* (Minneapolis: Fortress, 2003), 151–152.

30. Barnes, *Theology and the Dialogue of Religions*, 204.

Bibliography

"The Ad Hoc Committee Report on the 2010 Oberammergau Passion Play Script." http://www.ccjr.us/news/813-ccjr2010may14.

"Address of His Holiness Benedict XVI at the Meeting for Peace in Assisi." http://www.vatican.va/holy_father/benedict_xvi/speeches/2011/october/documents/hf_ben-xvi_spe_20111027_assisi_en.html.

Aliker, Stefan. "Intertextuality and the Semiotics of Biblical Texts." In *Reading the Bible Intertextually,* ed. Richard Hayes and S. Aliker, 3–21. Waco, TX: Baylor University Press, 2009.

Allen, James, Hilton Als, John Lewis, and Leon F. Litwack. *Without Sanctuary: Lynching Photography in America.* Santa Fe: Twin Palms Publishers, 2000.

Almond, Gabriel, R. Scott Appleby, and Emmanel Sivan. *Strong Religion: The Rise of Fundamentalisms around the World.* Chicago: University of Chicago Press, 2003.

Bacharach, Walter Zwi. *Anti-Jewish Prejudices in German Catholic Sermons.* Translated by Chaya Galai. Lewiston, NY: Edwin Mellen Press, 1993. Hebrew original, 1991.

Barnes, Michael. *Theology and the Dialogue of Religions,* Cambridge Studies in Christian Doctrine. Cambridge, UK: Cambridge University Press, 2002.

Barnett, Victoria J. "Dietrich Bonhoeffer's Relevance for Post-Holocaust Christian Theology." *Studies in Christian-Jewish Relations* 2 (2007): 53–67.

———. "The Role of the Churches: Compliance and Confrontation." *Dimensions* 12 (1998).

———. "Seelisberg: An Appreciation." *Studies in Christian-Jewish Relations* 2 (2007): 54–57.

Barry, Jonathan, Marianne Hester, and Gareth Roberts, eds. *Witchcraft in Early Modern Europe: Studies in Culture and Belief.* Cambridge, UK: Cambridge University Press, 1996.

Bauer, Yehuda. *Rethinking the Holocaust.* New Haven and London: Yale University Press, 2001.

Baum, Gregory. "The Social Context of American Catholic Theology." *Proceedings of the Catholic Theological Society of America* 41 (1986): 83–100.

Bentley, James. *Oberammergau and the Passion Play: A Guide and a History to Mark the 350th Anniversary.* New York: Penguin, 1984.

Bergen, Doris L. "Catholics, Protestants, and Christian Antisemitism in Nazi Germany." *Central European History* 27 (1994): 329–348.

———. "Nazism and Christianity: Partners and Rivals?" *Journal of Contemporary History* 42 (2007): 25–33.

———. *The Twisted Cross: The German Christian Movement in the Third Reich.* Chapel Hill: University of North Carolina Press, 1996.

———. "World Wars." In *The Oxford Handbook of Holocaust Studies,* ed. Peter Hayes and John K. Roth, 95–110. New York: Oxford University Press, 2010.

Bestul, Thomas H. *Texts of the Passion: Latin Devotional Literature and Medieval Society.* Philadelphia: University of Pennsylvania Press, 1996.

Bieringer, Reimund, and Didier Pollefeyt. "Open to Both Ways…? Anti-Judaism and Johannine Christology." In *Normativity of the Future: Reading Biblical and Other Authoritative Texts in an Eschatological Perspective,* ed. Reimund Bieringer and Didier Pollefeyt, 121–134. Leuven: Peeters, 2010.

Bishop, Claire Huchet. *How Catholics Look at Jews: Inquiries into Italian, Spanish and French Teaching Materials.* New York and Ramsey, NJ: Paulist Press, 1974.

Blaschke, Olaf . *Offenders or Victims? German Jews and the Causes of Modern Catholic Antisemitism.* Lincoln: University of Nebraska Press/Vidal Sassoon International Center for the Study of Antisemitism, 2009.

Bondi, Roberta C. *Memories of God: Theological Reflections on a Life.* Nashville: Abingdon, 1995.

Bonhoeffer, Dietrich. *No Rusty Swords: Letters, Lectures and Notes 1928–1936*, from the Collected Works of Dietrich Bonhoeffer. Vol. 1, ed. Edwin H. Robertson, trans. Edwin H. Robertson and John Bowden. New York: Harper and Row, 1965.

Borg, Marcus J., and John Dominic Crossan. *The Last Week: What the Gospels Really Teach about Jesus's Final Days in Jerusalem.* New York: HarperOne, 2006.

Boulton, Maureen. "Anti-Jewish Attitudes in French Literature." In *Jews and Christians in Twelfth-Century Europe,* ed. Michael A. Signer and John Van Engen, 234–254. Notre Dame, IN: University of Notre Dame Press, 2001.

Bowe, Barbara. "The New Testament, Religious Identity, and the Other." In *Contesting Texts: Jews and Christians in Conversation about the Bible,* ed. Melody Knowles, Esther Menn, John Pawlikowski, and Timothy J. Sandoval, 93–101. Minneapolis: Fortress, 2007.

Boyarin, Daniel. *Dying for God: Martyrdom and the Making of Christianity and Judaism.* Stanford: Stanford University Press, 1999.

————. *A Radical Jew: Paul and the Politics of Identity.* Berkeley: University of California Press, 1994.

————. "Semantic Differences; or, 'Judaism'/'Christianity.'" In *The Ways That Never Parted: Jews and Christians in Late Antiquity and the Early Middle Ages,* Texts and Studies in Ancient Judaism 95, ed. Adam Becker and Annette Yoshiko Reed, 65–85. Tübingen: Mohr Siebeck, 2003.

Boys, Mary C. "Does the Catholic Church Have a Mission 'with' Jews or 'to' Jews?" *Studies in Christian-Jewish Relations* 3 (2008): 1–19.

————. "Facing History: The Church and Its Teachings on the Death of Jesus." In *Christ Jesus and the Jewish People Today: New Explorations of Theological Relationships,* ed. Philip A. Cunningham, Joseph Sievers, Mary C. Boys, Hans Hermann Henrix, and Jesper Svartvik, 31–63. Grand Rapids: Eerdmans, 2011.

————. *Has God only One Blessing? Judaism as a Source of Christian Self-Understanding.* New York and Mahwah, NJ: Paulist Press, 2000.

————. "The *Nostra Aetate* Trajectory: Holding our Theological Bow Differently." In *Never Revoked: Nostra Aetate as Ongoing Challenge for Jewish-Christian Dialogue,* Louvain Theological and Pastoral Monographs 40, ed. Maryanne Moyaert and Didier Pollefeyt, 133–157. Leuven, Belgium: Peeters Publishers, 2009.

————, ed. *Seeing Judaism Anew: Christianity's Sacred Obligation.* Lanham, MD: Rowman and Littlefield, 2005.

Boys, Mary C., and Sara Lee. *Christians and Jews in Dialogue: Learning in the Presence of the Other.* Woodstock, VT: Sky Light Paths Publishing, 2006.

Brennan, Brian. "The Conversion of the Jews of Clermont in AD 576." *Journal of Theological Studies* 36 (1985): 321–337.

Brock, Rita Nakashima, and Rebecca Ann Parker. "Enemy and Ally: Contending with the Gospel of John's Anti-Judaism." In *Walk in the Ways of Wisdom: Essays in Honor of Elisabeth Schüssler Fiorenza,* ed. Shelly Matthews, Cynthia Kittredge, and Melanie Johnson, 161–180. Harrisburg, PA: Trinity International Press, 2003.

————. *Proverbs of Ashes: Violence, Redemptive Suffering, and the Search for What Saves Us.* Boston: Beacon, 2002.

Brown, Joanne Carlson, and Carole R. Bohn, eds. *Christianity, Patriarchy and Abuse: A Feminist Critique.* New York: Pilgrim Press, 1990.

Brown, Peter. "Christianization and Religious Conflict." *Cambridge Ancient History.* 13:632–664. Cambridge, UK: Cambridge University Press, 1998.

Brown, Raymond E. *The Death of the Messiah.* 2 vols. New York: Doubleday, 1994.

————. *The Gospel According to John, XII–XXI.* Garden City: Doubleday, 1970.

Brown, Robert McAfee. *Creative Dislocation: The Movement of Grace.* Journeys in Faith, ed. Robert A Raines. Nashville: Abingdon, 1980.

Brown-Fleming, Suzanne. *The Holocaust and Catholic Conscience: Cardinal Aloisius Muench and the Guilt Question in Germany.* Notre Dame, IN: University of Notre Dame Press, 2006.

Buber, Martin. *Autobiographical Fragments,* 2nd ed. New York: Routledge: 2007.

Bucher, Rainer. *Hitler's Theology: A Study in Political Religion.* Translated by Rebecca Pohl. Continuum Resources in Religion and Political Culture. New York: Continuum, 2001.

Burrows, William R. "Concluding Reflections." In *Redemption and Dialogue: Reading Redemptoris Missio and Dialogue and Proclamation,* ed. W. R. Burrows, 239–244. Maryknoll, NY: Orbis, 1994.

Byron, Gay L. *Symbolic Blackness and Ethnic Difference in Early Christian Literature.* New York: Routledge, 2002.

Callaway, Mary Chilton. "Exegesis as Banquet: Reading Jeremiah with the Rabbis." In *A Gift of God in Due Season: Essays on Scripture and Community in Honor of James A. Sanders,* ed. Richard D. Weis and David M. Carr, 219–230. Sheffield, UK: Sheffield Academic Press, 1996.

Camille, Alice. *The Seven Last Words: Lenten Reflections for Today's Believers.* Chicago: ACTA Publications, 2003.

Camille, Michael. *The Gothic Idol: Ideology and Image-making in Medieval Art.* Cambridge: Cambridge University Press, 1989.

Campbell-Johnston, Michael. "Martyrdom and Resurrection in Latin America Today." In *Truth and Memory: The Church and Human Rights in El Salvador and Guatemala,* ed. Michael A. Hayes and David Tombs, 44–58. Leominster, UK: Gracewing, 2001.

———. "Very Ordinary Saints." *The Tablet* (November 14, 2009): 14.

Carlo, Karyn. "The Cross and the Women of Galilee: A Feminist Theology of Salvation." Ph.D. diss., Union Theological Seminary in the City of New York, 2009.

Carroll, James. *Jerusalem, Jerusalem: How the Ancient City Ignited our Modern World.* Boston: Houghton, Mifflin, Harcourt, 2011.

Carroll, John T., Joel B. Green, Robert E. Van Voorst, Joel Marcus, and Donald Senior. *The Death of Jesus in Early Christianity.* Peabody, MA: Hendrickson, 1995.

Carter, J. Kameron. *Race: A Theological Problem.* New York and Oxford: Oxford University Press, 2008.

Carter, Warren. *Pontius Pilate: Portraits of a Roman Governor.* Interfaces, ed. Barbara Green. Collegeville: Liturgical Press, 2003.

———. *Roman Empire and the New Testament: An Essential Guide.* Nashville: Abingdon, 2006.

Castelli, Elizabeth A. *Martyrdom and Memory: Early Christian Culture Making.* New York: Columbia University Press, 2004.

Catholic Bishops of France. "Declaration of Repentance." In *Catholics Remember the Holocaust*. Secretariat for Ecumenical and Interreligious Affairs, National Conference of Catholic Bishops. Washington, DC: United States Catholic Conference, 1998.

Chapman, David W. *Ancient Jewish and Christian Perceptions of Crucifixion*. Grand Rapids: Baker, 2008.

Charlesworth, James. "From Old to New: Paradigm Shifts concerning Judaism, the Gospel of John, Jesus and the Advent of 'Christianity.'" In *Jesus Research: An International Perspective*, ed. Charlesworth and Petr Pokorný, 56–72. Grand Rapids: Eerdmans, 2009.

Chazan, Robert. *Medieval Stereotypes and Modern Antisemitism*. Berkeley: University of California Press, 1977.

The Church in the Present-Day Transformation of Latin America in Light of the Council. Vol. 2. Bogotá: CELAM, 1970.

Co, Maria Anicia. "Reading and Sense-Experiencing the Gospel of John." In *The Personal Voice in Biblical Interpretation*, ed. Ingrid Rosa Kitzberger, 86–96. New York: Routledge, 1999.

Cochrane, Arthur C. *The Church's Confession under Hitler*. Philadelphia: Westminster Press, 1962.

Cohen, J. D. *The Beginnings of Jewishness*. Berkeley: University of California Press, 1999.

Cohen, Jeremy. *Christ Killers: The Jews and the Passion from the Bible to the Big Screen*. Oxford: Oxford University Press, 2007.

Cohn, Norman. *Europe's Inner Demons: The Demonization of Christians in Medieval Christendom*, rev. ed. Chicago: University of Chicago Press, 1993.

Cohn, Yehuda B. *Tangled Up in Text: Tefillin and the Ancient World*, Brown Judaic Studies 35. Providence, RI: Brown University Press, 2001.

Cone, James H. *The Cross and the Lynching Tree* (Maryknoll, NY: Orbis, 2011).

———. *The Spirituals and the Blues: An Interpretation*. New York: Seabury, 1972.

———. "Strange Fruit: The Cross and the Lynching Tree." *Harvard Divinity Bulletin* 35 (2007): 46–54.

Connelly, John. "Catholic Racism and Its Opponents." *The Journal of Modern History* 79 (2007): 813–847.

———. *From Enemy to Brother: The Revolution in Catholic Teaching on the Jews, 1933–1965.* Cambridge, MA: Harvard University Press, 2012.

———. "Gypsies, Homosexuals, and Slavs." In *The Oxford Handbook of Holocaust Studies,* ed. Peter Hayes and John K. Roth, 274–289. New York: Oxford University Press, 2010.

Connerton, Paul. *How Societies Remember.* Cambridge, UK: Cambridge University Press, 1989.

Cook, Michael J. Review of *A Rabbi's Impressions of the [1900] Oberammergau Passion Play,* by Joseph Krauskopf. *Review and Expositor* 103 (2006): 243–245.

Cooley, Martha. *The Archivist.* Boston: Little, Brown and Company, 1998.

Coppa, Frank J. *The Papacy, the Jews, and the Holocaust.* Washington, DC: The Catholic University of America Press, 2006.

Cousins, Ewert. "The Humanity and the Passion of Christ." In *Christian Spirituality: High Middle Ages and Reformation,* World Spirituality, ed. Jill Raitt, 17:375–391. New York: Crossroad, 1987.

Crane, Richard Francis. *Passion of Israel: Jacques Maritain, Catholic Conscience and the Holocaust.* Scranton, PA: University of Scranton Press, 2010.

Criss, Nicholas C., and Jack Nelson, "Dr. King Slain by Sniper in Memphis." *Los Angeles Times* (April 5, 1968). http://encarta.msn.com/sidebar_761593843/dr_king_slain_by_sniper_in_memphis.html.

Crossan, John Dominic. *The Cross that Spoke.* San Francisco: Harper & Row, 1988.

———. "Roman Imperial Theology." In *In the Shadow of Empire: Reclaiming the Bible as a History of Faithful Resistance,* ed. Richard A. Horsley, 59–73. Louisville: Westminster John Knox, 2008.

Cullinan, Colleen Carpenter. *Redeeming the Story: Women, Suffering, and Christ.* New York: Continuum, 2004.

Cuming, Geoffrey J. *Hippolytus: A Text for Students.* Cambridge, UK: Grove Books, 1984.

Cunningham, Philip A. *Education for Shalom: Religion Textbooks and the Enhancement of the Catholic and Jewish Relationship.* Philadelphia: American Interfaith Institute, 1995.

D'Angelo, Mary Rose. "Re-membering Jesus: Women, Prophecy, and Resistance in the Memory of the Early Churches." *Horizons* 19 (1992): 199–218.

Davalos, Karen Mary. "The Real Way of Praying: The Via Crucis, *Mexicano* Sacred Space, and the Architecture of Domination." In *Horizons of the Sacred: Mexican Traditions in U.S. Catholicism,* ed. Timothy Matovina and Gary Riebe-Estrella, 41–69. Ithaca, NY: Cornell University Press, 2002.

Dear, John. "Oscar Romero, Presente!" http://www.commondreams.org/views05/0324-21.htm.

DeConick, April D. "Gospel of Truth," *New York Times* (December 1, 2007).

———. *The Thirteenth Apostle: What the Gospel of Judas Really Says.* New York: Continuum, 2007.

Delany, Sheila. "Chaucer's Prioress, the Jews and the Muslims." *Medieval Encounters* 5 (1999): 198–213.

deLange, Nicholas. *Origen and the Jews,* University of Cambridge Oriental Publications. Cambridge, UK: Cambridge University Press, 1976.

Dietrich, Donald J. *Catholic Citizens in the Third Reich: Psycho-Social Principles and Moral Reasoning.* New Brunswick, NJ: Transaction Books, 1988.

———. *Human Rights and the Catholic Tradition.* New Brunswick, NJ: Transaction Publishers, 2007.

Dolan, Archbishop Timothy. "Two Rabbis, an Archbishop and the Oberammergau Passion Play." http://catholicexchange.com/2010/08/12/133113/.

Dreyer, Elizabeth A. "Behold, the One You Seek Has Been Lifted Up." In *The Cross in Christian Tradition: From Paul to Bonaventure,* ed. E. A. Dreyer, 236–258. New York and Mahwah, NJ: Paulist Press, 2000.

Duffy, Eamon. *The Stripping of the Altars: Traditional Religion in England 1400–1580.* New Haven: Yale University Press, 1992.

Dyckman, Katherine, Mary Garvin, and Elizabeth Liebert. *The Spiritual Exercises Reclaimed: Uncovering Liberating Possibilities for Women.* New York and Mahwah, NJ: Paulist Press, 2001.

Dunn, James D. G. *The New Perspective on Paul,* rev. ed. Tübingen: Mohr Siebeck, 2005.

————. *The Partings of the Ways between Christianity and Judaism and their Significance for the Character of Christianity.* London: SCM and Trinity Press International, 2001.

Eck, Diana. *Encountering God: A Spiritual Journey from Bozeman to Banaras.* Boston: Beacon, 1993.

Egan, Harvey D. "Negative Way." In *The New Dictionary of Catholic Spirituality,* ed. Michael Downey, 700. Collegeville: Liturgical Press, 1993.

Ehret, Ulrike. "Catholicism and Judaism in the Catholic Defence against Alfred Rosenberg, 1934–1938: Anti-Jewish Images in an Age of Race Science." *European History Quarterly* 4 (2010): 35–56.

Elliott, Neil. *Liberating Paul: The Justice of God and the Politics of the Apostle.* Minneapolis: Fortress, 2006.

Elsbernd, Mary, and Reimund Bieringer. "Interpreting the Signs of the Times in the Light of the Gospel Vision and Normativity of the Future." In *Normativity of the Future: Reading Biblical and Other Authoritative Texts in an Eschatological Perspective,* ed. R. Bieringer and M. Elsbernd, 47–90. Leuven: Peeters Publishers, 2010.

Ericksen, Robert P. *Christian Complicity? Changing Views on German Churches and the Holocaust.* Washington, DC: United States Holocaust Memorial Museum, 2009.

————. *Complicity in the Holocaust: Churches and Universities in Nazi Germany.* Cambridge, UK: Cambridge University Press, 2012.

————. "Protestants." In *The Handbook of Holocaust Studies,* ed. Peter Hayes and John K. Roth, 250–264. Oxford: Oxford University Press, 2010.

————. *Theologians under Hitler: Gerhard Kittel, Paul Althaus and Emmanuel Hirsch.* New Haven: Yale University Press, 1985.

Ericksen, Robert P., and Susannah Heschel. "The German Churches and the Holocaust." In *The Historiography of the Holocaust,* ed. Dan Stone, 296–318. Basingstoke, Hants., UK: Palgrave MacMillan, 2004.

Eubank, Nathan. "A Disconcerting Prayer: On the Originality of Luke 23:34a." *Journal of Biblical Literature* 129 (2010): 521–536.

Everitt, Anthony. *Augustus: The Life of Rome's First Emperor.* New York: Random House, 2006.

Faulhaber, Cardinal Michael von. *Judaism, Christianity and Germany.* Translated by George D. Smith. New York: Macmillan, 1934.

Feiner, Shmuel. *The Jewish Enlightenment.* Translated by Chaya Naor. Philadelphia: University of Pennsylvania Press, 2004.

Feitlowitz, Marguerite. *A Lexicon of Terror: Argentina and the Legacies of Torture.* New York: Oxford University Press, 1999.

Felder, Cain Hope. *Race, Racism, and the Biblical Narrative.* Minneapolis: Fortress, 2002.

Feldman, Louis H. *Jew and Gentile in the Ancient World.* Princeton: Princeton University Press, 1993.

Fewell, Danna Nolan, Gary A. Philips, and Yvonne Sherwood, eds. *Representing the Irreparable: The Shoah, the Bible, and the Art of Samuel Bak.* Boston: Pucker Art Publications, 2008.

Fisher, Eugene J. *Faith without Prejudice: Rebuilding Christian Attitudes toward Judaism.* New York: Paulist Press, 1977.

Fisher, Jo. *Mothers of the Disappeared.* Boston: South End Press, 1999.

Flannery, Austin, ed. *Vatican II: The Conciliar and Post-Conciliar Documents,* new rev. ed. Vol. 1. Collegeville: Liturgical Press, 1975.

Fleischner, Eva. "Mauriac's Preface to Night: Thirty Years Later." *America* 159 (November 19, 1988): 411, 419.

Fredriksen, Paula. *Augustine and the Jews: A Christian Defense of Jews and Judaism.* New York: Doubleday, 2008.

———. *Jesus of Nazareth: King of the Jews.* New York: Vintage Books, 2000.

———. "What 'Partings of the Ways'? Jews, Gentiles, and the Ancient Mediterranean City." In *The Ways that Never Parted: Jews and Christians in Late Antiquity and the Early Middle Ages,* Texts and Studies in Ancient Judaism 95, ed. Adam Becker and Annette Yoshiko Reed, 35–63. Tübingen: Mohr Siebeck, 2003.

Fredriksen, Paula, and Oded Irshai. "Christian Anti-Judaism: Polemics and Policies." In *Cambridge History of Judaism,* ed. Steven T. Katz, 4: 977–1034. Cambridge, UK: Cambridge University Press, 2006.

Friedman, Saul S. *The Oberammergau Passion Play: A Lance against Civilization.* Carbondale, IL: Southern Illinois University Press, 1984.

Füllenbach, Elias H. "Shock, Renewal, Crisis." In *Antisemitism, Christian Ambivalence, and Holocaust*, ed. Kevin P. Spicer, 201–234. Bloomingdale, IN: Indiana University Press, 2007.

Gager, John. "Maccoby's Mythmaker." *Jewish Quarterly Review* 79 (1988–1989): 248–250.

Gallin, Mary Alice. "The Cardinal and the State: Faulhaber and the Third Reich." *Church and State* 12 (1970): 385–404.

Gailus, Manfred. "A Strange Obsession with Nazi Christianity." *Journal of Contemporary History* 42 (2007): 35–46.

Garnesy, Peter, and Richard Saller. *The Roman Empire: Economy, Society and Culture*. Berkeley: University of California Press, 1987.

Gaston, Lloyd. *Paul and Torah*. Vancouver: University of Vancouver Press, 1990.

Gaydosh, Brenda. "Seliger Bernhard Lichtenberg: Steadfast in Spirit, He Directed his Own Course." Ph.D. diss., The American University, Washington, DC, 2010.

Gebara, Ivone. *Out of the Depths: Women's Experience of Evil and Salvation*. Translated by Ann Patrick Ware. Minneapolis: Fortress, 2002.

Gerlach, Wolfgang. *And the Witnesses Were Silent: The Confessing Church and the Persecution of the Jews*. Translated by Victoria J. Barnett. Lincoln: University of Nebraska Press, 2000.

Gilbert, Martin. *The Righteous: The Unsung Heroes of the Holocaust*. Toronto: Key Porter, 2003.

Golden, Renny. "Oscar Romero: Bishop of the Poor." http://www.uscatholic.org/culture/social-justice/2009/02/oscar-romero-bishop-poor.

Goldenberg, David M. *Curse of Ham: Race and Slavery in Early Judaism, Christianity, and Islam*. Princeton: Princeton University Press, 2005.

Gordon, Mary. *Reading Jesus: A Writer's Encounter with the Gospels*. New York: Pantheon, 2009.

Green, Barbara. "The Old Text: An Analogy for Biblical Interpretation." *Biblical Theology Bulletin* (2006): 72–83.

Green, Joel B., and Mark D. Baker. *Recovering the Scandal of the Cross: Atonement in New Testament and Contemporary Concerns*. Downers Grove, IL: InterVarsity Press, 2000.

Greenebaum, Gary, and Noam Marans. "Jews Should Recognize When Christians Change." http://www.jewishjournal.com/opinion/article/jews_should_recognize_when_christians_change_2010 0809/.

Grieche-Polelle, Beth. *Bishop von Galen: German Catholicism and National Socialism.* New Haven, CT: Yale University Press, 2002.

Gremillion, Joseph B., ed. *The Gospel of Peace and Justice: Catholic Social Teaching Since Pope John.* Maryknoll, NY: Orbis, 1976.

Groppe, Elizabeth. "After Augustine: Humility and the Search for God in Historical Memory." In *Learned Ignorance: Intellectual Humility among Jews, Christians, and Muslims,* ed. James L. Heft, Reuven Firestone and Omid Safi, 191–209. New York: Oxford University Press, 2011.

Grufferty, Tom. "Through Death to Life." *The Tablet* (April 19, 2003): 20–21.

Gundlach, Gustav. "Antisemitismus." In *Lexikon für Theologie und Kirche,* 2nd rev. ed, ed. Josef and Karl Rahner, I: 504. Freiberg: Herder, 1930.

Haight, Roger. *Jesus: Symbol of God.* Maryknoll, NY: Orbis, 1999.

———. *The Future of Christology.* New York: Continuum, 2005.

Hall, Douglas John. *The Cross in Our Context: Jesus and the Suffering World.* Minneapolis: Fortress, 2003.

Hallie, Philip P. *Lest Innocent Blood be Shed: The Story of the Village of Le Chambon, and How Goodness Happened There.* New York: Harper & Row, 1979.

Hanson, K. C., and Douglas E. Oakman. *Palestine in the Time of Jesus: Social Structures and Social Conflicts.* Minneapolis: Fortress, 1998.

Harkins, Franklin T., ed. *Transforming Relations: Essays on Jews and Christians throughout History in Honor of Michael A. Signer.* Notre Dame, IN: University of Notre Dame Press, 2010.

Harkins, Paul W. *St. John Chrysostom: Discourses against Judaizing Christians.* Washington, DC: Catholic University of America Press, 1979.

Hauerwas, Stanley. *Cross-Shattered Christ.* Grand Rapids: Brazos, 2004.

Hayes, Diana L. *Were You There? Stations of the Cross.* Maryknoll, NY: Orbis, 2000.

Hayman, Marina. "Christ in the Work of Two Jewish Artists: When Art Is Interreligious Dialogue." *Studies in Christian-Jewish Relations* 4 (2009): 1–14.

Haynes, Stephen R. "Bonhoeffer, the Jewish People and Post-Holocaust Theology: Eight Theses." *Studies in Christian-Jewish Relations* 2 (2007): 36–52.

Hendrix, Holland Lee. "Benefactor/Patron Networks in the Urban Environment: Evidence from Thessalonica." *Semeia* 56 (1992): 39–58.

Herberer, Patricia, "Science." In *The Oxford Handbook of Holocaust Studies,* ed. Peter Hayes and John K. Roth, 39–53. New York: Oxford University Press, 2010.

Heschel, Susannah. *The Aryan Jesus: Christian Theologians and the Bible in Nazi Germany.* Princeton: Princeton University Press, 2008.

—————. "Nazifying Christian Theology: Walter Grundmann and the Institute for the Study and Eradication of Jewish Influence on German Life." *Church History* 63 (1994): 587–605.

Hexham, Irving. "Inventing 'Paganists': A Close Reading of Richard Steigmann-Gall's *The Holy Reich.*" *Journal of Contemporary History* 42 (2007): 59–78.

Hill-Fletcher, Jeannine. "Christology between Identity and Difference." In *Frontiers in Catholic Feminist Theology: Shoulder to Shoulder,* ed. Susan Abraham and Elena Procario-Foley, 79–96. Minneapolis: Fortress, 2000.

Hitchens, Christopher. *God Is Not Great: How Religion Poisons Everything.* New York: Twelve, 2007.

Hodge, Caroline Johnson. *If Sons, Then Heirs: A Study of Kinship and Ethnicity in the Letters of Paul.* New York: Oxford University Press, 2007.

Hoffman, Matthew. *From Rebel to Rabbi: Reclaiming the Jewish Jesus and the Making of Modern Jewish Culture.* Stanford: Stanford University Press, 2007.

Horsley, Richard A. "Introduction." In *Paul and the Roman Imperial Order,* ed. Richard A. Horsley, 3–5. Harrisburg, PA: Trinity Press International, 2004.

—————. *Jesus and Empire: The Kingdom of God and the New World Disorder.* Minneapolis: Fortress Press, 2003.

Huck, Gabe. *The Three Days: Parish Prayer in the Paschal Triduum*, rev. ed. Chicago: Liturgy Training Publications, 1992.

Hull, John M. *What Prevents Christian Adults from Learning?* London: SCM Press, 1985.

Isaac, Jules. *Teaching of Contempt: Christian Roots of Anti-Semitism.* Translated by Helen Weaver. New York: Holt, Rinehart and Winston, 1964.

Jantzen, Kyle. *Faith and Fatherland: Parish Politics in Hitler's Germany.* Minneapolis: Fortress, 2008.

Jessopp, Augustus, and Montague Rhodes James, eds. *The Life and Miracles of St. William of Norwich.* Cambridge, UK: Cambridge University Press, 1896.

Johnson, Elizabeth. "The Word Was Made Flesh and Dwelt Among Us: Jesus Research and Christian Faith." In *Jesus: A Colloquium in the Holy Land,* ed. Doris Donnelly, 146–158. New York: Continuum, 2001.

Johnson, Luke Timothy. *The Creed: What Christians Believe and Why It Matters.* New York: Doubleday, 2003.

———. "The New Testament's Anti-Jewish Slander and the Conventions of Ancient Polemic." *Journal of Biblical Literature* 108 (1989): 419–441.

Jones, Serene. *Feminist Theory and Christian Theology: Cartographies of Grace.* Guides to Theological Inquiry. Minneapolis: Fortress, 2000.

Justin Martyr. *Dialogue with Trypho.* Translated by Thomas B. Falls, ed. Michael Slusser. Washington, DC: Catholic University of America Press, 2003.

Kafka, Franz. *Letters to Friends, Family, and Editors.* Translated by Richard and Clara Winston. New York: Schocken, 1997.

Kahl, Brigitte. *Re-Imagining Galatians: Reading with the Eyes of the Vanquished.* Minneapolis: Fortress, 2010.

———. "Acts of the Apostles: Pro(to)-Imperial Script and Hidden Transcript." In *In the Shadow of the Empire: Reclaiming the Bible as a History of Faithful Resistance,* ed. Richard A. Horseley, 137–156. Louisville: Westminster John Knox, 2008.

Katz, Steven T. *The Holocaust in Historical Context,* vol. 1: *The Holocaust and Mass Death before the Modern Age.* New York: Oxford University Press, 1994.

Kautsky, John H. *The Politics of Aristocratic Empires.* Chapel Hill: University of North Carolina Press, 1982.

Kempe, Margery. *The Book of Margery Kempe,* edited by Lynn Staley. Kalamazoo, MI: Medieval Institute Publications, 1996.

Kertzer, David I. *The Popes against the Jews: The Vatican's Role in the Rise of Modern Anti-Semitism.* New York: Alfred A. Knopf, 2001.

Kieckhefer, Richard. "Major Currents in Late Medieval Devotion." In *Christian Spirituality: High Middle Ages and Reformation,* World Spirituality, ed. Jill Raitt, 17:75–108. New York: Crossroad, 1987.

Kimmelman, Reuven. "*Birkat Ha-Minim* and the Lack of Evidence for an Anti-Christian Jewish Prayer in Late Antiquity." In *Jewish and Christian Self-Definition, Vol. 2: Aspects of Judaism in the Graeco-Roman Period, 226–44,* ed. E. P. Sanders, A. I. Baumgarten, and Alan Mendelson. Philadelphia: Fortress, 1981.

Kiser, John W. *The Monks of Tibhirine: Faith, Love, and Terror in Algeria.* New York: St. Martin's Griffin, 2002.

Klassen, William. *Judas: Betrayer or Friend of Jesus?* Minneapolis: Fortress, 1996.

Klenicki, Leon. "Toward the Year 2000: Memory, Reckoning, and Reconciliation." *The Month* 32/4 (April 1999): 129–139.

Knight, Henry F. *Celebrating Holy Week in a Post-Holocaust World.* Louisville: Westminster-John Knox, 2005.

Kraeling, Carl H. "The Jewish Community at Antioch." *Journal of Biblical Literature* 51 (1932): 130–160.

Krieg, Robert A. *Catholic Theologians in Nazi Germany.* New York: Continuum, 2004.

———. "German Catholic Views of Jesus and Judaism, 1918–1945." In *Antisemitism, Christian Ambivalence, and the Holocaust,* ed. Kevin P. Spicer, 50–75. Bloomington, IN: University of Indiana Press, 2007.

———. "Karl Adam, National Socialism and Christian Tradition." *Theological Studies* 60 (1999): 432–456.

———. "Romano Guardini's Theology of the Human Person." *Theological Studies* 59 (1998): 457–474.

Kroeger, Catherine Clark, and James R. Beck, eds. *Women, Abuse, and the Bible: How the Bible Can Be Used to Hurt or Heal.* Grand Rapids: Baker, 1996.

Langer, Ruth. *Cursing the Christians? A History of the Birkat Haminim*. New York: Oxford University Press, 2012.

———. "Liturgy in the Light of Jewish-Christian Dialogue." *Studies in Christian-Jewish Relations* 4 (2009): 1–13.

Langmuir, Gavin. *Toward a Definition of Antisemitism*. Berkeley: University of California Press, 1990.

Lefebure, Leo D. *Revelation, the Religions and Violence*. Maryknoll, NY: Orbis, 2000.

Leiper, Henry Smith. "Churchmen Who Defy Hitler, I: Bishop von Galen of Germany." *The New York Times* (June 8, 1942). http://query.nytimes.com/mem/archive/pdf?res=FB0716FD3D5 A147B93CAA9178DD85F468485F9.

Levine, Amy-Jill. *The Misunderstood Jew: The Church and the Scandal of the Jewish Jesus*. New York: HarperOne, 2007.

Levine, Amy-Jill, and Marc Zvi Brettler, eds. *The Jewish Annotated New Testament*. New York: Oxford University Press, 2011.

Lewy, Günther. *The Catholic Church and Nazi Germany*. New York: McGraw-Hill, 1964.

Lieu, Judith. *Image and Reality: The Jews in the World of the Christians in the Second Century*. Edinburgh: T&T Clark, 1996.

Lifton, Robert Jay. *The Nazi Doctors: Medical Killing and the Psychology of Genocide*. New York: Basic Books, 1986.

Longerich, Peter. *Holocaust: The Nazi Persecution and Murder of the Jews*. Oxford: Oxford University Press, 2010.

Lopez, Davina C. *Apostle to the Conquered: Reimagining Paul's Mission*. Minneapolis: Fortress, 2008.

Luther, Martin. "Lectures on Galatians, 1535," In *Luther's Works*. Vol. 26, edited by Jaroslav J. Pelikan and W. A. Hansen. St. Louis: Concordia, 1963.

Luz, Ulrich. *Matthew in History: Interpretation, Influence, and Effects*. Minneapolis: Fortress, 1994.

Łysiak, Anna. "Rabbinic Judaism in the Writings of Polish Catholic Theologians." In *Antisemitism, Christian Ambivalence and the Holocaust*, ed. Kevin P. Spicer, 26–49. Bloomington: Indiana University Press, 2007.

Maccoby, Hyam. *The Mythmaker: Paul and the Invention of Christianity*. San Francisco: HarperSanFrancisco, 1986.

Mach, Michael. "Justin Martyr's *Dialogus cum Tryphone Iudaeo*." In *Contra Iudaeos: Ancient and Medieval Polemics between Christians and Jews*, Texts and Studies in Medieval and Early Modern Judaism 10, ed. Ora Limor and Guy G. Stroumsa, 27–48. Tübingen: J.C.B. Mohr, 1996.

Marcus, Jacob Rader. *The Jew in the Medieval World: A Sourcebook, 315–1791*, rev. ed. Cincinnati: Hebrew Union College Press, 1999.

Margolick, David, and Hilton Als. *Strange Fruit: Billie Holiday, Café Society and an Early Cry for Civil Rights*. Philadelphia: Running Press, 2000.

Markowski, Michael. "*Crucesignatus*: Its Origins and Early Usage." *Journal of Medieval History* 10 (1984): 157–165.

Marthaler, Berard L. *The Creed*. Mystic, CT: Twenty-Third Publications, 1987.

Marrus, Michael. "The Vatican on Racism and Antisemitism, 1938–39," *Holocaust and Genocide Studies* 4 (Winter 1997): 378–395.

Martin, J. Louis. *History and Theology in the Fourth Gospel*, 2nd ed., revised and enlarged. Louisville: John Knox, 1979.

Mastnak, Tomaž. *Crusading Peace: Christendom, the Muslim World, and Western Political Order*. Berkley: University of California Press, 2002.

Mattern, Susan P. *Rome and the Enemy: Imperial Strategy in the Principate*. Berkeley: University of California Press, 1999.

Mauer, Christian, and Wilhelm Schneemelcher. "The Gospel of Peter." In *New Testament Apocrypha*. Translated by R. McL. Wilson, rev. ed. W. Schneemelcher, 1:216–27. Louisville: Westminster, 1991; paperback reprint, 2006.

Mauriac, François. "Foreword." In Elie Wiesel, *Night*. Translated by Stella Rodway. New York: Avon Books, 1969.

Mavis, Brian. "Experience the Passion of the Christ." Vista, CA: Outreach, Inc., 2003.

———. "The Passion of the Christ: True or False?" Vista, CA: Outreach, Inc., 2003.

McGuckin, John. *St. Gregory of Nazianzus: An Intellectual Biography*. Crestwood, NY: St. Vladimir's Seminary Press, 2001.

McKenzie, Steven L. *How to Read the Bible: History, Prophecy, Literature— Why Modern Readers Need to Know the Difference and What It Means for Faith Today*. New York: Oxford University Press, 2005.

McManus, Dennis D. "Origen." In *A Dictionary of Jewish-Christian Relations*, ed. Edward Kessler and Neil Wenborn, 323. Cambridge, UK: Cambridge University Press, 2005.

McNutt, James E. "Vessels of Wrath, Prepared to Perish: Adolf Schlatter and the Spiritual Extermination of the Jews." *Theology Today* 63 (2006): 176–190.

Meeks, Wayne A., and Robert L. Wilken. *Jews and Christians in Antioch in the First Four Centuries of the Common Era*, Sources for Biblical Study 13. Missoula, MT: Scholars Press, 1978.

Meier, John P. *A Marginal Jew: Law and Love. Rethinking the Historical Jesus*. Vol. 4. New Haven: Yale University Press, 2009.

Meissner, William. *To the Greater Glory: A Psychological Study of Ignatian Spirituality*. Milwaukee: Marquette University Press, 1999.

Menn, Esther M. "No Ordinary Lament: Relecture and the Identity of the Distressed in Psalm 22." *Harvard Theological Review* 93 (2000): 301–341.

Merton, Thomas. *Courage for Truth: The Letters of Thomas Merton to Writers*. Thomas Merton Letters Series. Vol 4, ed. Christine M. Bochen. New York: Harcourt Brace, 1997.

Metz, Johann Baptist. "Between Remembering and Forgetting: The Shoah in the Era of Cultural Amnesia." Translated by L. J. Penta. In *Good and Evil after Auschwitz: Ethical Implications for Today*, ed. Jack Bemporad, John T. Pawlikowski, and Joseph Sievers, 21–28. Hoboken, NJ: KTAV, 2000.

———. *Emergent Church*. Translated by Peter Mann. New York: Crossroad, 1981.

Mitchell, Beverly Eileen. *Plantation and Death Camps: Religion, Ideology, and Human Dignity*. Minneapolis: Fortress, 2009.

Modras, Ronald E. *The Catholic Church and Antisemitism: Poland, 1933–1939*. London: Routledge/Vidal Sassoon International Center for the Study of Antisemitism, 1994.

Montaña, Constanza. "Passion Play Unites Pilsen." *Chicago Tribune* (March 26, 1991), 11.

Moore, R. I. *The Formation of a Persecuting Society: Power and Deviance in Western Europe 950–1250*. Oxford: Basil Blackwell, 1987.

Mork, Gordon R. "Christ's Passion on Stage: The Traditional

Melodrama of Deicide." *Journal of Religion and Society*, Supplement Series 1 (2004): 1–9.

Moses, A. Dirk. "Colonialism." In *The Oxford Handbook of Holocaust Studies*, ed. Peter Hayes and John K. Roth, 68–80. New York: Oxford University Press, 2010.

Mosse, George. *Nazi Culture: Intellectual, Cultural, and Social Life in the Third Reich.* New York: Grosset & Dunlap, 1966.

Murphy, Cullen. *God's Jury: The Inquisition and the Making of the Modern World.* Boston: Houghton Mifflin Harcourt, 2012.

Nanos, Mark. *The Irony of Galatians.* Philadelphia: Fortress, 2001.

Nava, Margaret M. "Via Crucis." *Commonweal* 136 (March 27, 2009): 30.

Neuhaus, Richard John. *Death on a Friday Afternoon.* New York: Basic Books, 2000.

Neusner, Jacob, William Scott Green, and Ernest S. Frerichs, eds. *Judaisms and their Messiahs at the Turn of the Christian Era.* Cambridge, UK: Cambridge University Press, 1987.

Noel, James A. "Were You There?" In *The Passion of the Lord: African American Reflections*, ed. Noel and Matthew V. Johnson, 33–50. Minneapolis: Fortress, 2005.

Norris, Kathleen. *The Cloister Walk.* New York: Riverhead Books, 1996.

Norris, Jr., Richard A. *The Christological Controversy.* Philadelphia: Fortress, 1980.

O'Connor, Jerome Murphy. "'Even Death on a Cross': Crucifixion in Pauline Letters." In *The Cross in Christian Tradition: From Paul to Bonaventure*, ed. Elizabeth A. Dreyer, 21–50. New York and Mahwah, NJ: Paulist Press, 2000.

Oesterreicher, John M. "Declaration on the Relationship of the Church to Non-Christian Religions." In *Commentary on the Documents of Vatican II*, ed. Herbert Vorgrimler, 3:1–136. New York: Herder and Herder, 1969.

O'Malley, John. *What Happened at Vatican II?* Cambridge, MA: Belknap Press of Harvard University Press, 2008.

Paffenroth, Kim. *Judas: Images of the Lost Disciple.* Louisville: Westminster-John Knox, 2001.

Panikkar, Raimon. *The Intrareligious Dialogue*, rev. ed. New York and Mahwah, NJ: Paulist Press, 1999.

Patterson, Stephen J. *Beyond the Passion: Rethinking the Death and Life of Jesus.* Minneapolis: Fortress, 2004.

Passelecq, Georges, and Bernard Suchecky. *The Hidden Encyclical of Pius XI.* Translated by Steven Rendall. New York: Harcourt, Brace & Company, 1977.

Pasto, James. "The Origins, Expansion, and Impact of the Hasmoneans in Light of Comparative Ethnographic Studies (and Outside of Its Nineteenth Century Context)." In *Second Temple Studies III: Studies in Politics, Class, and Material Culture,* ed. Philip R. Davies and John M. Halligan, 166–201. London: Sheffield Academic Press, 2002.

Pawlikowski, John T. "The Shoah: Its Challenges for Religious and Secular Ethics." *Holocaust and Genocide Studies* 3 (1988): 443–455.

———. "Historical Memory and Christian-Jewish Relations." In *Christ Jesus and the Jewish People,* ed. Philip A. Cunningham, Joseph Sievers, Mary Boys, Hans Hermann Henrix, and Jesper Svartvik, 14–31. Grand Rapids: Eerdmans, and Rome: Gregorian and Biblical Press, 2011.

———. "Honesty and Integrity in the Christian-Jewish Dialogue." In *Takt und Tacheles: Festschrift für Hanspeter Heinz,* ed. Johann Ev. Hafner, 224–237. Munich: Verlag Neue Stadt, 2009.

———. "We Remember: Looking Back, Looking Ahead." *The Month* 33 (2000): 3–8.

Pelikan, Jaroslav. *Credo: Historical and Theological Guide to Creeds and Confessions of Faith in the Christian Tradition.* New Haven and London: Yale University Press, 2003.

Peterson, Anna L. *Martyrdom and the Politics of Religion: Progressive Catholicism in El Salvador's Civil War.* Albany: State University of New York Press, 1997.

Phayer, Michael. *The Catholic Church and the Holocaust, 1930–1965.* Bloomington: Indiana University Press, 2000.

———. "The Catholic Resistance Circle in Berlin and German Catholic Bishops during the Holocaust." *Holocaust and Genocide Studies* 7 (1993): 216–229.

———. *Pius XII, the Holocaust, and the Cold War.* Bloomington, IN: University of Indiana Press, 2008.

————. "Saving Jews Was Her Passion; Serving Survivors Was Her Agony." *Commonweal* (August 18, 1995): 19–21.

Phayer, Michael, and Eva Fleischner. *Cries in the Night: Women Who Challenged the Holocaust.* Kansas City: Sheed and Ward, 1997.

Piper, Ernst. "Steigmann-Gall, *The Holy Reich.*" *Journal of Contemporary History* 42 (2007): 47–57.

Plaskow, Judith. *Standing Again at Sinai: Judaism from a Feminist Perspective.* San Francisco: Harper & Row, 1990.

Pollefeyt, Didier, ed. *Interreligious Learning.* Leuven: Leuven University Press, 2007.

Pollefeyt, Didier, and David J. Bolton. "Paul, Deicide and the Wrath of God: Towards a Hermeneutical Reading of 1 Thes 2:14–16." In *Paul's Jewish Matrix.* A Stimulus Book. Ed. Thomas G. Casey and Justin Taylor, 229–58. New York and Mahwah, NJ: Paulist Press, 2012.

Powell, Richard J. *Homecoming: The Art and Life of William H. Johnson.* New York: Rizzoli, 1991.

Pramuk, Christopher. "'Strange Fruit': Black Suffering/White Revelation." *Theological Studies* 67 (June 2006): 345–377.

Purvis, Sally B. *The Power of the Cross: Foundations for a Christian Feminist Ethic of Community.* Nashville: Abingdon, 1993.

Radcliffe, Timothy. *The Seven Last Words.* London: Burns and Oates, 2005.

Ratzinger, Joseph (Pope Benedict XVI). *Saint Paul.* San Francisco: Ignatius Press, 2009.

————. *Jesus of Nazareth: Part Two: Holy Week from the Entrance into Jerusalem to the Resurrection.* San Francisco: Ignatius Press, 2011.

Reed, Annette Yoshiko, and Adam H. Becker. "Introduction: Traditional Models and New Directions." In *The Ways that Never Parted: Jews and Christians in Late Antiquity and the Early Middle Ages,* ed. Adam H. Becker and Annette Yoshiko Reed, 1–34. Minneapolis: Fortress Press, 2007.

Reid, Barbara E. *Taking Up the Cross: New Testament Interpretations through Latina and Feminist Eyes.* Minneapolis: Fortress, 2007.

Reiser, William. "The Road from Aguilares." *America* 201 (November 16, 2009): 13–15.

Rhonheimer, Martin. "The Holocaust: What Was Not Said." *First Things* 137 (November 2003): 18–28.

Richardson, Peter. *Herod: King of the Jews and Friend of the Romans.* Columbia, SC: University of South Carolina Press, 1999.

Riley-Smith, Jonathan. *The Crusades, Christianity, and Islam.* New York: Columbia University Press, 2008.

———. "The First Crusade and the Persecution of the Jews." In *Persecution and Toleration*, ed. W. J. Sheils, 51–72. Oxford: Oxford University Press, 1984.

Rittner, Carol, and Sondra Myers, eds. *The Courage to Care: Rescuers of Jews During the Holocaust.* New York: New York University Press, 1986.

Rodriguez, Jeannette, and Ted Fortier. *Cultural Memory: Resistance, Faith and Identity.* Austin: University of Texas Press, 2007.

The Roman Missal in Latin and English, Arranged for the Use of the Laity to Which Is Added a Collection of Usual Public Prayers, 3rd ed. Tournay, Belgium: Society of St. John the Evangelist and Declée & Co., 1911. Reprint, New York: Benziger Brothers, 1925.

Ronan, Marian. "Coming Closer to the Cross: New Feminist Perspectives on the Passion of Jesus." Paper presented to the Protestant Akadamie at Bolder, Zurich, Switzerland, January 2008.

———. *Tracing the Sign of the Cross: Sexuality, Mourning, and the Future of Catholicism*, Gender, Theory and Religion. New York: Columbia University Press, 2009.

Rosenthal, Judith. "Margery Kempe and Medieval Anti-Judaic Ideology." *Medieval Encounters* 5 (1999): 409–420.

Roskies, David G. *Against the Apocalypse: Responses to Catastrophe in Modern Jewish Culture.* Cambridge, MA: Harvard University Press, 1984.

Ross, Ellen M. *The Grief of God: Images of the Suffering Jesus in Late Medieval England.* New York: Oxford University Press, 1997.

Rubin, Alexis P., ed. *Scattered Among the Nations: Documents Affecting Jewish History 49 to 1975.* Toronto: Wall and Emerson, 1993.

Rudin, A. James. "Oberammergau: A Case Study of Passion Plays." In *Pondering the Passion: What's at Stake for Christians and Jews?*, ed. Philip A. Cunningham, 97–108. Lanham, MD: Rowman and Littlefield, 2004.

Rutishauser, Christian. "The 1947 Seelisberg Conference: The Foundation of the Jewish-Christian Dialogue." *Studies in Christian-Jewish Relations* 2 (2007): 34–53.

Rutledge, Fleming. *The Seven Last Words from the Cross.* Grand Rapids: Eerdmans, 2005.

Saldarini, Anthony J. *Jesus and Passover.* New York: Paulist Press, 1984.

———. *Matthew's Christian-Jewish Community.* Chicago Studies in the History of Judaism. Chicago: University of Chicago Press, 1994.

———. *Pharisees, Scribes and Sadducees in Palestinian Society: A Sociological Approach.* Wilmington, DE: Michael Glazier, 1988.

Salmon, Marilyn. *Preaching without Contempt: Overcoming Unintended Anti-Judaism.* Minneapolis: Fortress Press, 2009.

Sanders, E.P. *Judaism: Practice and Belief, 63 BCE–66 CE.* London: SCM Press and Philadelphia: Trinity Press International, 1992.

———. *Paul and Palestinian Judaism: A Comparison of Patterns of Religion.* Philadelphia: Fortress Press, 1977.

Sanders, James A. "Intertextuality and Dialogue." *Biblical Theology Bulletin* 29 (1999): 35–44.

Sanders, Theresa. *Tenebrae: Holy Week after the Holocaust.* Maryknoll, NY: Orbis, 2006.

Saperstein, Marc. "Christian Doctrine and the Final Solution: The State of the Question." In *Remembering for the Future: The Holocaust in an Age of Genocide.* ed. John K. Roth and Elizabeth Maxwell, 2:814–841. New York: Palgrave, 2001.

———. *Moments of Crisis in Jewish-Christian Relations.* London: SCM and Philadelphia: Trinity Press International, 1989.

Sarans, Lieven. "The Attitude of the Belgian Roman Catholic Clergy toward the Jews prior to Occupation." In *Belgium and the Holocaust: Jews, Belgians, Germans,* ed. Dan Mikhman, 117–158. Jerusalem: Yad Vashem Publications, 1998.

Schlatter, Adolf. *History of the Christ: The Foundation for New Testament Theology.* Translated by Andreas Köstenberger. Grand Rapids: Baker, 1997.

Schmemann, Alexander. *Of Water and the Spirit: A Liturgical Study of Baptism.* Crestwood, NY: St. Vladimir's Seminary Press, 1974.

Schneiders, Sandra M. "Feminist Ideology Criticism and Biblical Hermeneutics." *Biblical Theology Bulletin* 19 (1989): 3–10.

Scholder, Klaus. *A Requiem for Hitler and Other New Perspectives on the German Church Struggle.* Translated by John Bowden. London: SCM Press, 1989.

Schreckenberg, Heinz. *The Jews in Christian Art: An Illustrated History.* Translated by John Bowden. New York: Continuum, 1996.

Schremer, Adiel. *Brothers Estranged: Heresy, Christianity, and Jewish Identity in Late Antiquity.* New York: Oxford University Press, 2010.

Schwartz, Daniel R. "Pontius Pilate." In *Anchor Bible Dictionary,* edited by David Noel Freedman et al., 5:395–401. New York: Doubleday, 1992.

Schwarz, Seth. *Imperialism and Jewish Society, 200 B.C.E. to 640 C.E.* Princeton: Princeton University Press, 2001.

Searle, Mark. *Christening: The Making of Christians.* Collegeville: Liturgical Press, 1980.

Seidman, Naomi. *Faithful Renderings: Jewish-Christian Difference and the Politics of Translation.* Chicago: University of Chicago Press, 2006.

Senn, Frank C. "Should Christians Celebrate the Passover?" In *Passover and Easter: The Symbolic Structuring of Sacred Seasons. Two Liturgical Traditions,* ed. Paul F. Bradshaw and Lawrence A. Hoffman, 6:183–205. Notre Dame, IN: University of Notre Dame Press, 1999.

Shapiro, James. *Oberammergau: The Troubling Story of the World's Most Famous Passion Play.* New York: Vintage Books, 2000.

Shaw, Brent D. "Rebels and Outsiders." In *The High Empire, A.D. 70–192,* Cambridge Ancient History 11, ed. Alan K. Bowman, Peter Garnsey, and Dominic Rathbone, 361–403. Cambridge, UK: Cambridge University Press, 2000.

Sherman, Franklin, ed. *Bridges: Documents of the Christian Jewish Dialogue, vol. 1, 1945–85.* New York and Mahwah, NJ: Paulist Press, 2011.

Signer, Michael A. "Speculum Concilii: Through the Mirror Brightly." In *Unanswered Questions: Theological Views of Jewish-Catholic Relations,* ed. Roger Brooks, 105–127. Notre Dame, IN: University of Notre Dame Press, 1988.

————, ed. *Humanity at the Limit: The Impact of the Holocaust Experience on Jews and Christians*. Bloomington: University of Indiana Press, 2000.

————, ed. *Memory and History in Judaism and Christianity*. Notre Dame, IN: University of Notre Dame Press, 2001.

Siker, Judy Yates. "Unmasking the Enemy: Deconstructing the 'Other' in the Gospel of Matthew." *Perspectives in Religious Studies* 32 (Summer 2005): 109–123.

Sloyan, Gerard S. *The Crucifixion of Jesus: History, Myth, Faith*. Minneapolis: Fortress, 1995.

Smith, Abraham. "Unmasking the Powers: Toward a Postcolonial Analysis of 1 Thessalonians." In *Paul and the Roman Imperial Order*, ed. Richard A. Horsley, 47–66. Harrisburg, PA: Trinity Press International, 2004.

Sobrino, Jon. *Archbishop Romero: Memories and Reflections*. Translated by Robert R. Barr. Maryknoll, NY: Orbis Books, 1990.

————. *Jesus in Latin America*. Translated by Robert R. Barr. Maryknoll, NY: Orbis, 1987.

Spicer, Kevin P. "Catholics." In *The Oxford Handbook of Holocaust Studies*, ed. Peter Hayes and John K. Roth, 233–249. Oxford: Oxford University Press, 2010.

————. *Hitler's Priests: Catholic Clergy and National Socialism*. DeKalb, IL: Northern Illinois University Press, 2008.

————. "Last Years of a Resister in the Diocese of Berlin: Bernhard Lichtenberg's Conflict with Karl Adam and his Fateful Imprisonment." *Church History* 70 (2001): 248–270.

————. "Bishop von Galen: German Catholicism and National Socialism." *Holocaust and Genocide Studies* 18, no. 3 (2004): 492–495.

Stacey, Robert C. "Jews and Christians in Twelfth-Century England: Dynamics of a Changing Relationship." In *Jews and Christians in Twelfth-Century Europe*, ed. Michael A. Signer and John H. Van Engen, 340–354. Notre Dame, IN: University of Notre Dame Press, 2001.

Stanton, Graham N. "Justin Martyr's *Dialogue with Trypho*: Group Boundaries, 'Proselytes' and 'God-fearers.'" In *Tolerance and Intolerance in Early Judaism and Christianity*, ed. Graham N. Stanton and Guy G. Stroumsa, 263–278. Cambridge, UK: Cambridge University Press, 1998.

Steigmann-Gall, Richard. "Christianity and the Nazi Movement: A Response." *Journal of Contemporary History* 42 (2007): 185–211.

———. *The Holy Reich: Nazi Conceptions of Christianity, 1919–1945*. Cambridge, UK: Cambridge University Press, 2003.

———. "Old Wine in New Bottles?" *Antisemitism, Christian Ambivalence and the Holocaust*, ed. Kevin P. Spicer, 285–308. Bloomington, IN: Indiana University Press, 2007.

Stendahl, Krister. *Paul among Jews and Gentiles, and Other Essays*. Philadelphia: Fortress, 1976.

Stowers, Stanley. *A Rereading of Romans: Justice, Jews and Gentiles*. New Haven: Yale University Press, 1994.

Stroumsa, Guy G. "From Anti-Judaism to Antisemitism in Early Christianity?" In *Contra Iudaeos: Ancient and Medieval Polemics between Christians and Jews*, ed. Ora Limor and Guy G. Stroumsa, 1–26.Tübingen: J.C.B. Mohr, 1996.

Suomala, Karla. "Healing the World and Mending the Soul." In *Covenantal Conversations: Christians in Conversation with Jews and Judaism*, ed. Darrell Jodock, 114–115. Minneapolis: Fortress, 2008.

Swidler, Leonard. "Oberammergau Passion Play 'inter-religiously triumphant." http://ncronline.org/news/global/oberammergau-passion-play-inter-religiously-triumphant.

Świebocki, Teresa and Henryk. *Auschwitz: The Residence of Death*. Translated by William Brand. Krakow and Oświęcim: Auschwitz-Birkenau State Museum and Bialy Kruk, 2003.

Taussig, Hal. *In the Beginning Was the Meal: Social Experimentation and Early Christian Identity*. Minneapolis: Fortress, 2009.

Taylor, Barbara Brown. "Table Manners." *Christian Century* 115 (March 11, 1998): 257.

Taylor, Mark Lewis. "American Torture and the Body of Christ." In *Cross Examinations: Readings on the Meaning of the Cross Today*, ed. Marit Trelstad, 264–277. Minneapolis: Augsburg Fortress, 2006.

Taylor, Miriam. *Anti-Judaism and Early Christian Identity: A Critique of the Scholarly Consensus*. Leiden: E. J. Brill, 1995.

Tec, Nechama. *When Light Pierced the Darkness: Christian Rescuers in Nazi-Occupied Poland*. Oxford: Oxford University Press, 1986.

"Ten Points of Seelisberg." http://www.jcrelations.net/en/?item=983.

Terrell, JoAnne Marie. "Our Mothers' Gardens: Rethinking Sacrifice." In *Cross Examinations: Readings on the Meaning of the Cross Today*, ed. Marit Trelstad, 33–49. Minneapolis: Augsburg Fortress, 2006.

Thatcher, Adrian. *The Savage Text: The Use and Abuse of the Bible*, Blackwell Manifestos. Oxford: Wiley Blackwell, 2008.

Thurman, Howard. *Deep River: Reflections on the Religious Insight of Certain of the Spirituals*, rev. and enlarged ed. New York: Harper and Brothers, 1955.

Thurston, Robert. *The Witch Hunts: A History of the Witch Persecutions in Europe and North America*, 2nd ed. New York: Pearson Longman, 2007.

Tigay, Jeffrey. "On the Term Phylactery (Matthew 23:5)." *Harvard Theological Review* 72/1–2 (1979): 45–53.

Timmerman, Jacobo. *Prisoner without a Name, Cell without a Number.* Translated by Toby Talbot. Madison: University of Wisconsin Press, 2002.

Toensing, Holly Joan. "Women of Sodom and Gormorrah: Collateral Damage in the War against Homosexuality." *Journal of Feminist Studies in Religion* 21 (2005): 61–74.

Tomson, Peter J. *Paul and Jewish Law: Halakha in the Letter of the Apostle to the Gentiles.* Assen: van Gorcum, 1990.

Tyerman, Christopher. *Fighting for Christendom: Holy War and the Crusades.* Oxford: Oxford University Press, 2004.

———. *God's War: A New History of the Crusades.* Cambridge, MA: Harvard University Press, 2006.

Tyson, Joseph B. "The Death of Jesus." In *Seeing Judaism Anew: Christianity's Sacred Obligation*, ed. Mary C. Boys, 44–55. Lanham, M.D.: Rowman & Littlefield, 2005.

Ventresca, Robert A. "Jacques Maritain and the Jewish Question: Theology, Identity and Politics." *Studies in Christian-Jewish Relations* 2 (2007): 58–69.

Viladesau, Richard. *The Beauty of the Cross: The Passion of Christ in Theology and the Arts, from the Catacombs to the Eve of the Renaissance.* New York: Oxford University Press, 2006.

————. *The Triumph of the Cross: the Passion of Christ in Theology and the Arts from the Renaissance to the Counter-Reformation.* New York: Oxford, 2008.

Volkov, Shulamit, *Germans, Jews, and Antisemites: Trials in Emancipation.* Cambridge, UK: Cambridge University Press, 2006.

von Kellenbach, Katharina. "God's Love and Women's Love: Prison Chaplains Counsel the Wives of Nazi Perpetrators." *Journal of Feminist Studies in Religion* 20 (Fall 2004): 7–24.

Vorster, Willem S. "Gospel Genre." In *Anchor Bible Dictionary,* ed. David Noel Freedman et al., 2:1177–1179. New York: Doubleday, 1992.

Vromen, Suzanne. *Hidden Children of the Holocaust: Belgian Nuns and Their Daring Rescue of Young Jews from the Nazis.* Oxford: Oxford University Press, 2008.

Walfish, Avraham. "Mishnah." In *The Oxford Dictionary of the Jewish Religion,* ed. R. J. Zwi Werblowsky and Geoffrey Wigoder, 471–472. New York: Oxford University Press, 1997.

Wegner, Paul Gregory. *Anti-Semitism and Schooling under the Third Reich.* New York and London: RoutledgeFalmer, 2002.

Weiss, John. *Ideology of Death: Why the Holocaust Happened in Germany.* Chicago: Ivan R. Dee, 1996.

Weitz, Eric D. "Nationalism." In *The Oxford Handbook of Holocaust Studies,* ed. Peter Hayes and John K. Roth, 54–67. New York: Oxford University Press, 2010.

Werner, Eric. "Melito of Sardis, the First Poet of Deicide." *Hebrew Union College Annual* 37 (1966): 191–210.

West, Colin. "Augustus." In *Anchor Bible Dictionary,* ed. David Noel Freedman et al., 1:524–528. New York: Doubleday, 1992.

————. "Roman Empire." In *Anchor Bible Dictionary,* ed. David Noel Freedman et al., 5:801–806. New York: Doubleday, 1992.

Wiesel, Elie. *A Jew Today.* Translated by Marion Wiesel. New York: Random House, 1978.

————. *All Rivers Run to the Sea: Memoirs.* New York: Schocken Books, 1995.

Wilken, Robert L. *The Christians as the Romans Saw Them.* New Haven: Yale University Press, 1984.

————. "The Jews and Christian Apologetics after Theodosius I *Cunctos Populos.*" *The Harvard Theological Review* 73 (1980): 451–471.

————. *John Chrysostom and the Jews: Rhetoric and Reality in the Late 4th Century*, The Transformation of the Classical Heritage. Berkeley: University of California Press, 1983.

————. *Judaism and the Early Christian Mind: A Study of Cyril of Alexandria's Exegesis and Theology.* New Haven: Yale University Press, 1971.

Williams, Delores S. "Black Woman's Surrogacy Experience and the Christian Notion of Redemption." In *Cross Examinations: Readings on the Meaning of the Cross Today*, ed. Marit A. Trelstad, 19–32. Minneapolis: Augsburg Fortress, 2006.

————. *Sisters in the Wilderness: The Challenge of Womanist God-Talk.* Maryknoll, NY: Orbis, 1993.

Williams, Demetrius K. "Identifying with the Cross of Christ." In *The Passion of the Lord: African-American Reflections,* ed. James A. Noel and Matthew V. Johnson, 77–110. Minneapolis: Fortress Press, 2005.

Williams, Monty. *The Gift of Spiritual Intimacy: Following the Spiritual Exercises of St. Ignatius.* Montréal: Novalis, 2009.

Williamson, Clark. *A Guest in the House of Israel.* Louisville: Westminster John Knox, 1993.

Williamson, Peter. *Catholic Principles for Interpreting Scripture: A Study of the Pontifical Biblical Commission's The Interpretation of the Bible in the Church.* Rome: Editrice Pontificio Istituto Biblico, 2001.

Willimon, William H. *Thank God It's Friday: Encountering the Seven Last Words from the Cross.* Nashville: Abingdon, 2006.

Wills, Garry. *Saint Augustine*, Penguin Lives Series. New York: Viking, 1999.

Wilson, Stephen G. *Related Strangers: Jews and Christians 70–170 C.E.* Minneapolis: Fortress Press, 1994.

Winter, Bruce W. *Seek the Welfare of the City: Christians as Benefactors and Citizens.* Grand Rapids: Eerdmans, 1994.

Wolf, Arnold. "Repairing *Tikkun Olam,*" *Judaism* 50 (1964): 479–482.

Wolf, Hubert. *Pope and Devil: The Vatican's Archives and the Third Reich*. Translated by Kenneth Kronenberg. Cambridge, MA: Belknap Press of Harvard University Press, 2010.

Woodward, Kenneth L. *Making Saints: How the Catholic Church Determines Who Becomes a Saint, Who Doesn't, and Why*. New York: Simon and Schuster, 1990.

Wright, N. T. *The Climax of the Covenant: Christ and the Law in Pauline Theology*. Minneapolis: Fortress Press, 1992.

————. *What Saint Paul Really Said: Was Paul of Tarsus the Real Founder of Christianity?* Grand Rapids: Eerdmans, 1997.

Yerushalmi, Yosef Hayim. *Zakhor: Jewish History and Jewish Memory*. New York: Schocken Books, 1989.

————. "Response to Rosemary Ruether." In *Auschwitz: Beginning of a New Era? Reflections on the Holocaust*, ed. Eva Fleischner, 97–107. New York: Ktav, 1977.

Yuval, Israel Jacob. *Two Nations in Your Womb: Perceptions of Jews and Christians in Late Antiquity and the Middle Ages*. Translated by Barbara Harshav and Jonathan Chipman. Berkeley: University of California Press, 2006.

Zanker, Paul. *The Power of Images in the Age of Augustus*. Translated by Alan Shapiro. Ann Arbor: University of Michigan Press, 1990.

Zetterholm, Magnus. *Approaches to Paul: A Student's Guide to Recent Scholarship*. Minneapolis: Augsburg Fortress, 2009.

Index